Essays on Austrian Economics and Political Economy

Advanced Studies in Political Economy

Series Editors: Virgil Henry Storr
and Stefanie Haeffele

The Advanced Studies in Political Economy series consists of republished as well as newly commissioned work that seeks to understand the underpinnings of a free society through the foundations of the Austrian, Virginia, and Bloomington schools of political economy. Through this series, the Mercatus Center at George Mason University aims to further the exploration of and discussion on the dynamics of social change by making this research available to students and scholars.

Essays on Austrian Economics and Political Economy

Karen I. Vaughn

MERCATUS CENTER
George Mason University
Arlington, Virginia

About the Mercatus Center

The Mercatus Center at George Mason University is the world's premier university source for market-oriented ideas—bridging the gap between academic ideas and real-world problems.

A university-based research center, the Mercatus Center advances knowledge about how markets work to improve people's lives by training graduate students, conducting research, and applying economics to offer solutions to society's most pressing problems.

Our mission is to generate knowledge and understanding of the institutions that affect the freedom to prosper, and to find sustainable solutions that overcome the barriers preventing individuals from living free, prosperous, and peaceful lives.

Founded in 1980, the Mercatus Center is located on George Mason University's Arlington and Fairfax campuses.

978-1-942951-62-9 (cloth)
978-1-942951-63-6 (paper)
978-1-942951-64-3 (ebook)

Mercatus Center at George Mason University
3434 Washington Blvd., 4th Floor
Arlington, VA 22201
www.mercatus.org
703-993-4930

Cover design: Jessica Hogenson
Editorial and production: Westchester Publishing Services

Dedication

To the memory of Laurence Moss, who first
introduced me to Austrian economics, and who left
this life all too soon, and to Garry—always.

Contents

Introduction

How I Became an Austrian Economist

My serious interest in Austrian economics began in June 1974 at the now famous Austrian conference at South Royalton, Vermont. During my Queens College days in the early 1960s, I had been introduced to both libertarianism and the writings of Ludwig von Mises by my longtime friend and colleague, Larry Moss. I had even attended two of Mises's lectures with Larry, one at his New York University seminar and another at a weekend conference at the Foundation for Economic Education. I was also fortunate at that time to meet Murray Rothbard, and I spent many interesting evenings in his apartment discussing Austrian economics and libertarian philosophy with him and other likeminded young people. There were not many of us at the time. Murray would quip that the majority of libertarians in New York City fit easily into his living room. Having been prompted by a previous acquaintance with the writings of Ayn Rand, I became a convinced libertarian. However, I was not at all sure how Austrian economics differed substantially from the conventional microeconomic theory I had fully embraced in my undergraduate education. As far as I could tell at that time, both neoclassical microeconomic theory and Austrian economics were showing that a market economy was the best of all possible economic structures for allowing people to live free and prosperous lives.

During my graduate years at Duke University and into the early days of my teaching career at the University of Tennessee, Knoxville, I harbored fond feelings for the Austrians, but these feelings were based on no real understanding of what the Austrian tradition had to offer. At Tennessee, with a department dominated by Clarence Ayres's version of Institutionalism, I thought of myself as a neoclassical microeconomist and taught the intermediate course with great enthusiasm. My primary research field of specialization was the history of economic thought, and my energies such as they were, were devoted to John Locke and the seventeenth century. But the truth was that I was getting bored with both. I realized that while I liked teaching micro, I had no ideas about how to contribute to the literature, and I was becoming increasingly impatient with Locke. I wrote a few desultory papers, none of which got published, and wondered if perhaps I was not cut out to be a professor of economics after all. Then, in the spring of 1974, I received the invitation to attend a week-long conference on Austrian economics held in South Royalton, Vermont, sponsored by the Institute for Humane Studies (IHS). Much has already been written about that conference, and elsewhere I have credited it with being the impetus for the Austrian Revival. For me, it was a life changer.

Initially, the prospect that most excited me was spending a week in early summer at an inn in Vermont in the company of interesting people. Having an opportunity to learn more about Austrian economics, of which I had only a cursory knowledge, was still important but perhaps only secondarily so. By the end of the week, that ordering changed.

The lectures by Israel Kirzner, Murray Rothbard, and Ludwig Lachmann, and the comments and discussions among participants, covered the full gamut of Austrian theory. I was most impressed by Israel Kirzner's talks. His carefully constructed arguments and dispassionate presentation contrasted with what seemed to me to be the "true believer" approach of Rothbard. As for Lachmann, his talks about market process and capital theory were a foreign language to me. Nevertheless, I found the whole experience invigorating. While I still did not see how Austrian economics differed substantially from the economics I imbibed in my school years, I was completely convinced that the Austrian approach merited some serious investigation. I never suspected that I would soon have reason to take up that investigation with a vengeance.

In November of that same year, Larry Moss organized a session at the Southern Economic Association meetings on the subject of "The Economics of Ludwig von Mises: Toward a Critical Reappraisal" (Moss 1976). The speakers were to be Murray Rothbard, Israel Kirzner, Larry Moss, and William Baumgarten, each speaking on a different aspect of Mises's work. Fritz Machlup was to be chair of the session. Moss asked me to serve as the sole discussant of all four papers in the session, a daunting prospect for an Austrian neophyte. Nevertheless, I accepted the challenge and spent months in the library giving myself a crash course in most aspects of Austrian theory. Of the four papers, one in particular engaged my interest: Rothbard's (1976) paper on the economic calculation debate. I had never before heard of that debate, but the more research I did into the Austrian response to the economics of socialism, the more I came to realize that the debate was the key to understanding the important theoretical differences between the then standard neoclassical economics and the view of the market process presented by Mises and Hayek. I cannot claim to have immediately grasped all of the implications of the debate, but it is no exaggeration to say that my research into the economic calculation debate sparked the development of my ideas for most of the rest of my career.

A word about why I was so intrigued by the calculation debate: When I first learned micro theory as an undergraduate, I felt that I had learned the secret of the universe. I loved the notions of market clearing, efficiency, and the apparent fairness that seemed to flow from people acting in their own interests in a market economy. Even before I read Adam Smith, the benefits of economic liberty seemed apparent to me. Microeconomics provided the organizing principle that helped me understand a complicated world, and it reinforced my youthful libertarianism. Imagine my chagrin, then, when in my graduate micro theory class, after a lecture on general equilibrium, I was told that general equilibrium theory proved that a socialist economy could be just as efficient as a market economy—and this from an otherwise conservative economist! I really did not believe it, but I had no tools to prove otherwise, so I just tucked it away for future reference. Learning about the economic calculation debate was a revelation. There really was something wrong, not only with socialist economics but possibly with neoclassical economics as well. The next twenty-five years of my career, more or less, consisted of an exercise in figuring out exactly what was wrong with both, a project greatly helped by my reading of Friedrich Hayek.

Hayek was, of course, a major force in the Austrian Revival, especially after winning the Nobel Prize in Economics in 1974. At first, I really only knew his work on the calculation debate and his knowledge essays. I admired the knowledge essays and incorporated "The Use of Knowledge in Society" (Hayek 1945) and "The Meaning of Competition" (Hayek [1946] 1948) into my micro theory course, but I was still thinking like a micro theorist—though with embellishments about knowledge problems. As far as I was concerned, market clearing was the important concept and as long as the market got there, that was all that mattered. Clearly, I still did not grasp the rudiments of market processes. Not surprisingly, I found "Economics and Knowledge," Hayek's (1937) most profound critique of equilibrium theory, elusive at best. I had yet to read *The Constitution of Liberty* (Hayek 1960) or the first volume of *Law, Legislation and Liberty* (Hayek 1973). Surprisingly, it was reading the third volume of *Law,*

Legislation and Liberty (Hayek 1979) that helped me understand how to think about market processes—but more on that later.

The 1970s and into the 1980s were exciting times to be a neophyte Austrian. Economists outside the Mises-Rothbard-Kirzner nexus were starting to take the Austrians—or at least Austrian ideas—seriously, despite not always agreeing with them. I was fortunate to meet some of them, scholars such as Axel Leijunhufvud, Robert Clower, Leland Yeager, and above all, James Buchanan, at a succession of Liberty Fund conferences held in the late 1970s. I was first introduced to Buchanan's work through a footnote reference to *L.S.E. Essays on Cost* (Buchanan and Thirlby 1981) in Rothbard's (1976) paper on the calculation debate. This in turn led me to read *Cost and Choice* (Buchanan [1969] 1999), a book that took Austrian arguments seriously. Because *Cost and Choice* was a difficult book for me to grasp, I had to read it several times before I finally thought I understood Buchanan's central arguments. However, what I immediately understood was that Buchanan, too, thought that the Austrians had important ideas. That may not seem like much all these many years later, but at the time it was enough to keep me studying the Austrian tradition. Austrian economics was clearly at the fringe of the economics profession. I was greatly attracted to its theories, but I was not sure I could trust my instincts. Was I right to think that there was real substance to the Austrian critiques of neoclassical theory? For me, reading Buchanan gave me confidence to follow my instincts.

In 1978, I accepted a position at George Mason University. Again, there were no Austrians on the faculty, but the work environment was congenial, and the names Mises and Hayek were at least familiar to a few. I still felt intellectually isolated—but not for long. In 1980, Richard Fink, director of the Austrian program at Rutgers University, Newark, accepted a position in our department and brought with him both his plan for an Austrian program and several of his Austrian students from Rutgers University, most notably undergraduates Daniel Klein and Tyler Cowen. Together that first year, Fink and I received permission from George Mason University to officially form the Center for the Study of Market Processes. We then persuaded the faculty to hire Don Lavoie and Jack High to become members of the center. If South Royalton had been a life changer for me, forming the Center for the Study of Market Processes was the event that made that change the guiding force of the rest of my career. We now had weekly seminars in Austrian topics and funds to bring in outside speakers, including such Austrian luminaries as Israel Kirzner, Ludwig Lachmann, Friedrich Hayek, and James Buchanan. I was immersed in discussions about the future of Austrian theory. Yet, while the Center for the Study of Market Processes was flourishing, it was doing so within an unknown and unremarkable university. The economics department was just starting to offer a PhD program. We were excited to admit our first graduate students, but we were also concerned for their future careers. No matter how good our program was, the future of our graduate students would be compromised by the status of the university as a whole. That worry disappeared when, much to everyone's amazement, James Buchanan and the entire Center for the Study of Public Choice moved to George Mason University. All of a sudden, our department went from being unknown to being the home of a prestigious academic center. The spillover benefits to the department, and especially to the Center for the Study of Market Processes, in both recognition and scholarly achievement were immeasurable. For me, however, the arrival of the Center for the Study of Public Choice was something of a mixed blessing. On the one hand, the intellectual stimulation that came from bringing Buchanan, who was a fount of ideas and greatly sympathetic to the Austrians, was enormous. But since I had been instrumental in negotiating the arrival of the Center for the Study of Public Choice, I was asked to serve as department chair, a position I held for seven long years. With all the administrative duties I had to assume, finding time to write was a challenge.

Before I became the department chair, I had published "Economic Calculation under Socialism: the Austrian Contribution" (chapter 1) and "Does It Matter That Costs Are Subjective?" (chapter 2), the two articles that provided the theoretical background to my understanding of Austrian economics. During my tenure as chair, I managed to publish several papers in Austrian economics: I co-authored "Hayek's Ricardo Effect: A Second Look" (chapter 3) with Larry Moss, as well as several papers on Public Choice themes, often from an Austrian perspective. The most significant Austrian piece that I wrote during those seven years was the entry on Menger in the *New Palgrave Dictionary of Economics* (Vaughn [1987] 2008), a piece that gives an historical account of the aspects of Carl Menger's writings, rather than an evaluation of them, from a contemporary perspective. When I was finally liberated from my seven years of indentured servitude as the department chair, I could then start thinking about contemporary Austrian economics more systematically. Since I was trained as an historian of economic thought, I naturally approached the subject historically.

Since I had recently written the Palgrave entry on Menger, it is not surprising that my first post-administrative effort was "The Mengerian Roots of the Austrian Revival" (chapter 5). Writing that paper helped me to clarify the central issues of contemporary Austrian theory and brought me back to a question that had dominated Austrian debates in the mid-1970s and throughout much of the 1980s: the role of equilibrium constructs in Austrian theory.

Shortly after the South Royalton conference, Israel Kirzner arranged for Ludwig Lachmann to visit New York University each spring semester for the better part of a decade, where Kirzner and Lachmann ran a colloquium on Austrian economics. A recurrent theme of their discussions was the nature of equilibrium theory and whether it had a role to play in Austrian economics. Kirzner argued that some notion of equilibrium was essential to explaining the order that emerges from economic action; without that, he believed, there was no defense of a market economy. The choice was between equilibrium explanations of the market and nihilism. Lachmann, on the other hand, emphasized the ongoing nature of market activity that never settles because of the subjectivism of not only preferences and costs, but also of expectations. He also talked about institutions as points of orientation, but in a rather nonsystematic way. In the beginning, I thought it was obvious that Kirzner was correct. Some notion of equilibrium was necessary to capture the orderly process of the market. One could explain the essentials of the market order by showing how price changes induced actors to move from one equilibrium to another. But after almost a decade of closer study of Menger, Hayek, and Lachmann, I was no longer so sure.

By 1992, the Kirzner-Lachmann debates were over, but as far as I was concerned, the issue had never been resolved. Kirzner was correct that the core of economics was explaining the spontaneous order that emerged from the unintended consequences of purposeful human action. But was the equilibrium metaphor really the best way to capture that order? Lachmann's arguments about the radical subjectivism of knowledge and the ongoing nature of economic action seemed to argue against any metaphor that was grounded in a state of rest, but unfortunately, he never specified an alternative construct. "The Problem of Order in Austrian Economics: Kirzner vs. Lachmann" (chapter 6) was my attempt to clarify the two viewpoints in my own mind. I had hoped it would allow me to come up with a way of explaining economic order without resorting to equilibrium notions. Unfortunately, I was successful in neither that essay nor in my larger work, *Austrian Economics in America* (Vaughn 1994). My "voilà" moment didn't come until several years later when, thanks to Hayek, I finally figured out what I thought about the whole equilibrium matter.

While my first acquaintance with Hayek in the late 1970s came from my study of the calculation debate, I soon started delving into his more philosophical works. I first read *Law, Legislation and Liberty* and *The Constitution of Liberty*. Then soon I was reading his books of published essays: *Studies in Philosophy, Politics and Economics* (Hayek 1967) and *New Studies in Philosophy, Politics, Economics and the History of Ideas* (Hayek 1978). I became a huge fan of Hayek. I was especially drawn to "Competition as a Discovery Procedure" (Hayek [1968] 1978), because it seemed to mark a real break from conventional economics. Market economies are about learning and change, not about achieving some equilibrium state. But still, how do we explain the orderly process that allows economically progressive learning and change to take place? I found my tentative answer in, of all places, Hayek's theory of social evolution. I had been reading a great deal about biological evolution during my years as the department chair. Austrians and some other nonmainstream economists were beginning to argue for an evolutionary account of market processes. I became convinced that an evolutionary framework was appropriate for Austrian economics, but I did not try to systematically explore my ideas. I wrote several papers examining Hayek's account of the evolution of rules from the perspective of constitutional economics, but nothing about the evolution of market economies.

After writing *Austrian Economics in America* (Vaughn 1994) and struggling with the problem of explaining order without equilibrium, I turned again to Hayek's social evolution. It then occurred to me that while, according to his critics, Hayek's account of the evolution of formal and informal social rules might be problematic, Hayek's evolutionary logic was a better fit when applied to a market order than to political and social interactions. Markets are indeed "discovery procedures." Actors are driven by competition to learn and experiment with new ways to satisfy consumer demands. Profit and loss are indicators of whether they are successful, and thus whether the innovation will persist. Hence, economic discovery leads to the growth of market institutions that codify the results of market discovery. Hayek ([1968] 1978) alluded to these market characteristics in his essay by that name, but he never attempted to develop a systematic economic theory that followed from his insights. "Hayek's Implicit Economics: Rules and the Problem of Order" (chapter 8) was my attempt to begin developing an evolutionary theory of markets from a Hayekian perspective, where equilibrium constructs were irrelevant to understanding the market order.

That article was a verbal account of market evolution from a Hayekian perspective, but in a profession that regards itself as scientific, verbal theory is more easily accepted when there is a systematic model that underlies it. So, when I began reading about the theory of complex adaptive systems, I believed I had found the appropriate model for Hayek's economics. After all, Hayek had been greatly interested in early cybernetic work and systems theory. He never directly applied systems theory to economics, but it seemed obvious to me that this is exactly what Hayek should have done. "Hayek's Theory of the Market Order as an Instance of the Theory of Complex, Adaptive Systems" (chapter 9) was my attempt to argue exactly that point. This article, along with "Hayek's Implicit Economics" (chapter 8), ended my search for the proper theoretical framework for Austrian economics. All that was left was to flesh out my arguments—or so I thought. To that end, I had hoped to write a book developing my ideas in more detail. Alas, life got in the way of my project, and I retired before I could finish it. Still, I regard these two papers as my most important contributions to Austrian economic theory.

The debates over the role of equilibrium in the 1980s and 1990s have long been over. Despite some initial skepticism on the part of some of my colleagues, it is now commonplace among Austrians and others who share many views with Austrians to think of the economy as a complex adaptive system. My specific emphasis on the nature and evolution of market institutions, however, initially did not seem to arouse much enthusiasm. Perhaps I was just writing what other Austrians already believed. I was disappointed but still, for me, these two essays were a personal achievement, the culmination of my twenty-five years of searching for the distinctiveness of contemporary Austrian theory.

Becoming an Austrian economist was a gradual process for me. At first, I was reluctant to be labeled by a set of ideas that I only partially understood. Besides, I greatly admired other economists, such as Milton Friedman, Armen Alchian, Douglas North, and Ronald Coase, all of whom did not exactly fit the Austrian mode. Indeed, Friedman and North were distinctly hostile to the Austrians. I continued to teach microeconomics in full confidence that I was imparting the core of economic theory. But each time I grappled with more of the contemporary Austrian literature, attended one of the frequent Austrian conferences that were being held at that time, or listened to contemporary Austrians explore various facets of Austrian theory, my neoclassical shell cracked a little more. When the Center for the Study of Market Processes was up and running at George Mason University, I finally realized that the aspects of the work of my non-Austrian heroes that I found attractive were exactly those aspects that were most reminiscent of Austrian theory. When I realized several years later that I could no longer teach intermediate micro with a clear conscience because I ceased to find the identification of equilibrium conditions to be a useful means of understanding market order, it occurred to me that I truly was an Austrian economist. I still do not particularly like the label, "Austrian." I would prefer Austrians highlight the substantive core of the tradition (such as market process economics) rather than their ancestry, but once given, labels are nearly impossible to change. Yet, despite the label, far from being a set of dogmas inherited from Menger and Mises as some early critics believed, Austrian economics is—to use an old-fashioned term—a progressive research program, a framework for developing an increasing understanding of the nature of the market order.

During a brief visit to the South Royalton conference, Milton Friedman provocatively quipped, "There is no such thing as Austrian economics, only good economics and bad economics." On the face of it, his claim was indisputable, but unlike Friedman, who clearly thought the Chicago version of neoclassical economics was the real "good" economics, it seems clear to me now that Austrian economics is in fact "good" economics. Indeed, I have come to realize that the Austrian approach to economics is far superior in its ability to understand and explain the consequences of human action in the marketplace than the neoclassical economics that so entranced me early in my career. The essays in this volume chronicle my transformative journey.

REFERENCES

Buchanan, James. M. (1969) 1999. *Cost and Choice: An Inquiry in Economic Theory.* Vol. 6 of The Collected Works of James M. Buchanan. Indianapolis, IN: Liberty Fund.

Buchanan, James M., and G. F. Thirlby, eds. 1981. *L.S.E. Essays on Cost.* New York: New York University Press.

Hayek, F. A. 1937. "Economics and Knowledge." *Economica* 4 (13): 33–54.

———. 1945. "The Use of Knowledge in Society." *The American Economic Review* 35 (4): 519–30.

———. (1946) 1948. "The Meaning of Competition." In F. A. Hayek, *Individualism and Economic Order*, 92–106. Chicago: The University of Chicago Press.

———. 1960. *The Constitution of Liberty.* Chicago: University of Chicago Press.

———. 1967. *Studies in Philosophy, Politics and Economics.* Abingdon, UK: Taylor & Francis.

———. 1973. *Law, Legislation and Liberty.* Vol. 1: *Rules and Order.* Chicago: University of Chicago Press.

———. 1978. *New Studies in Philosophy, Politics, Economics, and the History of Ideas.* Chicago: University of Chicago Press.

———. (1968) 1978. "Competition as a Discovery Procedure." In F. A. Hayek, *New Studies in Philosophy, Politics, Economics, and the History of Ideas*, 179–90. Chicago: University of Chicago Press.

———. 1979. *Law, Legislation and Liberty.* Vol. 3: *The Political Order of a Free People.* Chicago: University of Chicago Press.

Moss, Laurence S., ed. 1976. *The Economics of Ludwig von Mises: Toward a Critical Reappraisal.* Kansas City, MO: Sheed and Ward.

Rothbard, Murray. 1976. "Ludwig von Mises and Economic Calculation under Socialism." In *The Economics of Ludwig von Mises: Toward a Critical Reappraisal*, edited by Laurence S. Moss, 67–78. Kansas City, MO: Sheed and Ward.

Vaughn, Karen I. 1994. *Austrian Economics in America: The Migration of a Tradition.* Cambridge: Cambridge University Press.

———. (1987) 2008. "Menger, Carl (1840–1921)." In *The New Palgrave Dictionary of Economics.* London: Palgrave Macmillan.

Chapter 1
Economic Calculation under Socialism
The Austrian Contribution

Between 1920 and 1940, a body of economic literature developed which became known as the debate over economic calculation under socialism. It began with the publication of Ludwig von Mises's article, "Economic Calculation in the Socialist Commonwealth" (Mises 1920); it took form first primarily in the German literature and then reached full flower in English language journals and books during the 1930s. The ostensible subject of the debate was whether it was possible for a real economy to operate efficiently without free markets and without private ownership of capital and land, but at the core of the debate were issues that were far-reaching and profound in their implications for economic theory in general. That the issues involved are still some of the most difficult in contemporary economic theory and remain unresolved almost forty years after the conclusion of the debate makes the identification of the differences between the two sides of more than historical interest.

It is indicative of the nature of the controversy that those who argued most effectively in favor of socialism were not advocates of a labor theory of value but were economists operating within the dominant neoclassical paradigm.[1] A few took their inspiration from Marshall, more from Walras, but all agreed that given some "just" initial wealth distribution, equilibrium in the perfectly competitive model represented the maximization of human welfare, and all their programs for socialism were designed to reproduce the

Originally published in *Economic Inquiry* 18, no. 4 (1980): 535–54. Reprinted with permission.

conclusions of perfect competition in a centrally directed economy.[2] They preferred socialism to capitalism because they believed under socialism it would be possible to eliminate the imperfections that they found existing simultaneously with free markets: monopolies, externalities, business cycles, and unjust income and wealth distributions.[3] Thus, they believed that capitalism was undesirable because it did not measure up to the ideal of perfect competition.

Those most closely associated with the theoretical defense of capitalism,[4] on the other hand, were Ludwig von Mises, Friedrich Hayek and Lionel Robbins.[5] Of the three, Mises and Hayek were both Austrian economists, and Robbins, although English, was much influenced by Carl Menger and was, therefore, at least partly in the Austrian tradition. As Austrians, they worked with a perception of economic activity that differed markedly from that of mainstream economists. Primarily, they questioned the relevance and applicability of static equilibrium models in which all information is given and emphasized instead the process by which decentralized economic actors operating in a world of uncertainty and constant change bring about the coordination of production and consumption plans. Consequently, the debate was a contest of theoretical models in which a mutually satisfactory resolution was precluded from the outset.

Although it is conventional to treat the economic calculation controversy as a debate between those who favored socialism and those who opposed it, this is not descriptive of the actual course of events. During the 1920s there was a genuine debate between Mises and the German and Austrian socialists, but by the 1930s Mises had finished with the issue and it was Friedrich Hayek who took upon himself the role of critic of socialism in England. However, by that time, the real debate, in so far as one took place in the journals, was among the socialists themselves[6] who were busy hammering out a complete economic theory of socialism based on neoclassical static equilibrium analysis. Occasionally, Hayek's criticisms were noted in scholarly articles, but rarely for any purpose other than refutation. Mostly, Mises was ridiculed; and Hayek, on this issue seen as little more than Mises' apologist, was ignored. The unhappy result of this failure to see more than warmed-over Mises in Hayek's work was an almost total lack of recognition of the subtleties of the issues Hayek raised in criticism of market socialism. If I had to offer a crude synopsis of the economic calculation debate, it would be this: Mises wrote an article claiming that rational economic calculation was impossible under socialism. This prompted those who favored socialism to try to refute him and thus forced them to construct a model of rationally administered, centrally directed economy. Meanwhile,

Hayek wrote two sophisticated and penetrating critiques of the socialist schemes, which were in the main ignored. Mises seemed easy to refute, and so for twenty years, socialists continued to refute the same arguments, thereby avoiding consideration of the more difficult issues raised by Hayek.

In order to understand the principal issues raised in the literature on socialist economic calculation, it will be convenient to divide my discussion into four parts. The first part of this paper examines Mises's 1920 article to identify the sources of controversy; the second part briefly outlines the major developments in the economic theory of socialism during the 1930s; the third part presents Hayek's criticisms of socialist economic programs; and the fourth and final part attempts to summarize the theoretical problems raised during the debate in order to appreciate the relevance of the Austrian contribution to current problems in economic theory.

I.

The literature on the economics of socialism before 1920 is sparse. While there was no lack of scholarly (and not so scholarly) discussion of socialism as a social theory, Marxists, following the lead of Marx himself, paid little attention to the actual workings of a socialist economy. It was assumed that after the revolution was time enough to worry about the economic problem, assuming that one still existed after the demise of capitalism.[7] A few attempts were made to describe a theory of a centrally directed economy, but these attempts were significantly made by non-Marxist economists interested in a purely theoretical problem. F. von Wieser often made use of the construct of a centrally directed economy in explicating his economic theories, as did Pareto in his exposition of general equilibrium theory. Enrico Barone developed the most complete exploration into the economics of socialism, applying neoclassical tools to the problem of a centrally directed economy in an article written in 1908 (Wieser 1893, especially 60–64; Pareto 1906, especially 267–271; Barone 1908). None of these writers, however, were socialists and none were attempting to prescribe a formula for running a real socialist economy. More significantly, none of these efforts had any influence on socialists and Marxists prior to 1920.

What all these early attempts to construct a theoretical model of a centrally directed economy had in common was the realization that the same economic logic can be applied both to capitalism and socialism. Therefore, if socialist economic planners want to allocate resources efficiently, they must be able to calculate correct resource and product values, including those two much despised by Marxists, interest and profits. Hence in 1920, in a manner which suggested growing impatience with economically naive Marxists (some of whom were advocating a moneyless economy without exchange and denying the existence of resource scarcity), Mises wrote his famous article, "Economic Calculation in the Socialist Commonwealth."

Mises's article was concerned with establishing two principal propositions. The first was a restatement of the Wieser-Pareto-Barone argument that all the same economic variables that guide resource use in a capitalist economy must also necessarily be taken account of under socialism. He argued specifically that it was naive to expect money and prices to disappear for very long under socialism; that as long as people have differing preferences (and as long as socialist leaders strive to satisfy consumer preferences), the allocation of consumer goods would present problems which could only be solved by resorting to some system of money and prices. In fact, since consumer goods presumably would be owned by consumers themselves, the development of prices and markets in consumer goods was inevitable (Mises 1920, 90–93). The real problem, according to Mises, was in the allocation of capital goods—the means of production. Since these would not be privately owned, markets could not be utilized to determine resource prices, and hence there would be no way to evaluate relative resource scarcities (104–109). He conceded that while socialism may be possible in a static state where knowledge of unchanging economic parameters is universal and where the imputation problem, once solved, would remain solved forever, he emphasized that such a static state itself is only a "theoretical assumption corresponding to no real state of affairs" (104). In any real socialist world, the impediments to rational economic calculation are legion: the inevitability of change, the uncertainties that this implies in all economic decision-making (111), the problem of initiative without private property (116), and the necessary elimination of the "promoter and man of affairs" (119) who makes the market work to establish relevant prices. Mises's second proposition, then, was that without free markets based on private resource ownership, economic calculation would be totally impossible. It was this second proposition that infuriated socialists, challenged conventional economists, and became the focus of attempts to refute Mises.[8]

II.

Although there was much discussion of the problems Mises raised during the 1920s in the German literature,[9] the creation of an economic model of socialism along neoclassical lines was a product of English-speaking economists in the 1930s. Three men especially stand out as originators of socialist economics:

H. D. Dickinson, Oskar Lange, and Abba Lerner. Of the three, Dickinson was first in print with his preliminary model, Lange's work came to represent the "economic theory of socialism" (and incidentally was credited with offering the definitive refutation of Mises), and Lerner's marginal cost rule made a significant contribution to the work of the other two.[10]

Dickinson and Lange developed very similar models of socialist economy in which there would be private ownership of consumer goods and freedom of choice in occupation, but public ownership of all capital goods and nonhuman productive resources. Where their models differed most significantly, at least initially, was in the methods suggested for obtaining relative values to guide resource allocation. Dickinson's solution to the pricing problem was to set up selling agencies which would determine the prices of all goods by a combination of several methods: The prices for consumer goods would be set according to what the market would bear, the agencies "raising (prices) when stocks fell short, lowering when they accumulate" (1933, 239). In this way they would be able to determine statistically all the demand functions for all goods which, when combined with technologically determined production functions and a given supply of resources, would enable the central planning board to impute factor valuations (240). Dickinson also seemed to propose that the planning agency, operating within the "glass walls" of socialism (where all demand functions, production functions, and resource supplies are known to planners) would be able to construct a mathematical model of the economy which would be solved for resource prices using a system of simultaneous equations á la Barone (245).

Lange's solution to the pricing problem was simpler. He too, proposed setting up a central planning board to administer prices, but only resource prices. Consumer goods would be priced in free markets in order to provide accurate information for factor valuation (1938, 72–73). Factor prices would then be determined by a system of "trial and error" exclusively, the process partially adopted by Dickinson but originally proposed by F. M. Taylor in 1928. Lange's use of trial and error was a conscious attempt to overcome the myriad difficulties inherent in an attempt to solve for prices using statistical demand curves and econometric models, difficulties stressed by both Robbins and Hayek (Robbins 1933, 149; Hayek 1935, 212). In response to the critics, Lange argued forcefully that there was no need to set up systems of simultaneous equations to find factor prices as long as the planning board "fixes the prices so as to balance the quantity supplied and the quantity demanded of each commodity" (Lange 1938, 83). Lange believed that trial and error described the process by which prices are formed in real markets, and he patterned his method after a

Walrasian tâtonnement with the central planning board acting the part of the auctioneer (1938, 70, 82–83).

After Lange's work appeared in print, the socialists, as well as many nonsocialists, agreed that the problem of pricing under socialism had been solved by the trial-and-error process, and what remained to be explored was how these prices should be used in the actual production of goods and services. Hence, after the publication of Lange's article, the problem of what set of rules would induce managers of socialist firms to make decisions that would lead to appropriate resource allocation replaced the problem of pricing in the literature on socialist economics.

Lange's contribution to the question of managerial rules had been to point out that in pure competition, profit maximization and the freedom of entry and exit are the mechanisms which assure allocative efficiency. Thus, to duplicate the results of perfect competition, it was necessary to force socialist managers to behave like perfect competitors by imposing two rules of behavior on them: As an alternative to profit maximization, they would be instructed to minimize factor costs for the given set of resource prices, and to equate marginal cost to product price in the production of output. The first would guarantee efficient use of resources and the second, appropriate plant size. When applied to the industry as a whole, the second rule would also control the size of the industry (Lange 1938, 75–79). As long as socialist managers observed the "parametric function of price," that is, as long as they, like perfect competitors in genuine markets, treated resource and product prices as parameters rather than dependent variables, his rules would lead to the same resource allocation as perfect competition (81).[11]

By the end of the decade, the outline of a neoclassical economic theory of market socialism was complete. Consumer goods are priced in genuine markets, communally owned resource prices are determined by a central planning board through the trial-and-error process, and managers at both firms and industries are told to produce where the marginal cost of output equals the price of the product produced and the price of any resource employed equals the marginal contribution of that resource to output. Any change in parameters will manifest itself as a change in price, which will cause managers to alter firm production and industry size accordingly. Clearly, these neoclassical socialists believed they had shown that economic calculation was just as possible under socialism as it was under capitalism. That in order to do so they had to create a socialism that bore no resemblance to any existing political states, and which had nothing to do with Marxist economics, was irrelevant. Their economic model was still within the spirit of socialism although it retained many important features of capitalism.[12] In addition, they believed their brand of socialism was both economically and morally superior to free market capitalism. With a system of market socialism, one could more rationally direct economic growth through appropriate manipulation of the rate of interest, and production in general would increase because of the elimination of monopoly power and the waste associated with business cycles and inappropriate coordination of private production plans. Furthermore, income distribution under socialism would be morally superior to capitalism because of the absence of income derived from property ownership, and because of the ability of the central authority to adjust wages to eliminate rents (Lerner 1937, 269–270). Certainly, they believed Mises had been decidedly refuted many times over by the end of the decade.[13]

III.

So far, we have considered only the socialists' contribution to the debate over economic calculation. It has been possible to review the development of the economic theory of socialism without reference to Hayek's writings because despite the fact that the socialists apparently read his essay, there was very little notice taken of the criticisms he offered of the socialist schemes. Hence, it is more in keeping with the actual course of the controversy to treat Hayek's comments as a critique apart from the development of socialist economic theory.

What seemed to trouble Hayek the most about neoclassical socialist economics was what he regarded as an inappropriate application of static equilibrium models to the formation of a new economic order. He respected the usefulness of the concept of equilibrium for limited explanatory purposes but believed that the socialists were overstepping those limits by venturing into the realm of planning on the basis of equilibrium models. While the high level of abstraction of the Walrasian general equilibrium model in particular might be an advantage in explaining precisely the end point of a market process, this level of abstraction which is an asset in simplifying explanation also precludes the model's usefulness as a blueprint for constructing a different, nonmarket economy.[14] What this model omits—considerations of the process by which equilibrium is approached, the effects of uncertainty on the conclusions of the model, consideration of what constitutes economic information and to whom it is available—are each one sufficient to guarantee that an economic order resulting from conscious planning according to that model will be far different from the one envisioned by the planners. Thus, Hayek argued specifically that while the models the socialists were using to arrive at their solution to the pricing problem were not logically contradictory and socialism was not therefore impossible in the sense of being theoretically inconceivable, it was nevertheless practically impossible since the socialist models bore no relationship to the manner in which prices were formed in the real world.[15] In general, the market socialists misunderstood the nature of the market economy and were misapplying the market models they were using.

It is true that Hayek never said this in so many words all in one place; it unfortunately is the fate of a critic to have his own vision revealed only piecemeal and in reaction to the work of others. Yet this was the heart of Hayek's argument against the socialists, and whether or not he was correct, his argument was a profound one that deserved careful attention. Instead, there apparently was some confusion over what Hayek meant by the possible versus the practical in economic model building because Lange took Hayek's work to represent a "second line of defense" of capitalism. Lange claimed that Hayek now admitted that Mises had been wrong, that socialism *was* possible "in theory," but that there were just practical objections to its implementation (1938, 63).

At the center of the confusion was a failure to agree on what constituted a theoretical objection to socialism (or any model meant to tell us something about the real world) and what was "merely" a practical one. The socialists (and most of the economics profession at the time) seemed to believe that the demonstration that the same economic logic applies to both capitalism and socialism was sufficient proof that socialism was "theoretically possible," and hence they pointed to Pareto and Barone as having refuted Mises' claim that socialism is impossible (Lange 1938, 59). Neither Mises nor Hayek ever argued that the socialist models were inconsistent given their assumptions, however. What they argued was that the ability to calculate rationally under socialism was "practically impossible" because the theory, while logically consistent, did not capture enough important features of the real world to make it applicable. This is hardly a "practical" objection in any useful sense of the word. Certainly, this kind of "practical" objection cannot be shrugged off as trivial. Nevertheless, it was Lange's simplistic interpretation of Hayek's sophisticated insight that was accepted by the profession with the unhappy result that the really interesting and important question of what constitutes an appropriate model for a socialist economy was never formally discussed.[16]

The major source of Hayek's criticisms of the wholesale application of general equilibrium models to socialist economies was his perception of the role of information in economic decision-making, a problem which has only recently been recognized in the theoretical literature.[17] Standard neoclassical models begin with the assumption of given utility and production functions which, when ground through the maximization model, imply a set of relative product and resource prices. Lange pointed out that the same information which guided economic decisions in capitalism would also be available in a socialized economy.[18] To Hayek, saying that the information was "available" was just the beginning of the problem of demonstrating the possibility of a nonmarket economy. The real problem of any economic model is to show how the information necessary for rational decision-making, which exists in the minds of millions of separate individuals, can be transmitted to appropriate decision makers in such a way as to permit an orderly economy to emerge (Hayek 1948, 210).[19] The market is one highly successful means of encouraging the production, transmission, and use of information because it takes advantage of decentralization of knowledge and of decision-making (83–87). Hayek referred to this as the division of knowledge (50). The burden of proof therefore was on the socialists to show that centralization could improve upon the market's production and use of information.

Hayek's emphasis on the role of information in the economic process is well illustrated in his discussion of the Dickinson-style mathematical solution to the pricing problem. Hayek objected to the mathematical solution in part because of the practical difficulties involved in solving what would necessarily be a formidable set of equations once the data are given. This was the objection upon which the socialists concentrated their rebuttals. However, Hayek's more profound criticism was that given the way in which information is discovered and used in a market economy, it would be physically impossible for a planning board to acquire the information necessary to specify those equations (Hayek 1935, 208–212).

The information that individuals use to guide their economic activity is vast, detailed, and necessarily incomplete (212–213). It is not neatly summarized in objective demand and cost functions which need only be revealed to central planners in order for them to take over the task of economic decision-making. Even if it were possible to arrive at useful demand functions for consumer goods, it would not be possible to obtain objective production functions and cost functions which represent those which describe a free market. The major reason Hayek gave was that such information is not given but is the subject of continuous discovery. Neoclassical economics emphasizes "engineering knowledge" or knowledge of production techniques as if it were the only information relevant to business decisions. In fact, efficient resource use depends as much upon knowledge of "time and place"—the ability to perceive opportunities others miss and to know when to take advantage of them (Hayek 1948, 80). Further, some information may be no more than a "technique of thought" which enables a producer to "find new solutions rapidly as soon as he is confronted with a new constellation of circumstances" (1935, 196). Market prices are the result of transactions among individuals with unique and fragmented knowledge and are a means by which this decentralized knowledge is coalesced into a coordinated whole. To try to summarize all this information into a set of simultaneous equations would be quixotic at best.

Hayek's perception of the role of information in economic analysis also provided the basis for his criticism of the Lange-Taylor trial-and-error method of pricing—the socialists' solution to the difficulties inherent in trying to operate an economy using econometric models. Hayek argued that trial-and-error pricing would not be able to duplicate free market pricing for two reasons: One had to do with the timing of price changes and the other, with the problem of specifying the product accurately. As for the first, neither Lange nor Dickinson (who also adopted the trial-and-error techniques in his 1939 book, *The Economics of Socialism*) made clear at what intervals the central planning board would change prices in response to surpluses and shortages. Hayek pointed out that only if the price of every good was to be changed immediately whenever some imbalance was perceived would a planning board come close to approximating the market. More likely, however, there would be some accounting period at the end of which prices would be adjusted. Since the data are always changing, in between these accounting periods the official prices would be disequilibrium prices, which would prolong excess demands and supplies and hence also prolong resource misallocation. Of course, he was not implying that market-determined prices are never in disequilibrium: Rather, the implication was that market prices will be in disequilibrium less often than centrally controlled prices and will always be changing in the "right" direction, thus giving correct market signals even if they are technically in disequilibrium. Markets enable buyers and sellers to react more quickly to changing data because the path by which information must travel in order for corrective price changes to be effected is shorter than it would be under socialism (Hayek 1948, 187–188, 192–194).

In addition to the problem of slower reaction time, Hayek also pointed to the problems a planning board would have with trying to specify the products to be assigned prices, and again this was a problem that refers to the kind of data available to decision makers. In effect, Hayek argued that there are more dimensions to the objects of exchange than price and quantity. In the real world, unlike the model of perfect competition, many products are not standardized with uniform, competitive prices. In capital markets especially, products are often physically unique, and where they are physically similar, they vary according to location, time of availability, and concomitantly offered services. It would be unlikely that any planning board would be able to take account of all these characteristics in defining products for which to set prices. Hence, a central planning board would be setting prices for aggregates of goods that were not representative of all the different products subject to economic exchange. This would necessarily reduce the informational content of prices, the adaptiveness of resources to various production processes and the variety of production techniques employed (Hayek 1935, 209; 1948, 188, 193).

Of these three criticisms Hayek offered of socialist pricing schemes, the misunderstanding of the character of the information which guides economic activity, the difference in the speed of adjustment to changing data between socialism and capitalism, and the difficulty in defining what a "product" is for accounting purposes, the first was not dealt with by the socialists (and apparently was not acknowledged to be a genuine problem by those who later evaluated the controversy),[20] and the second two were considered to be minor empirical objections to socialism which could be worked out and which in any case would not lead to serious distortions in resource allocation.

Even if the pricing problem were solved, Hayek, taking his cue from Mises, still believed that there would be great difficulties in attempting to operate an economy without private ownership of the means of production. Hence, he believed that even Lange's "competitive socialism" would necessarily fall short of the level of economic well-being the market is capable of yielding. Lange had claimed that all that was necessary to show that socialism was capable of allocating resources as well as capitalism was to refer to the "parametric function of price" (1938, 80). That is, all that was necessary for socialism to work was to ensure that managers of firms and industries behave like perfect competitors and treat resource and product prices as if they were independent of the producers' production decisions. The problem, aside from the question of whether or not the "parametric function" actually describes the way prices operate in a competitive economy, is that socialist managers would not really be perfect competitors. While there might very well be many firms in an industry with firm managers making output decisions on the basis of given prices, Lange's plan also required the existence of industry managers who would make decisions regarding the growth or decline of the industry as a whole. The industry manager, then, would really be in a position of a monopolist who knows his output decisions will affect the price of his product. Only if he could be convinced to ignore his effect on the price of the product, could Lange's solution be consistent with his model. Lange's method of dealing with the problem was for the Central Planning Board to impose an "accounting rule," which would instruct industry managers that "All accounting has to be done as if prices were independent of decisions taken" (80). Both Mises and Hayek questioned the likelihood of managers actually following such a rule when it easily could work contrary to their own personal long-run interests.

Mises especially had argued that the role of the manager in a socialist state was crucial to the success or failure of the system. One of the reasons Mises gave for the "impossibility" of socialism was that managers could never be substitutes for private businessmen: that one had to risk one's own income on the consequences of the decisions one makes if the market is going to yield the most efficient outcome (1920, 116–122). One particular socialist argument that Mises took pains to contradict was that managers in socialist enterprises would be no different from managers of private corporations who are not themselves owners of stock in the company. Mises acknowledged that this might be partially true, but countered that the most successful corporations were those whose managers did have a direct stake in the success of the business either through bonuses or shareholding (119). While this claim is open to empirical testing, Mises also hinted at a more sophisticated theoretical argument against identifying corporation managers with socialist managers: that it is the capital markets which keep private managers in line, that the owners of private capital can shift resources from unprofitable to more profitable ventures and thus put poor managers out of a job (1922, 139). Where profit or loss no longer serves as an objective test of managerial success, as it likely would not under socialism, it becomes exceedingly difficult to weed out inefficient managers.

Hayek enlarged on this theme when he argued that under socialism, where a manager's decisions are not subject to the objective test of profit or loss to determine their correctness, one's success as a manager would therefore depend upon convincing the planning board that the decisions he made in the past were the best given the alternatives available. As a result, managers would be less likely to make risky decisions regardless of their potential profitability because the consequences of failure far outweighed the benefits of success to their careers.[21]

While the actual propensity to take risks depends upon the constraints facing individual socialist managers and an argument can be made that they will be either more or less prone to risk taking than private entrepreneurs (in fact, Mises [1922, 140] had argued that managers would be more prone to risk taking than private entrepreneurs since they did not have potential loss of personal wealth to constrain their behavior), the problem both Mises and Hayek were approaching was essentially one of the effects of different specifications of property rights on individual economic decision-making. The issue of property rights, which has provided such a fruitful framework for modern analysis of socialist economies,[22] was only touched on in the early literature on socialism. It was generally contained under the rubric of "incentives," with the critics arguing that without private property, people would have no incentive to produce, and the early socialists countering with descriptions of the change in human nature which would occur after the abolition of the evils of the capitalist system. The later socialists tended to dismiss the problem of the relationship between managerial incentives and managerial decision-making entirely as being more in the province of sociology than economics.[23] Instead they concentrated their energies on defining a set of managerial rules which would lead to efficient levels of output without considering how to induce people to follow the rules they devised.

Even granting that a planning board could devise appropriate managerial rules and induce managers to follow them, Hayek implied that determining whether or not the rules had been followed was not as easy a task as it might seem at first blush. The socialists' managerial rules, as we have seen, generally involved instructing the manager to equate the "parametric" price to some measure of cost to achieve optimal output. The most theoretically satisfying rule was Lerner's, which instructed managers to expand output (or input use) to that point where price equals marginal cost at every decision point (Lerner 1937, 251). Hayek criticized the workability of even this rule, however, and in so doing implicitly criticized all rules that assumed that costs could be treated as objective data (Hayek 1935, 226; 1948, 196). In fact, only current prices are objective data available to producers while costs are ultimately subjective evaluations of the utility of forgone alternatives, the value of what could have been produced with the resources now being used to produce one's product. Hayek argued that in full market equilibrium, the values of forgone alternatives were accurately measured by market prices of resources, but in the real world where static equilibrium conditions do not obtain, the values of forgone alternatives can only be individual estimates of the possible effects of different courses of action (Hayek 1935, 226).[24]

The relevance of this thoroughly "Austrian" view of costs to socialist economy is most pronounced in the valuation and use of capital in a nonmarket setting. Capital creation and use necessarily depends upon an entrepreneur's subjective estimates of future values. Since a socialist manager's estimates of current capital value would be based only partly on current prices, but more so on his estimates of possible market changes, conjectures about the planning board's response to these changes, his evaluation of the risks involved in his decisions, and his propensity to take risks, it would be impossible for costs perceived by the manager to be objectively measured by some outside observer. If marginal cost is a subjective estimate that has no "correct" value, then the planning board would have no way of discovering if the firm had followed its directive. Hence, Hayek argued that the planning board would have to engage in detailed audits of the firm's books to see if at every decision point the manager took the "best" course of action available to him. But "best" would now mean best according to the planner, who would have to substitute his judgment for that of the socialist manager in the evaluation of costs (Hayek 1935, 236–237; 1948, 198–199). There were no simple rules for judging managerial success in a non-market setting.

IV.

To the modern reader who is aware of the empirical record of the last thirty years of East European and Russian Communism, the early work of Lange and Dickinson (as well as the professional acclaim accorded them)[25] seems naive at best. For the greater part of the short history of communist states, price has not been used as the primary allocative mechanism. Output quotas instead have been the rule rather than the exception, with all the concomitant problems of resource misuse and sheer waste that even the socialists of the 1930s predicted. It is only recently that attempts have been made in the more liberal of the communist countries to move closer to Lange-type market socialism in a belated vindication of both the Austrians and the market socialists.[26] However, one feature which stands out in the modern literature of market socialism is the attention paid to incentive structures. Despite an almost contemptuous dismissal of the problem during the original debate, even Lange in his later work put incentives in the forefront of the problems of socialist economy still to be solved.[27] The major problem now seems to be whether or not rational incentive structures can be built into a socialist economy so that economic agents actually do what the planners want them to do: whether there can be a good substitute for profits to make the system function effectively. Gone are the blithe assertions of the superiority of socialism in reaching the "perfection" of perfect competition more easily than capitalism.

It is not only as a predictor of actual economic events that Lange's 1936 work suffers by comparison to Hayek's essays but also as a contribution to theoretical economics. Of course, it is unfair to criticize Lange for failure to perceive all the problems inherent in the wholesale application of Walrasian general equilibrium to a socialist economy since he was writing before the major work on such models was even begun. In fact, when one considers the state of the art in 1936, Lange's use of Walras in comprehending and describing an economic system is a formidable achievement indeed. Yet, recognition of the greatness of Lange's work can only increase one's respect for Hayek's. Today Hayek seems more modern than Lange precisely because he was able to pinpoint many of the most crucial defects in Lange's exposition long before the economics profession came to recognize these same criticisms in their attempt to refine and extend simpler Walrasian models. In fact, a listing of Hayek's major criticisms of market socialism—the failure to take account of adjustment processes, the misunderstanding of the problem of decentralized and incomplete information, the lack of appropriate incentive structure—reads like a research program for general equilibrium theorists for the last three decades.[28]

To dwell for a moment on a single, far-reaching example, one has only to consult the growing literature on the economics of information to see the contemporary relevance of Hayek's work. The modern literature asks "how individuals should and do behave when imperfectly informed"[29] and then goes on to construct models based on different assumptions about economic behavior and the amount of knowledge available to market participants. While it shows that it is possible to construct models with imperfect information which converge toward an equilibrium, the equilibria vary with the assumption about the knowledge and market behavior. These models are a far cry from Lange's "parametric function of price," and in them we see partly why Hayek's early work, in which the information problem was always central, is quoted and referred to today with increasing frequency in the theoretical literature.

I began this essay by claiming that the controversy between the advocates of socialism and their critics was at heart a contest of theoretical models based on differing perceptions of what a market economy really was. The socialists seemed to regard the market as a mechanism, the salient features of which were accurately captured in a simple general equilibrium model. Human beings were assumed to react automatically to market signals and could be counted on to react just as automatically to commands from a central planning agency. The institutional structure and the system of incentives implicit in the structure were assumed to have no effect on economic behavior. Hayek, on the other hand, understood the market to be fundamentally entrepreneurial in nature. Equilibrium models, he argued, could be no more than a useful preliminary to the study of the main problem (1948, 44–45), which was to show how the market enables profit-seeking individuals to make choices in an environment of decentralized and incomplete information and uncertainty about the future, and in which they bear the consequences of their choices. To Hayek, the market economy is essentially a spontaneously evolved institutional response to the difficulties of coordinating economic activity in a complex and changing world. Because the real world is so complex and so changeable, it was clear to him that the simplistic models constructed by the market socialists, if used to operate a real socialist economy, were doomed to produce an economic environment far different from, and far inferior to the one they envisioned in their plans.

NOTES

1. The people most responsible for developing the economic theory of socialism and who are referred to here are Fred Taylor, H. D. Dickinson, Oskar Lange, Abba Lerner, E. M. F. Durbin, and Maurice Dobb. While many other economists wrote on the economics of socialism, these were the most influential writers on the subject and the ones whose work was accepted as a refutation of Mises.

2. The exception was Maurice Dobb, who was far more Marxist than the others and who challenged the "sacredness of consumer preferences" (1933, 591) and who argued that reproducing the conclusions of perfect competition under socialism missed the point. As he put it, "Either planning means overriding the autonomy of private decisions or it apparently means nothing at all." (1937, 279).

3. A belief in the superiority of socialism over capitalism both as it exists and as it is described in ideal models is implicit in all the socialists' writings, but the best specific statement is found in Lange (1962, IV:98–120, "The Economist's Case for Socialism"). There he claims that "only a socialist economy can distribute incomes so as to attain the maximum social welfare," (IV:99). In regard to externalities, a socialist economy would be able to "take into the cost accounts all the alternatives sacrificed . . . by doing so it would avoid much of the social waste connected with private enterprise." (IV:104). He further asserts that "as a result of the possibility of taking into account all the alternatives a socialist economy would not be subject to the fluctuations of the business cycle" (IV:105). See also Dickinson (1933, 247).

4. I will use the terms "socialism" and "capitalism" to designate the opposing economic systems under debate. Although the words have no clearly recognized scientific definition (and even to the participants in the debate, the meanings shifted frequently between theoretical and empirical states), I will try to be consistent with the following meanings. *Socialism* will refer to any theoretical model which provides for collective ownership of land and capital goods, and which designates some kind of planning board to oversee resource allocation and set official policy for capital accumulation and growth. This is a loose enough definition to encompass all the systems proposed by socialist economists during the debate. *Capitalism* will mean a theoretical model where all resources are privately owned and where resource allocation, consumption patterns, and capital accumulation are all determined by the coordination of individual preferences in unregulated markets. This definition seems closest to what Mises and Hayek had in mind when they talked about capitalism and capitalist methods of production.

5. Although he has not received nearly the publicity the others have, we should also include Hawtry in this list. In *The Economic Problem* (1926) he described a socialist model which closely resembled that developed by Dickinson and Lange a decade later and criticized it along much the same lines as Hayek criticized the later ones in 1935 and 1940. See especially pp. 336–340.

6. For instance, Dickinson's 1933 article drew sharp criticism from Maurice Dobb (1935). Dobb's criticism of Dickinson brought a stinging rebuke from Abba Lerner (1935). Lange managed to get by pretty much unscathed by his fellow socialists, but Durbin and Lerner had a somewhat hostile interchange on the subject of Durbin's 1936 article (Lerner 1937; Durbin 1937; Lerner 1938).

7. For a description of early socialist and Marxist literature which makes this point, see Schumpeter (1954, 877–885). This is not to say that there was no socialist economics before 1920. Rather, there was no attempt by socialists to deal with the problem of efficient resource use and growth within the context of a consistent model before 1920. In his excellent review article of W. O. Henderson's *Life of Friedrich Engels*, T. W. Hutchison points out that Engels in his later work showed that he understood very well the vital importance of a competitive pricing mechanism when criticizing other socialists as "utopian," but

ignored it when describing his and Marx's view of the workings of the economy after the Revolution. Hutchison comments, "Surely no one in the whole of intellectual history can have looked a major, pressing intellectual and practical problem so clearly and piercingly in the face and then so blithely and confidently passed on without a word." Hutchison (1978, 317).

8. One reason Mises infuriated socialists is that he deliberately chose to clothe his arguments in highly polemical garb. He claimed, for example, that "Every step that takes us away from private ownership of the means of production and from the use of money also takes us away from rational economy" (1920, 104), and "Where there is no free market, there is no pricing mechanism; without a pricing mechanism, there is no economic calculation" (111). He even went so far as to claim that the absence of free markets under socialism would lead to the end of "rationality and logic in thought itself" (105). While it is true that in so stating his arguments, he was using polemic to answer polemic, the result of his emotionally charged style was that the style was better remembered than the cogency of the argument.

9. Accounts of some of these clearly socialist responses can be found in Hayek (1935, 1–40), and Hoff (1949, chap. IV, V).

10. Dickinson's model was first published as an article in the *Economic Journal* in 1933. He later expanded and refined it in his booklength *The Economics of Socialism* (1939). Lange's major contribution was his two part article, "On the Economic Theory of Socialism," published in the *Review of Economic Studies* (1936; 1937) and later reprinted together with Fred Taylor's "The Guidance of Production in a Socialist State." See Lange and Taylor (1938). Lerner contributed several articles to the development of socialist economics, but perhaps his most famous is "Statics and Dynamics in Socialist Economies" (1937). Lerner has charmingly recalled the genesis of the marginal cost rule he proposed in that article and his personal conversations on the subject with Lange, in Lerner (1973).

11. The problem of managerial rules was also addressed by E. M. F. Durbin in his 1936 article in the *Economic Journal*, although his instructions for socialist managers were somewhat different from Lange's. Durbin would tell them (a) to produce the largest output possible in any existing plant that is consistent with making normal profits, and (b) where normal profits could not be earned, to equate price to marginal cost (686). Hence he, even more than Lange, was attempting to reproduce the symptoms of static equilibrium in perfect competition in a socialist economy. Lerner effectively attacked this position in Lerner (1937). There he formulated his famous marginal cost rule in which he argued that in so far as the goal of socialism is the maximization of the value of production, one should assure that no resources be used to produce a commodity which can be used to produce a more highly valued commodity elsewhere. This can be accomplished by equating prices to marginal cost at every decision point. (251).

12. Mises would not have agreed with this statement. To him, socialism and markets were mutually exclusive categories (as they were to many Marxists at the time when Mises was writing). Hence any move to restore markets in a collectivist economy was a step away from original socialist aspirations. See Mises (1936, 705–706).

13. An interesting illustration of the degree to which Mises was anathema to the socialists was Lerner's comment in "Statics and Dynamics in Socialist Economics" (Lerner 1937). Although he thoroughly and very effectively criticizes the many flaws in Durbin's formulation of managerial rules, he nevertheless introduces his comments by saying Durbin "refutes anew the well-known thesis of Professors Mises, Hayek and Halm that a socialist economic calculus is impossible" (251).

14. Hayek published only three articles dealing specifically with the problem of economic calculation under socialism. The first two were original contributions to his volume of essays, *Collectivist Economic Planning* (1935). The lead essay in this volume (1–40) was a review of the controversy until 1935, and the concluding summary was a critical article, "The Present State of the Debate" (201–243). The third and final article which Hayek published on the subject was his 1940 review of Dickinson's and Lange's books on socialist economics (Hayek 1948, 181–208). However, in order to understand Hayek's position more fully, one should also consult several other articles he published during the 1930s and 1940s, "Economics and Knowledge" (1948),

33–56), "The Use of Knowledge in Society" (1948, 77–91) and "The Meaning of Competition" (1948, 92–106). Although not strictly directed to the debate, they all dealt in a more abstract manner with exactly the kinds of criticisms Hayek made of the socialist programs.

15. This is, for example, the sense of his statement that "all the difficulties which have been raised are 'only' due to the imperfections of the human mind. But while this makes it illegitimate to say that these proposals are impossible in any absolute sense, it remains not the less true that these very serious obstacles to the achievement of the desired end exist and that there seems to be no way in which they can be overcome." Hayek (1935, 238). Hayek further developed his concept of the nature of economic equilibrium and its relationship to knowledge in "Economics and Knowledge" (1948, 33–56).

16. This might not have been so serious an omission if the market socialists were doing no more than playing theoretical games of market simulation. Instead, they were purporting to describe the potential design and operation of a real economy, which made exploration of the differences between capitalism and socialism, and the implications of these differences for modeling the economic structure, vastly important.

17. See for example, Rothschild (1973).

18. See for instance, Lange (1938, 60–61).

19. Gerald O'Driscoll, in his recent (1977) study of Hayek's contributions to economics, has dubbed this "the coordination problem."

20. Schumpeter (1942) believed that "In any normal situation, it (the socialist economy) would command information sufficient to enable it to come at first throw fairly close to correct quantities of output in the major lines of production, and the rest would be matter of adjustments by informed trial and error" (185). In addition, he claimed that since uncertainties about competitors' reactions and general business climate would be eliminated, solving practical business problems under socialism would be easier (186). See also Bergson (1948).

21. Hayek (1940, 199; 1935, 234–237). See also Hayek (1935, 219) and Hayek (1948, 198).

22. For a summary treatment of the property rights approach to study of socialist economies, see Furubotn and Pejovich (1972, 1154–1157).

23. See for example, Lerner (1937, 267); Lange (1938, 109); and Durbin (1937, 687).

24. Buchanan (1969), in his sympathetic treatment of the Austrian role in the economic calculation controversy, criticizes Hayek for failure to see the full implications of his theory of subjective costs by concentrating too much on the conditions of equilibrium in markets (22).

25. Professional evaluation of the calculation controversy in the 1940s was overwhelmingly that the socialists had the best of the argument. See, for example, Bergson (1948). Perhaps Schumpeter (1942) best summed up the current consensus when he stated that "as a matter of blueprint logic, it is undeniable that the socialist blueprint is drawn at a higher level of rationality" (185) (which in effect meant that a Walrasian general equilibrium model was more descriptive of socialism than it was of capitalism). While he later warned that this might have nothing to do with the workability of either capitalism or socialism (Schumpeter 1954, 989) he nevertheless believed that the theoretical case for socialism was stronger than the one for capitalism.

26. There has been a wealth of articles describing and analyzing "soviet-type" economies in light of the reforms which took place during the late sixties. Representatives of just a portion of this group are Belassa (1970), Bornstein (1974), Furubotn and Pejovich (1970), and Prybyla (1966). For a favorable reevaluation of Hayek's original criticisms in light of the historical experience of socialist economies, see Bergson (1967).

27. Lange (1962, 19). "It seems that the greatest obstacle to further progress results from the lack of proper economic incentives in . . . bureaucratic, centralist-type management." And "There are also other economic laws which must be observed by the plan. These are the laws which result from the operation of economic incentives under the circumstances created by the plan . . . By utilizing economic means planning makes use of the automatic character of

people's responses to given incentives" (24). It is interesting to note that at least one socialist economist has suggested a means by which some form of profits might be incorporated into socialist incentive structures. See Bajt (1968).

28. A good summary of modern attempts to take into account adjustment processes, information content of models, and incentive structures can be found in Hurwicz (1973).

29. Rothschild (1973, 1286). This article suggests that current work in models with imperfect information is a direct outgrowth of Stigler's 1961 article, "The Economics of Information." One major difference between the modern approach and Hayek's view of information is that Hayek saw incomplete and decentralized information to be the distinguishing feature of markets and the reason for their existence; while the modern literature, following the implications of earlier general equilibrium models, still sees imperfect information as a defect that needs to be explained away within the context of maximization models.

REFERENCES

Bajt, A. 1968. "Property in Capital and the Means of Production in Socialist Economies." *Journal of Law and Economics* 11 (April): 1–4. Reprinted in 1973, in *The Economics of Property Rights*, edited by Eirik G. Furubotn and Svetozar Pejovich, 253–256. Pensacola, FL: Ballinger.

Belassa, Bela. 1970. "The Economic Reforms in Hungary." *Economica* (February):1–22.

Bergson, Abram. 1948. "Socialism." In *A Survey of Contemporary Economics*, vol. 1, edited by Howard Ellis, 412–488. Homewood, IL: Richard D. Irwin, 1948.

———. 1967. "Market Socialism Revisited." *Journal of Political Economy* 75 (October): 655–673.

Bornstein, Morris. 1974. "Soviet Price Theory and Policy." In *The Soviet Economy*, edited by Bornstein and Fusfeld, 85–115. Homewood, IL: Richard D. Irwin.

Buchanan, James. 1969. *Cost and Choice*. Chicago: Markham.

———, and G. F. Thirlby. 1973. *L.S.E. Essays on Cost*. London: Weidenfeld and Nicholson.

Dickinson, H. D. 1933. "Price Formation in a Socialist Community." *Economic Journal* 43 (June): 237–250.

———. 1939. *The Economics of Socialism*. Oxford: Oxford University Press.

Dobb, Maurice. 1933. "Economic Theory and the Problems of a Socialist Economy." *Economic Journal* 43 (December): 588–598.

———. 1935. "Economic Theory and Social Economy; A Reply." *Review of Economic Studies* 2 (February): 144–154.

Durbin, E. M. F. 1936. "Economic Calculus in a Planned Economy." *Economic Journal* 46 (December): 676–690.

Furubotn, Eric, and Svetozar Pejovich. 1970. "Property Rights and the Behavior of the Firm in a Socialist State: The Example of Yugoslavia." *Zeitschrift fur Nationalokonomie* 30:431–454.

———. 1972. "Property Rights and Economic Theory: A Survey of Recent Literature." *Journal of Economic Literature* 10 (December): 1137–1162.

Hawtry, R. G. 1926. *The Economic Problem*. London: Longmans, Green.

Hayek, F. A. 1935. *Collectivist Economic Planning*. London: Routledge.

———. 1948. *Individualism and Economic Order*. Chicago: University of Chicago Press.

Hirshleifer, J. 1973. "Where Are We in the Theory of Information?" *The American Economic Review* 63 (May): 31–39.

Hoff, Trygve J. B. 1949. *Economic Calculation in the Socialist Society*. London: William Hodge.

Hurwicz, Leonid. 1973. "The Design of Mechanisms for Resource Allocation." *The American Economic Review* 63 (May): 1–30.

Hutchison, T. W. 1978. "Friedrich Engels and Marxist Economy Theory." *Journal of Political Economy* 86 (April): 303–320.

Lange, Oskar, and Fred M. Taylor. 1938. *On the Economic Theory of Socialism.* New York: McGraw-Hill.

———. 1962. *Problems of Political Economy of Socialism.* New Delhi, India: People's Publishing House.

Lerner, Abba. 1934. "Economic Theory and Socialist Economy." *Review of Economic Studies* 2 (October): 51–61.

———. 1937. "Statistics and Dynamics in Socialist Economics." *Economic Journal* 47 (June): 251–270.

———. 1938. "Theory and Practice in Socialist Economics." *Review of Economic Studies* 6 (October): 71–75.

———. 1977. "Marginal Cost Pricing in the 1930s." *The American Economic Review* 67 (February): 235–239.

Mises, Ludwig von. 1935. "Economic Calculation in the Socialist Commonwealth." In *Collectivist Economic Planning,* edited by F. Hayek, 87–130. London: Routledge. (Originally published in 1920 as "Die Wirtschaftsrechnung im Sozialistischen Gemeinwesen.")

———. (1949) 1963. *Human Action: A Treatise on Economics.* New Haven, CT: Yale University Press.

O'Driscoll, Gerald P. 1977. *Economics as a Coordination Problem.* Kansas City, MO: Sheed, Andrews and McMeel.

Prybyla, Jan. 1966. "Soviet Command: From Liberman to Liberalism?" *Bulletin Institute for the Study of the USSR* 13 (July): 19–77.

Robbins, Lionel. 1933. *The Great Depression.* London: MacMillan.

Roberts, Paul Craig. 1971. *Alienation in the Soviet Economy.* Albuquerque: University of New Mexico Press.

Rothschild, Michael. 1973. "Models of Market Organization with Imperfect Information: A Survey." *Journal of Political Economy* 81 (November/December): 1283–1308.

Rothbard, Murray N. 1976. "Ludwig von Mises and Economic Calculation under Socialism." In *The Economics of Ludwig von Mises,* edited by Laurence S. Moss, 67–68. Kansas City, MO: Sheed and Ward.

Samardzija, Milos. 1969. "The Market and Social Planning in the Yugoslav Economy." In *Comparative Economic Systems,* edited by J. S. Prybyla, 340–349. New York: Appleton-Century-Crofts.

Schumpeter, Joseph. (1942) 1963. *Capitalism, Socialism and Democracy.* New York: Harper and Row.

———. 1954. *History of Economic Analysis.* New York: Oxford University Press.

von Wieser, Friedrich. 1971. *Natural Value.* New York: Augustus M. Kelley.

Chapter 2
Does It Matter That
Costs Are Subjective?

I. INTRODUCTION

The subjectivist interpretation of cost has a history at least as long as that of neoclassical economics itself. The concept of opportunity cost, the subjective value of alternatives forgone, was implicit in the writings of Carl Menger, made explicit in the work of Friedrich von Wieser, developed by Phillip Wicksteed, and explored in depth by economists at the London School of Economics during the 1930s and 1940s. Although the concept of opportunity cost is widely accepted in the profession as a whole (and is, in fact, often regarded as the benchmark of "economic thinking"), the peculiarly subjectivist interpretation has not found many adherents, and is actively discussed by only a small subset of the economics profession today. The general fate of the subjectivist interpretation of cost has been neglect rather than confrontation, and indeed, it is likely that most economists practicing today are not even aware of any subjectivist tradition which differs from accepted neoclassical cost theory found in most textbooks on economic theory. Cost, it is presumed, is something that economists understand very well, even if accountants do not.

That most economists fully understand the meaning and implications of cost was a proposition directly challenged by James Buchanan in his 1969 book, *Cost and Choice*. Here (and in later writings), Buchanan traced the evolution of the subjectivist interpretation of cost from von Wieser to the present and argued forcefully for the essential correctness of this tradition.

Originally published in *Southern Economic Journal* 46, no. 3 (1980): 702–715. Republished with permission.

To Buchanan cost, properly defined, is not limited to that which can be revealed in traditional cost curves in micro-economic theory. Rather, cost is an all-pervasive concept that reaches to the core of economic thinking. Economic decision-making is an exercise in choosing among alternatives, and cost can only be understood to be a personal subjective evaluation of the consequences of choice. Specifically, Buchanan summarizes his view of cost as follows:

> Simply considered, cost is the obstacle or barrier to choice, that which must be got over before choice is made. Cost is the underside of the coin, so to speak, cost is the displaced alternative, the rejected opportunity. Cost is that which the decision-maker sacrifices or gives up when he selects one alternative rather than another. Cost consists there-fore of his own evaluation of the enjoyment or utility that he anticipates having to forego as a result of choice itself (Buchanan and Thirlby 1973, 14).

While this explanation of cost might seem a bit metaphysical to some, it is nevertheless a description which would meet with very little criticism from most economists, at least at some level of abstraction. Most would agree completely that costs are displaced alternatives, and when pushed, might also agree that, fundamentally, costs are personal, subjective evaluations of the utility of forgone alternatives; yet few would see any reason, after agreeing to the subjective nature of cost, for modifying one bit of standard neoclassical cost theory. That is, while most economists might agree that costs are at heart subjective, few would see that this makes any difference to economic theory and what economists do with it.

Part of the reason for the lack of impact the subjectivist view of cost has had on even those mainstream economists who know of its existence stems from a failure to perceive the implications of subjective cost for the more conventional cost theory used and taught by most economists. Buchanan lists several implications drawn from the subjective theory of cost, all of them at odds with the general interpretation given to cost in standard economics:

1. Cost must be borne exclusively by the person who makes decisions; it is not possible for this cost to be shifted to or imposed on others.

2. Cost is subjective; it exists only in the mind of the decision maker or chooser.

3. Cost is based on anticipations; it is necessarily a forward-looking or ex ante concept.

4. Cost can never be realized because of the fact that choice is made; the alternative which is rejected can never itself be enjoyed.

5. Cost cannot be measured by someone other than the chooser since there is no way that subjective mental experience can be directly observed.

6. Cost can be dated at the moment of final decision or choice (Buchanan and Thirlby 1973, 14–15).

It is obvious from this list of implications that the subjectivist understanding of cost is fundamentally different from the way cost is treated in standard neo-classical microeconomics. The question to be addressed here is whether or not this difference is important enough to alter standard economic theory. Does it matter in any important sense that costs are subjective?

II. CURRENT CONFUSIONS IN THE THEORY OF COST

The concept of opportunity cost is fundamental to economics and underlies the whole corpus of neoclassical cost theory, but it is opportunity cost viewed in an objective rather than in a subjective sense. While it may be acknowledged at some level of discourse (most prominently at the Principles level) that costs are ultimately the value of opportunities forgone by the individual facing a decision, whether or not these costs should be evaluated in terms of utilities forgone or in terms of money values is often not specified. For example, it is common to introduce students to the concept of opportunity cost by asking them to consider all the alternatives they had to going to class that morning, and then to conclude that going to class must have been at least as valuable to them as the next best alternative they rejected (e.g., sleeping late). However, this is generally the extent of any subjectivism in the standard exposition of the theory of cost.[1] From there, it is likely that the instructor or the textbook in use goes on to stress objective measures of opportunity cost by evaluating the cost of pursuing one activity in terms of the income forgone in the next best alternative, as if the income forgone fully measures the costs to the individuals.

In applying the cost concept to the theory of the firm, it is taken for granted that all costs facing an entrepreneur are fully measured by the market prices of resources. Sometimes the transition from the subjective to the objective level is made explicit by stating the assumption that all entrepreneurs value alterna-tives at market prices and all resource prices fully reflect marginal opportunity costs of resources.[2] Often, however, the assumption is implicit, making it difficult for students to see any connection between the concept of opportunity cost and the imposing array of cost curves drawn to explain market behavior of firms. It becomes easy for them (and perhaps also for us) to fall into the habit of thinking of opportunity cost as one thing, and the "real" costs facing a firm as it produces output for sale as quite another. Even implicit costs are treated as the market value of resources owned by the entrepreneur and used in production, while normal profit, the return available on the next best alternative investment, is treated as an observable market return.

That these assumptions are not impervious to challenge is perfectly obvious to anyone who has ever had to face a class of students in intermediate price theory and try to explain exactly what economists do mean by normal profit or implicit costs in general. The limitation of the definition (and of the supposed objectivity of the measurement of implicit costs) is intuitively felt by students who ask, "But what if Mr. A. happens to like his business so much that he will not give it up even if he doesn't make a 'normal profit'?" The only way out of that one is to agree that such a possibility exists, in which case Mr. A. is earning "psychic profits" (he is a utility maximizer rather than a profit maximizer), and to claim that most people are not like Mr. A. That is, as long as there are people at the margin who are profit (or income) maximizers, our assumption that opportunity costs are fully reflected in market prices makes sense. The theory of cost then reduces to a simple matter of showing how given production functions and given resource prices generate well-behaved cost curves, and the theory of the firm reduces to picking an easily identifiable point on the marginal cost curve to maximize profits. There is no uncertainty, no judgment to exercise; the future can be easily discounted to the present at known discount rates, production functions are known, and costs are the same for all firms. While the theory of the firm in standard microeconomics is actually intended to describe broad patterns of market outcomes and is not meant to say anything about actual decision-making within a firm, the simplifying assumptions we make about firm behavior seem to abstract from the economic problem itself. If costs are market prices of resources, and all alternatives are known to everyone, the only problems facing the firm are trivial, and failure to produce the optimum rate of output at minimum average cost in the optimum firm size can only be taken to be sign of gross incompetence on the part of the managers. Costs are not barriers to overcome in this model, because there are in effect no real choices to be made. There is only correct and incorrect behavior.

It is not only in the theory of the firm that the subjective nature of human choices and evaluations of costs is slighted. Where the theory of the firm tends to assume away the subjective nature of cost, the theory of consumer choice ignores it altogether. Since the theory of consumer choice is ostensibly based on assumptions about consumers' subjective evaluation, the realization that the concept of cost is absent from the analysis is indeed startling. In standard theory, indifference curves are purported to show an individual's subjective assessment of the value of a marginal unit of one good in terms of the number of units of another he is willing to give up for it. While this sounds very much like a theory of opportunity cost, the choices along the indifference curves are not real alternatives but are only imagined at a moment in time. These hypothetical trade-offs, moreover, are defined for a given level of utility and are measured in commodity space. The marginal value of a unit of x is so many units of y one is willing to forgo. Costs, however, must be viewed as the utility losses associated with genuine alternatives, and hence the closest we can come to a notion of opportunity cost in standard indifference curve analysis is described by a movement along a budget line as one passes through higher and higher indifference curves. The budget line represents real market choices open to an individual, and the cost of acquiring one bundle of goods is the utility level associated with the next best bundle one could have consumed along the budget line.

Finally, probably the most egregious misuse of the concept of opportunity cost takes place not at the micro level so much as at the macro level, where production possibilities curves measure the cost of one commodity in terms of the amount of other commodities that could have been produced with the same resources. While this pedagogical device may help students to understand the broad concept of trade-offs, calling these trade-offs opportunity costs is misleading at best. Defining opportunity cost as forgone commodities rather than forgone utilities contains an inherent contradiction. Opportunity cost refers to the value of the next best alternative forgone, but "best" implies a value judgment of some kind. With a simple two commodity production possibilities curve, the problem is obscured since more guns necessarily involves less butter and there are not other alternative products. The number of commodities forgone, then, can be taken as a proxy for the values of the commodities. However, in a more complex economy, there are many possible alternatives to any chosen state, and choosing more guns will imply less butter, eggs, automobiles, theater tickets, or a whole variety of other possible goods one could have instead. Thus, some valuation process must be employed in order to identify the next best alternative.

One might conclude at this point that all I am complaining about is the failure of economists to keep their terms straight; cost is used to represent too many different concepts. That is a part of the problem that both Buchanan and Armen Alchian have gone far to correct. Alchian (1969, 404–415) wants to reserve the word *cost* for the true opportunity cost notion, the individual evaluation of forgone alternatives, and call the negative consequences of a decision an *outlay.* For example, when a firm chooses to invest in a new piece of equipment, the cost is incurred at the time of the decision in the sense that obtaining the equipment precludes choosing some other potentially profitable course of action. Once the decision is made, however, the firm will be faced with a stream of expenditures as a result of its acquisition of the machine that are merely outlays, not costs in the true sense. This distinction provides a more consistent usage of the term *cost* which makes the actual decision process within a firm more understandable, but it is not sufficient to clear up the confusion which characterizes most standard treatments of cost. Even using Alchian's classification, one could still treat costs as measurable, objective entities, and miss the important subjective implications of cost as the inevitable coincident of individual choice.[3]

Buchanan has suggested a slightly different redesigning of our definitions of cost. Although the terms he uses are perhaps a bit clumsy, they do help to focus more on the essential problem of cost. He distinguishes between choice-influencing cost (the anticipation of utility losses which affect the individual decision before it is actually made) and choice-influenced cost (utility losses which flow from the decision once it has been taken (Buchanan 1969a, 44–45). We can illustrate this distinction with an example given by Alchian (1969). If one is trying to decide whether or not to build a backyard swimming pool, choice-influencing costs would include the anticipated forgone utility of any alternative expenditure of time and money which, in order for the decision to be made, would have to be compared to the expected net utility gained from actually building the pool—including both the pleasures derived from owning and swimming in the pool and the disutility associated with maintaining the pool and suffering the increased backyard noise level as neighborhood children suddenly reveal themselves to be your own children's best friends. In this framework, then, pains or disutilities are not costs, but they do get calculated in the form of reducing anticipations of the utility of any proposed action. After the pool is actually built, Alchian would regard the disutilities actually suffered to be nothing more than consequences of the past decision (subjective outlays, perhaps), while Buchanan would call them choice-influenced cost. Either set of definitions will suffice to order our thinking as long as the essential point is kept in mind: Costs, either choice-influencing or choice-influenced, are subjective estimates of utility losses, either anticipated in the case of choice-influencing cost or realized in the sense of ex post choice-influenced cost. Thus, there is no presumption at this point that costs perceived by an individual decision maker either ex ante or ex post are objectively represented by any set of market prices.

III. EQUILIBRIUM AND SUBJECTIVE COST

There is, of course, a logic which connects opportunity costs in the subjective sense to measured outlays of firms and individuals in our standard models, although the logic is rarely spelled out to students except in the frequently neglected chapters on general equilibrium theory at the end of most micro textbooks. In those chapters, an economy is characterized by given individual utility functions and technologically determined production functions. Numeraire prices adjust in product and factor markets until there are no excess demands in any market. This implies that each consumer has adjusted his consumption bundle until marginal rates of substitution equal price ratios for all goods. All producers are earning zero economic profits and (what amounts to the same thing) are just covering all costs where these costs represent marginal opportunity costs to all factors of production. Hence, the subjective valuations of individuals both as consumers and owners of input services are fully reflected in market input and product prices. That is, market adjustments made by rational individuals guarantee that subjective evaluations of forgone alternatives are represented by objectively observable market prices. It would seem then, that if one objects to treating costs as measurable entities, ultimately one is objecting to the use of equilibrium models themselves to explain economic activity. If so, our problem is more methodological than theoretical.

But is it really true that equilibrium theory provides the necessary bridge between subjectively felt states and objectively observable market exchange ratios? Buchanan argues (1969a, 85–86; Buchanan and Thirlby 1973, 10–11) that it is true that if all conditions of full general equilibrium are met, then subjective costs will equal measured outlays, but only in the same sense that relative prices equal marginal rates of substitution. That is, costs are even indirectly measurable in terms of prices only because individuals can freely adjust their consumption and production in a market setting to those prices and, in the process, have some marginal effect on the level of prices themselves. Outlays then become the representation of individually felt costs just as prices are the representation of individually felt marginal utilities. However, it is the relative prices that are the objective, observable entities, not the costs or the marginal utilities. Buchanan further argues that such an understanding of costs in full general equilibrium really doesn't tell us very much since, "The whole purpose of the economic theory in which cost is relevant is to demonstrate how choices made in nonequilibrium settings will generate shifts toward equilibrium. And choices in disequilibrium must be informed by opportunity costs that cannot, even indirectly, be represented by measured outlays" (1969a, 49). That is, equilibrium theory, because it describes an end point rather than the process which leads to this end point, may be largely irrelevant to an understanding of the true nature of cost.

Perhaps the problem will stand out more clearly if we consider some of the necessary requirements for all costs to be measurable in general equilibrium in even the limited sense described above.[4] First of all, not only must all utility and production functions be known, but all individuals must be assumed to make rational choices based solely on pecuniary considerations. Otherwise, utility maximizers may be earning quasi-rents which make income payments to them an overestimate of the cost of employment to them. There must be no unexploited profits existing anywhere in the system or else measured outlays and implicit costs valued at market prices will underestimate true costs. All adjustments must be made marginally, and, most significantly, there must be no uncertainty about the future because uncertainty will lead to divergence in individual estimations about the probability and value of future outcomes. The implication of true uncertainty is that costs will be evaluated differently by different individuals, and there is no objective way of discerning a priori whose evaluation is correct. Hence, even more sophisticated equilibrium models which bring in imperfect information and uncertainty about the future must assume that all individuals choose a rational amount of ignorance (as if one can rationally choose a specific amount of ignorance when one does not know the limits of the knowledge one could in total acquire), and that all individuals perceive the same probabilities of the likelihood of future outcomes of current decisions.[5] If any one of the above conditions do not hold, then subjective evaluations of cost will not necessarily equal observed outlays.

The fact is, of course, that the requirements for general equilibrium are never met in any real economy. Individuals always make choices on the basis of only partly understood preference functions under conditions of total ignorance of the future. One makes educated guesses, perhaps, but one does not really calculate future profits if that implies accounting for predictable streams of income and outlays. Real market adjustments are never capable of being infinitesimal, and unexploited profit opportunities are always present somewhere in a real economy and are constantly being discovered and acted upon by entrepreneurs.

If we grant both of these propositions: (a) that in full market equilibrium with no uncertainty about the future, subjective evaluations of forgone opportunities are represented by objectively measureable outlays on goods and factors, and (b) that at no time is any real economy operating in full market equilibrium, how, then, can equilibrium theory help us to say anything useful about the costs of anything? It appears that if we want to understand the nature and function of cost in economic theory, we must either treat equilibrium as an interesting special case in the analysis of an ongoing market process, admitting the implication that costs are never fully measurable by anyone other than the person incurring the costs, or we must contend that equilibrium closely approximates the conditions of the real world at any moment in time and retain the theoretical assumption that costs are measurable at market prices.[6] Both propositions have found adherents, but it is the second one that is most characteristic of the implicit beliefs of the majority of the economics profession, probably with good reason.

If we choose the first option, we must develop an economic logic in which genuine choice in the sense of nonpredictable decisions is the distinguishing feature of economic theory, and we must abandon much of what has been useful in standard equilibrium economics: tractability of analysis, mathematical rigor, simplicity of assumptions, and predictability of outcomes. If we choose the second option, we must ignore the logical difficulties of our standard models and proceed as if they were scientifically useful representations of reality with the understanding that the results of the empirical research and economic policy based on these models may well be very wrong in many important cases.

The first option is that chosen by the present-day Austrians; Mises, Hayek, Kirzner, Lachmann, and Rothbard.[7] All of these economists work within a framework where the market is understood as a process of entrepreneurial adjustment to constant change and characterized by the piecemeal elimination of pervasive ignorance and error.[8] Individual economic actors always operate under conditions of uncertainty, and in such an environment, error is the norm and the correction of error the raison d'être of markets. In this setting, there can be no question that subjective evaluations of cost bear little predictable relation to objectively measured outlays. Each person evaluates alternatives open to him within the context of uncertainty about the likelihood of expected outcomes, ignorance of the total realm of alternatives open to him and the possibilities of error in judgment about the value to him of the alternatives he does perceive. In such a world, it would seem to be purely happenstance if two separate individuals were to evaluate the same set of alternatives in the same ways. Thus, the central problem of economic analysis in this context is to explain how millions of separate individuals with differing perceptions of reality and differing valuations and expectations about the future ever manage to achieve any kind of coordination of economic activity.[9] With such an understanding of the purpose of economic theory, it is the very subjectivity, ignorance, error, and uncertainty confronting man that helps to explain the development and persistence of markets as corrective and coordinating institutions. That is, markets enable individuals to compare their subjective judgment with the evaluations of others in a continual process of giving and receiving information relevant to economic decision-making.

But what if we ignore the logical difficulties involved in the second option to us and assume that all costs are fully represented by market prices? What do we gain and what do we lose? William Baumol (1970), in his review of *Cost and Choice*, argued for this alternative when he claimed that Buchanan's exposition of the nature of cost was logically correct, but that he overstated his case. Baumol argued that

> There surely is a wide variety of circumstances in which the objective data do constitute a reasonable approximation to the subjective opportunity costs . . . For few other economic magnitudes is there quite so strong a presumption that the available figures often approximate reasonably the information we really want (1210).

In other words, Baumol's position seems to be that indeed, cost is a subjective concept, but the fundamental subjectivity is irrelevant to how economists should ply their trade. Models which assume measurability of costs at market prices, he implies, closely approximate the real world, or closely enough for the problem at hand. Have we come down to an empirical question, then, of how closely the real world approximates the conditions of equilibrium states? In part the question is an empirical one, but I believe there are deeper methodological implications which must be explored.

Consider what it means to ask if costs are fully measured by observed outlays even in equilibrium. Measured by whom and for what purpose? For the individual contemplating any act of choice, the question of whether or not the costs of any proposed action can by quantified is meaningless. Individuals compare different expected subjective states in the future. These subjective states are presumed in most market transactions to be highly influenced by both current prices and expected future prices, but no two individuals ever need evaluate the costs of the same activity in the same way. In fact, markets exist in part because individuals do all have differing evaluations and expectations about the future. As observing economists, however, we cannot directly compare mental states of different individuals, so we make assumptions about the factors which influence individual choice. In order to explain market activity, we assume that individuals have primarily pecuniary motivations, which enables us to assume that costs are evaluated in terms of market prices of alternatives forgone. We may agree that the assumption is incomplete, but if our aim is to explain market behavior, the assumption is good enough. As long as there are those in every market who will respond to purely pecuniary motivations, those who are "at the margin," we can with some confidence explain the direction of change of prices, profits, and resource movements for any change in parameters.[10] Costs can be described by a series of marginal and average cost curves as long as it is understood that their purpose is to explain equilibrium conditions and directions of change to new equilibria. That inframarginal units exist for which market prices do not fully reflect subjective costs is unimportant for this limited purpose of economic theory. We can say, for example, that as long as economic profits are perceived by competitors to exist in an industry, resources will flow into that industry, without having to specify what the magnitude of economic profit is and how the perceptions are formulated (the perceived profits could be simply market expectations about the future profitability of a firm, for example, that will be capitalized into its present value even though current revenues and outlays do not seem to justify such a high net worth). The point is that as long as our purpose is restricted to explaining market behavior and making conditional predictions about the direction of change within a market, the identification of cost with market resource prices is a useful fiction. The subjective formulation is perhaps more logically consistent than the objective one and should therefore be preferred, but there is simplicity of exposition on the side of the cost curves that argues strongly for their retention at least on a pedagogical level. However, once we move beyond the pedagogical level to the practical application of economic theory, the divergence between the subjective and objective views of cost become more significant.

When Baumol suggests that the cost figures we have are close approximations of the magnitudes we want to know, he is implying that we want to know the magnitudes in order to conduct economic analysis for the purpose of pursuing public policy. However, economic policy requires not only that we be able to explain the market actions of individuals in some coherent pattern, but also that we be able to measure the magnitude of the effects of various actions in order to fashion legislation to change economic activity in predictable and desirable ways. Hence, policy requires that we move out of the range of economics as a logic of choice (as Hayek has called it) and into the realm of economics as a predictive science.[11]

Certainly, economists are interested in developing a quantitatively predictive science for reasons other than the pursuit of public policy. Econometric research can aid in our understanding of the real world through measuring the magnitude of effects which can only be guessed at a priori. Not all variables are equally important in influencing economic action, and econometrics can help us to eliminate from consideration those whose effects are small and insignificant. While econometric studies aimed at estimating cost functions for a particular firm or set of firms will of necessity ignore the subjective element of cost, except insofar as it is reflected in observable magnitudes (thereby generating cost functions which are little more than an accountant's and engineer's view of the state of the firm), this is not useless, only incomplete, and for some purposes (e.g., explaining why some firms have been more successful in the past although not necessarily predicting which ones are likely to be successful in the future) even this might be complete enough. It is only when econometric analysis which assumes all costs both to firms and to individuals are fully measured by current market prices is used to manipulate economic variables and to control outcomes that neglecting the subjectivism of costs and values is most questionable. For, as we have already shown, even theoretically, costs can be taken to be represented by market prices only at the margin and only in full equilibrium. Yet it is precisely in those areas in which equilibrium in markets is least likely to obtain the economic policy that is most often pursued.

I am suggesting here that we are in the middle of a paradox. Costs may be taken to have some objective measurability at the margin in full market equilibrium when all economic actors are permitted to adjust their consumptions and resource supplies to take account of market prices, but the minute we move out of equilibrium or away from freely adjusting markets, choice-influencing costs take on more subjective content, and there is less uniformity in individual evaluations of forgone opportunities. Yet economic policy is almost exclusively interested in dealing with nonmarket problems or with attempts to alter the consequences of market behavior. Obviously, if there were no desire to alter markets or move decisions from a market to a nonmarket setting, there would be, in effect, no economic policy. Furthermore, when the goal is to manipulate markets in order to achieve policy goals, the presumption must be (when economic welfare as defined by purely competitive models is the criterion for judgment) that the markets that need manipulation are either functioning poorly or are out of equilibrium. If this is the case, however, there must be at least a tacit recognition that the costs that enter into our calculations for the purpose of framing policy are not fully represented by the market prices of resources. In fact, Baumol (1970) makes this concession by claiming that the magnitudes we are interested in measuring are only reasonably close to the measurement available to us. Yet Buchanan has argued that by ignoring the subjective elements in cost, policy economists are likely to be "wildly inaccurate" in their estimates of social cost (Buchanan 1969a, 58). Is any a priori resolution of this difference of opinion about the characteristics of the real world possible? I can only suggest an answer: that the further we move away from purely competitive markets, and the more government decisions preempt market decisions, the less likely will policy based on models of markets in full equilibrium lead to accurate evaluation of alternatives and to outcomes desired by the policy makers.

A concrete example will help illustrate the relevance of subjective costs to economic policy making. In *Cost and Choice*, Buchanan provided many such examples, including the difficulty of determining the cost of the provision of public goods where public goods are decided upon by political rather than economic processes (Buchanan 1969a, 51–69), the problem of giving any precise meaning to social cost where subjective elements in choice are recognized (70–83),[12] and the problems inherent in measuring costs of decisions made in non-market settings (84–102). Rather than covering the same ground again, let me focus on just one further example in which recognition of the subjective nature of cost makes an important difference in appropriate government policy toward business: the regulation of monopolies.

It should be immediately obvious that when one is dealing with problems of monopoly regulation, there is no question that we are operating in a realm where competitive equilibrium models don't apply. Monopolies by definition do not set prices that represent marginal opportunity costs for resources employed in production—this is the whole rationale behind regulation of monopoly pricing in the first place. Yet regulatory policies recommended by economists usually require administrators to set prices based on some measure of cost, as if the measurability of costs which follows from competitive equilibrium applies to monopoly as well.[13] The familiar marginal cost pricing rule is a good example of a policy designed to improve social welfare by regulating monopoly price in accordance with the economist's understanding of cost. The familiar argument for marginal cost pricing is that because monopolists perceive marginal revenue to be less than price, they "underproduce," and the appropriate corrective policy is to require regulated monopolies to expand output to the point where price equals marginal cost so that marginal social benefits equal marginal resource costs. (We neglect here the problem of decreasing marginal cost.) The problem is illustrated by drawing cost curves which are completely definable for each level of output and are based on given techniques of production and given resource prices. But what are the marginal costs facing a regulated monopoly? And how does the regulatory agency know what they are?[14] The fact that standard regulatory practice is rate base pricing rather than marginal cost pricing suggests that the question of what costs actually are is far more complex than our theoretical analysis implies. In fact, the literature is replete with examples of the difficulties of defining the rate base and verifying that the rate base is not manipulated to the advantage of the monopolist.[15] The implication is that it is difficult for the regulatory agency to ascertain what the costs facing a regulated firm are, even when costs are viewed as measurable entities. We can take this one step further and suggest that there is also a problem facing the monopolist himself in discerning what his costs are and providing a suitable accounting of them to any outside observer.

As we have already suggested, for a real-world monopolist (as for any real-world business decision maker), the costs which influenced decision making are only partly a function of the prices of resources that will be consumed as a result of the decision. The forgone profits of alternative actions must also be estimated and this will be dependent upon estimates of future prices. The future is unknown, and decisions are made in the present to unfold in the future. Cost is the value of the alternatives forgone, but for any decision maker, both the alternatives actually facing him and the present value to him of the alternatives are only estimated. Hence, if a producer is faced with the problem of whether or not to begin a new product line, for example, the decision will be partly based on whether or not the profit opportunities foreclosed by that decision are greater or less than the profits expected from the new line. But the profits are estimates of future prices, and these estimates are only partly influenced by knowledge of current product and resource prices.

In a competitive market, those who evaluate costs and revenues poorly, who fail to choose the most profitable alternatives, will find themselves eliminated by competitors who have made better choices. The important point, however, is that there is really no way one can know ex ante which choices will turn out to be correct. Even if one could apply a set of probabilities to various future outcomes, they are only probabilities, not certainties. There could be a whole range of outcomes with an approximately equal chance of occurring, and at the moment of decision, even a risk minimizer has no choice but to guess (or exercise his informed judgment). Information about which decisions were correct, and with it the information about what constitutes profit maximization and cost minimization, is only revealed in retrospect through the market process. Competition is the screening mechanism that allows cost minimizers to survive and prosper, and it is this process which indirectly provided information as to what costs are. In short, costs are inseparable from the process of decision-making and cannot be fully revealed to a third party.

Obviously, in the case of pure monopoly, market checks on producer behavior are greatly reduced. Both monopolists and competitors are obliged to estimate future outcomes to calculate costs of current decisions, but the monopolist has less relevant information upon which to form his judgment than does a firm in a competitive market. He does not have competitors' actions to check against his own, nor does he have his competitors' prices to serve as an indication of his own success at cost control. Hence, a monopolist might find it easier to avoid the utility reducing activity of engaging in cost minimization. That is, a monopolist is in a more favorable position to satisfy the non-pecuniary elements in his utility function by choosing to indulge in the luxury of not working so hard, or may be more able to make "wrong" decisions, and without direct competitors, he may do so without even realizing that he is not behaving as a cost minimizer.[16] Part of the problem facing any producer is to discover what minimum costs are, and a monopolist, being subject to less direct market pressure than a competitive firm, can be expected to experience greater difficulty in attempting to do so.

While all these problems in determining the nature of the cost function apply to open monopolies, they are compounded in the case of regulated (or closed) monopolies. Open monopolies are at least partly constrained by the threat of potential competition and stockholder retaliation: there is a limit to how much slack an open market monopoly can tolerate and still retain its market and its capital value. Regardless of any economies of scale a monopolist might in principle enjoy, if he doesn't take advantage of them, he leaves room for someone who better perceives the nature of the cost function to take away his market of his business.[17]

For regulated monopoly, even this limited market check on monopoly behavior is missing. The major check on poor cost management in regulated monopoly is the vigilance of the government regulatory agency. But the regulatory agency is an outsider to the firm that is required to make judgments about costs that it can only guess at second hand. Regulators might be able to measure resource outlays for whatever production plan the monopolist is currently following, but they have little information about what alternative plans were rejected and how the value of these forgone alternatives affect cost. If regulators are required to set prices for regulated monopolists based on some measure of cost, they need to be able to verify the cost data supplied by the firm, but even with a general willingness of the monopolist to comply, it will be unlikely that the costs perceived by the regulators will be the same as those perceived by the regulated.[18]

There is, first of all, the obvious potential for differing estimations of future outcomes of current decisions made by the monopolist and the regulator. Costs are the value of anticipated alternatives. In a world of uncertainty, no future outcome can be fully anticipated, and the probabilities assigned to the expected outcomes can differ between regulated and regulator. Further, there could be vastly different judgments about the value of alternative outcomes. Current outlays are the consequences of previous choices, and the regulatory agency must find itself in the position of always having to second guess decisions made by the monopolist sometime in the past.[19] It is also likely that nonpecuniary costs to the regulated and the regulator will bear little resemblance to one another unless the regulator adopts exactly the same goals as the regulated monopolist (a charge that is often made against regulatory agencies, by the way, but which if true defeats the intentions of regulation). This goes beyond the simple difference that the regulator wants to set prices below those which the monopolist would charge were he unencumbered by regulation, and the monopolist wants to charge a price that will maximize profits. The regulator wants lower prices in order to satisfy a political constituency, which implies a whole set of cost considerations that would not ordinarily inform business decision-making. And the regulated monopolist wants to maximize profits, but within the constraint of the politically relevant regulation. One needn't go further than a priori argument to be convinced of the importance to a regulated monopoly of trying to outguess the policies of the regulatory agency. Hence, even if the monopolist scrupulously attempted to follow a pricing rule, the cost he perceived would be influenced by his judgment about the consequences of his action on future regulatory policy. Thus, the process of regulation itself will change the course of economic activity, and the political content of regulatory behavior will guarantee that pricing policies, even the most unobjectionable in theoretical terms, will not fulfill the conditions necessary to increase social welfare.[20] In fact, the subjectivist interpretation of cost suggests that there is no way of knowing if society is better or worse off with even supposedly theoretically sound regulatory pricing policies based on some measure of cost.

IV. CONCLUSION

I have tried to argue four points in this paper: (1) that the only interpretation one can give to the concept of opportunity cost as the value of the next best alternative is a subjective one; (2) that it is only in full, timeless, certain, general equilibrium that subjective cost can be represented by money outlays; (3) that the real world is never in equilibrium; and (4) that the real world's divergence from equilibrium is most significant when economic theory is used in the service of public policy. When the purpose of economics is seen to be the construction of abstract models to explain resource allocation in market equilibrium, the conceptual gulf between subjective costs and measurable outlays can be ignored for the sake of convenience of exposition. But when economic theory is used to formulate policy for real economies, to ignore the fact that the costs we are trying to measure are calculated by human beings who make choices in partial ignorance and uncertainty about the future will be perilous indeed. Perhaps one might still argue that assuming costs are fully represented by measured outlays is "close enough" (that the only thing worse than cost/benefit analysis is no cost/benefit analysis, for example), but the arguments offered in support of this position so far are not convincing. When costs and benefits are mainly subjective and evaluations are made by third parties who do not directly suffer the consequences of their choices, it is just as possible that public policy undertaken in even the best scientific spirit will have perverse effects on social welfare.

NOTES

I wish to thank Richard B. McKenzie and Garrett A. Vaughn for the very helpful comments which have improved the paper greatly, and I wish to thank Laurence S. Moss for stimulating conversation when the paper was in its formative stages.

1. By "standard exposition of the theory of cost" I mean the explanations found in almost all micro economic texts at the intermediate level. It has been my impression, gathered from a cursory review of relevant texts, that the level of subjectivism in the theory of cost is inversely related to the teaching level of the text.

2. Charles Baird's (1975) is one of the few texts that makes the assumption explicit. At the other end of the subjective-objective spectrum, Ferguson and Gould (1975, 181) is notable for including no subjectivism in their discussion of costs at all. Opportunity cost is identified with social cost and measured as "foregone product."

3. Alchian (1969) himself recognizes the subjectivity of the valuing process in his definition of cost as the "highest valued opportunity necessarily forsaken" which is "a logical implication of choice among available options." However, when he applies the concept of cost to market decisions, aside from the warning that "in actual practice, the measurement is very imprecise in that it involves estimates of uncertain future events" (407), he treats costs as being fully represented by market prices. He can do this because of his assumption that "the incentive to increase one's wealth induces shifts of resources to their higher-valued use until their cost is at least matched by the value of their currently yielded product" (405). In other words, Alchian is assuming purely pecuniary motivations on the part of individual choosers.

4. Buchanan (1969a, 49–50, 88–89) spells out the highly restrictive nature of the requirements for full general equilibrium in detail. The requirement that there be only pecuniary

motivations in utility functions perhaps needs a word of explanation. If there are nonpecuniary elements in individual utility functions, the prices of resources will reflect opportunity costs at the margin, but not the opportunity costs of inframarginal units. Hence, marginal cost and average cost will diverge, and total resource costs cannot be measured by summing resource prices.

5. See Rothschild (1973) for a summary of some of these models.

6. We might also argue that equilibrium constructs help us to discern the direction of change of costs as parameters shift. If we don't start from a position of equilibrium, however, the direction of change may not be predictable.

7. In addition, G. L. S. Shackle (1976) in his recent works has explored the subjective nature of choice in the context of disequilibrium. See also Littlechild (1978), Wiseman (n.d.), and Pasour (1978).

8. Israel Kirzner's (1973) work has been most concerned with examining the role of the entrepreneur in the market process.

9. This was the point of several of Hayek's articles written during the 1930s and 1940s, now collected in *Individualism and Economic Order*. In "Economics and Knowledge" he frames the problem as follows: "The question why the data in the subjective sense of the term should ever come to correspond to the objective data is one of the main problems we have to answer" (Hayek 1948, 39). And "How can the combination of fragments of knowledge existing in different minds bring about results which, if they were to be brought about deliberately, would require a knowledge on the part of the directing mind which no single person can possess?" (54).

10. This seems to be the essence of what Buchanan (1969a) argues in chapter 3 of *Cost and Choice*.

11. Actually, Hayek distinguishes between economics as a logic of choice and economics as an empirical science whereby "empirical science" he means statements which are in principle capable of verification. Hayek claims that the statement that the economy tends toward equilibrium is an empirical proposition which "gives our somewhat abstract statement a rather plausible common-sense meaning." The statement itself, however, tells us nothing about (a) "the conditions under which this tendency is supposed to exist and (b) the nature of the *process* by which individual knowledge is changed" (1948, 44–45). Buchanan (1969b, 48–55) distinguishes among three ways of regarding economic theory: as a logic of choice in the Hayekian sense of a system of tautologies which helps us to understand economic activity; as an abstract science of behavior in which the motivations of individual actors are specified; and as a predictive science in which the propositions of the abstract science are tested empirically. However, insofar as the abstract science of behavior makes statements about qualitative changes, it too is predictive in a sense. Hence, I would distinguish between the tautological logic of choice, the qualitatively predictive science, and the quantitatively predictive science. It is only within the quantitatively predictive science that the measurability of costs becomes an important question.

12. See also Littlechild (1978).

13. The problems involved in attempting to formulate a pricing rule for a firm when costs are recognized to be subjective are explored by Buchanan and Thirlby (1973, 165–198).

14. These questions are dealt with by Wiseman (n.d., 248–255).

15. See, for example Kahn (1970) on problems of determining the "rate base" and in supervising and controlling operating costs and capital outlays.

16. He may be able to measure resource outlays for various kinds of business plans, but he may not explore as many plans or as many resource combinations as he otherwise would were his entrepreneurial instincts not dulled by his monopoly position.

17. This implies that non-regulated monopolies can only maximize profits subject to the constraint of potential competition. Hence, they would not charge a price which equalized current marginal cost and marginal revenue if that price were subject to being undercut by potential competitors.

18. The presumption of willingness to comply is a major abstraction considering the enormous profit potential in overstating costs when rate-based pricing is practiced. Indeed, because of the difficulties involved in judging costs second hand, the monopolist may well be able to obscure his true costs sufficiently to enable him to profit maximize regardless of the pricing rule he is supposed to follow.

19. Hayek made this same point with respect to the ability of central planners to monitor the activities of managers of socialist firms (1948, 198–199).

20. Tarascio (1977) makes a similar point when he argues that "economic policy involves expected change which itself produces unexpected change. . . . The result of the above is that government policy may be change producing but in a way not anticipated" (286). Tarascio argues that attempts to "plug loop-holes" to get people to behave as government policy wants them to behave can only succeed, even in theory, by virtually eliminating human freedom.

REFERENCES

Alchian, Armen. 1969. "Cost." In *Encyclopedia of the Social Sciences*. Vol. 3, 405–415. New York: Macmillan.

Baird, Charles. 1975. *Prices and Markets*. Los Angeles: West Publishing.

Baumol, William. 1970. "Review of *Cost and Choice*." *Journal of Economic Literature* (December).

Buchanan, James M. 1969a. *Cost and Choice*. Chicago: Markham Publishing.

———. 1969b. "Is Economics the Science of Choice?" In *Roads to Freedom: Essays in Honour of Friedrich von Hayek*, edited by Erich Streissler. London: Routledge and Kegan Paul.

———, and G. F. Thirlby. 1973. *L.S.E. Essays on Cost*. London: Weidenfeld and Nicholson.

Ferguson, C. E., and J. P. Gould. 1975. *Microeconomic Theory*. Homewood, IL: Richard D. Irwin.

Hayek, F. A. 1948. *Individualism and Economic Order*. Chicago: University of Chicago Press.

Kahn, Alfred E. 1970. *The Economics of Regulation: Principles and Institutions*. Vol. 1. New York: John Wiley and Sons.

Kirzner, Israel. 1973. *Competition and Entrepreneurship*. Chicago: University of Chicago Press.

Littlechild, S. C. 1978. "The Problem of Social Cost." In *New Directions in Austrian Economics*, edited by Louis P. Spadaro, 77–93. Kansas City, MO: Sheed, Andrews and McMeel.

Pasour, E. C., Jr. 1978. "Cost and Choice—Austrian vs. Conventional Views." *The Journal of Libertarian Studies* (Winter): 327–336.

Rothschild, Michael. 1973. "Models of Market Organization with Imperfect Information: A Survey." *Journal of Political Economy* (November–December): 1283–1308.

Shackle, G. L. S. 1976. "Time and Choice." *Proceedings of the British Academy* 62:306–329.

Tarascio, Vincent J. 1977. "Theories of Behavior and Public Policy." *Spoudai* 27 (2): 279–290.

Wiseman, Jack. N.d. "Costs and Decisions." Unpublished paper.

Chapter 3
Hayek's Ricardo Effect
A Second Look
with Laurence S. Moss

I. INTRODUCTION

In this article we review a long-standing controversy in twentieth-century economic thought: the debate over Hayek's Ricardo effect. Hayek developed his interpretation of the Ricardo effect in the context of his theory of business cycles primarily in the late 1930s and early 1940s. At that time Hayek's use of the familiar proposition was held up to close scrutiny by many talented critics, including Nicholas Kaldor, H. D. Dickinson, and R. G. Hawtry; all of whom, according to Hayek, failed to understand what he was saying.[1] In each case Hayek countered their criticism with a restatement of his proposition which in turn failed to satisfy the critics.[2] Indeed, this apparent miscommunication was still taking place as late as 1969 when Hayek wrote his last piece on the Ricardo effect in answer to a criticism leveled by Sir John Hicks.

The purpose of our article is to discover whether in this debate it was Hayek who was out of step with the profession or the profession that was out of step with Hayek. We shall argue that the reason that Hayek's argument seemed so elusive to his contemporary colleagues (and some later critics) was that his method of analysis was foreign to their way of thinking. While English economists in the 1930s (especially after Keynes published the *General Theory*) were concerned primarily with the static problem of balancing income and expenditure flows at acceptable levels of employment, Hayek was attempting to

Originally published in *History of Political Economy* 18, no. 1 (1986): 545–565. Copyright 1986 Duke University Press. All rights reserved. Republished by permission.

develop a dynamic theory of business cycles that involved tracing out the path of adjustment of the capital stock of an economy from one equilibrium state to another. This problem of describing the transitional process only became the subject of serious professional attention long after the debate over the Ricardo effect was concluded.[3]

In the course of our exposition, we will demonstrate that Hayek's Ricardo effect was not, in Blaug's words, "only another instance of the vice of neoclassical economics: the hasty application of static theorems to the real world."[4] Indeed, we shall argue that this is the *last* accusation one could logically hurl at Hayek's analysis. The very reason why Hayek encountered so much difficulty in communicating his message was precisely that he was not presenting an exercise in comparative statics but was rather hypothesizing a particular adjustment process where the final equilibrium state depended upon the particular path of adjustment followed in the economy.

In recent years the founders of the "new classical economics" have praised the broad outlines of Hayek's approach to the business cycle. Robert Lucas pointed out that as early as 1929, Hayek articulated what remains today the single most important theoretical question in business cycle research. Hayek asked, How can cyclical phenomena be incorporated "into the system of economic equilibrium theory?"[5] Lucas goes on to regret the unfortunate Keynesian diversion of research effort from a thoroughgoing theory of the business cycle to what, in Lucas's words, is the "simpler question of the determination of output at a point in time."[6] It is well known that Hayek also regretted the unfortunate "Keynesian diversion" and resisted the redirection of research away from what he considered to be one of the most important macroeconomic questions: how production structures adjust to the underlying demand conditions and savings patterns of the community. It was this concern that made him wary of an economic theory that made it appear possible to push an economy into a perpetual state of boom.[7] He feared that instead of perpetual boom, inflationist policies would only result in short-term, illusory gains followed by a collapse with all its undesirable macroeconomic effects.

Hayek's approach (much like the modern approach of Lucas and others) was to derive macroeconomic consequences from an analysis of the self-interested behavior of market participants. This was a continuation of the Misesian research program of reducing aggregate relationships to statements about individual action in markets.[8] Hayek's particular analytic structure combined elements of a Wicksellian cumulative expansion that included Cantillon effects with an "Austrian" description of production as consisting of a succession of stages that had to be synchronized and coordinated with each other through appropriate price signals.[9] This framework allowed Hayek to argue that changes in the quantity of money would have nonneutral effects on individual prices and on the allocation of resources. All this led Hayek to admit the stimulative impact of Keynesian monetary policies but severely criticize the Keynesian claim that unemployment could be permanently cured by government-engineered expansions of aggregate demand. If governments try such engineering, they will be thwarted by the Ricardo effect.

We have organized our discussion as follows. In section II we identify two uses of the Ricardo effect in Ricardo's *On the Principles of Political Economy and Taxation*, each of which bears a certain similarity to the mechanism Hayek finally developed. In section III, we trace the intellectual roots of Hayek's theory to the "reverse movement" problem in the trade cycle theory of Ludwig von Mises. Mises's theory was itself a variant of the "cumulative process" analysis first presented by K. Wicksell at the turn of the century. In section IV, we summarize Hayek's main concern during the 1930s, that economic development required voluntary savings on the part of the economy and that government-created booms would prove to be self-defeating. The Ricardo effect served as the trigger that would bring on the crisis. In section V we review the substance of the Hayek-Kaldor debate over the micro foundations of the Ricardo effect. This debate was especially important to the development of Hayek's theory. It was by responding to Kaldor's formidable criticisms of that mechanism that Hayek finally realized why the comparative static approach based on perfect information was totally out of step with the type of phenomena Hayek was trying to model.

II. RICARDO'S RICARDO EFFECT

As a proposition in comparative statics, the Ricardo effect compares two equilibrium states of the economy—before and after a change in relative factor prices has induced a switch in production techniques. As part of a dynamic theory, the Ricardo effect examines the path by which an economy reestablishes equilibrium after a disequilibrating shock to the system occurs. Both uses of the Ricardo effect appear in Ricardo's *Principles*, and both uses influenced Hayek in naming his own composite mechanism of relative price changes after the work of his English predecessor.[10] It may be helpful to explain the Ricardo effect as it appeared in Ricardo's *Principles* so as to better appreciate the way in which the mechanism functions in Hayek's trade cycle theory.

Comparative Static Statement

In his famous first chapter "On Value" in the *Principles*, Ricardo explained why the labor theory of relative commodity prices breaks down in a capital-using economy. It breaks down because of different durabilities of capital or, as Ricardo noted elsewhere, the varying role of time in the production of commodities.[11] More specifically, Ricardo demonstrated why a sudden across-the-board rise in wages must raise the prices of commodities manufactured with labor-saving machinery by a lesser amount than that same wage increase will raise the prices of commodities produced without any machinery at all. His analysis proceeded in two steps.

First, at the "firm level," the manager finds himself indifferent between two techniques of production, Technique A and Technique B, each capable of producing a given volume of output at the same identical cost. Technique A consists of a $5,000 machine lasting one year and capable of performing 100 man-years of work. Technique B consists of directly hiring 100 man-years of labor to do the work unaided by any machinery at all. At a supposed wage of $50 per man-year, both techniques cost $5,000. Ricardo explained that it is obviously a "matter of indifference" to the manager which of the two techniques is used.[12]

The second step of Ricardo's argument requires that we upset this state of indifference by supposing wages unexpectedly rise from $50 per man-year to $55 per man-year—a 10 percent rise in wages. Technique B, the labor-intensive technique, will now cost $5,500. The machine-intensive technique, Technique A, will also increase in price, but not by as much. The price of the machine cannot increase to $5,500 because if it was formerly profitable to sell those machines at $5,000 (the price of the machine prior to the rise in the price of labor), then each machine had to have contained *less than* 100 man-years of labor to allow for profits to the machine makers. As a general rule, a machine must contain less labor than it displaces; and so a rise in wages will raise its price by *less than* 10 percent.[13] Faced with a cheaper way of getting the work done, the manager will substitute the machine method for the direct-labor method of production.

Now moving from the firm level of analysis to the economic system as a whole, Ricardo was quite explicit about the role competition plays in keeping machine producers from increasing the prices of their machines by the full 10 percent. Such an effort would elevate profits among machine manufacturers above the going rate established by the productivity of marginal investments in agriculture.[14] This would create a situation in which an "unusual quantity of capital" would flow into machinery manufacture, expanding the supply of machines and forcing their prices down.[15] Competitive forces would therefore drive the price of machines down again.

A corollary of Ricardo's argument is that the substitution of machinery for labor causes the prices of commodities produced with machines to decline relative to the prices of commodities produced entirely with direct labor. In other words, the adoption of labor-saving machinery by capitalist-managers, in an effort to maximize profits, eventually results in a decline in specific consumer-goods prices.[16] Thus, we can summarize the conclusions of the comparative static version of Ricardo's Ricardo effect as follows:

(i) A rise in wages will encourage managers to substitute machine-intensive for labor-intensive methods of production; and

(ii) In the new equilibrium position, the prices of consumer goods made with (labor-saving) machinery will decline relative to the prices of other commodities.[17]

The Ricardo Effect in a Dynamic Context

Hayek refers to a second place in Ricardo's *Principles* to support his use of the Ricardo effect: chapter 31, "On Machinery." In that now famous chapter, Ricardo addressed the problem of whether the introduction of a new technology could ever make workers worse off. Added only in the third edition, his surprising conclusion was that under certain circumstances, the introduction of a technological innovation could reduce the real wages of labor and lead to unemployment in the short run.[18] He argued that if the introduction of the new technology is sudden and there is no growth in the economy, the fact that labor will have to be diverted from the production of consumer goods to the production of capital will lead to a reduction in the real wage of labor and to reduced employment.[19] That is, during the transition period while new capital goods are being produced, less food can be produced with the same total resources as one had before. Hence in the next time period, workers find that there is less for them to buy with their money, reducing their real wages, and they find that some of the labor that was previously employed has now become "redundant" because of the increased productivity of the new machinery. Here we have the germ of the idea that later appears in the Austrian theory of the boom—that capital-intensive methods of production cannot be instantly installed; rather, a costly transition period must be financed and this financing requires real savings on the part of the community. It was an idea, however, that Ricardo himself did not explore further.

After raising this extremely interesting problem about the process by which new capital goods are financed, Ricardo assured his readers that the practical significance of his example of an innovation crisis was slight. These conditions could occur only in an economy without net investment, and even then it would only be during the temporary transition period that the workers would experience distress.[20] As a practical matter, sudden switches from "circulating to fixed capital" occur concurrently with capital accumulation. This meant that there is typically enough real community savings available to sustain the flow of consumer goods while some labor is being diverted to constructing capital goods. In the context of capital accumulation all that happens is wages rise less quickly than they otherwise would. The financing of the new capital goods does not require that wages fall absolutely. Thus, with net investment, the introduction of new technology during the process of accumulation improves the economic welfare of the workers. The worker's wage is lower than it would otherwise be, but higher than it was in the past.

Hayek's Version

As recently as 1969, Hayek articulated his Ricardo effect theorem that "an increase in the demand for consumer goods will lead (in conditions of full employment) to a decrease in the demand for the kind of investment goods appropriate only to more highly capital-intensive modes of production."[21] Hayek demonstrated that the Ricardo effect can be presented as a theorem in comparative statics by comparing two equilibrium positions identical in all respects except one—the ratio of product-to-factor prices is higher in one than in the other.[22] But as the rest of his 1969 restatement made clear, Hayek's Ricardo effect was employed to do a great deal more than simply compare the logic of choice under varying patterns of relative prices. The raison d'être of the mechanism was to explain why the end of the boom phase of the trade cycle nearly always consists of a depression.

Much as Ricardo had used his proposition to draw out the possible disequilibrium consequences of the attempt to introduce a new technology before adequate savings are available, Hayek used the Ricardo effect as an important component of a dynamic theory of the trade cycle to elucidate the implications of a disequilibrium phenomenon. Drawing on the comparative static proposition in Ricardo's chapter I, Hayek employed the notion that changing real factor prices induce entrepreneurs to switch from labor-saving methods of production back to labor-intensive methods, thereby ending the boom.

But what is it that caused the factor prices to change in the first place? As early as 1931, Hayek elaborated that successfully switching from a labor-intensive to a labor-saving technology requires that there be a diversion of national product from consumption to investment so as to "finance the transition." According to Hayek it was "voluntary savings" that provided this "diversion" and nothing else could do as well. An inflationary process seldom succeeds, because it relies on "forced savings" rather than voluntary savings, and forced saving is rarely if ever adequate. As we shall explain below, the inadequacy of forced savings manifests itself in a change in factor prices ultimately inducing the switch back to labor-intensive methods of production and the crises.

Hayek referred his readers to *both* chapters in Ricardo's writings to support his analysis. Several commentators compare Hayek's mechanism to Ricardo's first version and fail to emphasize the close connection between the argument of Ricardo's chapter "On Machinery" and the central problem of Hayek's theory.[23] In addition to the influence of Ricardo's *Principles* on Hayek, we must also consider the impact of a particular unresolved problem in the so-called Austrian theory of the business cycle on Hayek's thinking about economic problems.

III. THE REVERSE MOVEMENT PROBLEM

During the 1920s Ludwig von Mises's "circulation-credit" theory of the business cycle (now commonly called the "Austrian" theory) was widely regarded as the most important of the contributions of the younger generation of Austrian writers to modern, neoclassical economics.[24] Mises took issue with the phenomenon Wicksell described in his *Interest and Prices* of a steady and evenly accelerating increase in prices so long as the market rate of interest is held below the natural rate and the quantity of money steadily increased.[25] According to Mises, the injection of new money into the economy has to raise certain prices ahead of others as entrepreneurs try to construct more capital-intensive investment projects. When new money enters the economy through the loan market, after a period of economic expansion consumer goods prices will rise ahead of wages, and this will encourage entrepreneurs to substitute labor-intensive for capital-intensive techniques of production. This will discourage the sales of capital goods and bring about an economic crisis. The process of capital goods construction cannot go on indefinitely. Mises insisted that a "reverse movement" must inevitably set in, ending the boom and ushering in the crisis even if entrepreneurial expectations were to remain optimistic and even if the operation of the international gold exchange standard did not produce contractionary pressures on the banking system.[26] Mises's discussion of the reverse movement problem was incredibly terse:

> This is one of the ways in which the equilibrium of the loan market is reestablished after it has been disturbed by the intervention of the banks. The increased productive activity that sets in when the banks start the policy of granting loans at less than the natural rate of interest at first causes the prices of production goods to rise while the prices of consumption goods, although they rise also, do so only in a moderate degree, viz., only insofar as they are raised by the rise in wages. Thus the tendency towards a fall in the rate of interest on loans that originates in the policy of the banks is at first strengthened. But soon a counter-movement sets in: the prices of consumption goods rise, those of production goods fall. That is, the rate of interest on loans rises again, it again approaches the natural rate.[27]

While this analysis set forth a broad outline of a theory of the trade cycle, it left several theoretical questions unanswered. The most important from the Austrian point of view were these: What was the market mechanism that could bring about the countermovement? How can one explain how each entrepreneur pursuing his own interest can be led to make decisions which, when reconciled with the decisions of other managers, produce the end of the boom and the subsequent crisis? In other words, what are the microeconomic foundations for the "spontaneous *disorder*" that seems to characterize the business cycle?

Shortly after Hayek arrived in London, he was invited to deliver the special university lectures at the London School of Economics (1930–1931). Hayek used this occasion to elaborate on the Mises account of the boom and crisis in a way that made more explicit use of the Austrian description of production as a succession of stages through which resources must pass toward their ultimate destination of becoming consumer goods. This course would enable him to explain, he believed, why a credit-financed boom would necessarily have to end in crisis. The 1931 published version of his lectures, *Prices and Production*, immediately attracted the interest and commentary of most of the leading economists of his day and led to his appointment to the prestigious Tooke chair at the London School.[28]

Hayek analyzed the reverse-movement problem in Lecture 3. According to Hayek, a credit-induced boom leads entrepreneurs to bid resources away from consumer-goods industries without any compensating voluntary savings on the part of consumers. This resulting relative decrease in the supply of final goods and services at a time when wage incomes are rising due to the newly created money causes final goods prices to rise faster than the price of labor. There is a consequent decline in the real wage of labor (where real wage means the ratio of product price to per-unit labor cost). This is most pronounced in the stage of production nearest to the consumer and leads to a surge in profits on short-term investment projects. This surge encourages entrepreneurs to turn away from machine-intensive methods of production in favor of more labor-intensive methods, thereby discouraging sales of capital goods.[29] Entrepreneurs, determined to complete their endangered long-term capital projects, turn to the banks for more bank credit, and a tug of war begins. Producers seek new bank loans, the banking system accommodates the new loan demand by creating new money, product prices rise ahead of wage costs. In each market period the process repeats itself, with product prices always rising ahead of wages.[30] Hayek argued that any attempt to reduce the flow of bank credit will bring this process of competing errors to a halt, turning the boom into a bust and leading to a readjustment of the capital-goods industry to a new equilibrium consistent with real patterns of consumer demand.[31]

In his 1969 restatement of the Ricardo effect, Hayek objected to Hicks's description of the mechanism presented in *Prices and Production* as being predicated on wages "lagging" behind consumer-goods prices.[32] Hayek argued that his explanation did not depend upon a lag, if that meant that one incorrect market value is somehow trying to catch up with a correct value with which it must be in harmony. Rather, *both* product prices and wages are incorrect in the sense of being inconsistent with the underlying objective conditions of supply and demand for consumer goods. The fact that consumer expenditures are ultimately used to pay for intermediate goods creates the objective conditions in the market that generate a particular price sequence. As he argued in 1939 and 1942, when capital creation is financed through expanding bank credit, the signals that communicate the objective conditions to entrepreneurs are distorted, and incorrect investment decisions are made. The incorrect decisions are corrected by way of a crisis.

In essence, the Ricardo effect as Hayek described it occurred in the context of a process of genuine macroeconomic disequilibrium in which a crisis could not be averted. The crisis, he argued, was a necessary consequence of a boom brought about by money creation and characterized by a constant incompatibility between relative prices and the growing structure of real capital.

IV. THE INEVITABILITY OF THE CRISIS

The first major point Hayek was making during his lectures and in several articles he published in the years immediately following *Prices and Production* was simply that any real growth in the capital stock takes time and requires voluntary net savings. There is no way for an expansion of the money supply in the form of bank credit to short-circuit the process of economic growth. His second major point was more difficult. He argued that forced savings can only distort the mix of capital and consumer goods, by generating false relative price signals. These false signals throw the economy into a genuine macroeconomic disequilibrium that cannot be sustained over time. Eventually, the underlying consumer preferences will reassert themselves. All that credit can do is to encourage competition between consumers and producers for the same pool of scarce resources, leading ultimately to a state of affairs in which producers switch from capital-intensive to labor-intensive methods of production. This switch, when carried out by a large number of managers, will choke off investment and bring on a full-scale crisis. But was either the switch or the crisis inevitable? Hayek argued that they are, but most of his early critics disagreed.[33]

Suppose the inflation caused by an expansion of bank credit could only last for, say, twenty-two months, but that a larger (i.e., "more roundabout" or "deeper") capital structure could be erected in less time. Wouldn't that mean that even when the eventual halt to credit expansion came, the economy would be richer with a larger per capita capital stock that could potentially produce enough income to generate the savings to maintain itself without collapse? If this scenario were possible—say, under conditions of less than full employment of resources—it would seem that a deliberate policy of credit creation could bootstrap the economy into a permanently larger flow of consumer goods without suffering the consequences of a disruptive crisis.[34]

At one place Hayek did agree that under certain restricted conditions a credit expansion could occur that did not end in collapse with a misplaced collection of capital goods. He warned, however, that the conditions were so stringent that they were unlikely to have much empirical relevance. This happy state of affairs could only occur in a "progressive economy" where credit expansion did not lead to increased prices, but only managed to keep price levels constant as output grew. In this case, where voluntary saving was already high and the proportion of capital formation financed by forced saving was very low, it was just possible that a crisis could be averted if the credit expansion had been gradual and the contraction equally gradual. However, even in this case, he argued, forced saving did not actually increase the capital stock that can be accumulated in the long run, but only speeded up the process of creating it, since once the credit expansion stopped, "for a time the current voluntary savings will be used to take over, as it were, the capital created by means of forced saving; and current savings would then have to serve, not to make further new investment possible, but merely to maintain capital which has been formed in anticipation of these savings."[35] Under these circumstances, there would still be a relative price change for real wages and real cost of capital that would trigger a switch of techniques. But in this case, the switch would not lead to a crisis. Thus, as a theoretical matter, the crisis need not inevitably follow the boom. The likelihood of such a set of events, however, was extremely limited. As Hayek explained, this was not a scenario upon which to build one's plans for smooth economic growth, since the conditions under which it might obtain were extremely restrictive. As a practical matter, credit expansions followed by economic crises were the norm, not the exception.

In Hayek's early book, *Monetary Theory and the Trade Cycle*, he presented a theory of trade cycles that made them endogenous to a monetary economy.[36] Cyclical fluctuations were simply the consequences of information problems inherent in an economic system that relied on credit banking. In *Prices and Production*, he described a process of economic growth that consisted of a time-consuming transition from one full-employment equilibrium to another. Business cycles were a consequence of attempting to finance this transition process by an expansion of the money supply via bank credit creation. In both these books, Hayek was well on his way to working out a macroeconomic theory that incorporated money and time into a theory of growth from one equilibrium state to another.

However, after the publication of Keynes' *General Theory*, the rules of the game changed and professional attention shifted from the problem of economic growth as a transition process from one equilibrium to another, to the problem of the determination of flows of income and expenditure at a moment in time. The limelight shifted from Hayek to Keynes.

In 1939 Hayek produced a restatement of his view of the trade cycle more in line with these contemporary trends. Instead of starting from a position of full-employment equilibrium as he had before, he tried to meet Keynes and his followers on their own ground by making standard Keynesian assumptions of unemployment, rigid wages and interest rates, immobile labor, in order to show how the economic system would nevertheless still find itself unable to sustain a boom.[37] It was here that he first used the term the "Ricardo effect" to underline the venerable pedigree of the mechanism that figured so prominently in his attempt to give a microeconomic account of how individual maximizing decisions on the part of entrepreneurs will lead to the switch of techniques that brings about an economic crisis. In 1939, then, the debate over the Austrian theory of the business cycle focused explicitly on the choice-theoretic foundations of the turning point in business cycles.

V. MICROFOUNDATIONS OF THE RICARDO EFFECT

Let us suppose along with Hayek that during the boom, consumer product prices do rise ahead of wages, and hence real wages fall. Is this alteration in relative prices by itself sufficient to produce a crisis? As we have shown, Hayek believed that the price effect would induce entrepreneurs to substitute labor-intensive for labor-saving methods of production. Although each entrepreneur makes the decision to alter investment priorities independently of other entrepreneurs, the aggregative effect of their decisions is to produce a decline in net investment (that is, a decline in the sales of capital goods) and the onset of the crisis. By 1939 Hayek was arguing that the crisis will begin even if the monetary authorities stand ready to continue to supply bank credit at less than the natural rate.[38] Indeed, one important corollary of Hayek's Ricardo effect was to show that while a commodity standard (that is, a gold standard) might by itself be sufficient to arrest a boom, it was by no means necessary. A boom would end because of the incentives created by changes in the relationship among wages, prices, and profits.

In order to appreciate the choice-theoretic foundations of Hayek's Ricardo effect, it will be helpful to think of entrepreneurs as managing a number of on-line investment projects. In fact, the firm itself may be construed as a "portfolio of investment projects" rather than, as in standard Marshallian terms, an organization that produces a single product.[39] Now each investment project can be identified with a particular product and calculable rate of return. The entrepreneurs are assumed to reshuffle the amount of liquid capital available to them so as to maximize the present value of the firm: they calculate the rate of return on each separate project and then allocate money capital among the projects so as to equalize returns at the margin.[40]

In his 1939, 1942, and 1969 expositions of the Ricardo effect mechanism, Hayek started his analysis (much as Ricardo did) with the firm in "long-period investment equilibrium" earning the same rate of return on the investments in each different project. In some projects, capital turns over rapidly (bakery products), while in other projects (selling rare books) funds are typically tied up for years on end. Offsetting these "waiting periods" of varying lengths are the actual returns on the different projects which differ in absolute amounts so as to yield an identical internal rate of return among all projects. The internal rate of return (I) is equal to the product of the rate of turnover (T) and the profit margin (M). In equilibrium then, $M = I/T$ for all projects.[41]

Now, let us disturb this equilibrium situation by permitting a sudden unexpected rise in product prices (relative to wages) and we discover that the rate of return on quick turnover projects will have risen relative to the returns on slow turnover projects. Entrepreneurs would obviously attempt to shift their money capital to quick turnover projects in which the returns are now relatively greatest. These quick turnover projects are necessarily more labor-intensive, and hence the demand for capital investment relative to labor will fall. Now it is absolutely vital to keep in mind the following arithmetic facts in order to appreciate the controversy surrounding Hayek's mechanism: (i) the internal return on quick turnover projects has indeed risen relative to slower turnover projects but (ii) all rates of return are necessarily higher than they were prior to the rise in product prices.[42]

The second of the two facts led T. Wilson, Nicholas Kaldor, and the majority of Hayek's critics after 1940 to accuse Hayek's theory of being *logically inconsistent*.[43] According to Hayek's critics, the rational firm-manager would not simply switch from one kind of project to another but would try to invest more in each and every project. If before the rise in product prices all returns were equal to the firm's cost of capital, then in the next equilibrium position the scale of the firm must increase because the firm will invest in all its investment projects until each internal rate of return falls back down to equal the cost of capital.[44] The cost of capital remains fixed throughout the analysis because Hayek has assumed that during the boom the banking authorities are making loanable funds freely available at a rate of interest below the natural rate.

According to Kaldor:

> [Hayek committed the same fallacy as those who argue
> that] a rise in demand for a commodity will cause a rise
> in its price, and the rise in price causes a restriction in

demand (because less is bought at a higher price than a lower price), the increase in demand will lead to a reduction in the amount bought. No doubt the rise in price will make the increase in purchases (following upon the increase in demand) less than it would have been if the price had not risen. But it cannot make it less than before, since the price has only risen because the amount bought has gone up. In the same way, the reduction in capital intensity will make the rise in investment expenditure less than it would have been if capital intensity had remained constant. But it cannot eliminate it altogether because capital intensity would not have fallen if investment expenditure had not risen.[45]

In short, Kaldor claimed that Hayek had assumed a situation in which the substitution effect outweighed the scale effect, a situation which a comparative static analysis of the Ricardo effect mechanism demonstrated to be impossible.

Hayek responded to Kaldor's criticism by claiming that it missed the point. Kaldor along with other critics seemed unable to understand his mechanism for two basic reasons: (i) their stubborn attachment to the "perfect competition" model of market structure even when the descriptive realism of that model was at odds with the particular market under study and (ii) their insistence on evaluating his Ricardo effect mechanism solely within a comparative statics framework.

Consider the first charge. If the loanable funds market were perfect in that the cost of capital facing the firm were to remain constant regardless of the absolute volume of funds the firm wished to borrow, then the rational manager would indeed expand the size of the firm in all directions as Kaldor insisted he would. But, Hayek argued, the market for loanable funds is not and cannot be modeled as "perfect" under these conditions. Under any real conditions, the cost of capital facing the firm could not remain equal to the external market rate of interest while the firm expanded in size; there is a "limit beyond which [the firm-owner] can raise capital only at higher costs."[46] Loans to the same borrower will never represent the "same commodity" in the sense in which the term is used in theory of competition. Bankers will not lend infinite amounts of bank credit to any single borrower at a uniform rate because they will perceive an increased risk associated with a higher debt-to-equity ratio.[47] But are the bankers' perceptions based on an understanding of the real underlying conditions that prevail in the market or are their perceptions based instead on the imperfect and incomplete information available to the creditors at the time the applications for the loans are received?

Hayek later clarified this point. He admitted that creditors "misjudge" the creditworthiness of borrowers because they fail to take into consideration the favorable impact inflation will have on the firm's revenues. In the long run, increasing product prices might imply that the creditworthiness of a firm has increased and therefore should justify increased loans at no additional risk premium. But long before creditors perceive that this sort of long-run equilibrium adjustment has occurred, the Ricardo effect will have already asserted itself. Hayek's argument then rested on the assumption that increasing product prices increased the firm's demand for loanable funds more quickly than the banks could subjectively reevaluate the creditworthiness of the firm itself. Under these circumstances, the firm is constrained by the upward-sloping portion of the supply curve of credit, which acts as a brake on the firm's expansion.[48] Hence, with incomplete knowledge the scale effect cannot outweigh the substitution effect as Kaldor maintained. In this way Hayek readily admitted what several of his critics had pointed out: the upward-sloping supply of credit to the firm acted as a kind of rationing device to constrain the growth of the firm. The manager adjusts by investing his limited capital in short-term (that is, labor-intensive) investment projects.

Hayek's resort to this kind of credit rationing was by no means *ad hoc*. The credit rationing was a rational response to the informational lags that occur during a period of accelerating inflation. The assessment of the creditworthiness of the firm in one period imposes a "finance constraint" on the amount it can borrow (at the old interest rate) in the next period.[49]

Consider, now, the merits of Hayek's charge that his critics misunderstood his theory because of their preoccupation with perfectly competitive equilibrium conditions and comparative statics. According to Hayek, even if the supply of credit were infinitely elastic to the economy as a whole, the Ricardo effect would still occur because of the finance constraints encountered along the path of business expansion. However, one cannot see that point simply by comparing two equilibrium states. Such a comparison, Hayek argued, would disguise precisely the mechanism he was interested in discussing. As he put it:

> The situation which we consider . . . is indeed the clas-
> sical instance of a cumulative process. . . . the perfectly
> elastic supply of credit at a rate of interest lower than the
> internal rate of all or most of the firms will be the cause of
> continuous changes of prices and money incomes where

> each change makes further changes necessary. There is
> no point in saying with respect to such a situation that "in
> equilibrium there must" exist such and such a relationship,
> because it necessarily follows from the assumptions that
> the relationship between at least some prices must be out
> of equilibrium.[50]

This disequilibrium is a situation in which the different price-determining tendencies in the economy are inconsistent with one another and lead to perpetual change. Hayek tried to explicate his problem by resorting to an imaginative analogy: "The question is rather similar to that whether, by pouring a liquid fast enough into one side of a vessel, we can raise the level at that side above that of the rest to any extent we desire." Of course, we cannot, since this depends upon the viscosity of the liquid itself. Hence, "the speed at which an increase of incomes leads to an increase in the demand for consumers' goods limits the extent to which, by spending more money on factors of production, we can raise their prices relative to those of the products."[51] In the end, real wages will have to fall, if for no other reason than the unavailability of consumer goods to meet the demand; and hence it is inevitable that the Ricardo effect will be triggered.

To throw Hayek's problem into relief, consider the subsequent Hicksian construct of the "progressive economy."[52] In a progressive economy the managers expect the demand for their products to be rising. Based on this expectation they proceed to invest and expand the scales of their firms. They do this over a market period long enough for the net investment that takes place to generate exactly enough extra income and new savings for savings and investment to remain equal to each other. In Hicks's progressive economy, investment generates income without delay—the period of construction of capital goods is assumed to be zero.[53] In the new equilibrium position, managers find out that they have constructed exactly the quantity and variety of capital goods they wished to have at the beginning of the market period. Thus, the economy started out in stock equilibrium and ended up in stock equilibrium. In addition, the flow of net investment during the market period was exactly matched by a flow of net savings. Flow and stock equilibrium occur together in the progressive economy. The boom, to return to Hayek's terminology, has proceeded smoothly and without the slightest possibility of ending in crisis.

Now clearly this construction of a progressive economy rules out the Mises-Hayek crisis phenomenon as a matter of definition. If all plans are coordinated at the beginning of the market period and also at the end, then where is the "cluster of business errors" that constitutes the crisis? In this sense, Hayek was quite correct when he objected to Kaldor's use of comparative static methodology. The methodology of comparing isolated equilibrium states rules out precisely the phenomenon of the crisis.

Suppose on the other hand, that Hayek's entrepreneurs only *believe* they are in a progressive state. The lowering of the interest rate suggests that consumers have provided a larger amount of real savings and the managers eagerly begin the task of constructing the new equipment.[54] But the entrepreneurs have only been deceived into thinking the flow of new voluntary savings is larger than it really is because (as we know) it is only the money supply that is increasing. Now the flow of actual net savings is brought exactly into balance with the flow of actual net investment through the familiar forced-saving mechanism. Still, at the end of the period the actors come to realize that their stocks of capital goods are inappropriate to satisfy consumer demand. In old-fashioned terminology, there is too much fixed capital and not enough circulating capital—a realization brought on by Hayek's Ricardo effect mechanism. In summary, we have stock equilibrium at the beginning of the market period, flow equilibrium within the period, and stock *dis*equilibrium at the end.

Hayek's point is that precisely because the entrepreneurs are mistaken about the true real savings of the consumers, a time must come when they have evidence of their mistakes and take steps to correct them. A comparative static analysis of the economy at two points in time, where the capital structure at T_2 is larger than at T_1, compares two equilibrium situations. Hayek preferred a market period approach over a comparative static analysis because it enabled him to identify the sequence of events by which the entrepreneurs come to realize that the equilibrium toward which they are all heading is no longer economic. They come to that conclusion because the underlying structure of production makes the simultaneous realization of their business plans impossible. This information is transmitted to the entrepreneurs through the price system by way of the internal rates of return on investment projects. Hayek's objection to applying comparative statics to this problem of dynamical change and adjustment seems to us remarkably cogent. The problem is not to learn about maladjustments by comparing states of equilibrium but rather to ask if the conditions prevailing at T_1 make the transition to T_2 at all possible. Kaldor's approach indeed assumed away the very problem that Hayek's theory was designed to analyze, the problem of the transition an economy undergoes in moving from one coordinated capital structure to another. The revival in the 1970s of interest in modeling this transition process gives Hayek's favorite mechanism a decidedly modern ring.[55]

VI. CONCLUSION

By emphasizing the inapplicability of the perfectly competitive model especially in the supply of loanable funds, and by insisting on the disequilibrium
nature of the cumulative process, Hayek was speaking a different language from
his peers in the 1930s, 1940s and, surprisingly, in the late 1960s as well. Hayek
challenged the relevance and appropriateness of comparative static analysis
to an expanding economy. His struggle to free himself from the precepts of
comparative static analysis constitutes, in our view, the elusive element in his
thinking and explains why so much miscommunication occurred. Hayek's
most formidable opponent, Kaldor, seemed unable to structure the problem
except in comparative static terms, and this we believe is what prompted Hayek
to focus on their methodological differences.

It is gratifying that by the 1970s Hayek's favorite problem of the process of
adjustment from one coordinated state of equilibrium to another was finally
recognized and tackled by some of the finest minds in the profession, including one of Hayek's own critics—Hicks.[56] While the particular solution and
the methods of analysis Hayek proposed may be controversial, there is now
no longer any question that the problem Hayek raised about the feasibility of
reaching one equilibrium based on the conditions prevailing prior to reaching that equilibrium is an important one. The issues Hayek raised during the
1930s have their counterpart in the modern debates about the structural limits
placed on short-run macroeconomic policy. This, of course, remains a central
concern of the "new classical economists," some of whom have recognized
Hayek as a pioneer investigator.[57] We have taken a second look at Hayek's
Ricardo effect in order to illuminate certain novel elements in Hayek's thinking and their relevance to contemporary economic theorizing.

NOTES

1. A partial list of English language writers includes, in chronological order, N. Kaldor, "Capital
Intensity and the Trade Cycle," *Economica* (February 1939): 40–66, reprinted in Kaldor, *Essays
on Economic Stability and Growth* (Glencoe, IL: The Free Press) 120–147; T. Wilson, "Capital
Theory and the Trade Cycle," *Review of Economic Studies* 7 (1940): 169–179; H. D. Dickinson,
"Review of Hayek's *Freedom and the Economic System*," *Economica* (November 1940): 435–437;
R. G. Hawtrey, "The Trade Cycle and Capital Intensity," *Economica* (February 1940): 1–22; H.
Townshend, "Review of Hayek's *Profits, Interest and Investment*," *Economic Journal* (March 1940):
99–103; N. Kaldor, "Professor Hayek and the Concertina Effect," *Economica* (November 1942),
359–382, reprinted in Kaldor, *Essays on Economic Stability*, 148–176; S. Tsiang, *Variations of
Real Wages and Profit Margins in Relation to the Trade Cycle* (London: Pitman and Sons, 1947),
reprinted by Kraus, West Germany, 1970; S. Tsiang, "Rehabilitation of Time Dimension of
Investment in Macrodynamic Analysis," *Economica* (August 1949), 204–217; W. J. Baumol,
"Income Effect, Substitution Effect, Ricardo Effect" *Economics* (February 1950), 69–80; F. Lutz
and V. Lutz, *The Theory of Investment of the Firm* (Princeton, NJ: Princeton University Press,

1951), 137–142; R. G. Hawtrey, *Capital and Employment* (1937; London, 1952), 248–255; J. Hicks, "The Hayek Story," in Hicks, *Critical Essays in Monetary Theory* (Oxford: Oxford University Press, 1967), 203–215; M. Blaug, *Economic Theory in Retrospect* (Homewood, IL: Richard D. Irwin, 1968), 543–548; W. A. Johr, "Note on Professor Hayek's 'True Theory of Unemployment,'" *Kyklos* 30 (1977): 713–723; and David H. Howard, "Review of Hayek, *Denationalisation of Money*," *Journal of Monetary Economics* 3 (1977): 483–485.

2. Hayek adopted the name "Ricardo effect" toward the end of the 1930s, but the effect itself is discussed in some detail in the following references: F. A. Hayek, *Prices and Production* (London, G. Routledge & Sons, 1935), 69–100 and 148–157; F. A. Hayek, *Profits, Interest and Investment* (Clifton: Augustus M. Kelley, 1975), 3–71; F. A. Hayek, "A Comment," *Economica* (November 1942), 383–85; F. A. Hayek, "Three Elucidations of the Ricardo Effect," *Journal of Political Economy* (1969): 274–285.

3. E. Burmeister, *Capital Theory and Dynamics* (Cambridge: Cambridge University Press, 1980).

4. Blaug, *Economic Theory in Retrospect* (1968), 548.

5. F. A. Hayek, *Monetary Theory and the Trade Cycle* (London, 1933), 33n. The German edition of Hayek's essay appeared in 1929. Cf. R. E. Lucas, Jr., "Understanding Business Cycles," in K. Brunner and A. Meltzer, eds., *Stabilization of the Domestic and International Economy* (Amsterdam, 1977), reprinted in R. E. Lucas, Jr., *Studies in Business Cycle Theory* (Cambridge, MA: MIT Press, 1981), 215.

6. Lucas, "Understanding Business Cycles," 215.

7. See, for example, the selected passages from Hayek's writings in F. A. Hayek and S. Shenoy, *A Tiger by the Tail* (London, IEA, 1978); Hayek, *Full Employment at Any Price?* (London, IEA, 1976).

8. On the Misesian "research program," see L. S. Moss and K. I. Vaughn, "Ludwig von Mises and the Austrian Tradition," paper read at the 1990 meeting of the American Economic Association in Denver, MS; and L. S. Moss, "The Monetary Economics of Ludwig von Mises," in L. S. Moss, *The Economics of Ludwig von Mises: Toward a Critical Reappraisal* (Kansas City, MO: Sheed and Ward, 1974), 13–49.

9. G. O'Driscoll, *Economics as a Coordination Problem* (Kansas City, MO: Sheed and Ward, 1977), xv–xxi, 1–11, and 153–155.

10. See D. Ricardo, *On the Principles of Political Economy and Taxation*, in *The Works and Correspondence of David Ricardo* (Cambridge: Cambridge University Press, 1951) 1:39–43, and 386–397, hereafter referred to as *Principles*. Hayek cited both places in Ricardo's *Principles* as the location of what he (Hayek) termed the "Ricardo effect" (see Hayek, "The Ricardo Effect" in F. A. Hayek, *Individualism and Economic Order* (Chicago: University of Chicago Press, 1948), 220. G. O'Driscoll, a recent commentator, emphasized the dynamic Wicksellian nature of Hayek's analysis in "The Specialization Gap and the Ricardo Effect: Comment on Ferguson," *History of Political Economy* 7, no. 2 (1975): 261–269, but did not emphasize the close connection between the argument of Ricardo's machinery chapter and Hayek's Ricardo effect mechanism; cf. G. O'Driscoll, *Economics as a Coordination Problem*, (Kansas City: Sheed Andrews & McMeel, 1977), 92–128.

11. D. Ricardo, Letter to McCulloch, June 13, 1820; cf. P. Sraffa, "Introduction to Ricardo's *Principles*," in *The Works and Correspondence of David Ricardo* (Cambridge: Cambridge University Press, 1951), xlv.

12. Ricardo, *Principles*, 40.

13. Ricardo, *Principles*, 40.

14. On Ricardo's so-called agricultural theory of profit, see P. Sraffa, "Introduction to Ricardo's *Principles*," xxx–xxxvii. For an application of that theory to how it "regulates" the overall market rates on competing investments and a summary of the recent doctrinal debate surrounding that application, see L. S. Moss, "Professor Hollander and Ricardian Economics," *Eastern Economical Journal* 5 (December 1979): 503.

15. Ricardo, *Principles*, 41. Our discussion is entirely consistent with S. Hollander's claim that Ricardo's "intention" was to show that a once-and-for-all rise in wages would not raise the level of prices, but only alter relative commodity prices; cf. L. Moss, "Professor Hollander and Ricardian Economics," 503–506.

16. Ricardo, *Principles*, 37–38.

17. Although Ricardo did not specifically discuss the economic impact of a sudden decline in the wages of labor, we can infer from his comparative-static framework that a once-and-for-all decline in wages will encourage managers to substitute labor-intensive or direct methods of production (Technique B) for labor-saving (i.e., capital-intensive) methods of production (Technique A). Also, the decline in wages will bring about a decline in the prices of consumer goods made without machinery relative to the prices of consumer goods manufactured with the aid of machinery. This is the form of Ricardo's comparative-static theorem that most closely resembles the one Hayek tried to develop—see the text.

18. On the details of Ricardo's controversial chapter, see P. Sraffa, "Introduction to Ricardo's *Principles*," lvii–lx; and S. Hollander, "The Development of Ricardo's Position on Machinery," *History of Political Economy* 3, no. 1 (1971): 105–135.

19. Ricardo, *Principles*, 390.

20. Ricardo, *Principles*, 395.

21. Hayek, "Three Elucidations of the Ricardo Effect," 275–277. See also Hayek, *Profits, Interest and Investment*, 3–72.

22. Hayek, "Three Elucidations of the Ricardo Effect," 275–276.

23. Except for this omission, see G. O'Driscoll's useful critique of Ferguson's remarks about Hayek's version of the Ricardo effect in "The Specialization Gap and the Ricardo Effect." Hayek refers to both of Ricardo's versions in F. A. Hayek, "The Ricardo Effect," *Economica* 34 (May 1942): 127–152 n. 3. One major difference between the two versions has to do with Ricardo's suggestion that technological changes induce the substitution of machines for labor, while Hayek's analysis is restricted to a choice of techniques that is induced by a change in factor prices.

24. G. Haberler, *Prosperity and Depression* (Geneva, Switzerland: League of Nations, 1941), 33–35; H. S. Ellis, *German Monetary Theory 1905–1933* (Cambridge, MA: Harvard University Press, 1934), 335–374.

25. Knut Wicksell, *Interest and Prices* (1898; London: Macmillan, 1936), 102–121.

26. L. Mises, *Theory of Money and Credit* (Indiana: Liberty Fund, 1980), 362–363. Cf. J. S. Mill, *Principles of Political Economy with Some of Their Applications to Social Polity*, 2 vols. (London: Longmans, Green, Reader, and Dyer, 1878), 2:528 n.

27. Mises, *Theory of Money and Credit*.

28. According to Abba Lerner, "I had just learned about the average period of production from Professor Friedrich von Hayek's first course at the London School of Economics on capital theory [1931–1932]. At the time, a group of my fellow students (who were avid discussants of economic theory in the third year undergraduate study room) were very excited about my essay and its three-dimensional diagram. We persuaded the editor of the *Clare Market Review*, the LSE student magazine to print it in the magazine." Lerner, shortly before his death, revised the exposition under the title "Paleo-Austrian Capital Theory," and it has been published posthumously in A. Lerner, *Selected Economic Writings of Abba P. Lerner*, edited by D. Colander (New York: New York University Press, 1983), 563–583. Other responses to the main argument of Hayek's *Prices and Production* include J. R. Hicks, "Equilibrium and the Trade Cycle," *Zeitschrift für Nationalökonomie* 4 (June 1933), reprinted in *Economic Journal* 18 (October 1980): 523–534; H. Neisser, "Monetary Expansion and the Structure of Production," *Social Research* 1 (November 1934): 434–457; and E. F. M. Durbin, *Purchasing Power and Trade Depression: A Critique of Underconsumption Theories* (London: Cape, 1934); R. G. Hawtrey, *Capital and Employment* (London: Longman, Green, 1936), 220–255. Last, but by no means least, was P. Sraffa's stinging review, "Dr. Hayek on Money and Capital," *Economic Journal* (March 1932):

42–53. Also cf. F. A. Hayek's response, "Money and Capital: A Reply," *Economic Journal* (June 1932): 236–249, followed by P. Sraffa's "Rejoinder," *Economic Journal* (June 1932): 249–251. The Sraffa–Hayek debate has only in recent years inspired discussion; see M. Desai, "The Task of Monetary Theory: The Hayek–Sraffa Debate in Modern Perspective" (working paper at Institut des Sciences Economiques in Belgium); M. Milgate, "On the Origin of the Notion of 'Inter-temporal Equilibrium,'" *Economica* 46 (February 1979): 1–10; and L. M. Lachmann, "Austrian Economics under Fire: The Hayek–Sraffa Duel in Retrospect" (MS, 18 pp.).

29. See F. A. Hayek. "The Paradox of Savings," in F. A. Hayek, *Profits, Interests and Investment* (New York: Augustus M Kelly, 1975), 199–263. See C. Menger's discussion of the various "order" of production in his *Principles of Economics* (Glencoe, IL: Richard D. Irwin, 1950), 149–174. Cf. Hayek, *Prices and Production*, 32–50; and J. R. Hicks, *Capital and Time* (Oxford: Oxford University Press, 1973), 3–26.

30. Hayek always emphasized that the appropriate measure of real wages was the nominal wage divided by the price of the immediate product that labor helped produce. To distinguish this concept of the real wage from the usual nominal wage divided by the price index, Hayek spoke of the "own-wage" of labor. We have glossed this distinction in the text, since none of our conclusions is affected by it. See F. A. Hayek, "The Ricardo Effect" in F. A. Hayek, *Individualism and Economic Order*, 251–253.

31. Hayek, *Prices and Production*, 90–94. On the tug-of-war thesis, see M. N. Rothbard, *America's Great Depression* (Princeton, NJ: D. Van Nostrand, 1963), 17–21.

32. Hayek, "Three Elucidations of the Ricardo Effect," 278–279. Curiously, Hayek had earlier described his theory as involving "lags"; see Hayek, *Prices and Production*, 146.

33. Apparently, consumers must change their *flow* of savings in order to build up a *stock* of capital. Once the stock is built up (i.e., completed), savings can be reduced. H. Neiser, "Monetary Expansion," 439–442, and also P. Sraffa, "Dr. Hayek on Money and Capital," 46–48. Cf. Haberler, *Prosperity and Depression*, 54–56. Cf. L. Lachmann, *Capital and Its Structure* (New York: New York University Press, 1981), 100–127.

34. Hayek, "The Present State and Immediate Prospects of the Study of Industrial Fluctuating," translated from the German, "Der Stand and die nächste . . . ," in Hayek, *Profits, Interest and Investment*, 180.

35. Hayek, *Profits, Interest and Investment*, 180.

36. Hayek, *Monetary Theory and the Trade Cycle*, 147.

37. This claim was asserted by Mises in *The Theory of Money and Credit* (Indiana: Liberty Fund, 1980) and restated toward the end of the 1930s by Hayek. See esp. *Profits, Interest and Investment*, where Hayek states: "What I am concerned with is to show how [the rate of profit] would act if the rate of interest failed to act at all" (6–7). At another place in his essay Hayek concludes, "We might get the trade cycle even without changes in the rate of interest" (64). Cf. O'Driscoll, *Economics as a Coordination Problem*, 94–96.

38. Hayek, *Profits, Interest and Investment*, 64.

39. Members of the Austrian school were never endorsers of the Marshallian firm/industry distinction. See M. Rothbard, *Man, Economy and the State*, 2 vols. (Princeton, NJ: D. Van Nostrand, 1962), 1:304–308). The modern "management view" of the firm (similar to the Austrian view) sees the firm as a bundle of investment projects; see B. Henderson, *Henderson on Corporate Strategy* (Cambridge, MA: Harvard University Press, 1972), 145–166. In the example taken from Hayek (to be discussed below) Hayek speaks of three "firms" rather than three investment projects within a single firm. This modification allows us to clarify our exposition considerably.

40. See Tsiang, *Variations of Real Wages*, 133–34. Hayek, "The Ricardo Effect," 227. Hayek's firm-manager tries to maximize the "internal rate of return on investments"; see Lutz and Lutz, 16–26. For a general critique of using the internal rate of return as an index of investment success see J. Hirshleifer, *Investment, Interest and Capital* (Englewood Cliffs, NJ: Prentice-Hall, 1970), 51–56, and K. E. Boulding, "The Theory of a Single Investment," *Quarterly Journal of Economics* 49 (May 1935).

41. According to Hayek, "the per annum net percentage return on the whole capital of a firm (or on any part of it for which we find it necessary to compute separately), net of 'wages of management' and of risk premium, we shall designate as the 'internal rate of return.'" Initially, the internal rate of return is equal on all projects. Hayek explained: "If we call the internal rate of return I, the rate of turnover T. and the profit margin M, the relationship will be presented by $I = TM$ or $M = I/T$. If . . . the internal rate is 6 percent, [then] the profit margin of a firm turning over its capital six times a year will have to be 1 percent, while a firm turning over its capital only once in two years will have to earn 12 percent on all sales, and a firm turning over its capital only once in every ten years will have to earn a profit of 60 percent" (Hayek, "The Ricardo Effect," 227).

42. "For the three [investments] which we have just considered by way of illustration, the first (with an annual rate of turnover $T = 6$) will find its profit margin increased from 1 to 6 percent; the second [with $T = \frac{1}{2}$] from [12] to [17] percent; and the third (with $T = \frac{1}{10}$) from 60 to 65 percent. Multiplying these profit margins by the corresponding rates of turnover, we obtain the new internal rates of return of $6 \times 6 = 36$ percent for the first, $[\frac{1}{2} \times 17 = 8.5]$ percent for the second, and $\frac{1}{10} \times 65 = 6.5$ percent for the third [investment activity]." Hayek, "The Ricardo Effect," 227.

43. Kaldor, *Essays in Economic Stability*, 2:148–176.

44. Kaldor, *Essays on Economic Stability*, 2:148–176. See also Wilson, "Capital Theory and the Trade Cycle," 177; Hawtrey, *Capital and Employment*, 240–245; and Tsiang, *Variations of Real Wages*, 141–144.

45. Kaldor, *Essays on Economic Stability*, 2:148–176.

46. Hayek, "The Ricardo Effect," 237.

47. Hayek, "The Ricardo Effect," 236. Cf. M. Kalecki, "The Principle of Increasing Risk," *Economica* (November 1937).

48. Hayek, "The Ricardo Effect," 235–237.

49. Cf. M. Kohn, "In Defense of the Finance Constraint," *Economic Inquiry* 19 (181): 177–195.

50. Hayek, "The Ricardo Effect," 239.

51. Hayek, "The Ricardo Effect," 241. Cf. Hayek, "Three Elucidations of the Ricardo Effect," 281.

52. I. R. Hicks, *Capital and Growth* (Oxford: Oxford University Press, 1956), 90–93. This is not to be confused with Hayek's use of the term "progressive economy," referred to earlier in this article.

53. Hicks, *Capital and Growth*, 91.

54. Hayek, *Monetary Theory and the Trade Cycle*; and cf. Rothbard, *America's Great Depression*, 16–17.

55. Hicks, *Capital and Time*. 47–80. See also Burmeister, *Capital Theory and Dynamics*. See, however, Lachmann's "A Reconsideration of the Austrian Theory of Industrial Fluctuations," *Economics* 7 (May 1940); in Lachmann, *Capital Expectations and the Market Process* (Kansas City, MO: Sheed and Ward, 1977), 267–286.

56. Hicks, *Capital and Time*, 81–150. Hicks, like Hayek, harks back to Ricardo's machinery chapter for doctrinal precedent. See Hicks.

57. Hayek did not reach the same conclusion as certain radical exponents of the "new Classical economics." For one thing, Hayek would not agree that a fully announced set of policy changes will have no effect on real macroeconomic variables as has been maintained by T. Sargent and N. Wallace in "'Rational Expectations': The Optimal Monetary Instrument and the Optimal Money Supply Rule," *Journal of Political Economy* 83 (April 1975): 241–254. Hayek argued that Keynesian stimulative policies would have short-run beneficial effects. Hayek disagreed with Keynes when Hayek insisted these beneficial effects would be at the expense of long-run disruptions.

Chapter 4
Profit, Alertness, and Imagination

The events of the last year in Eastern Europe and in the Soviet Union have signaled a widespread recognition of the superior productive capacity of capitalism. Country after formerly communist country has amazed and delighted the West with its rapid rush toward decentralization and the institution of some form of market economy. It seems finally that the debate over the relative efficiency of markets and central planning that was begun by Austrian economists earlier in this century has been settled and capitalism has won. There is another debate, however, that has hardly been engaged at all, and yet this debate is perhaps even more important than the debate over the relative efficiency of capitalism and socialism. That is the debate over the moral status of capitalism. At the same time that we hear praise from the formerly communist countries for the economic productivity of capitalism, we also hear wary warnings about the moral pitfalls of an unhampered capitalist system. Indeed, if anything is capable of derailing the continuing liberalization of the Eastern European economy, it is the fact that the values capitalism seems to stand for appear to many to be harsh and at variance with simple sentiments of justice and charity. At a time like this, a clear statement of the positive moral values projected by a capitalist economic system would go a long way toward settling this second debate. Israel Kirzner's new book, *Discovery, Capitalism, and Distributive Justice* (1989), takes an important step in that direction.

Originally published in *Journal des Économistes et des Études Humaines* 1, no. 2 (1990): 183–188. Republished with permission.

It is especially fortunate that Israel Kirzner, of all people, has chosen to explore the moral justification of capitalism since his insights into the nature of the capitalist process add a theoretically important and morally relevant dimension to generally received economic theory. For the last twenty-five years (since the publication of *Competition and Entrepreneurship* in 1973), Kirzner has been recognized as one of the foremost modern contributors to the theory of entrepreneurship. In contrast to the standard theory of economic behavior as the unproblematic maximization of known utility functions subject to fully known resource constraints, Kirzner has consistently explained the market process as emanating from the unique and unpremeditated actions of alert entrepreneurs who exploit opportunities neglected by others. As such, he has called attention to the importance of genuine human action and unpredictable choice in a way that is largely missing from standard neoclassical economic theory. Since it is the peculiarly entrepreneurial aspects of market economies that are least understood and most often criticized by moral critics of capitalism, Kirzner's insights into the moral status of capitalism promise to be most helpful.

The argument of Kirzner's new book is straightforward. First, he argues, capitalism is not solely a system of allocating known resources among competing and known ends. It is also and more profoundly a process of discovering and exploiting new profit opportunities that have been overlooked in the past. And since discovery of a new opportunity is equivalent to an act of creation, the capitalist process is one of continuing creation of new resources, new ways of combining resources, and ever new ways of satisfying consumer demand. Secondly, Kirzner identifies a widely shared moral sentiment among the population that is colloquially known as "finders-keepers." That is, most people agree that if someone finds something that no one else owns and that no one else knows about, the finder has claim to what he finds. Finally, Kirzner concludes, because in capitalism, profits are *found* by entrepreneurs, if one subscribes to the finders-keepers moral sentiment, one should also accept the morality of profits under capitalism.

While the nub of the argument can be stated quickly, Kirzner builds his case slowly and carefully through seven chapters ranging from a discussion of the meaning of discovery, through the market as a discovery process to an exposition of the finders-keepers rule, to the *ethics* of a finders keepers rule until finally, in chapters six and seven, he actually applies the finders keepers rule to capitalism. (So slow and careful is Kirzner's approach that the reader can't help occasionally wishing that he would just get on with his argument.) While there are many fascinating ideas that one would like to discuss at great length in this book, there are a few issues that I find of particular interest.

Over the years, Kirzner's understanding of the entrepreneurial enterprise has undergone a subtle evolution. In *Competition and Entrepreneurship,* the entrepreneur was placed clearly within the comparative static framework of neoclassical economics. His role was to notice opportunities that were available to all who would but look and, by exploiting these opportunities, to bring the market closer to neoclassical equilibrium. The clear implication of Kirzner's approach was that these opportunities existed somehow "out there." They were objectively present in much the same way that resources are objectively present whether or not one has found them. These opportunities could be noticed by anyone at all who was alert, and why one person might notice them and another not was totally unexplainable. In subsequent essays, Kirzner responded to the challenge presented by Shackle and Lachmann and others concerning the subjective and creative nature of choice by increasingly acknowledging that the entrepreneur was doing more than just noticing what was out there for the taking. He was in fact engaging in a discovery process that was in some sense creative as well. However, Kirzner (1972, 148) maintained that there was no real essential difference between the two ways of describing entrepreneurship and continued to label the significant aspect of entrepreneurship as "alertness."

In this latest effort, Kirzner has moved even further into the Shacklean camp by especially emphasizing the creative aspects of entrepreneurship, yet he still tries to retain his earlier language. It has become obvious to this reviewer that the old language no longer fits his new theoretical insights.

To my mind, one of the major problems with the language of alertness and "noticing" opportunities is that it implies a certain randomness in who makes any particular discovery. Kirzner justifies his characterization of the entrepreneurial enterprise by arguing that when an alert entrepreneur notices something that has escaped the attention of others, he is making a discovery that is in a very practical sense the equivalent of bringing something brand new into the world. An unnoticed opportunity is nonexistent from the human perspective. While I agree with the direction of Kirzner's argument, he does not go far enough in pointing to the implications of the creative nature of entrepreneurship. Consequently, he fails to serve his own purpose of justifying entrepreneurial profits by showing the essential unity between the entrepreneur's creative act of discovering profit opportunities and the creativity of an artist transforming paint and canvas into a work of art.

What is it that the artist and the entrepreneur have in common? Certainly, it is not a matter of noticing a use for inputs that no one else had noticed before, or even noticing the possibility of using something as an input that no one else had thought of (like using oil for energy, perhaps, or burlap for a collage). The nub of both creative acts is not *noticing* per se but imagining and acting upon one's imagination. One imagines a future different from the present and one acts purposefully to bring this imagined alternative future about. And contra Kirzner, the purposeful action to bring about one's vision of the future is not simply a matter of production, but an integral and inseparable part of the entrepreneurial enterprise. While this may be dismissed as merely a difference in rhetoric, I think here the rhetoric is important. Each artist will use his media differently. There are no repeatable creative acts of artistry, and it is *not* true that an infinite number of monkeys with an infinite number of typewriters will eventually write *Hamlet*. The same is true of entrepreneurial acts. No two will be alike because all entrepreneurial acts are products of the entrepreneur's imagination, and each imagination is unique. One doesn't notice opportunities that are there, one imagines opportunities that no one else even in principle could imagine in exactly the same way.

By focusing on alertness rather than imagination as the essence of entrepreneurial action, Kirzner tends to imply that what gets noticed and who notices it is largely accidental. The purpose of Kirzner's language is to emphasize the costlessness of entrepreneurial opportunity to distinguish it from deliberate search, but the consequence is to make the entrepreneur almost a hapless beneficiary of fortune. Kirzner does claim that more than mere luck is involved in entrepreneurial discovery, that not everyone will be equally alert, but the argument strikes me as thin, especially since all his examples are examples where luck plays a large role in discovery. If discovery is completely costless and unexpected, in what way isn't it the product of pure chance? Here again, an emphasis on imagination rather than alertness could provide the way to an answer. Imagination, as I have argued, is a unique product of an individual's brain. What one creates out of one's imagination is far more genuinely one's own than what one simply picks up off the street.

This point would not be worth belaboring had it not implications for Kirzner's moral argument. Kirzner hangs his argument on the claim that a finders-keepers ethic is deeply ingrained in public sentiment, and while this may be a promising starting point, it is not clear to me that invoking finders-keepers is going to be terribly convincing to anyone who is not already convinced by other arguments for capitalism. Perhaps for simple circumstances like finding a coin in the street, finders-keepers suffices as a moral argument for ownership. Once the circumstances become more complicated, however, so do public moral sentiments. For example, if one were to find, not a coin, but a million dollars in the street, public support for finders-keepers might be considerably weakened by a belief that some effort should be made to find the original owner. The public would be even less likely to support a finders-keepers ethic if a passerby were to find a vial of rare and expensive prescription medicine or a pedigree dog of great value. In fact, my reading of public sentiment is that finders-keepers applies most strongly when the gains are the most trivial. On the other hand, no one ever disputes the gains earned by painters or writers no matter how large they may be. Perhaps the public ethical sentiment that would most strongly undergird a capitalist system isn't so much finders-keepers, then, as it is "creators-keepers," a sentiment fully in line with Kirzner's own understanding of the nature of capitalist discovery.

I am skeptical about the finders-keepers ethic for yet another reason. Kirzner develops his finders-keepers ethic almost exclusively through parables of isolated individuals. So for example, he starts his exposition by asking us to imagine a man (Jones) stuck at the bottom of a hole who notices some lumber, nails, and tools and uses them to construct a ladder. Jones has, according to Kirzner, behaved entrepreneurially by discovering the raw materials and, by the finders-keepers rule, as long as no one has a prior claim to the raw materials, he should own the raw materials and the resultant ladder. Yet, how relevant is this story to any real-world problem? Most of the questions of the morality of property are not about isolated individuals using unnoticed scraps to solve a problem or about individuals gathering acorns in the woods or discovering that the fruit of some common vine is good to eat; they are about conflicting claims over the use of the same property.

Reconsider Jones, for example, who now is at the bottom of the hole with four other people. Jones by himself first notices the materials for building a ladder and proceeds to construct it to liberate himself from his predicament. How far would the finders-keepers ethic be generally accepted if Jones then proceeded to drag the ladder up after him and leave everyone else there? Would the community acknowledge his right to do so in this case? Or what if after building the ladder, he then charged everyone a fee for escape that was equal to their total net worth? Would the rest of the people in the hole say, "Oh well, finders-keepers" and pay up? And what if Smith also noticed the lumber et al.

a split second after Jones and yet was denied the opportunity to build the ladder? How would he feel about finders-keepers in such a desperate situation? I can imagine the others acknowledging Jones's right to some profit from his discovery, but the right acknowledged would also undoubtedly be tempered by community considerations of end-state fairness and overall public benefit. Perhaps finders-keepers can be proposed as a starting point for a capitalist ethic, but if so, other moral precepts will have to be brought in very quickly to make the moral case for capitalism.

Kirzner correctly sees himself building on Nozick's entitlement theory of property (what one acquires through a just process is justly one's own) by providing a theory of original entitlement through entrepreneurial discovery. He also distinguishes his argument for initial entitlement from Locke's famous labor theory of property. Locke's theory, Kirzner argues, assumes that one acquires property by mixing one's labor with given and known resources, while Kirzner's entrepreneur creates property by discovering resources that no one else has seen before. At this level, Kirzner is correct to emphasize his difference from Locke. Locke presumed that the world was given to men in common for their use, and his problem was to explain how bits of this common inheritance could be partitioned off into private property for an individual's exclusive use. Because he explained private property as the product of a process of an individual mixing his labor with common resources, one common interpretation of Locke is that he meant that only brute labor was necessary to create title to property. Yet, given the whole context of Locke's account of property in the state of nature, Locke's argument is closer to Kirzner's than it might appear.

Locke, too, was appealing to common moral sentiments to try to explain how a right to private property could have come about in the "original state." He was appealing to his audience's sense of self-ownership to show how property legitimately could have been created out of unowned resources. But while Locke framed his argument in terms of labor-mixing, his emphasis was in showing that human agency was responsible for creating something new out of formerly worthless natural resources. Locke's discussion of labor-mixing then was very much like Kirzner's emphasis on discovery: to point to the novelty that flows from property creation rather than to a simple mechanical transformation of resources into output. Locke also didn't rest his argument on entitlement alone. He also provided a utilitarian argument for property by claiming that everyone was better off as a result of private ownership—thereby appealing to self-interest as well as moral sentiments.

Kirzner correctly notes a long-standing problem in Locke's argument that seems to undercut his justification of capitalist ownership: the limitation imposed on property creation in the state of nature by the famous Lockean proviso (that property was only legitimate if it created no scarcity of resources for others). Kirzner points out that this proviso places serious limitations on Locke's support for capitalism since it seems to suggest that one can only acquire legitimate title to property in a world of no scarcity. Since all important questions of capitalist property pertain to a world of scarcity, Kirzner finds Locke's justification of property unhelpful. However, before we accept Kirzner's criticism, it should be noted that Locke overcame his own proviso in the *Second Treatise of Government* (1689) by introducing market exchange and money into his analysis. Money makes unequal distributions of wealth permissible and market exchange makes it possible for people to mix their labor with the property of others to create their own wealth. The market was a moral means of creating wealth in Locke's thought just as it is in Kirzner's. Unfortunately, by using the language of labor mixing as if in a recipe, Locke's important message of property as creation tended to get overlooked. Instead, his argument was used to provide the basis for the mechanical labor theory of value and for a moral argument against private ownership of the means of production. Here is an instructive example of how rhetoric matters. By speaking of entrepreneurial discovery, rather than labor-mixing, Kirzner has clearly taken us in a more promising direction for justifying private property under capitalism. If he would also speak in terms of creation and imagination instead of alertness, he would take us even further toward his goal of providing a convincing justification for capitalist ownership.

In his penultimate chapter, Kirzner takes pains to clarify his purpose in writing this important new book. He tells us that "To declare a finders-keepers rule just is to recognize that such a rule gets us, morally speaking, to a stage whence we can hope, possibly, to proceed further" (Kirzner 1989, 131). Even if one were to reject his argument in favor of finders-keepers, however, he has nevertheless succeeded in achieving this desired stage. He has begun the much-needed rethinking of the morality of capitalism in light of our post-Hayekian knowledge about the market process. By centering his moral inquiries on the role of entrepreneurship as creativity and discovery rather than on the role of prices in bringing about allocative efficiency in the marketplace, he has started from the central attribute of capitalism. I have long harbored the optimistic belief that if people truly understood the nature of the market process, they would find it to be a system that embodies some of our most cherished moral sentiments. If such an understanding is to come closer to reality, it will be in large part because of the pioneering work of Israel Kirzner.

REFERENCES

Kirzner, Israel M., ed. 1972. *Method, Process and Austrian Economics: Essays in Honor of Ludwig von Mises*. Lexington, MA: Lexington Books.

Kirzner, Israel M. 1973. *Competition and Entrepreneurship*. Chicago: Chicago University Press.

———. 1989. *Discovery, Capitalism, and Distributive Justice*. New York: Basil Blackwell.

Locke, John. 1689. *Second Treatise of Government*.

Chapter 5
The Mengerian Roots of the Austrian Revival

I. INTRODUCTION

The thesis of this paper is straightforward. The Austrian revival in the United States is the continuation of a research program begun by Carl Menger in 1870 but truncated in the early part of the twentieth century as the economics profession became more and more entranced first with Marshall and then with Walras. Despite the richness and complexity of Menger's economics, by the 1930s economists in the English-speaking world, at least, knew of Menger only indirectly through his students. If he was thought of at all, his contribution was considered to be little more than a nonmathematical version of marginal utility analysis. The real substance and importance of Menger's work had to be rediscovered by Friedrich Hayek in the middle decades of the twentieth century. Although at first the debt to Menger was often unconscious, the rediscovery of Mengerian ideas was the root of the revival of interest in Austrian economics by an increasing number of younger economists beginning in the 1970s. Further, Mengerian ideas form the basis for some of the most interesting aspects of current Austrian theory.

II. CARL MENGER AND THE INCOMPLETE SUBJECTIVIST REVOLUTION

After nearly one hundred years of his being identified with Jevons and Walras as marginal revolutionaries, the reevaluation of Menger's contributions to

Originally published in *History of Political Economy* 22 (Suppl. 1990):379–407. Copyright 1990 Duke University Press. All rights reserved. Republished by permission.

economics began in earnest in 1972. Erich Streissler's 1972 article "To What Extent Was the Austrian School Marginalist?" was followed by Hicks and Weber's edited volume of essays, *Carl Menger and the Austrian School of Economics* in 1973 and by William Jaffé's "Menger, Jevons and Walras Dehomogenized" in 1975. In 1978 an entire issue of the *Atlantic Economic Journal* was devoted to Carl Menger and included a piece by Ludwig Lachmann entitled "Carl Menger and the Incomplete Revolution of Subjectivism." The point of all these essays was that Menger had been misrepresented by economists who thought of him as a marginal utility theorist who used words instead of mathematics. Streissler argued that Menger's *Principles of Economics* was really more a treatise on economic development than on marginal utility theory (1972, 430). Jaffé showed the importance of ignorance and error in Menger's theory (1975, 521), and Lachmann argued that Menger's contribution had been more to begin a subjectivist revolution than to carry it out in full (1978, 59). These writers all helped to illuminate the aspects of Carl Menger that form the backbone of the Austrian revival.

The principal reason that Menger was for so long lumped with the "marginal revolutionaries" was that value indeed was the central unifying principle of his economics. Like Jevons in England and like the German Historical School, which for so many subsequent decades Menger regarded as the enemy, Menger was convinced that the labor theory of value of the Ricardian school was dangerously incorrect, yet unlike the German Historical School, he was convinced that a correct theory of value was a necessary prerequisite to any analysis of real, historical economic phenomena. Hence, he set out in *Principles* to develop a theory of value that began from the subjective valuations of individuals concerning the usefulness of goods for the purpose of fulfilling their needs. Like other discoverers of the principle of diminishing marginal utility, Menger proposed that people rank-ordered their needs and applied successive units of goods to satisfying less and less urgent needs. The value of any part of a stock of goods was equal to the least important use to which a portion of the stock was put (Menger 1981, 122–28). This theory, only later termed "diminishing marginal utility" by Wieser (1893), was what earned Menger the reputation of having been one of the coparticipants in the marginal revolution.

Of course, it was pointed out several times that Menger's formulation of diminishing marginal utility was imprecise.[1] The numerical scales of value that he included to illustrate why an individual would consume combinations of valued goods, rather than exhausting his desire for the most important before moving on to the less important good, were incomplete. Since he included no given income endowment, it was impossible from his table to figure out the equilibrium consumption basket. It was assumed that the many interesting examples of allocating increasing quantities of the same good to successively less important uses were just imprecise verbal elaboration on the same theme. Nevertheless, despite the supposed imprecision of Menger's presentation, at least he was credited with developing the basic idea, and that was that. The incredibly rich and suggestive context within which this admittedly central part of Menger's theory was couched seems to have been overlooked by most of the subsequent evaluators of Menger's work until the reevaluation referred to above. Yet it is only when Menger's theory of value is read within the larger context of his *Principles* that one truly appreciates his greatness. And it is only then that it becomes apparent that differences between Menger and the neoclassical revolution are what is really important about him.

Three themes that recur throughout Menger's *Principles* form the basis of his particular view of economics. They are, roughly, (1) knowledge and plan, (2) the primacy of process, and (3) spontaneous order and the progress of civilization.

Jaffé argued that Menger, far from viewing man as a rational "lightning calculator," saw him as a "bumbling, erring, ill-informed creature, plagued with uncertainty, forever hovering between alluring hopes and haunting fears, and congenitally incapable of making finely calibrated decisions in pursuit of satisfactions" (1975, 521). One does not have to agree with Jaffé all the way in order to recognize an important truth in this description. To Menger, rationality did not mean omnipotence or omniscience. Humans were born into ignorance and had as their primary task to learn the "causal connection between things and the satisfaction of their needs" in order to make reasonable decisions about their economic well-being. Further, they not only had to acquire knowledge, they also had to have the power to do something about their knowledge.[2]

Knowledge and power: throughout the *Principles*, Menger stresses the importance of acquiring knowledge and power to economic behavior.[3] Economic life is built around gaining knowledge and power: knowledge of causal relationships between things and satisfactions (1981, 52), knowledge of the relationship between goods of a higher order and goods of the first order (56–57), knowledge of available quantities of goods (89), knowledge of trading opportunities (179), knowledge of the "economic" situation (224), and the power to make the best use of one's knowledge. The acquisition of knowledge was an integral part of the economic problem; it was not a problem to be assumed away in the confines of *ceteris paribus*.

This leads to the second theme of importance in Menger's *Principles*, the primacy of process. That man is ignorant and constantly must try to improve his knowledge implies that his economizing activities cannot be passive and reactive. Insofar as men recognize their ignorance and try to overcome it, they must engage in some process that leads to a future different from the past. That process consists of either imagining a future different from the past or noticing something previously overlooked and taking steps to act on this new knowledge to one's advantage.[4] We see exactly such a process described in the introductory sections of Menger's much-celebrated theory of value.

Menger's theory of value was far more complex than simply a theory of how people make choices with given information. The theory of marginal use is preceded by a discussion of an individual's need to plan to meet his requirements for an uncertain future (1981, 80–84). In order to meet their requirements adequately, men must anticipate their needs and their resources over a planning period so that they can take steps to correct any potential shortfall in resources. The plan includes the recognition that, over time, needs may change; hence men must plan for a variety of contingencies. Once the estimation is made, they must then actively seek out additional resources if they believe their currently anticipated supplies are inadequate. Obviously, Menger recognized that men live in time and must plan through time.[5] Economizing behavior is more than just allocating given resources among competing ends. In order to economize over time, men must seek out information and take action to improve their potential well-being. These actions include producing goods, seeking out sources of supply, and participating in economic institutions that gather information about the availability of goods.

The human being that is the subject of Menger's study is neither Veblen's lightning calculator nor a passive reactor to changing constraints. Certainly he cannot be summarized by a static and fully defined preference function. He is ignorant of the world around him, but he seeks to remove as much of that ignorance as he can. He is an active creator both of himself and of his world. And creation is a process rather than a state of affairs.

Menger fills his writing with examples of active processes. The most important of these, of course, is his theory of exchange. In the two chapters devoted to exchange and price formation, it seems obvious that Menger is not interested solely in deriving equilibrium prices for different market structures.[6] Rather, he describes a process whereby men seek out trading partners for the purpose of better satisfying their needs and then engage in a process of bargaining to get the best deal they can.

> The same principle that guides men in their economic
> activity in general, that leads them to investigate the use-
> ful things surrounding them in nature and to subject them
> to their command, and that causes them to be concerned
> about the betterment of their economic positions, the
> effort to satisfy their needs as completely as possible, leads
> them also to search most diligently for this relationship
> wherever they can find it, and to exploit it for the sake of
> better satisfying their needs. (Menger 1981, 180)

Menger's men are not simply solving a maximization problem. They actively search out trading partners and exploit the differences in valuation between them. And since the activity of trading requires knowledge and effort, not everyone will come to the same conclusions. Actual trades will depend on actual circumstances that will differ from individual to individual. The economist's job is to show the principles by which individuals bargain with one another once a trading partner is found, and to develop general principles for the formation of prices in more developed markets. Hence, Menger's theory of price described the limits of economic prices and did not attempt to determine equilibrium prices.[7]

In a modification of typical neoclassical procedure, Menger begins with isolated monopoly and then shows how the range of potential prices would narrow with increases in the numbers of buyers and sellers in the market. However, even here he was not so much deducing equilibrium prices under different market models as he was giving an analytic and a historical account of how increasing competition leads to lower prices, greater output, and the more complete exploitation of every economic opportunity. In fact, Menger's chapter on price formation is more an analysis of the characteristics of economic progress than it is an analysis of equilibrium prices.[8]

I do not want to exaggerate the nonequilibrium character of Menger's work. He implies the notion of an individual equilibrium (1981, 74–76), and he uses the idea of an equilibrium between needs and requirements as the goal of individual plans (97). Further, he makes passing mention of an equilibrium between future and present consumption (159n.) and describes prices as "symptoms of an economic equilibrium between the economies of individuals" (191). The whole notion of setting the limits to economic exchange implies some equilibrium toward which actions are progressing. However, economic equilibria are at best partial and ephemeral. The world is characterized more by constant flux than by equilibrium states, although equilibrium may obtain from time to time:

> the foundations for economic exchanges are constantly changing, and we therefore observe the phenomenon of a perpetual succession of exchange transactions. But even in this chain of transactions we can, by observing closely, find points of rest at particular times, for particular persons, and with particular kinds of goods. At these points of rest, no exchange of goods takes place because an economic limit to exchange had already been reached. (Menger 1981, 188)

While the passage above pretty clearly describes a notion of partial equilibrium, Menger also makes reference in his *Investigations* to "economic prices," a notion that bears some resemblance to prices in general equilibrium (1985, 71). Prices are "correct" to Menger only when everyone protects his economic interests, people have complete knowledge of their goals and means of achieving them, they understand the "economic situation" (all market opportunities are known and taken into account in personal calculation), and they have the freedom to pursue their goals.[9] However, he views economic prices as the benchmarks for measuring the deviations of real prices and as the direction toward which civilization is progressing, not as an underlying characteristic of the economy at any moment in time.[10] Menger seems to have believed that as civilization progressed, people's economic knowledge would improve so as to make real prices more closely approximate economic prices. In fact, so much of Menger's observations have to do with the way in which civilization progresses that I must agree fully with Streissler (1972) that Menger was fundamentally providing a theory of economic development in the *Principles* and not a theory of static economic allocation.[11] Once one reads the *Principles* with this purpose in mind, it is difficult to see how it could ever have been read in any other way.

The importance of knowledge and process come together in Menger's concern with progress and development. We see this in his identification of economic progress with the increase of human knowledge and with his persistent interest in the nature and origin of various phenomena, from value to economic institutions. The opening paragraph of the *Principles* states the relationship between progress and knowledge very clearly:

All things are subject to the law of cause and effect. This
great principle knows no exception, and we would search
in vain in the realm of experience for an example to the
contrary. Human progress has no tendency to cast it in
doubt, but rather the effect of confirming it and of always
further widening knowledge of the scope of its validity.
Its continued and growing recognition is therefore closely
linked to human progress. (1981, 51)

Throughout the *Principles* we see repeated examples of how increasing knowledge of the causal relationship between goods and their ability to contribute
to want satisfaction contributes to human progress. In fact Menger, explicitly
criticizes Adam Smith for too narrowly identifying the "progressive division
of labor" as the source of wealth (1981, 72). Rather, Menger argues,

The quantities of consumption goods at humans' disposal
are limited only by the extent of human knowledge of the
causal connections between things, and by the extent of
human control over these things. . . . the degree of economic progress of mankind will still, in future epochs,
be commensurate with the degree of progress of human
knowledge. (1981, 72)

In fact, Menger's zealous adherence to the idea that economic progress was
caused by the growth of knowledge has opened him up to the criticism by
Lachmann (1978, 58) that he was not sufficiently subjectivist.

In one sense Lachmann is correct. Menger believed that there were objective laws of nature and that goods had objective properties that made them
more or less capable of fulfilling human needs. Hence, people need to learn
of the causal relationship between the properties of a good and its ability to
satisfy needs. However, people could make mistakes about a good's properties.
For instance, at a more primitive time people could believe that witch doctors
cured disease, but with the advancement of knowledge they would come to
realize that such a belief is in error. Hence Menger included in his lexicon the
category of "imaginary goods" (1981, 53).

For a pure subjectivist this category is problematic. If goods are defined by
individual subjective evaluations, why would any good be more imaginary
than any other? The answer, it seems to me, is that Menger's theory of development required that he make room for error in perceptions and consequent

learning, and this meant that he had to judge some past beliefs as mistaken if there were to be any meaning in the notion of improved knowledge. If one is going to talk about progress, one must be able to define it. Menger could not define it in terms of national wealth, since he did not think one could aggregate the wealth of individuals in a sufficiently precise way as to come up with a meaningful measure of national wealth (1981, 109–13). The measure of progress had to be an individual one, yet if one held that an individual's subjective evaluations could never be incorrect even in light of his own later knowledge, how could one ever speak of "progress"? Hence Menger took the position that people value goods according to their subjective assessments of the relationship between the good and the need it could satisfy, but that they can be mistaken in their understanding in the sense that once they acquire better information, they will recognize their mistake. Witch doctors objectively do not cure disease. Progress means that people come to realize this and, as a result, will substitute better forms of medicine. Here, then, Menger's theory of imaginary goods is not so much a truncating of subjectivism as it is an extension of subjectivism to knowledge.[12]

While Menger repeatedly identifies progress with the growth of knowledge, it is interesting that the process he describes by which much progress takes place is not necessarily an intentional one. Some economic progress emerges as the intentional outcome of individuals' seeking solutions to economizing problems by, say, organizing firms to collect information about availability of supplies (Menger 1981, 91–94). In other cases, the individual search for economic improvement leads to the emergence of institutions that were planned by no one and yet serve the interests of all. This second kind of progress is the kind that Smith and the Scottish Enlightenment referred to as outcomes that were the product of human action but not of human design and which Friedrich Hayek was later to refer to as a "spontaneous order."[13]

The most famous example of a spontaneous order in Menger is his theory of money. Money is the unintended outcome of individuals' attempts to improve their chances to get what they want through barter. They find that if they trade less marketable commodities for more marketable ones, they can increase the barter opportunities open to them. Eventually one commodity emerges as the most marketable and becomes institutionalized as money (Menger 1981, 257–60). Notice that this is a process in which the outcome is neither deliberately designed nor predictable in advance. An increase in knowledge results, but it is not knowledge that is searched for. Such processes are mentioned again and again in Menger.[14] The outcome of all of them is a new convention or institution that aids individuals to satisfy their wants better by following some new pattern. It is not an exaggeration to think of Menger as developing a theory of economic institutions grounded in a theory of individual economizing action.

Knowledge, process, and development: all are key concepts in Menger's work, and all had to be rediscovered in the twentieth century.

If this reading of Menger is correct, it is legitimate to ask why these major contributions were overlooked as neoclassical economics was undergoing its formation in the late nineteenth and early twentieth century. There are several convincing reasons to offer. First, Menger was known in the English-speaking countries primarily through the work of his colleagues, Wieser and Böhm-Bawerk. Those two were most known for those aspects of their work that contributed to the growing neoclassical orthodoxy. Wieser (1893) developed the theory of marginal utility further and articulated the principle of opportunity cost to which it gives rise. He further worked on extending Menger's sketchy notions of general equilibrium in a manner more consistent with Walras than with Menger's intent (Wieser 1927). Böhm-Bawerk became best known for his capital theory, which Menger regarded as a grave error because it reintroduced classical aggregative notions into economics.[15] Hence, even the disciples chose to glean from Menger's work ideas that were not true to its overall thrust. And Menger could not speak for himself to the increasingly important English-speaking audience, for the *Principles* was not translated into English until 1950.

The second- and third-generation Austrians retained some of Menger's message, but in order to be part of the greater scholarly community they were increasingly obliged to develop their ideas in neoclassical parlance. Clearly this was true of Haberler, Machlup, and Morgenstern, for example. Schumpeter was an even more extreme case. While retaining much of the Austrian concern with process and institutions, he nevertheless embraced the static equilibrium economics of Walras as the epitome of economic science.[16] Even Ludwig von Mises, the most identifiably Austrian thinker of this period, was more concerned with equilibrium theorizing than Menger had been.[17] And Friedrich Hayek, who had been Mises's student in Vienna, went to England and tried to convey an Austrian theory of capital and the trade cycle in neoclassical terms.[18]

III. ECONOMIC CALCULATION AND THE REDISCOVERY OF MENGERIAN THEMES

Modern Austrian economics owes its demise and rebirth to a putative failure: the debate over the economics of socialism.[19] This watershed event in the evolution of the Austrian tradition was a classic example of miscommunication in the economics profession. Interestingly, when he technically started the debate in 1920, Mises believed that the arguments he produced to support his famous contention that economic calculation under a socialist regime was impossible, were not particularly Austrian but were simply good economic arguments. Perhaps even more than Mises, Hayek viewed himself as part of a broad scholarly community that had progressed beyond distinctions as to school and country of origin. Hence it was in a spirit of professional unity that Hayek in 1930–1931 delivered a series of lectures on the topic of capital theory to an intrigued and receptive audience at the London School of Economics.[20]

At first after his arrival in London there was no small enthusiasm for Hayek's ideas. However, during the 1930s and early 1940s Hayek lost two important debates: first, he lost out to Keynes over the question of the trade cycle, and then, more important to our story, he lost out to Oscar Lange over the issue of the economics of socialism. That he lost out so completely was largely due to the fact that he had a fundamentally different understanding of market economies from his English colleagues. The economics profession during these years was becoming more and more entranced with Walras, while Hayek at root was a Mengerian—although it took him almost a decade to rediscover his Mengerian roots.

Perhaps it was easy for Hayek in the early "years of high theory" to believe he was part of one scholarly community when the questions under discussion were limited to how one defined capital or what the role of bank money was in a trade cycle. Differences of opinion are the stock in trade of science, and one expects to encounter opposition to new ideas and to argue hard for one's new theory. Besides, when arguing over specific pieces of theory, one generally assumes the basic framework. However, the debate over socialism was different. When arguing over the feasibility of replacing a market economy with a centrally planned economy, the totality of an economist's understanding of markets is called into play. It is not a surprise, then, that the very basic differences of world view between Hayek and the market socialists would hamper communication.

As is now well known, Mises began what was later referred to as the economic calculation debate by pointing out in an article in 1920 that Marxist plans to do away with markets, money, and prices in the post-revolutionary society were naive (see Mises [1920] 1935). Every economy required a set of market prices in order for economic calculation to be possible. Without money or markets, Mises claimed, economic prices could not be known, and hence socialist economies were doomed to suffer inefficiency at best and chaos at worst.

Mises's challenge was taken up by a number of conventional English-speaking economists, who first attempted various ways of solving the pricing problem in central planning, ranging from estimating demand and supply equations from empirical data in order to compute economic prices to Oscar Lange's version of "market socialism."

Lange's market socialism attempted to answer Mises's criticism by deriving shadow prices from market information in much the same way that Lange believed it was accomplished in real markets. His scheme (Lange and Taylor 1938) required that there be a real market in consumer goods but that all producer goods, "the means of production," were to be collectively owned. Prices for factor inputs would be decreed by a Central Planning Board (CPB), and all production would take place in state-owned firms. The managers of all state-owned firms would be instructed to behave as perfect competitors and maximize profits based on the prices dictated by the CPB.

The crux of Lange's plan, and the feature that won him the most praise from his colleagues, was his plan for arriving at economic prices. He imagined that actual pricing in real markets took place according to a Walrasian *tâtonnement*, with the auctioneer arriving at the market-clearing price by trial and error. Hence, Lange argued, the CPB would act as an auctioneer and adjust prices according to trial and error as well, increasing prices in response to shortages and decreasing prices in response to surpluses. Information about shortages and surpluses would be obtained from the managers of state-owned firms. Since Lange believed his scheme duplicated all the important features of the market (the parametric function of price, trial-and-error pricing, and profit maximization), there was no reason to believe his brand of market socialism would be any less efficient than capitalism. Hence, he was able to enlist neoclassical general equilibrium theory in the service of socialism.

Hayek first wrote on the economics of socialism in response to the early plans to estimate demand and supply curves statistically. His critique of market socialism continued after Lange published his work and went on until about 1944. Over the course of these eight years, he became increasingly frustrated in his attempts to explain to his colleagues why he was convinced that their plans for redesigning society would not succeed. All his best arguments were considered either trivial or irrelevant. It was not so much that the profession thought he was wrong in anything he said. They just did not see how what he said mattered.

As one reads through the calculation articles of this period,[21] it becomes not entirely surprising that Hayek was not understood. Despite some extremely insightful comments, it seems obvious that Hayek was himself struggling with locating the theoretical source of his intuitive rejection of the market social-ists' plan. His critiques are often poorly organized, almost musing in nature. Themes are introduced in one article only to be developed in later writings as their importance becomes clearer to him. Even more damning, his arguments were too philosophical or detailed to seem like good economic theory. In ret-rospect it is obvious that Hayek was not playing the game by the same rules as everyone else, and that he was himself unaware of the gulf that separated him from the rest of the profession.

All of Hayek's criticisms of market socialism center around two famil-iar Mengerian themes: the role of knowledge in society, and the dynamic nature of market economies. Neither of these was important to neoclassical economics at the time. Consider first his argument against the earlier social-ist solution of estimating supply and demand equations statistically (Hayek 1935). At the time, Hayek was understood to have made a practical objection to such a plan—that it would be too difficult to make the required compu-tations given the existing state of technology. What he was really arguing, however, was that one could not even set up such an estimation problem. First, he questioned the nature of the information required to set up the equation system. He argued that in trying to specify the goods to be priced, many important details automatically accounted for in market transactions would be lost. The goods specified would be aggregates rather than descrip-tions of the variety of attributes people actually value. In addition, the social-ist presumption seemed to be that technological information was somehow available and given.

In response to this, Hayek argued that technological knowledge was dis-persed among many minds and had to be discovered through competition. There was no relevant sense in which it was "there." Secondly, he argued that the equations solution to the pricing problem under socialism implied that prices were generally in equilibrium and did not change rapidly. In fact, he argued, markets are characterized by constant change:

> The essential thing about the present economic system is that it does react to some extent to all those small changes and differences which would have to be deliberately disre-garded under the system we are discussing if the calcula-tions were to be manageable. In this way, rational decision would be impossible in all these questions of detail which in the aggregate decide the success of productive effort. (Hayek [1935] 1948, 156–57)

Hayek raised a number of other important questions in this article: Will the managers of state-owned firms behave as private entrepreneurs would? How can a regulator get enough information to regulate a state-owned firm? What are the criteria by which one allocates resources to state-owned firms, when much decision-making must be based on estimates of future probability rather than past performance, and how can a regulator measure success or failure without genuine profits? While most critics took all of these objections to be concerned primarily with the question of incentives, in fact every one was a variation on the theme of knowledge and process. These themes reappeared again and again during the next decade in Hayek's writing.

Hayek explored these themes explicitly the next year in one of his most famous articles, "Economics and Knowledge" ([1937] 1948, 33–56).[22] Here he began with an exploration of the meaning of "equilibrium" that in effect redefined the concept. Equilibrium for an individual, he argued, in order to have any meaning, had to refer to a consistent plan rather than a particular consumption basket. The implication of this, however, was that the concept of a social equilibrium was problematic, an idea Menger had lightly touched on in the *Principles*. Social equilibrium had to mean not a state of affairs but a set of mutually compatible plans. But in that case one had to ask what people had to know in order for mutually compatible plans to exist, and by what process they would come to know what they needed to know. This led him to the question of how people acquire knowledge in a market economy and to propose, as Menger had implied, that the crucial feature of markets was that they permitted individuals to take advantage of the existing division of knowledge.

In this discussion we see the beginning of the exploration of the connection between knowledge and process. Once it is recognized that knowledge is not a given but must be acquired, one cannot help but ask what are the implications of changing knowledge for social action. That leads inexorably to questions of process and the role of equilibrium theory.[23] Not surprisingly, in this article Hayek proposed a fundamentally different notion of equilibrium from the static equilibrium assumed by his neoclassical colleagues. There seems to be no indication that he realized he was doing so.

Hayek continued to explore the implications of knowledge and process in his direct answer to Oscar Lange written in 1940, and in two culminating articles in 1945 and 1946, "The Use of Knowledge in Society" (1948, 77–91) and "The Meaning of Competition" (1948, 92–106). Hayek's critique of Lange repeated some of his earlier objections to "statistical" socialism which Lange's scheme failed to address. Lange's plan still would require that products be defined in such a way as to obscure real market differences, and it still presumed that production functions somehow would be known, at least well enough for the CPB to be able to monitor the behavior of state firms. It also still presumed that equilibrium prices persist for long periods of time. Hayek, on the other hand, continued to argue that prices in real markets are always changing. Unless Lange's CPB would adjust all prices continuously in response to surpluses and shortages, it would have no hope of coming close to matching the efficiency of the market. Since surpluses and shortages would always need to be reported to the CPB before prices could change, it is obvious that CPB prices could never respond as quickly to changing demand and supply patterns as market prices could. Even more important, the need for firm managers to accept listed prices as parameters meant that under Lange's scheme "there will be less differentiation between prices of commodities according to the differences of quality and the circumstances of time and place" (1940, 192). In addition, unless it was recognized that many important managerial decisions are based on anticipations of the future that could never be second-guessed by the CPB, the chances of success for market socialism, Hayek concluded, were slim indeed.

Rather than writing in reaction to socialist plans, Hayek addressed the problem of knowledge head on in "The Use of Knowledge in Society" ([1945] 1948, 77–91). There he redefined the economic problem so that instead of being a question of allocating known resources among known ends, it is "how to secure the best use of resources known to any members of society, for ends whose relative importance only these individuals know" (78). Economic efficiency required the greatest use of existing knowledge. The real questions were what kind of knowledge was usable and important and what kind of institutions were most likely to generate the knowledge necessary to act economically. Socialists seemed to think that only scientific knowledge matters, but in fact the market functions because people can profit from their particularized knowledge of special circumstances—knowledge of time and place, as Hayek called it. It was this kind of knowledge that was most important to everyday economic decision-making. The socialists' failure to appreciate the importance of this kind of knowledge, Hayek charged, was directly linked to their assumption that change was infrequent in the market. In fact, all real economic problems are problems of adjusting to change. Markets only function because of the constant deliberate adjustment to change that economic actors engage in. The only way to take advantage of the particularized knowledge of individuals that allows that constant adjustment to change take place is to use the decentralized decision-making feature of markets.

The following year Hayek published the final article in this nine-year series. In "The Meaning of Competition" ([1946] 1948, 92–106) he launched his final (albeit indirect) attack on the socialists, this time challenging their underlying assumptions about the nature of competition by offering his own alternative. Competition, he claimed, is the "moving force of life" (93), and yet it is completely omitted from economic models of perfect competition. It is a "dynamic process whose essential characteristics are assumed away" (94). The wishes and desires of consumers, including the kinds of goods and services they want and the prices they would be willing to pay for them, are not implications of some set of given equations. They are problems to be solved by competition. In the rush to homogenize and theorize, economists forget that the real world is characterized by diversity and personal relationships. The proper question for economists to ask is what institutional arrangements are required to get the most suitable people for each task. It is clear that Hayek believed the market economy goes a long way toward solving that problem.

In these last two essays, finally, the distinctive Hayekian (and not surprisingly, Mengerian) message emerges.[24] Markets are about knowledge and change. The knowledge important for market decisions is specialized, detailed, particularized according to time and place. It is also sometimes tacit and unreportable.[25] The information that is generally assumed in economic models is really the product of a market process in which competition is rivalry among partially ignorant suppliers who through a genuine process of trial and error seek to earn profits by learning about and providing information to partially ignorant consumers. Since even the best market socialists' plans assumed the existence of knowledge that was yet to be discovered and provided no satisfactory means to duplicate the market process in generating that knowledge, market socialism must be presumed to be unsatisfactory. Lange had not even touched the hem of the robe.

Unfortunately, Hayek's critique of Lange was unappreciated by his colleagues.[26] They understood him to be claiming that incentive structures in bureaucratic firms might cause managers to shirk—a problem Schumpeter called political. They also believed he was making trivial criticisms by pointing to the specialized nature of many of the capital goods that would be priced by the CPB. His larger exploration of the problem of knowledge seemed to fall on deaf ears. His pointing to the difficulty of monitoring state-firm behavior when decisions had to be based on estimations of the future profitability of alternatives again was interpreted to be a matter of incentives. It is no wonder that Hayek ceased writing primarily for an audience of economists by the end of the 1940s. He was simply not in the same conversation as everybody else. He had to wait twenty more years for his message to be heard.

IV. THE QUIET YEARS

To speak of an Austrian revival is to suggest an Austrian economics that was once at death's door. The patient went into cardiac arrest and was revived only by the workings of an outside force. That is an apt metaphor for the reawakening of interest in Austrian economics in the closing quarter of the twentieth century. By the end of World War II, any kind of distinctively "Austrian" economics was certainly dead to the economics profession. The loss of the calculation debate was devastating. During the 1950s and into the 1960s, if not completely dead, Austrian economics was certainly comatose. Austrian economics became associated with failed arguments and outdated theories and methods.

After his intellectual losses to Keynes in the 1930s and to Lange in the 1940s, Hayek left England altogether. He eventually joined the Committee on Social Thought at the University of Chicago, where he concentrated his efforts in the fields of philosophy, jurisprudence, psychology, and the history of ideas. While hindsight allows us to recognize that Hayek's excursions into these other fields were simply a further part of the intellectual inquiry he began in the socialism debate, at the time it seemed as if he had given up economics all together.[27]

Although Hayek emigrated to America in the late 1940s, it was his older colleague Mises who was responsible for bringing Austrian economics to America. While I believe Hayek's ideas ultimately proved more important in shaping the Austrian revival, it was because of Mises that there was a revival at all. For that reason, a quick look at Mises's biography is in order.

Mises had been a student of Böhm-Bawerk's at Vienna.[28] Instead of joining the academy after his student years, he instead became a major economist for the Austrian Chamber of Commerce and Industry from 1909 to 1938. He claimed that an orthodox academic career was closed to him because of his outspoken anti-statist views, so he chose a less orthodox route to carry on his intellectual life. He became a *Privatdozent* at Vienna in 1913 and received the rank of associate professor in 1918. Although he served, unpaid, in this capacity throughout his life in Vienna, his real contributions as a teacher were made in the private seminar that he ran at the Chamber from 1920 until his departure from Vienna in 1934. His students included some of the most famous economists to have come out of Austria, including Gottfried Haberler, Friedrich Hayek, Fritz Machlup, Oskar Morgenstern, Paul Rosenstein-Rodan, and also the philosopher Alfred Schütz. This seminar apparently was all that kept the Austrian intellectual tradition alive during those years, even in Austria.

Mises was by his own account always an outsider to academic circles. The only formal teaching position that he ever held was as professor of international relations at the Institut Universitaire des Hautes Etudes Internationales in Geneva from 1934 to 1940. Despite his claim that he found the teaching there satisfying, his general despair at the political collapse of Europe in front of the Nazi invasions led him to emigrate to the United States in 1940.

In the United States, Mises once again secured an unofficial position with a university, this time with New York University, where he held a chair that was financed by the Volker Fund, a conservative organization that knew of his lifelong anti-statist fight. At NYU he conducted a weekly seminar which, along with the publications flowing from his pen during the two decades following 1945, *was* the Austrian School in the United States.

Although continuing to teach and write during this time, Mises was so far out of the mainstream of economic thought in the United States as to be virtually nonexistent. Perhaps this explains in part why his masterly treatise, *Human Action,* published in 1949[29] and serving as a complete summary of his lifework, attracted little more than a flurry of attention. It was a treatise in the grand style: comprehensive, philosophical, nonmathematical, deductive, explicitly critical of Marxist and interventionist ideology, and hence completely out of step with the times. Further, it was contemptuous of the currently fashionable positivist methodology and held instead that empirical data (or "history" as Mises referred to it) had to be organized according to a priori theory. While this is a more acceptable position to take today (and was also the position taken by Menger during the *Methodenstreit*; see Vaughn 1987, 443), at the time it seemed as if Mises was opposed to scientific method. His claim that praxeology, the science of human action, was not only a priori but apodictically certain did nothing to calm the scientific outrage of the economics profession. His insistence on the apodictic certainty of praxeological theory made it seem as if the superiority of the free market over interventionism was also apodictically certain and earned him the reputation of a conservative ideologue.

Unfortunately, because of the emphatic style Mises used in his writing and because of the insistence on the certainty of theory, he was read by some as doing little more than rewriting neoclassical economics in words rather than mathematics and as adding arcane philosophy and irrelevant observations about the human condition. This was particularly unfortunate because large sections of *Human Action* are direct continuations and elaborations of

Menger's ideas. Mises builds time, uncertainty, and process right up front in his system. He understands the problem of social cooperation in much the same way that Menger did and expands on Mengerian insights in light of twentieth-century European philosophy.[30] Indeed, Mises also made one tremendously important addition to Mengerian thought by insisting on the impossibility of economic calculation without money.[31] More than Menger, Mises integrated money into the theory of markets. While his theory of prices in chapter 16 does seem more determinate than Menger's, it is not so much so that he deserved the superficial reading by contemporary eyes that he so often received.[32] In a way, he was suffering the same fate as Menger almost a hundred years earlier. He was read in light of what the profession as a whole already believed, and hence the interesting bits that did not fit into the neoclassical framework were ignored: the bits about the importance of time and process, about knowledge and ideology, about the meaning of action—the Mengerian themes that were also ignored in Menger.

Mises himself was partly to blame for this misreading. He did pay more attention to equilibrium theorizing than had Menger, and he was more concerned with the certainty of theory than with exploring the consequences of ignorance and error. While the knowledge problem may be in Mises implicitly, it is not an explicit concern of his. One has to know the Mengerian tradition in advance in order to find it easily in Mises. Like Hayek, he was presuming the ideas in that tradition rather than stating them for the uninitiated. To make matters worse, Mises was also drawing on a sophisticated European intellectual background that was totally unknown to his American audience. To this day, *Human Action* strikes me as an odd mixture of polemic and dispassionate analysis. Mises was at once dedicated to *Wertfreiheit* and a passionate defender of the free market. This political stance, coupled with his unfamiliar understanding of economic theory, clearly estranged him from any potential professional audience in the 1950s.

Indeed, Mises's name primarily became associated with free-market causes and extreme conservative politics. Private foundations eager to keep alive arguments supporting free-market policies at a time when the profession was enamored of "indicative planning" and "fine tuning" supported Mises's work. He was touted by such diverse groups as the John Birch Society and the followers of Ayn Rand (who finally broke with Mises because his subjectivist economics seemed to contradict Rand's philosophy of objectivism). His seminar attracted a variety of people, from serious students of economics to political conservatives who saw Mises as an island of sanity in an increasingly insane world. And as the radical 1960s got under way, Mises became something of an underground hero to a group of "libertarian anarchists" who believed that his economics provided a complete and self-sufficient argument against all state intervention.

During the 1950s and 1960s, then, Austrian economics was understood mostly as odd methodology and free-market advocacy. Mises's writing during this time consisted of some methodological essays and some public policy articles.[33] In both of these his style seemed to get more and more polemical as he saw the statism he had unsuccessfully combated in Europe taking over the intelligentsia of his newly adopted country. This time it was Mises who was in the wrong conversation.

If Mises's seminar during these years *was* Austrian economics, at least in the United States, its future depended on the students who attended. The two most notable in the history of Austrian economics in America were Murray Rothbard and Israel Kirzner. Rothbard, himself a dedicated advocate of the free market, became Mises's faithful interpreter to the radical libertarian fringe, while Kirzner, against overwhelming odds, attempted to carry on Mises's work in the context of the mainstream academic community. Kirzner published three books during these middle years, and Rothbard two,[34] but other than that there was little professional scholarship in American Austrian circles. Certainly there was almost no communication with the rest of the profession. However, Mises, Rothbard, and Kirzner must have had something of importance to say, because despite the almost total professional silence about these Austrian economists, by the time the 1960s erupted into the early 1970s, there had emerged a host of young people, many of them free-market radicals, dedicated to economics but dissatisfied with the reigning orthodoxy, who had discovered the work of Mises (and to a lesser extent Hayek), who had listened to the Austrian folklore at Murray Rothbard's knee, and who were ready to change the world—as most young people were in those days.[35]

V. THE AUSTRIAN REVIVAL

If one had to set a specific date for the Austrian revival in America, I would choose 1974, although rumblings of a reawakening of interest in Austrian economics were heard several years before. Specifically, in 1969 James Buchanan published *Cost and Choice*, in which he claimed that the Austrians really had won the calculation debate because they understood the subjective nature of cost whereas the market socialists did not. This exploration of subjectivism for economic theory and policy was a shot across the neoclassical flagship's bow. In 1972 Erich Streissler's article on Menger was published in *HOPE*, and George

Shackle, a sympathetic fellow traveler, published *Epistemics and Economics*, which broke new ground in subjectivist theory and provided a set of problems for further Austrian research. In 1973 more help came from England: Sir John Hicks, having recently found some interesting bits in Menger concerning time, edited *Carl Menger and the Austrian School of Economics*, and in the United States that same year, Israel Kirzner attempted to delineate an Austrian theory of market processes in *Competition and Entrepreneurship*.[36] This was one of the first books by a committed Austrian that self-consciously tried to explain Austrian theory to the profession at large. It carved out room in neoclassical orthodoxy for entrepreneurship and change and raised a wealth of questions about the further implications of change for understanding markets. The publication of these books not only raised important questions but also made Austrian themes and ideas respectable again. In October 1974, when Hayek won the Nobel Prize in Economics (shared, ironically, with Gunnar Myrdal), the time surely seemed ripe for a revival of Austrian economics.

As important as these academic events were to the revival of Austrian ideas, the catalyst for the revival came from another source. In 1974 the Institute for Humane Studies sponsored a week-long conference on Austrian economics in South Royalton, Vermont.[37] This conference brought together a varied group of economists and current graduate students whose unifying characteristic was that they had expressed some interest in the work of Mises or Hayek. The main speakers were Murray Rothbard, Israel Kirzner, and Ludwig Lachmann, who was introduced to American Austrians for the first time at that conference. The papers were an odd mix. They ranged from the history of the Austrian School, its method, and particular characteristics, to policy and the ethical implications of Austrian economics.[38] The interesting feature of the papers, however, was the implicit assumption by all the speakers and participants (with the possible exception of Lachmann) that Austrian economics was something given that had to be learned, rather than a line of inquiry that was to be developed and created.

Perhaps this was a necessary fiction in the early days of the Austrian revival, especially considering the composition of the revivers. With the exception of the three speakers, most of the enthusiasts for Austrian ideas at that conference (or anywhere else) were either graduate students or young assistant professors. Most young students of economics, no matter where they are educated, usually believe that they have discovered truth and that their job is to apply truth to the world around them. This attitude was doubly evident at South Royalton, where the young Austrians also believed their truth was being unjustifiably ignored by a mistaken academic community. There was an aura of crusade enveloping

South Royalton, and for years afterward even Austrian sympathizers were to comment upon the "siege mentality" of the young Austrians. In retrospect that attitude of virtue wronged was probably necessary in order to give these young, mostly unknown economists the courage to pursue an eccentric research program that flew in the face of received orthodoxy. It enabled them to undertake the difficult work of actually building a coherent Austrian paradigm. And much in the same manner as Hayek explains the evolution of the common law, the attempt on the part of the young Austrians to "learn" the theory led inexorably to the emergence of new ideas.[39] It seems clear today that what has been happening over the last fifteen years has been a creative development, not a scholastic repetition, of a line of inquiry begun by Menger more than one hundred years before.

VI. MODERN AUSTRIAN ECONOMICS: THE MARKET PROCESS

From the beginning of the revival there was consensus on several cornerstones of Austrian economics. And since the revival was brought about by students of Mises, Mises's phraseology became the language of that consensus.[40] Where neoclassical economics was concerned with describing equilibrium states, Austrians were concerned with disequilibrium processes. Where neoclassical economics was static and timeless, Austrian economics took account of time and change. Where neoclassical economics was based on full knowledge and certainty, Austrians were interested in the implications of ignorance and uncertainty. As opposed to neoclassical beliefs in the importance of empirical testing of theoretical propositions, Austrians argued that theory was a priori and all testing was simply interpretations of historical data. Austrians rejected mathematical modeling because it limited the kinds of questions that could be asked, and it necessarily abstracted away from too many real-world considerations. They rejected using macroeconomic aggregates because they tended to obscure the micro foundations of macro problems. And everyone agreed that government intervention was always worse than the market alternative.

Despite the initial agreement on basic propositions there was no clear understanding, it seemed to me, of what those propositions implied about how to do economics. One knew there was much wrong with modern economics, but one did not yet know how to put it right. It was necessary first to explore the propositions themselves for internal coherence and relative importance, and to figure out what difference this "Austrian perspective" made for understanding the real world. To the much-asked question "What is Austrian economics?" there was simply not a ready answer. It has taken almost fifteen years, and a growing body of literature, much of it produced by the young scholars from South Royalton, to begin to answer that question, and it is being answered in at least two different ways.[41]

To draw the difference between the two answers with broad brushstrokes, one way of conceiving of the Austrian contribution is as a supplement to or a reinterpretation of neoclassical economics. Here the presumption is that neoclassical economics began on a sound footing with its recognition of the subjective nature of value but then took a wrong turn toward overconcern with formalism, mathematical modeling, and macroeconomic aggregative reasoning. The task of Austrian economics is to make a midcourse correction by pushing conventional economics in the direction of greater attention to subjectivism and process. Equilibrium is a necessary construct as long as one does not concentrate exclusively on equilibrium conditions. Equilibrium theory must keep prominent all the variations of behavior and detailed adjustments that make equilibrium possible. And certainly, policy conclusions should not be based on too literal a translation of economic theory to economic reality. While many contemporary Austrians accept this view, it is probably best exemplified in the early work of Israel Kirzner.

In *Competition and Entrepreneurship* (1973), for example, Kirzner focused on how entrepreneurial alertness to hitherto unnoticed profit opportunities would bring the system closer toward equilibrium, thus providing a supplement to conventional theory. In that volume his entrepreneur does not create or discover anything that is genuinely new. One can still think of a world of given tastes and given resources where the function of the entrepreneur is to notice that given resources are not being fully exploited. The entrepreneur may even be said to exploit differences in knowledge, but it is knowledge that in some sense exists. Hence Kirzner's entrepreneur supplies a moving force to bring the system from disequilibrium to equilibrium. While the later Kirzner (e.g., 1985) is willing to agree that the entrepreneur may in fact be said to discover opportunities, he does not believe this is in principle different from saying that the entrepreneur "notices" what already exists. Yet the difference between noticing what is already there and creating what is yet to be is the crux of the difference between the two ways of understanding Austrian economics.

The other interpretation sees Austrian economics as a radical departure from neoclassical economics. While still approving of the subjectivist revolution, this view does not think there is much salvageable in the basic framework of contemporary economic theory. This view, along with Shackle, is impressed with the "kaleidic" nature of reality and the genuine creativity of choice (see Shackle 1972). It also takes seriously Lachmann's worry about the implications of the subjectivity of expectations and Hayek's admonitions about the subjectivity of knowledge itself. To this view, the implications of the problems of knowledge and process require a very different way of organizing our understanding of economic reality. The implication of "radical subjectivism" is to jettison the conventional notion of equilibrium in favor of some idea of ordered process. That is, to follow the implications of the Austrian insights into the human condition is to cease speaking of end states at all and to look only at processes.

This view of Austrian economics is more tentative and less coherent than the first. While it bespeaks a dissatisfaction with static, engineering notions of equilibrium, it has not yet developed an alternative organizing principle that is widely accepted. One attempt to develop an alternative is Lachmann's *Market as an Economics Process* ([1986] 2020). Here, rather than trying to come up with a general theory of market behavior, Lachmann instead disaggregates markets and analyzes them according to such features as the importance of stocks versus flows, the kind of product sold, and the information characteristics of the particular market. Rather than trying to predict outcomes, to Lachmann ([1986] 2020, 3) the best the economist can do is to understand and describe "what men do in markets." There is not even a presumption that all market activities will be coordinated, since "competitive market forces will cause discoordination as well as coordination" (Lachmann 1986, 5).

While Lachmann's work is insightful and largely convincing, it also is narrow in scope. Others have argued that Austrian economics need not stop with limited market studies; it can be folded into a more formal framework without doing violence to its understanding of human action. Specifically, Langlois (1983) and Boettke, Horwitz, and Prychitko (1986) have argued that an evolutionary framework is the most congenial setting for an Austrian theory of the market process. Biological evolution provides a model of ordered change where there are no predictable end states and no notion of an ideal outcome. Evolutionary theory rests on the basis of "three interrelated factors: selection, memory and variation or mutation." We can find the economic analogues to these in competition, habits, or institutions, and entrepreneurship and creativity (Langlois 1983, 5). Such an analogy allows us room to explore the origin and nature of institutions, the source of creative change, and the role of competition in good Mengerian and Hayekian fashion. Knowledge becomes not an addendum to the theory but the central element in the evolutionary process. This is perhaps what Hayek (1979, 258) had in mind when he referred to the "twin concepts of evolution and spontaneous order."

Interestingly, both paths of development of Austrian ideas have their roots in Menger. Certainly, the "Austrian economics as supplement to and conscience of modern economics" view can claim Menger as its legitimate ancestor. Menger did write of equilibrium states as well as processes, and his emphasis on knowledge can be interpreted as discovery rather than creation. Yet if the reading of Menger offered here is correct, it is the second vision of modern Austrian economics that seems more consistent with the spirit of Menger's inquiry. Once we examine Menger's concept of spontaneous order in the context of the problem of knowledge in society (as Hayek did in the 1930s and 1940s), we are led to recognizing just how deeply the problems of incomplete, decentralized, and inarticulate knowledge cut in the social world. The unraveling of the implications of the knowledge problem, both to people's intentional choices and to the unintended social consequences of human action, then becomes the main task of economics. We are led to construct theories of institutional emergence and development where the important questions are not ones of optimal end states but of the processes by which humans interact to create and adapt to their social environment. And we are inexorably led to asking, and with luck answering, the same question that moved Adam Smith and Carl Menger: what causes the growth and development of the wealth of nations?

NOTES

1. In fact, Menger's translators, Dingwall and Hoselitz, felt compelled to point out Menger's "error" in a lengthy footnote on p. 126. I argue in Vaughn (1978, 440) that the scale of values tables that Menger includes in his text are meant only to be illustrative of a general principle and do not substitute for analysis. His genuine analysis of the principle of marginal use is found in the verbal discussion following the tables.

2. Menger points out that useful things become goods when four conditions are met: there must be a human need, there must be a causal connection between the useful thing and the ability to satisfy the need, humans must know of this causal connection, and they must have command over the use of the good (1981, 52).

3. It should be noted that when Menger uses the term "power" in this context, he is referring to the power people can acquire over things and not power over other people.

4. Notice that both these ways of describing a process of introducing novelty into an economic system have recently been explored in the literature. Kirzner has consistently examined the relevance of entrepreneurial "alertness" to market processes (1973, 1979, 1985). Shackle has argued that in order for choice to be genuine, it must be an imaginative leap from the present to an as yet uncreated future (1972). Both these ideas are implicit in Menger's writings.

5. "The idea of causality, however, is inseparable from the idea of time. A process of change involves a beginning and a becoming, and these are only conceivable as processes in time. Hence it is certain that we can never fully understand the causal interconnections of the various occurrences in a process, or the process itself, unless we view it in time and apply the measure of time to it" (Menger 1981, 67).

THE MENGERIAN ROOTS OF THE AUSTRIAN REVIVAL

6. Laurence Moss points out that Menger calls his theory a theory of price formation rather than price determination to underscore the indeterminateness of the outcome of exchange (1978, 26ff.).

7. It should also be pointed out that Menger consciously abstracted from error and ignorance in his theory of competitive price (1981, 224). The implications of this are discussed in Kirzner (1978), Moss (1978), and Vaughn (1978).

8. "The manner in which competition develops from monopoly is closely connected with the economic progress of civilization" (Menger 1981, 217).

9. In Appendix 6 to the *Investigations* (1985, 216–19), Menger gives an account of the "economic situation" that amounts to a verbal description of constrained optimization. There he argues that given the goals of an individual and the constraints he faces, there is really only one theoretically correct economic solution. However, he also points out that real individual action will deviate from this solution for reasons of "volition, error and other influences" (217).

10. This is why Streissler wrote, "Menger's tâtonnement is a social process and a most laborious one to boot. One might, perhaps, condense the contrast between Menger and Walras thus: Walras's tâtonnement takes a minute; Menger's tâtonnement takes a century! Needless to say, with Menger we are most of the time out of equilibrium in the sense that the equilibrium price has not yet been found" (1972, 440).

11. In this respect, Menger's *Principles* has far more kinship to *The Wealth of Nations* than to Ricardo, Jevons, or Walras. Menger himself seemed to be aware of the affinity since he criticized Smith on two key points—the causes of the wealth of nations (1981, 71–74) and the propensity to truck, barter, and exchange (175)—both issues that are central to Menger's theory of growth.

12. That is, Menger does not assume that individuals have a direct pipeline to truth about the world around them. They form theories about the nature of the real world and act upon these theories. Eventually, Menger believes, these theories are either supported or falsified by experience.

13. Hayek (1973, 36ff). I am not claiming that the growth of the "professional class which operates as an intermediary in exchanges and performs for the other members of society not only the mechanical part of trading operations . . . , but also the task of keeping records of the available quantities" (Menger 1981, 91) is not also an example of the product of a "spontaneous order." The emergence of new market institutions must be viewed as such. However, there does seem to be a difference in that such institutions are the product of someone's deliberate idea that perhaps had some consequences not imagined but was still recognizable as part of the plan. Money, on the other hand, emerged purely as the unintended consequences of human action that no one planned or even could have envisioned before its emergence. These examples seem to be at two different places on a continuum of emergent institutions rather than being two different kinds of processes.

14. While the *Principles* is full of analysis of the "origin and nature" of various phenomena, in the *Investigations*, Menger extends his notion of spontaneous orders to "law, language, the state, money, markets" (1985, 147) and in fact develops the theory of spontaneous order more fully than in the *Principles*. See book 3, ch. 2, "The theoretical understanding of those social phenomena which are not a product of agreement or of positive legislation, but are unintended results of historical development" (1985, 139–60).

15. Menger is reported by Joseph Schumpeter to have regarded Böhm-Bawerk's theory of the period of production as a grave error (1954, 847 n. 8). It is also interesting to note that Mises believed that Wieser never understood subjectivism (Mises 1978, 36).

16. This is Schumpeter's claim in his *History of Economic Analysis* (1954, 827). His enchantment with Walras is also evident in his assessment of the calculation debate, where he argues that "as a matter of blueprint logic, it is undeniable that the socialist blueprint is drawn at a higher level of rationality" (Schumpeter 1942, 185). This could only be said by someone who believed Walras's logic was somehow more "scientific" than Menger's.

17. I think this is true of the *Theory of Money and Credit* (1934), where Mises used a framework of analysis that was more neoclassical than Menger's framework had been. Despite the more

Mengerian part to *Human Action* (Mises 1966), it can also be read as another exercise in equilibrium theory.

18. Here I am referring to *Prices and Production* (Hayek 1931).

19. For a full account of the debate from an Austrian perspective, see Vaughn (1980), Lavoie ([1985] 2015), and Kirzner (1988). See also the recent article by Caldwell (1988), in which he also argues that the calculation debate was instrumental in Hayek's "transformation." I see it not so much as a transformation as a rediscovery of what he learned from Menger through Mises.

20. The demise of a particularly Austrian perspective is underscored in the volume resulting from that series of lectures, *Prices and Production* (Hayek 1931). Because of the static equilibrium framework within which Hayek developed his theory in that volume, it reads more like a neoclassical rendering of some Austrian insights than a work in Austrian economics as we have come to think of it today. On Hayek's experiences in London see Hicks (1967). For an account of the effect of Hayek's capital theory debates on his professional development, see O'Driscoll (1977).

21. All of the articles relevant to the calculation debate are collected in *Individualism and Economic Order* (Hayek 1948).

22. As Caldwell points out (1988, 513), Hayek himself regarded his essay "Economics and Knowledge" as the beginning of his "transformation" from accepting pure technical economics to pursuing his life-long attempt to articulate the principles of a spontaneous order.

23. Here we see an intermediate stop between Menger and the modern controversy surrounding the proper role of equilibrium theory.

24. In fact, the best statement of Hayek's view of competition was not published until 1969, the German version of "Competition as a Discovery Procedure." The English version did not appear until 1978, when Hayek published *New Studies in Philosophy, Politics, Economics and the History of Ideas*. In this important essay he clearly and concisely expresses the central point of all the earlier articles on knowledge and competition published in the 1930s and 1940s: the main task of competition is to generate the knowledge that static equilibrium assumes is given (Hayek 1978).

25. Hayek was anticipating some of the arguments made by Michael Polanyi in *Personal Knowledge* (1958). In fact, the tacit nature of much market knowledge only became clear after Polanyi. It is necessary, then, to regard Polanyi as a major force in the development of the Austrian understanding of the knowledge problem.

26. See, for example, the summary review of the debate by Abram Bergson, in which he argues that Mises's original claim is totally without force, that Hayek had exaggerated the difficulties inherent in monitoring state firms, and that the questions about knowledge, while "a wholesome antidote to the tendency to regard a CPB as superman," probably did not imply too much limitation to the ability of socialist economies to plan (Bergson 1948, 412, 335–37).

27. Caldwell (1988) also points out the continuity of Hayek's research after 1948. His work in psychology stemmed from his exploration of the knowledge problem, his work on spontaneous social orders from his recognition of the dynamic nature of markets, and his political philosophy from his exploration of the shortcomings of planning.

28. Information about Mises's biography is taken from his own *Notes and Recollections* (1978).

29. *Human Action* was a completely revised and rewritten version of a book Mises published in German in 1940 entitled *Nationalökonomie: Theorie des Handelns und Wirtschaftens*.

30. It is ironic that O'Driscoll and Rizzo's (1985) attempt to explore a Bergsonian notion of time to support Austrian economics garnered so much criticism when they were simply following up on a hint Mises has left in *Human Action* (100n.).

31. Mises's claim that one cannot have economic calculation without money prices caused him to be held up to ridicule during the calculation debate, yet I think it is one of his most important contributions to economics. We have still to plumb the depths of its implications.

Jack High (1983, 8–9) also recognizes the importance of Mises's integration of money into his theory of markets.

32. This misreading was not only the fault of hostile contemporaries. Mises's student Murray Rothbard, who was influential in the early days of the Austrian revival, wrote a textbook translation of *Human Action* that reads very much like a rendition of neoclassical economics in nonmathematical language (Rothbard 1962).

33. The two works that come to mind are *The Ultimate Foundations of Economic Science* ([1962] 1978) and *Economic Policy: Thought for Today and Tomorrow* (1979).

34. Kirzner's works during this time were *Market Theory and the Price System* (1963), *An Essay on Capital* (1966), and *The Economic Point of View* (1967), which was essentially an exploration in the history of economic thought. The history of thought is a convenient vehicle for airing unpopular views. Rothbard published *Man, Economy and the State* (1962) and *America's Great Depression* (1963), an attempt to apply an Austrian theory of the trade cycle to that great American tragedy.

35. I can only offer personal testimony as to why the Austrian School attracted young followers in the late 1960s and early 1970s. As an undergraduate I was frankly attracted by the free-market message that I believed was inherent in Austrian economics. It was only much later, as the revival got under way, that I also began to be interested in Austrian economics as an intellectual system apart from policy or political philosophy. I suspect my experience was not unusual. Interestingly, I now find the "free-market" aspects of Austrian economics the least intriguing of all the intellectual challenges it offers.

36. In this list of important books that heralded in the Austrian revival, I should also mention *L.S.E. Essays on Cost* (Buchanan and Thirlby 1973). This book traced a tradition of subjective cost theory that began in the 1930s at the London School of Economics as an outgrowth of the work of Hayek and Lionel Robbins and continued to survive into the 1970s through the writings of Jack Wiseman and G. F. Thirlby.

37. The Institute for Humane Studies ran two more conferences in Austrian economics over the next two years whose purpose was to articulate an Austrian research program. The third conference, at Windsor Castle, England, produced a volume entitled *New Directions in Austrian Economics* (Spadaro 1978).

38. The papers for this conference were collected and published by Edwin Dolan, who had organized it. The title was descriptive of what we all thought was being discussed there: *The Foundations of Modern Austrian Economics*.

39. One good example of how new ideas grow out of attempts to restate the old is the writing of O'Driscoll and Rizzo's *Economics of Time and Ignorance* (1985). In 1980, O'Driscoll and Rizzo delivered a paper at the AEA meetings in Denver on the topic "What is Austrian Economics?" There was a surprisingly large audience for their paper, indicating some widespread interest in Austrian themes. They argued that Austrian economics was subjectivist and paid attention to real time and to expectations, to heterogeneity of products, and to market processes rather than equilibrium states. As a result of that paper, they commenced to write their book. They expected to have it finished in about a year, but instead it took about five years. Part of the trouble was simply the problem of trying to articulate what Austrian economics is. They began their project by thinking of it as something there that must be explained rather than as a theoretical system that must be developed. By the time of its completion, the book broke new ground in developing a coherent Austrian paradigm (and consequently was criticized by many Austrians who "knew" it was not faithful to Austrian principles); but the authors struggled precisely because they began by thinking they were reporting and articulating rather than creating.

40. Hayek was not mentioned very much at South Royalton except in the context of his capital theory. The reasons were partly that Murray Rothbard did not think much of Hayek's politics or economics and partly that the first volume of *Law, Legislation and Liberty* (1973) had not been out long enough to make an impact on the group. However, once Hayek won the Nobel Prize later on that year, he obviously came into the limelight. His works were discussed more

and more as the Austrian conferences continued and as the group of participants became more immersed in the literature of Austrian economics.

41. The literature produced by the Austrian revival falls into three broad categories: intellectual history of the Austrian School, criticism of neoclassical economics, and some small amount of constructive theorizing. It is probably not surprising that so much of the work done so far has been in the first two categories. First, it was necessary to learn what the Austrian tradition was before one could presume to work in it. Also, given the problems of publishing unusual work in the major journals, doing history of thought was often the only way to get exposure for Austrian ideas. Criticism of the orthodoxy is also a necessary step in locating the distinctiveness of an alternative paradigm. It is also constructive in the sense that through the process of criticism one explores the robustness of one's own theory. Constructive theorizing is the most difficult and is only beginning to play a part in the Austrian literature. Examples of the latter type of work are of course Kirzner (1973; 1979; 1985); Lachmann ([1986] 2020); O'Driscoll and Rizzo (1985); and White (1984). Lavoie is currently reexamining the methodology of the Austrian School in light of modern continental philosophy that carries forward the methodological positions taken by Menger and Mises. There are also several unpublished doctoral dissertations coming out of George Mason University that promise to add to the corpus of new Austrian theoretical works.

REFERENCES

Bergson, Abram. 1948. Socialist Economics. In *A Survey of Contemporary Economics*, edited by Howard S. Ellis, 1:412–448. Homewood, IL: Richard D. Irwin.

Boettke, Peter, Steven Horwitz, and David Prychitko. 1986. "Beyond Equilibrium Economics." *Market Process* 4 (2).

Böhm-Bawerk, Eugen von. (1888) 1959. *The Positive Theory of Capital*. Translated by George Huncke. South Holland, IL: Libertarian Press.

Buchanan, James M. 1969. *Cost and Choice: An Inquiry into Economic Theory*. Chicago: University of Chicago Press.

———, and G. F. Thirlby, eds. 1973. *L.S.E. Essays on Cost*. New York: New York University Press.

Caldwell, Bruce J. 1988. "Hayek's Transformation." *HOPE* 20 (4): 513–542.

Dolan, Edwin G., ed. 1976. *The Foundations of Modern Austrian Economics*. Kansas City, MO: Sheed & Ward.

Hayek, F. A. 1931. *Prices and Production*. London: George Routledge & Sons.

———. 1935. *Collectivist Economic Planning*. London: George Routledge & Sons.

———. 1948. *Individualism and Economic Order*. Chicago: University of Chicago Press.

———. 1973. *Law, Legislation and Liberty*. Vol. 1. Chicago: University of Chicago Press.

———. 1978. *New Studies in Philosophy, Politics, Economics and the History of Ideas*. Chicago: University of Chicago Press.

———. 1979. *Law, Legislation and Liberty*. Vol. 3. Chicago: University of Chicago Press.

Hicks, J. R. 1967. *Critical Essays in Monetary Theory*. Oxford: Clarendon Press.

———, and W. Weber, eds. 1973. *Carl Menger and the Austrian School of Economics*. Oxford: Clarendon Press.

High, Jack. 1983. "The Market Process: An Austrian View." *Market Process* (1): 1.

Jaffé, William. 1975. "Menger, Jevons and Walras Dehomogenized." *Economic Inquiry* 14 (4): 511–524.

Kirzner, Israel M. 1963. *Market Theory and the Price System*. Princeton, NJ: D. Van Nostrand.

——. 1966. *An Essay on Capital*. New York: Augustus M. Kelley.

——. 1967. *The Economic Point of View*. Kansas City, MO: Sheed & Ward.

——. 1973. *Competition and Entrepreneurship*. Chicago: University of Chicago Press.

——. 1978. "The Entrepreneurial Role in Menger's System." *Atlantic Economic Journal* 6 (3): 31–45.

——. 1979. *Perception, Opportunity and Profit*. Chicago: University of Chicago Press.

——. 1985. *Discovery and the Capitalist Process*. Chicago: University of Chicago Press.

——. 1988. "The Economic Calculation Debate: Lessons for Austrians." *Review of Austrian Economics* 2:1–18.

——, ed. 1982. *Method, Process and Austrian Economics: Essays in Honor of Ludwig von Mises*. Lexington, MA: Lexington Books.

——, ed. 1986. *Subjectivism, Intelligibility and Economic Understanding: Essays in Honor of Ludwig M. Lachmann on His Eightieth Birthday*. New York: New York University Press.

Lachmann, Ludwig M. 1978. "Carl Menger and the Incomplete Revolution of Subjectivism." *Atlantic Economic Journal* 6 (3): 57–59.

——. (1986) 2020. *The Market as an Economic Process*. Reprint, Virginia: Mercatus Center at George Mason University.

Lange, Oscar, and Fred M. Taylor. 1938. *On the Economic Theory of Socialism*. New York: McGraw-Hill

Langlois, Richard N. 1983. "The Market Process: An Evolutionary View." *Market Process* 1 (2).

Lavoie, Don. (1985) 2015. *Rivalry and Central Planning: The Socialist Calculation Debate Reconsidered*. Reprint, Virginia: Mercatus Center at George Mason University.

Menger, Carl. (1871) 1981. *Principles of Economics*. Translated by James Dingwall and Bert F. Hoselitz. New York: New York University Press.

——. (1883) 1985. *Investigations into the Method of the Social Sciences with Special Reference to Economics*. Translated by Francis J. Nock. Edited by Lawrence White. New York: New York University Press.

Mises, Ludwig. (1920) 1935. *Economic Calculation in the Socialist Commonwealth*. In Hayek, *Collectivist Economic Planning*, 87–130. London: George Routledge & Sons.

——. (1934) 1980 . *Theory of Money and Credit*. Indianapolis, IN: Liberty Classics.

——. (1949) 1966. *Human Action: A Treatise on Economics*. 3rd ed. New York: Henry Regnery.

——. (1962) 1978. *The Ultimate Foundations of Economic Science: An Essay on Method*. Kansas City, MO: Sheed, Andrews & McMeel.

——. 1978. *Notes and Recollections*. Translated by Hans F. Sennholz. South Holland, IL: Libertarian Press.

——. 1979. *Economic Policy: Thoughts for Today and Tomorrow*. South Bend, IN: Regnery/ Gateway.

Moss, Laurence S. 1978. "Carl Menger's Theory of Exchange." *Atlantic Economic Journal* 6 (3): 17–29.

Nelson, R. Richard, and Sidney G. Winter. 1982. *An Evolutionary Theory of Economic Change*. Cambridge, MA: Harvard University Press.

O'Driscoll, Gerald P. 1977. *Economics as a Coordination Problem: The Contributions of Friedrich Hayek*. Kansas City, MO: Sheed, Andrews & McMeel.

——, and Mario J. Rizzo. 1985. *The Economics of Time and Ignorance*. Oxford: Basil Blackwell.

Polanyi, Michael. 1958. *Personal Knowledge: Towards a Post-Critical Philosophy*. Chicago: University of Chicago Press.

Rizzo, Mario J. 1979. *Time, Uncertainty and Disequilibrium: Exploration of Austrian Themes.* Lexington, MA: Lexington Books.

Rothbard, Murray N. 1962. *Man, Economy and the State: A Treatise on Economic Principles.* Los Angeles, CA: Nash.

———. 1963. *America's Great Depression.* Princeton, NJ: D. Van Nostrand.

Schumpeter, Joseph. 1934. *A Theory of Economic Development.* Translated by R. Opie. Cambridge: Cambridge University Press.

———. (1942) 1963. *Capitalism, Socialism and Democracy.* New York: Harper & Row.

———. 1954. *History of Economic Analysis.* Edited by E. B. Schumpeter. Oxford: Oxford University Press.

Shackle, George. 1972. *Epistemics and Economics: A Critique of Economic Doctrines.* Cambridge: Cambridge University Press.

Spadaro, Louis M., ed. 1978. *New Directions in Austrian Economics.* Kansas City, MO: Sheed, Andrews & McMeel.

Streissler, Erich. 1972. "To What Extent was the Austrian School Marginalist?" *HOPE* 4 (2): 426–441.

Vaughn, Karen I. 1978. "The Reinterpretation of Carl Menger: Some Notes on Recent Scholarship." *Atlantic Economic Journal* 6 (3): 62–64.

———. 1980. "Economic Calculation under Socialism: The Austrian Contribution. *Economic Inquiry* 18:535–554.

———. 1987. "Carl Menger." In *The New Palgrave: A Dictionary of Economics*, edited by John Eatwell, Murray Milgate, and Peter Newman, 438–444. London: Macmillan.

White, Lawrence. 1984. *Free Banking in Britain: Theory, Experience and Debate, 1800–1845.* Cambridge: Cambridge University Press.

Wieser, Friedrich von. (1893) 1971. *Natural Value.* New York: Augustus M. Kelley.

———. (1927) 1967. *Social Economics.* New York: Augustus M. Kelley.

Chapter 6
The Problem of Order in
Austrian Economics
Kirzner vs. Lachmann

I n their recent book, O'Driscoll and Rizzo depict Austrian economics as
the *Economics of Time and Ignorance* (1985). They claim that what distinguishes Austrian economics from conventional, mainstream economic
analysis is its rejection of static theorizing and its embrace of a theory of processes. Since all human action takes place in time, the outcomes of such action
must of necessity be uncertain and fraught with error. Consequently, market
activity, they argue, can be "made intelligible as a process of attempting to correct errors and coordinate behaviour" (O'Driscoll and Rizzo 1985, 5). They
then go on to characterize the market as a continuing process with no stable
endpoint to which it must lead and no single path that it must follow.

In so characterizing the Austrian vision of the market process, O'Driscoll
and Rizzo are taking sides in a debate among American Austrians about the
theoretical implications of the "Austrian paradigm." While all Austrians agree
in general that economics should not abstract either from real time or ignorance if both the raison d'être and the actual functioning of markets is to be
understood, the precise way in which time and ignorance are to be incorporated into market analysis is still a topic of controversy. Both sides of this
controversy point to Hayek and von Mises as their intellectual heirs, and both

Originally published in *The Review of Political Economy* 4, no. 3 (January 1992). Reprinted by permission of the publisher (Taylor & Francis).

sides share an overriding belief in the efficacy of markets in satisfying the wants of consumers as compared with other possible forms of social organization. Yet, despite this apparent agreement, there are real differences in how each side of the debate understands the market process. Both sides think of the market process as fundamentally orderly and coherent, but they disagree about how to conceptualize that order. One side more or less conceives of economic order in the conventional sense of a system converging toward equilibrium inherent in the existing data; the other side thinks of the system, as O'Driscoll and Rizzo state, as one "with no stable point" and "no single path that it must follow."

These are not trivial differences of opinion. In grappling with the implications of time and ignorance for economic order, Austrians are in fact attempting to define their paradigm and their relationship to the neoclassical orthodoxy. Furthermore, they are implicitly reexamining the basis for the traditional Austrian belief in the benefits of "the pure market economy."[1] The notion of economic order that underlies one's understanding of market behavior is crucial to how one evaluates the performance of the system.

In the pages that follow, I will explicate and critique the conception of order underlying both sides to the current Austrian debate by concentrating on the central figures representative of each side: Israel Kirzner and Ludwig Lachmann. I will show that the underlying notion of order that informs the work of each man affects the relationship he sees between Austrian economics and the mainstream. Kirzner sees the role of Austrian economics to supplement a largely correct but seriously incomplete neoclassical economics, a view that derives from his teacher, Ludwig von Mises, and is widely shared in Austrian circles. Lachmann, on the other hand, sees Austrian economics as a radical challenge to neoclassical orthodoxy and draws on his reading of Hayek, Keynes, and Shackle to support his view. I conclude that neither Kirzner nor Lachmann provides a satisfying view of economic order that reflects the Austrian assumptions of time and ignorance, and that more work needs to be done in specific directions to fully articulate an Austrian paradigm.

I. KIRZNER'S ENTREPRENEUR

Israel Kirzner has been a vocal critic of neoclassical orthodoxy all of his professional life, yet his criticisms have been more in the nature of family feuds than all out warfare. His stated view is that neoclassical economics started off on the right track during the marginal revolution when it explained price as the consequence of the subjective valuations of individual actors, rather than as the product of some objective criteria. It took an unfortunate turn in the middle of the twentieth century, however, when as a consequence of a growing preoccupation with an excessive formalism in theoretical constructs, neoclassical economics lost sight of its subjectivist roots. The consequence, according to Kirzner, was that neoclassical economics developed an "excessive preoccupation with the conditions of equilibrium,"[2] and thereby limited itself to the description of static states. Echoing the earlier attitude of the founder of the Austrian school, Carl Menger, Kirzner argues that equilibrium prices, while important, are merely epiphenomena to the real meat of economic theory— market processes (Kirzner 1973, 6).

But how is one to theorize about a market process? For Kirzner, this means providing an explanation of how equilibrium in principle is capable of being achieved in real markets. The static equilibrium theories of conventional economics with their presumptions of homogeneous knowledge and maximizing behavior can only tell us what equilibrium is implied by a set of parameters; it can never explain how partially ignorant maximizing agents act to bring about an equilibrium. For that one needs a theory of a prime mover in markets, which to Kirzner means a theory of entrepreneurship.

II. ENTREPRENEURSHIP AS DIFFERENTIAL KNOWLEDGE

Kirzner first introduced his theory of the entrepreneur in his 1973 book, *Competition and Entrepreneurship*, where he laid out a theoretical structure that had two purposes: to provide a reformulation of microeconomic theory which takes account of the core insights of Austrian economics and to do so in a way that would communicate with neoclassical economists. In the course of almost 20 years of subsequent explanation and clarification, Kirzner's original structure has remained essentially unchanged. One can regard all of Kirzner's post-1973 work on entrepreneurship as so many footnotes to his path-breaking book.

To Kirzner, entrepreneurship is a particular kind of action distinct from maximizing behavior and without which a market process would be unexplainable. Economists generally model human action as the maximization of utility subject to constraints, a form of behavior he calls "Robbinsian maximizing" after Lionel Robbins's famous definition of economics (Robbins 1932).[3] But Robbins's definition of economics as the study of the allocation of scarce means among competing ends, Kirzner argues, is incomplete. Pure "Robbinsian maximizers" can only operate within a known means-ends framework. They can never be the source of change in the means-ends framework. In fact, they could never even be counted on to bring about a general equilibrium since that would require acting on special information about price differentials. How would any simple "Robbinsian maximizer" come to recognize that price differentials exist? For this, Kirzner argues, one needs to invoke a kind of behavior that is not strictly maximizing yet is purposeful, motivated by the chance for gain and yet not simply reactive to a given means-ends framework. In short, economics needs a theory of entrepreneurial action (Kirzner 1973, 32–34).

Entrepreneurs, to Kirzner, are the embodiment of a quality he refers to as "alertness" (1973, 35). They notice opportunities for profit that others have missed, and through their alertness to profit opportunities, they redefine the means-ends framework. Kirzner emphasizes that the profit opportunities they notice are there for the taking, but they are not equally obvious to every purposeful human actor. In fact, entrepreneurship is only understandable as the differential perception among actors of past error, past failure on the part of Robbinsian maximizers to recognize that an opportunity for profit exists (Kirzner 1973, 67). Hence, in Kirzner's system, the entrepreneur functions as a means of discovering and disseminating particularized and decentralized information in the market order. He carries out this function by acting as an arbitrageur, buying cheap and selling dear and profiting from the differential. And, just as for an arbitrageur, an unintended consequence of his exploiting his profit opportunity is that he brings the market closer to equilibrium (Kirzner 1973, 73).[4]

Entrepreneurship is pure, unplanned, and unplannable alertness to opportunities that cannot be predicted in advance, cannot be hired and deployed by another or invested in. But, if entrepreneurship cannot be planned or predicted, does this mean that it is the result of pure luck? Kirzner argues not (1979, 155). While it is serendipitous discovery, it is not luck because some people are more alert than others and/or condition themselves to being in a state of alertness. People are alert in the sense that they tend to notice what is in their interests. However, since interests and particularized knowledge differ, people will notice different profit opportunities. Hence, while one cannot predict what anyone or any group of people may notice, one can be sure that "opportunities come to be noticed" (Kirzner 1979, 170).

Interestingly, Kirzner does not consider the possibility that entrepreneurs could be incorrect in their hunches. Error only enters Kirzner's system as the failure to notice an opportunity that is available (1979, 130), not through faulty perceptions. Hence, it seems that it is impossible in Kirzner's system for an entrepreneur to be destabilizing.[5]

III. KIRZNER AND SCHUMPETER

Obviously, Kirzner's system differs markedly from Schumpeter's explanation of the entrepreneurial process, a difference Kirzner himself emphasizes (1973, 7). While Schumpeter was an Austrian by birth and learned his economics in Vienna, he soon abandoned Menger and adopted a Walrasian understanding of economic order. This is evident in his early attempt to explain the capitalist process in *The Economics of Development* (1934), where he described the entrepreneur as the disrupter of existing equilibria. Here, entrepreneurial innovation is the source of change in an otherwise featureless repetition of economic equilibrium. Entrepreneurs destroy old patterns of behavior as they introduce their creations into the system (Schumpeter 1934, 92). Hence, entrepreneurship is inherently innovative and therefore destabilizing in Schumpeter's view.

It was exactly this view of the economy that Kirzner determined to oppose with his theory of entrepreneurship. Where Schumpeter saw entrepreneurs as innovators and promoters, Kirzner saw them as equilibrators who notice that which was already present to be noticed. Entrepreneurs do not destroy old equilibrium patterns nor create opportunities in Kirzner's system, they take advantage of existing discoordination to bring the system closer to equilibrium (Kirzner 1973, 72–73). While this might seem a semantic quibble to some, for Kirzner the differing implications of the two views of entrepreneurship were significant.

At least according to Kirzner, Schumpeter's view seems to imply that an economy could function very nicely without entrepreneurs: that given any set of parameters, central planners could eventually arrive at equilibrium prices and thereby plan and control an economy. In Kirzner's view, the economy is never actually in equilibrium because there are always profit opportunities inherent in *somebody's* data that could be exploited. Indeed, without the entrepreneur, an economy would always be worse off than it could be even within the framework of the existing opportunities. Prices would be in perpetual disequilibrium without entrepreneurs to set them right. In this way, Kirzner's response to Schumpeter was another round in the economic calculation debate that had been fought 30 years before Kirzner wrote (1979, 119–129).

Seen in this light, one can understand Kirzner's insistence that the entrepreneur creates nothing *ex nihilo*. If he were to create *ex nihilo*, an economy would function efficiently without him (although perhaps not as affluently). On the other hand, if one sees the economic problem as one of coordinating information as well as setting uniform market prices, then entrepreneurship was the means of uncovering and eradicating differences in information within the system. Entrepreneurs then become guarantors of co-ordination rather than disrupters of economic life.[6]

Kirzner's entrepreneur obviously fills one requirement of the Austrian research program; his theory starts with selective ignorance in the market and posits an adjustment process that serves to eliminate that ignorance and bring the market into greater coordination. However, Kirzner's insistence on the coordinating nature of entrepreneurship raises problems associated with the other requirement of the Austrian program—the serious consideration of the implications of time. Indeed, in order to save the entrepreneur as unquestionable coordinator, Kirzner must largely ignore investigating the consequences of the passage of time.

IV. ENTREPRENEURSHIP AND TIME

While Kirzner's obvious differences with Schumpeter's version of entrepreneurship are interesting but not particularly surprising, his differences from his teacher, Ludwig von Mises, are both. Mises viewed the entrepreneurial function as dealing with uncertainty: "acting man in regard to the changes occurring in the data of the market" (Mises 1949, 254) and profit the reward for successfully dealing with uncertainty. The future is always uncertain, and all action takes time. Hence every entrepreneur must be a speculator. "His success or failure depends on the correctness of his anticipations of uncertain events" (1949, 291).

While Kirzner never denies the fact that the world is uncertain, it is certainly not an emphasis of his early works on entrepreneurship. Indeed, despite Kirzner's frequent reminders that entrepreneurs operate in time, the argument of *Competition and Entrepreneurship* is fully worked out on the assumption of a one period world. Kirzner argues that the single period model is perfectly generalizable to entrepreneurship through time. Others are not so certain.

Kirzner first addressed the issue of uncertainty and entrepreneurship in 1982[7] in a paper in which he examined to what degree his theory of entrepreneurial alertness differs from Mises's emphasis on uncertainty bearing. He argues that his understanding of entrepreneurship as alertness to opportunities for arbitrage is fully compatible with the problem of uncertainty. While entrepreneurial activity is indeed speculative as Mises argued, "far from being numbed by the inescapable uncertainty of our world, men act upon their judgements of what opportunities have been left unexploited by others" (Kirzner 1982, 41).

Entrepreneurship is based on discovering error, but we can distinguish two meanings of entrepreneurship. The first is "selecting the means-ends framework." Because of the uncertainty of the "human predicament," one cannot be sure of the relevant framework for calculating, but the entrepreneur can benefit by choosing the correct framework. The second meaning, "noticing missed opportunities" refers not to current uncertainty but to earlier error and hence is not affected by the recognition of uncertainty (Kirzner 1982, 147–148). The entrepreneur's role here is to be "alert to the future," to make his view of the future close to the real future. The closer his view is to the real view of the future, the greater will be his chance of making a profit. Hence, once again, the entrepreneurs' role is to coordinate the market; but now, he co-ordinates over time. He will be able to accomplish this because he is "motivated" to be correct about the future (Kirzner 1982, 149–151).

The coordinating ability of entrepreneurs over time is crucial to sustaining Kirzner's view of the market process, yet how convincing is his case? This argument, while appearing to deal with issues of uncertainty, seems to avoid it all together. It seems here as if Kirzner cannot come to grips with what the passage of time really implies for human action. Having fully digested the implications of heterogeneous knowledge and consequent scope for error in economic activity, he neglects time all together. Certainly entrepreneurs *try* to choose the right means-ends framework, certainly they *try* to recognize past error, certainly they *try* to make their anticipation of the future "the" correct one. But what guarantee do we have that they will succeed? Certainly, being motivated to succeed does not ensure success. They simply may be mistaken in their judgment about the course of future events.

Perhaps the problem of uncertainty is not most usefully captured by referring to it as a problem of choosing the "right" means-end framework. At one level, uncertainty can refer to the uncertainty as to whether or not the entrepreneurial hunch was correct. Entrepreneurs may feel something akin to certainty, but subsequent events may well prove them wrong. Their interpretive framework may be faulty, or their information incorrect. It seems unreasonable to dismiss this as "nonentrepreneurial" simply because the entrepreneur was in error. This is a form of uncertainty that does not emphasize the passage of time, simply imperfect information despite the noncalculative character of the entrepreneurial act.

However, if we do consider the passage of time, another kind of uncertainty comes into the picture. If we take seriously von Mises's dictum that the passage of time implies changes in knowledge, then even if entrepreneurs are correct in their identification of past market errors, there is no guarantee that their ventures to exploit those errors will succeed. If the "data" are continually changing as Mises argued (1963, 245), the opportunity that entrepreneurs think they see can well disappear before they can fully exploit their vision. People's tastes may change, someone else may make a discovery that changes the potential profitability of one's venture, people may pursue their own plans in an unpredicted way. In this more realistic world, one can be alert and still be incorrect. Speculators often lose money.

Indeed, in this scenario, it seems unhelpful even to speak of entrepreneurs striving to formulate the "correct" vision of the future as if the future were something already implicit in the "data" and one's only problem is to guess correctly what that future will be. Even if, in some purely formal sense, at any moment in time there might be a future inherent in "the data," the actual future that emerges is surely the product of the unpredictable discoveries of Kirzner's entrepreneurs. Given that all opportunities cannot be expected to be discovered in some predictable pattern, nor even discovered at all, each actual discovery, in Kirzner's system, should change the future in totally unpredictable ways. And again, what was an opportunity at one moment in time could turn into a failure in the next. In such a world, what could possibly be the "correct" anticipation of the future except in a purely *ex post* sense?

Kirzner's treatment of uncertainty is troubling because he fails to consider those aspects of uncertainty that would challenge his system. If entrepreneurs can be wrong, not in the simple sense of missing opportunities, but in the far more important sense of using resources in ways that lead to losses, how can they be seen as the unequivocal driving force bringing the system toward equilibrium? If they can be wrong, perhaps they can be a destabilizing influence on the market and perhaps that instability can persist for long periods of time. This was, after all Keynes's argument. Certainly, it requires some answer other than calling on the fact that entrepreneurs will be motivated to be correct.

One might argue that the problem here is one of emphasis. Kirzner in part is saying that without entrepreneurs, it is unlikely that there will be any intertemporal co-ordination at all. Someone has to make the judgments about the future and take risks based on that judgment. One cannot avoid dealing with uncertainty, one can only change who it is that will bear the consequences. Entrepreneurs who specialize in bearing risk will tend to be more successful than those who accept risk by default. Entrepreneurial action, then, need not be perfect, only on balance more correct than an economic system without markets and entrepreneurs. The problem with this argument, however, is that it fails to supply arguments about why entrepreneurs in an uncertain world should on balance be correct enough to drive the system towards equilibrium. If the data are constantly changing, what does equilibrium mean, anyway?

There are signs that for a time, at least, Kirzner himself was troubled by the introduction of uncertainty into his model. In an article published in 1983, he described the market as "a sequential, systematic process of continual adjustment, incessantly buffeted and redirected by exogenous changes" (Kirzner 1985, 156). There, he identifies two kinds of discoordination: the first with respect to information already known and the second with respect to future discoveries. He argues that "current market activities may be fully coordinated with each other, yet be very imperfectly coordinated with future activities *as these will turn out to be informed by as yet undiscovered truths*" (Kirzner 1985, 159). Although even here, entrepreneurs are identified as "correctly perceiving elements to be calculated" (Kirzner 1985, 157). Instead of bringing about equilibrium, they are responsible for bringing about whatever "allocative balance" exists in the market (Kirzner 1985, 162). The implication here seems to be the more modest one that entrepreneurs are necessary not to guarantee equilibrium, but only to bring about whatever approximation to equilibrium is possible in the real world of time and ignorance.

In an even later article, Kirzner (1985, 84–85) distinguishes among three types of entrepreneurship: arbitrage, speculation, and innovation all of which, he argues, are adequately described by his term, "alertness," although in another place, he suggests that each of these may be the product of a completely different thought process (Kirzner 1985, 116). One might, from these articles, conclude that Kirzner, reacting to the influence of Lachmann and indirectly through Lachmann of Shackle, was beginning to rethink some of his earlier ideas on equilibrium and entrepreneurship, and was perhaps ready to question more closely the relationship of Austrian economics to the neoclassical mainstream. However, in the introduction to *Discovery and the Capitalist Process* (1985) he reasserts with full vigor his position of 1973. He argues that his work is a reaction to the "stark options" in which entrepreneurship is regarded either as an automatic response to market demand as in neoclassical economics, or as originative, spontaneous, and unexplained as in the writings of Shackle. Kirzner aims to show that through the concept of "alertness" one can "incorporate entrepreneurship into the analysis without surrendering the heart of microeconomic theory" (Kirzner 1985, 11). Indeed, microeconomics needs his conception of the entrepreneur in order to be complete. He rejects once again the notion that entrepreneurs create anything *ex nihilo*, instead arguing that by discovering opportunities already "there" to be discovered, they are introducing genuine novelty into the system. He reasserts that "human alertness at all times furnishes agents with the propensity to discover information that will be useful to them" (Kirzner 1985, 12), and this will result in a continuous discovery process that "in the absence of external changes in underlying conditions, fuels a tendency toward equilibrium." His parting shot is aimed directly at Shackle and Lachmann: to accept the view that ignorance is an "indelible feature of the situation . . . is to give up systematic market processes" (Kirzner 1985, 13). Entrepreneurs must eliminate ignorance untainted by their own error in order for market processes to be systematically explainable.

Kirzner appears to have largely succeeded in his goal to provide a theory of the entrepreneur that accounts for the missing link in neoclassical price theory; his entrepreneur inserts an element of undetermined action in an otherwise fully determinate model of price adjustment. Indeed, at one level, Kirzner has simply formalized a set of verbal stories countless economics professors tell their introductory students as they try to explain how some particular market reaches equilibrium. This is in itself no small accomplishment since it also permits him to reinterpret the neoclassical notion of competition and monopoly in a way that brings more congruence between neoclassical and Austrian theory.[8] Yet, Kirzner seems to have succeeded by taking inadequate account of half the Austrian research program. By incompletely examining the implications of the passage of time in the world, he may have succeeded in improving upon a model of market behavior that still fails to capture the central problem of human action.

V. LACHMANN AND THE KALEIDIC WORLD

Although both agree on many of the important presuppositions of Austrian economics and especially on the central importance of market processes in economic theory, Ludwig Lachmann's writings present a stark contrast to Kirzner's. Where Kirzner can be seen as attempting some reconciliation between Mises and conventional microeconomic theory, Lachmann's work reflects different influences and interests. A student first in Germany and then in England, early on in his studies he read Menger and Mises, but he also read Max Weber whose ideas became a major source of inspiration to his own. He studied with Hayek in England, but he also was influenced by Keynes—or at least by the subjectivist parts of Keynes's *General Theory*. And finally, as a student of subjectivism, he was very sympathetic to the work of G. L. S. Shackle, who helped carry Lachmann's own subjectivist inclinations to new heights.

Whereas Kirzner approached a theory of the market process through the phenomenon of the arbitraging entrepreneur, Lachmann's way in was through capital theory. Or rather, through the theory of capital, which he argued was a very different thing. Conventional capital theory after Keynes had come to mean a theory of interest, but for Lachmann a theory of capital should rather examine how individuals chose to create particular kinds of intermediate goods at particular times and how these intermediate goods led to the eventual production of consumer goods. He thus saw himself as carrying forth Hayek's program of examining "what type of equipment it will be most profitable to create under various conditions, and how the equipment existing at any moment will be used, rather than to explain the factors which determine the value of a given stock of productive equipment and of the income that will be derived from it" (Lachmann 1987a, vii).

Obviously, Lachmann, as both Menger and Hayek before him, saw capital as a collection of heterogeneous goods whose structure and alternative uses were fundamental to describing the contours of a market economy. Capital was the outcome of conscious plans of entrepreneurs to construct equipment that would only yield a return in the future. Hence the decision to invest in any particular kind of capital structure is a consequence of an entrepreneur's assessment of current economic conditions and his expectations about the future. One can readily appreciate how his work in capital theory would draw his attention to problems of time and futurity in economics.

Lachmann was also fascinated with the fact that the existing capital stock is continuously reshuffled and reused. Entrepreneurs make production plans, but these plans often are impossible to complete because of mistaken expectations about the plans of others. Where people have differing expectations about the future, it is impossible for them all to be correct. Hence a certain incompatibility of plans is natural to the market process. Some investments will turn out to have been mistaken from the perspective of the investor. Nevertheless, investment, good or bad, leads to the creation of material objects that exist regardless of the success or failure of the plan. These objects, "fossils" of former projects (Lachmann 1986, 61) or tracks of history are ultimately used for purposes other than those they are originally constructed to serve. While such reshuffling of the capital stock into alternative occupations is a testament to the flexibility of the market process, it nevertheless inevitably results in some "waste" in the system (Lachmann 1976c, 149). Such considerations made Lachmann mindful of the problem of disequilibrating tendencies in market economies as well as equilibrating ones.[9] Considerations both of time and disequilibrating tendencies figure prominently in his scattered attempts to develop an alternative economic paradigm to the static equilibrium framework of contemporary economic theory.

To Lachmann, the nature of the market process is such that it makes no sense to attempt to describe equilibrium states for the market as a whole. This was a method appropriate, perhaps, to the classical school that saw value as a real phenomenon where prices could be imagined to converge to a "centre of gravity," but once value is understood as a consequence of utility, the economist's job is to assess the mental acts of multitudes of consumers, and the notion of a center of gravity ceases to be helpful (Lachmann 1986, 14). Instead, the market is better understood as "a particular kind of process, a continuous process without beginning or end, propelled by the interaction between the forces of equilibrium and the forces of change" (Lachmann 1976a, 60). In fact, rather than a mechanical resolution of forces that equilibrium conjures up, a better metaphor for the market is Shackle's "kaleidic society," a notion that may seem alien to Austrians at first, but is completely consistent with their assumptions (Lachmann 1976a, 61). That is, the kaleidic society is a metaphor that captures the implications of human action within the context of real time and heterogeneous and imperfect knowledge.

VI. INDIVIDUAL ACTION IN REAL TIME

Like Shackle, Lachmann regards the future as undetermined, the unpredictable consequence of creative and undetermined choices to pursue ends within the constraints of means and obstacles in the present. Hence, one can never "see" into the future, one can only imagine and conjecture, interpret the present and form expectations about the future. As Lachmann repeats many times in his writing, "The future is unknowable, but not unimaginable" (1976a, 55). While the undetermined nature of the future makes it unknowable, the reason it is not unimaginable is that there is some consistency in human action that makes some futures more likely to emerge than others. However, it is impossible for either the actor or the social scientist to predict which of the many possible futures one could imagine will actually occur. Hence uncertainty is a fact of life, and all expectations are subjective estimations of possible futures.

But why is human action undetermined or unpredictable? Kirzner, while arguing forcefully for a kind of undetermined action in his theory of entrepreneurship, was willing to accept fully determined Robbinsian maximizing as a theoretical proposition once a means-ends framework was established. Lachmann is less willing to go even this far toward rapprochement with neoclassical modeling. As a true student of Shackle, he emphasizes that all action, except "routine action" is undetermined creative choice.[10] Shackle emphasizes the importance of imagination in choice where choice is an undetermined cut between past and future. Lachmann accepts this view but goes further than Shackle by providing an explanation for the indeterminate nature of choice rooted in a theory of mind that is reminiscent of Hayek's work on the sensory order.

The reason that choice can never be fully predicted, Lachmann would argue, is that no two minds are alike; neither in the bits of knowledge they contain nor in their method of interpreting the information they receive. The world does not present itself to human minds in an unproblematic way. Sensory data must be interpreted, and this interpretation process is subjective and never exactly duplicated from one mind to another. Hence, the means-ends framework and the obstacles that individuals perceive is itself subjective in that the same "information" will invoke differing interpretations among human beings (Lachmann 1971, 39).

While human action is not determinate, neither is it arbitrary. Lachmann sees human action as "free within an area bounded by constraints" (1971, 37). Since the purpose of economic theory in Lachmann's view is to make the world intelligible in terms of human action, it would seem to be imperative to develop a theory of action that specifies the areas of freedom as well as the constraints. To Lachmann, the way forward is not to focus on momentary acts of choice or the solution to maximizing problems. Rather, he reinterprets praxeology, the study of how human beings use means to achieve ends, as the study of how human beings devise and act upon the plans to use means to achieve ends. Whereas the simpler Misesian formulation could potentially be construed in a static timeless manner, the notion of devising and acting upon plans focuses us squarely on the importance of acting in time.[11] The notion of a plan, Lachmann argues, is particularly appealing to praxeology since it is a human phenomenon that has no counterpart in nature. Inanimate objects do not plan,[12] yet human action can only be understood in terms of the plan of which it is a part. People carry an image of what it is they want in their minds. Action is the carrying out of the project designed to bring about imagined ends. Indeed, concepts like success and failure only make sense as the outcomes of some plan (Lachmann 1971, 29–30).

While people formulate and act upon plans, as Lachmann emphasized in his theory of capital, this does not mean that plans can always be carried out unproblematically. Plans are, after all, carried out in time, and the passage of time implies that knowledge and circumstances will change. Lachmann especially emphasizes the degree to which knowledge is affected by the passage of time. Problems of time and knowledge are inseparable to Lachmann, as they were in principle (although perhaps not in practice) to von Mises.

Lachmann repeats often the dictum that "As soon as we permit time to elapse we must permit knowledge to change, and knowledge cannot be regarded as a function of anything else" (1977, 92). The passage of time (and presumably action in time), means that people will learn more about both their ends and means, and more about the plans that other people are undertaking. This will imply that initial plans must be revised, often many times in light of new knowledge. Revision of plans, then, is the norm rather than the exception in human action. In such a world, it would be extremely unlikely that all plans would ever be "coordinated." It is for this reason that Lachmann describes the market as "a sequence of individual interactions, each denoting the encounter (and sometimes collision) of a number of plans, which, while coherent individually and reflecting the individual equilibrium of the actor, are incoherent as a group. The process would not go on otherwise" (Lachmann 1976b, 131). For Lachmann, it seems this process is such that we cannot even predict the direction of change.

Lachmann's view about the market process, stated so baldly, seems to contradict the very notion of order that informs economic analysis. Without a tendency toward equilibrium, how can we theorize about the market process at all? What can we say about it other than that change happens? So ingrained are familiar notions of equilibrium in the economics profession, that Lachmann's arguments have led others, both within and without Austrian circles, to charge him with nihilism; with denying the possibility of theory all together. Yet Lachmann claims that he does not deny theory, simply the wrong kind of theory.[13] In several places (Lachmann 1971, 1986) he gives us clues to his view of an alternative theory of the market process. Whether these clues amount to a case is an open question.

VII. LACHMANN'S THEORY OF INSTITUTIONS

Unfortunately, Lachmann never wrote a systematic treatise to integrate his understanding of economic theory. Those interested in Lachmann's positive program for economics must attempt to piece together a system from several sources. Primary among them are *The Legacy of Max Weber* (1971) and his last book, *The Market as an Economic Process* (1986). While there are some real differences in Lachmann's sentiments as expressed in these two books, there is enough continuity to get a glimpse of what he thinks a viable alternative to neoclassical economics would look like.

The Legacy of Max Weber is an undeservedly neglected book. As the title indicates, it is not so much an explication of Weber's thought as it is an attempt to build upon some aspects of Weber's work that pertain to economic theory. Specifically, Lachmann wishes to ground Weber's use of ideal types in a theory of human action based on the notion of the plan and hence render ideal types more a theoretical than strictly historical construct. More important for our purposes, Lachmann intended to bring some coherence to Weber's widespread remarks about institutions by outlining a general theory of institutions; how they evolve and what function they serve in human social life. Lachmann's theory of institutions developed in chapter 2 of *The Legacy of Max Weber* provides one basis for Lachmann's claim that his view of the market process is not nihilistic: that order can be explained without recourse to general equilibrium constructs.

Lachmann begins here with his notion of "the plan" as the basic unit of analysis of human action with all of its implications for unpredictability, failure and revision. However, within this world of unpredictable unfolding of a multitude of human plans, Lachmann sees institutions serving as "points of orientation." Institutions are "recurrent patterns of conduct" (Lachmann 1971, 75) that "coordinate activities to a common signpost" (Lachmann 1971, 49). They enable us to predict some actions of others with a fair amount of confidence. As such, they help to reduce the potential chaos that might ensue in an undetermined world.

Lachmann illustrates his point by referring to Menger's theory of institutions. Specifically, the price system is an institution that provides a sufficient level of predictability of action and interpretation to allow people to pursue their plans with some possibility of success. In addition, the price system allows enough flexibility of action to permit useful market institutions to emerge. Within markets, "profits . . . are sign posts of entrepreneurial success. In symbolic form they convey knowledge . . ." (Lachmann 1978a, 102). The price system works because "some men realize that it is possible to pursue their interests more effectively than they have done so far and that an existing situation offers opportunities not so far exploited. In concert with others, they do exploit them. If they are successful their example will find ready imitators, at first a few, later on many." The mechanism for such crystallization is imitation, "the most important form by which the ways of the élite become the property of the masses. Once an idea originally grasped by an eager mind has been 'tested' and found successful, it can be safely employed as a means to success by minds less eager and lacking in originality. Institutions are the relics of the pioneering efforts of former generations from which we are still drawing benefit" (Lachmann 1971, 68).

None of this implies either perfection in outcome or unqualified "efficiency" in markets, however. Market processes are not clockworks. The price system may offer "points of orientation," but it does not guarantee any particular outcome. What the price system does offer is a method for carrying out plans in an orderly, coherent process, a method for detecting error and the flexibility to correct errors when they are perceived.

The price system is one kind of institution in society that allows the generation of other, subsidiary market institutions like firms, financial intermediaries, wholesalers, stock markets, and so forth. Similarly, the price system operates within the context of other social institutions such as families and, most important, the legal structure. Neoclassical economists define order and efficiency with respect to the price system as the achievement of general equilibrium, a construct that Lachmann finds fantastic for all his previously articulated reasons of subjectivity, knowledge, and time. Markets can be orderly without tending toward or achieving general equilibrium. However, he addresses the problem of coordination and order that neoclassical economics tries to solve with a theory of general equilibrium, but at a different level of social organization. While individual plans and actions will never be completely coordinated as is required in general equilibrium theory, it is legitimate to question the coherence and co-ordination of the social institutions that people take as signposts for their actions (Lachmann 1971, 70).

Lachmann envisions the social world as a series of nested institutions, all of which affect human plans and projects. In a world of uncertainty and change, institutions face two challenges: they must be permanent enough to serve their function as points of orientation for human plans, but they also must be flexible enough to change with changed circumstances. No society can function with continual flux in its institutional structure, but a society that never permits its institutional structure to change will suffer increasing inefficiencies (Lachmann 1971, 89). Further, in order to enable individuals to act with efficacy, the institutional structure must be compatible within itself (Lachmann 1971, 75). For society to flourish, finally, Lachmann argues that it must possess a few fundamental institutions that change infrequently and provide the firm outer structure of society, but it must also possess wide scope for freedom of contract to allow the emergence of new institutions to serve new problems (Lachmann 1971, 90).

Lachmann is addressing several problems at once with his discussion of institutions. He alludes to questions of how an institutional structure emerges (both as the unintended byproduct of purposeful human action as in Menger and through conscious design) (Lachmann 1971, 69), he describes potential characteristics of an institutional structure, and he posits a set of characteristics for a well-functioning institutional structure. Yet no clearly articulated theory of institutions emerges from all of this, at least no theory that translates easily into analysis and policy.

In the end, Lachmann says many tantalizing things about institutions without developing a full-blown theory to give us confidence in the coherence of the market order. We have learned something of the importance of institutions, but we have no account of how institutional permanence, coherence, and flexibility might arise. Lachmann still has not solved his problem of order. He has just moved it to another level of social interaction.

VIII. THE MARKET AS AN ECONOMIC PROCESS

In Lachmann's last book, *The Market as an Economic Process* (1986), he tries again to give us a coherent alternative economic system. Here he draws together most of his earlier themes such as the unknowability of the future; the concomitant uncertainty within which everyone acts; the unpredictability of choice and the inability of economics to be a predictive science; the subjectivity of knowledge, interpretation, and expectations; and the inappropriateness of equilibrium theorizing. Instead of continuing his promising program of developing a theory of institutions, however, in this book the role of institutions recedes into the background. It forms an indispensable presence but is not a conscious focus.

Ironically, in his last book, Lachmann once again invokes the legacy of Max Weber, but from a different and less self-conscious perspective. Where in the *Legacy*, Lachmann had criticized Weber's use of the ideal type as being insufficiently sensitive to the causes of human action, here he argues that the appropriate way to theorize about economic phenomena is to employ the construct of the ideal type (Lachmann 1986, 34).[14]

An ideal type, according to Lachmann, is not a pure abstraction or generic concept such as "horse" or "father" that abstracts from all particular horses or fathers. Rather it is a construct that accentuates "certain properties found either in reality, or in our imagination, even though we also have to abstract from other properties found there." Since this may not be a perfectly pellucid definition, an example might help. A financial intermediary is an ideal type in that it is an abstract notion that nevertheless is only useful in certain historical instances. The ideal type of "financial intermediary" would make no sense in a noncredit economy. An ideal type is "a foil against which to hold real events so as to bring out particular properties of the latter by comparison" (Lachmann 1986, 34). There needs to be some grounding in a real phenomenon and some comparison to reality possible in order for a construct to be an ideal type. In this sense, *homo economicus* is not an ideal type, but a pure abstraction.[15]

An example of an ideal type used in neoclassical economics, according to Lachmann, is the model of perfect competition (Lachmann 1986, 35). It takes certain properties of some real markets such as price taking, widespread knowledge, and shared technical information, and exaggerates them into an ideal type. Unfortunately, neoclassical economics does not know what to do from there. The proper procedure is to use the ideal type to examine the deviations from it in the real world. Hence, when Jevons introduced recontracting and Walras, the auctioneer, they were identifying a problem that was solved in some fashion or other by real types. The ideal type of the auctioneer should have started a research effort to learn what the real-life counterpart was to this ideal type (Lachmann 1986, 39–40). (And had they done so, neoclassical economics might have immediately focused on the importance of explaining market processes rather than limiting its fire power to equilibrium states.)

Ideal types are empirically relevant constraints. Hence, the usefulness of an ideal type depends on the events one wants to study. The ideal type of a financial intermediary is only useful, for example, in a credit economy. But when it is empirically relevant, the ideal type allows us to identify real counterparts or "real types." So, for example, a financial intermediary is an ideal type that allows us to identify the Victorian merchant banker as a real type (Lachmann 1986, 36). Such reliance on the empirical grounding of ideal types and the historical relevance of real types, Lachmann implies, will permit economics to perform its legitimate function, providing classificatory and theoretical schema for historical research. Economics is not like physics. We cannot predict the future, but we can explain the past. Hence, our theoretical constructs are best thought of as aids to the interpretation of the history.

In the rest of the book, and especially in his chapter on markets and the market, Lachmann pursues his program of disaggregating typical economic concepts from abstractions to ideal types. In particular, he implicitly argues, instead of examining the world through the lens of the abstraction called "the market," we need to develop ideal types of particular kinds of markets: asset markets versus production markets, fix-price markets or flex-price markets, markets dominated by merchants versus markets dominated by salesmen. Such distinctions will make a difference as to how markets adjust to change. Austrians, he claims, should be interested not in questions of price determination but, as Menger showed us, in questions of price formation. What price emerges is less interesting than how prices emerges; who sets the price, what information is available, to what signals does one respond? Rather than focusing on the empirically irrelevant case of equilibrium prices, it is far more important to ask what the consequences of particular kinds of price setting are over time (Lachmann 1986, 128).

Lachmann addresses some of his questions and in the course of doing so says some interesting things about particular markets. For instance, as he wrote several times before, asset markets are more volatile than production markets because in asset markets value depends purely on expectations and owners can "change sides" at will, as bulls become bears and vice versa. The function of the price system in these markets is to divide the bulls and the bears, which perhaps means to allow people to hold the assets they wish based on their expectations about the future. In such a setting, one side or the other is bound to be right.

He further argues that where markets are characterized by fix-price rather than flex-price, quantity adjustments will be the norm. (He makes the unsupported claim that almost all markets are fix-price markets now, a belief he apparently picked up from the post-Keynesians.) Where markets are dominated by salesmen, prices will be more rigid than where they are dominated by merchants; once again, because merchants can change sides (Lachmann 1986, 133–134).

But where does this leave us with respect to the problem of order in society? Is there anything we can say about the market process that allows us to assert its fundamental coherence and order? If we are not to speak of "equilibrium" can we still speak, then, as did Adam Smith, of a "simple system of natural liberty" in which the invisible hand, *any* invisible hand, is operative? Or are we forced to conclude that the market system is simply one institutional order among many in society that may or may not be coherent on its own, and may or may not be compatible with the other institutions of society? In a reversion to neoclassical language, Lachmann tells us that markets are subject to both disequilibrating and equilibrating tendencies (Lachmann 1986, 37), but he takes no position on which kinds of tendencies tend to dominate the system. In the end, as with *The Legacy of Max Weber,* we are left frustrated and dissatisfied. We have agreed with Lachmann on all aspects of his description of the human condition, we have followed his criticism of the conventional orthodoxy and we have been eager to follow him in his examination of real markets, but we feel that we have taken a tour of individual trees and have missed the forest. Lachmann leaves us with detailed understanding of some market processes, but no overall theory of the market process itself.

So, both Kirzner and Lachmann appear to have failed to fulfill their prom-ise. Kirzner, in an attempt to inject entrepreneurship into an equilibrium model of markets, can do so only at the price of ignoring the consequences of real time. He is true to only one half of the Austrian project. Lachmann, in an attempt to take seriously the challenge of real time, tries to devise an alter-native to equilibrium theorizing that leaves us with no overarching abstract theory at all.

IX. CONCLUSION

It seems that we have reached a very uncomfortable impasse. Apparently, we must conclude that Austrian economics must either be an adjunct to neo-classical economics that provides an account of equilibrating within the con-ventional static framework of fixed preferences and analytic instantaneous adjustments, or it must be a philosophically oriented account of the implica-tions of time and uncertainty with no theoretical structure underpinning it. Neither position succeeds in fulfilling the promise of the proposed Austrian project to develop a theory of an orderly market process that starts not only from individual action to satisfy preferences within resource constraints, but also recognizes that economizing activity takes place within a world of partial ignorance and real time.

If we must choose sides between two unsatisfactory projects, the Kirznerian side seems the safest. On this side is the weight of established economic the-ory to which Austrian insights can serve as useful addenda. But after hav-ing described the role of the entrepreneur and pointed out the limitations placed on one's theoretical and policy pronouncements by the problems of ignorance and time, there does not seem to be much left for Austrians to do. This might be an appealing prospect if it were not for the nagging suspicion that Lachmann perhaps had a point or two. If, as Mises argued, wants are continuously being reevaluated, if time passes and knowledge changes, then the neoclassical research program plus Austrian addenda seem likely to mis-understand important market processes. Although the risk of failure is great, a search for an alternative paradigm to take account of these apparent facts of reality promises to have huge payoffs. Such a search, moreover, would not entirely be a voyage into the heart of darkness. There are some clues, even within the Austrian tradition, to guide our way forward.

Consider, first, Menger's conceptualization of the market process. To Menger, the market process was primarily an engine for generating new knowledge and growing quantities of economic goods. Questions of equilibrium were far less important to Menger than accounts of how the attempts of individual actors led to the unintended consequences of greater wealth and greater knowledge. Growth, further, was an evolutionary process, a process of trial and error and of imitation.

Virtually every Austrian writer since Menger has alluded to trial and error processes in describing markets, but no one has self-consciously attempted to recast the usual Austrian arguments into an evolutionary framework.[16] While there are many problems one would expect to encounter in attempting to execute such a recasting (what, if anything, are the economic analogues to evolutionary concepts like genes, mutations, crossovers, selection, replication, etc.), and the borrowing of terms and concepts would have to be selective with respect to the purposes of social science, there are enough similarities in problems and structure to make evolutionary theory a far more promising metaphor for market activity than physics or mechanics. For example, human action shares with natural history an explainable, patterned history, problems of indeterminate futures, path dependency, and a penchant for exhibiting both stability and rapid change. While others (Nelson and Winter 1982; Hirschleifer 1977, 1982) have argued for adopting an evolutionary framework for economics, Austrians here have even more reason than most for following through on such a program.

Another avenue to explore in developing an alternative Austrian paradigm would be to follow up Lachmann's suggestions about institutional structure. Here, again, there is a long Austrian pedigree stretching back to Menger and forward to Hayek in the analysis of the evolution and structural coherence of market institutions. Indeed, the study of institutions is not an alternative to evolutionary analysis, as Hayek has taught us, but a part of it, where institutions provide the ballast, the source of stability in society, while freedom of contract provides the avenue for the introduction of change. An analysis of how market institutions evolve to solve specific problems of ignorance and time, and how these institutions are conditioned by the other institutional structures of societies seems a promising field of inquiry. Once again, Austrians are far from alone in pursuing such a project, but their emphasis on problems of time and ignorance rather than efficiency suggests a possible unique contribution to a theory of institutions.

One particular Austrian variant to a study of institutions, moreover, would serve to provide a more suitable framework for a favorite Austrian theme: the study of the nature of "free" markets. As Hayek has begun to show us, the evolution and interaction of specific legal and customary contexts is not fully separable from study of the economy. Further, the collapse of faith in central planning suggests that there is no longer a stark alternative between planned and free economies at the theoretical level. All societies exhibit market behavior within the context of varying rules structures. A good Austrian program would be to bring its particular insights into the nature of human action to bear on analysis of the interaction of market, political, and cultural institutions.

While these are still tentative suggestions that I am in the process of trying to develop further, it seems certain that any creative Austrian research program will have to combine aspects of evolutionary theorizing and the analysis of institutions. The irony in all this does not escape me. Menger spent most of his productive life arguing the case for pure theory against the historical school. Mises spilled much ink in his similar case against the institutionalists. Yet, the work of both Hayek and Lachmann seems to indicate that the way forward with the recently articulated Austrian research program requires careful attention to the historicity and institutional structure of society. Perhaps soon, more than a hundred years later, the *Methodenstreit* will finally be over.

NOTES

I wish to thank Richard Wagner, Warren Samuels, Robert Ekelund, Roy Cordato, members of the Austrian Colloquium sponsored by the Ludwig von Mises Institute and an anonymous referee for helpful comments on an earlier draft of this paper. Of course, errors and misinterpretations are fully my responsibility. © Edward Arnold 1992

1. Belief in the benefits of the "pure market economy" was most forcefully argued by Mises (1963). Although he used the concept of the pure market economy, an economic system characterized by private property, freedom of contract, and minimal government intervention in the contracts formed by individuals, as an abstraction against which to compare existing market orders, he also came to regard it as the ideal social arrangement for achieving consumer sovereignty (Mises 1963, 237).

2. This is a paraphrase of Hayek's assessment of his opponents' errors during the socialist calculation debate in the 1930s and 1940s (Hayek 1940, 188). It became a common Austrian criticism of neoclassical economics.

3. Ironically, when Robbins wrote *The Nature and Significance of Economic Science*, he was attempting to bring Austrian insights to English economics. Robbins had traveled to Austria where he both met with faculty members at the University of Vienna and participated in Mises's private seminar for a time.

4. Despite the fact that he speaks of "the entrepreneur," Kirzner is clear that he is describing a function rather than a kind of person—just as laborers and capitalists are themselves functions in economic theory. That is, entrepreneurship describes a kind of behavior that exists in some degree in all human actions (Kirzner 1973, 31), and it provides an explanation for a source of income: labor receives wages, capitalists receive interest, and entrepreneurs receive profit (Kirzner 1973, 48). However, although entrepreneurship is a function in this sense, it cannot strictly be said to be a factor of production that earns a "return." Unlike other factors of production, it cannot be invested in, searched for, or calculated within a production plan nor does it have a price.

5. The stabilizing function of entrepreneurs in Kirzner's system is partly definitional. What he means by entrepreneurship is the noticing of genuine profit opportunities that others miss. Hence, if one is incorrect about the profitability of an opportunity, one is simply not behaving as an entrepreneur. While this definition makes his system tautologically complete, it does not help us to understand the kinds of mistaken perceptions and evaluations that cause so many business enterprises to fail every year. I shall return to this point later.

6. While Schumpeter's version of entrepreneurship still seems to dominate Kirzner's, there is a sense in which Kirzner has the stronger case, especially when it is examined against the back-drop of central planning. Schumpeter's version would hold, "as a matter of blueprint logic," that once equilibrium prices were arrived at by the central planners, they could be repeated *ad infinitum* without any loss of efficiency albeit without economic growth either. In Kirzner's story, however, the central planners could never arrive at those equilibrium prices in the first place. The only way to approach an equilibrium is through the actions of alert entrepreneurs who "notice what is in their interests to notice" and who can profit from exploiting those interests. Central planning will have no profits and no room for entrepreneurs; hence prices will always reflect incomplete information.

7. The occasion for the presentation was a conference Kirzner organized for Liberty Fund to honor Ludwig von Mises's 100th birthday. It was already evident during that conference that a rift was developing between those who, like Kirzner, wanted to preserve a strong link to conventional economics and the Lachmannians who were willing to pursue subjectivism wherever it should lead.

8. Following Hayek, Kirzner identifies competition with rivalry in the market. Competition occurs when entrepreneurs engage in such practices as price cutting, product differentiation and product innovation. Once the market settles down to the standard description of a perfectly competitive equilibrium, competition ceases. This implies, however, that competition can be fully compatible with the existence of downward sloping demand curves for particular products whose existence is the result of entrepreneurial alertness. Additionally, profits may be the consequence of some temporary advantage entrepreneurs are enjoying and not a symptom of persistent monopoly power. Hence, Kirzner argues, the conventional theory of monopoly as market power or discretion over prices is not helpful in distinguishing the short-term consequences of entrepreneurship and the existence of disequilibrium from long-run persistent monopoly power. A better classificatory system would be to define monopoly in terms of barriers to entry, which to Kirzner means monopoly ownership of some crucial resource necessary to the production of a product. In that way, profits that were subject to being eroded by competition could not be construed as evidence of monopoly while those that were protected by right could be so construed.

9. Obviously, Lachmann sides with Hayek in maintaining that it is unhelpful to think of capital as the source of a continuous income stream, as Frank Knight argued in his debates with Hayek. For capital to produce any income at all requires acts of judgment based upon assessment of the current situation and expectations of the future. It is just as easy for capital to lead to loss as profit for any individual producer. While one might focus as Knight did on the potential permanence of income producible by the capital stock for some kinds of questions, Lachmann would argue that it is misleading to abstract from the human actions that use capital to produce income for most questions of economic theory and policy.

10. It is not clear to what extent Lachmann's "routine" overlaps with Kirzner's Robbinsian maximizing. On the one hand, in the context of Lachmann's discussion, "routine" seems to suggest unthinking repetition as in brushing one's teeth or driving a car, while Kirzner's Robbinsian maximizing covers all those fully conscious rational economic calculations of neoclassical economic theory. If this interpretation is correct, Lachmann would seem to deny the possibility of determinate calculation in Kirzner's sense. On the other hand, Lachmann might simply be stressing Kirzner's notion of undetermined entrepreneurial behavior to a greater degree than Kirzner did.

11. Ironically, it is also more consistent with Mises's notion of subjective time as the "real present." Mises argued that although time may be conceived as a continuous flow in which the present moment has no duration, people experience duration differently and identify as

the "real present" the span of time relevant to their plans or expectations about change (Mises 1963, 100–101).

12. Lachmann does not address the question of whether or not animals can be said to plan, although his identification of planning as distinctively human seems to indicate that he would place animal behavior in the deterministic category. However, his argument does not require that all animals except man be considered reactors rather than planners. One might be able to develop a praxeology of ape behavior that might have similarities to humans, although the behaviorists would deny this. Of course, behaviorists might deny that humans plan creatively as well.

13. "As regards 'nihilism,' this appears to be a term more appropriate to describing the mentality of those who, blind to the variegated activity of human minds when engaged in the formation of expectations, are frantically searching for links of mechanical causation where there are none, than to that of those who do their best to draw the attention of their colleagues to the problems we all face" (Lachmann 1986, 140).

14. Lachmann appreciated the role that ideal types were meant to play in Weber's view of social science. According to Lachmann, Weber wanted idea types to be useful as ordering devices in understanding social phenomena, "measuring rods" to allow us to gain knowledge of reality by understanding the distance between the ideal type and the real phenomenon under investigation (Lachmann 1971, 26–27). However, he thought Weber's use of the ideal type was far too broad to make it useful for analytic purposes, as it encompassed rational schemes of action (of which Lachmann approved), irrational schemes, historical generalizations, actions, and ideas. Lachmann argued that Weber's concept had to be narrowed to be useful and suggested that at least some distinction needed to be made between rational schemes of actions (Lachmann's plans) and historical generalizations. Lachmann (1986) carried this through by distinguishing between abstractions (figments of imagination), ideal types that had to have some grounding in historical reality and real types that were generalizations from reality.

15. Actually, here I must disagree with Lachmann. I have had a few colleagues over the years who have been embodiments of *homo economicus* and, alas, they were all too real and not the least bit abstract.

16. Ulrich Witt has argued that evolutionary theory is the most promising route for further work in Austrian economics (Witt 1991).

REFERENCES

Hayek, F. A. 1940. "Socialist Calculation III: The Competitive 'Solution.'" *Economica* 7. Reprinted in Hayek, 1948: *Individualism and Economic Order*, 181–208. Chicago: University of Chicago Press.

Hirschleifer, J. 1977. "Economics from a Biological Point of View." *Journal of Law and Economics* 20:1–52.

———. 1982: "Evolutionary Models in Economics and Law." *Research in Law and Economics* 4:1–60.

Kirzner, I. M. 1973. *Competition and Entrepreneurship*. Chicago: University of Chicago Press.

———. 1979. *Perception, Opportunity and Profit*. Chicago: University of Chicago Press.

———, ed. 1982: *Method, Process, and Austrian Economics: Essays in Honor of Ludwig von Mises*. Lexington, MA: D. C. Heath & Co.

——— 1985. *Discovery and the Capitalist Process*. Chicago: University of Chicago Press.

Lachmann, L. 1971. *The Legacy of Max Weber*. Berkeley, CA: Glendessary Press.

———. 1976a. "From Mises to Shackle: An Essay." *Journal of Economic Literature* 14:54–62.

———. 1976b. "On the Central Concept of Austrian Economics: The Market Process." In *The Foundations of Modern Austrian Economics*, edited by E. Dolan, 126–132. Kansas City, MO: Sheed and Ward.

———. 1976c. "On Austrian Capital Theory." In *The Foundations of Modern Austrian Economics*, edited by E. Dolan, 145–151. Kansas City, MO: Sheed and Ward.

———. 1977. *Capital, Expectations and the Market Process.* Kansas City, MO: Sheed, Andrews and McMeel.

———. 1978. *Capital and Its Structure.* Kansas City, MO: Sheed, Andrews and McMeel, Inc. First published 1956.

———. 1986. *The Market as an Economic Process.* Oxford: Basil Blackwell.

Mises, Ludwig. 1963. *Human Action: A Treatise on Economics.* New Haven, CT: Yale University Press. First published 1949.

Nelson, R. R., and S. G. Winter. 1982. *An Evolutionary Theory of Economic Change.* Cambridge, MA: Harvard University Press.

O'Driscoll, G. P., and M. J. Rizzo. 1985. *The Economics of Time and Ignorance.* Oxford: Basil Blackwell.

Robbins, L. 1932. *An Essay on the Nature and Significance of Economic Science.* London: Macmillan. Reprinted 1962.

Schumpeter, J. A. 1934. *The Theory of Economic Development.* New York: Oxford University Press. Reprinted 1961.

Witt, U. 1991. "Evolutionary Theory—The Direction Austrian Economics Should Take?" In *Austrian Economics: Tensions and New Developments*, edited by B. Caldwell and S. Boehm. Dordrecht, Netherlands: Kluwer Academic Press.

Chapter 7
Should There Be an Austrian Welfare Economics?

I. INTRODUCTION

For most of the history of Austrian economics, concerns with economic welfare have been tacit issues compared to the more overt theorizing about human action within market contexts. Austrians have generally been advocates of free market economies, and indeed, one of the most impressive achievements of Austrian economics in the twentieth century has been its theoretical refutation of central planning. Yet, despite the demonstrations that central planning is an impossibility, Austrians have not spent much time developing a corresponding theory of welfare to support their view of the superiority of market economies over interventionist regimes. There is a good reason for this apparent lacuna in Austrian economics; the particular issues addressed in conventional welfare economics, market failure and distributional concerns, are dictated by a neoclassical view of markets that is foreign to Austrian theorists. However, the broader questions of the economic well-being of participants in a market economy are equally as important to Austrians as to neoclassical economists. To what extent do markets "work" to provide benefits to market participants? What counts as a benefit? What constitutes a market failure? And most importantly, what kind of remedies are available to correct identified market failures that don't themselves lead to more problems than are solved? These questions require answers that don't rely on the unacceptable assumptions of neoclassical economics for answers. Indeed, an Austrian welfare

Originally published in *Advances in Austrian Economics*, vol. 2, part A (London: JAI Press, 1995), 109–123. Copyright Elsevier. Republished with permission.

economics needs to redefine the questions asked in order to be consistent with an overall Austrian perspective.

Recently, a few voices have been raised to begin the process of articulating a welfare economics from an Austrian perspective (Kirzner 1973, 1979, 1985a, 1985b, 1992; Cordato 1992; Cowen 1990; Hamlin 1994; Prychitko 1994). While each of these authors takes a somewhat different tack in approaching the problem, for our purposes, Kirzner's work is foundational, both from his earliest explorations of the welfare implications of Austrian theory (1973) to his clear statement of the requirements of an Austrian welfare economics in one of his more recent essays (1993).

A. Foundational Assumptions for an Austrian Welfare Economics

In a recent article (1992), Kirzner has concisely and accurately laid out the three fundamental assumptions that must undergird any Austrian welfare economics. They are:

1. Methodological individualism: we shall refuse to recognize meaning in statements concerning the "welfare of society" that cannot, in principle, be unambiguously translated into statements concerning the individuals in society (in a manner which does not do violence to their individuality).

2. Subjectivism: we shall not be satisfied with statements that perceive the economic well-being of society as expressible in terms (such as physical output) that are unrelated to the valuations and choices made by individuals.

3. An emphasis on process: we shall be interested in the economic well-being of society not merely in terms of its level of economic well-being (however defined) but also in regard to the ability of its institutions to stimulate and support those economic processes upon which the attainment of economic well-being depends (181).

On the basis of these familiar Austrian assumptions—methodological individualism, subjectivism of the preferences, expectations and knowledge of market actors, the fact that market action is a process in time—Kirzner goes on to criticize former standards of well-being from Smith's measure of material wealth to Pareto optimality for violating one or more of his criteria. He offers as a substitute a standard of welfare based on the ability of a system to facilitate market coordination. Kirzner's discussion is relatively brief, but it opens up some important issues that need to be examined more closely before we can be satisfied that we are on the right road to an Austrian welfare economics. I hope to show that Kirzner's alternative to contemporary welfare economics is not only important but has far deeper implications for an Austrian evaluation of market economies than have so far been plumbed, even by Kirzner himself. However, I will also argue that an Austrian understanding of markets in all its richness and empirical relevance casts doubt on the whole enterprise of welfare economics as it is generally understood in the economics profession.

B. Pareto Optimality as a Criterion for an Austrian Welfare Economics

Before we explore the requirements and limitations of an Austrian welfare economics, it will be useful to note some similarities between the standard Pareto welfare apparatus and Kirzner's foundational assumptions. Despite Kirzner's dismissal of the Pareto criterion for assessing welfare, at first blush it is not obviously incompatible with Austrian assumptions.

Pareto's criterion for assessing welfare, that a welfare improvement requires that at least one person gain and nobody lose in a transaction, is clearly individualistic. That is, it accepts the personal valuations of market participants as the criterion for judging the welfare properties of an economy. All individual actors are given equal standing in the evaluation. While Kirzner points to the fact that it is "society's" welfare that is said to have improved (1992, 183), where the welfare of society is composed of the sum of individuals' welfare, it is a semantic issue whether or not the criterion is supra-individualistic.

The Pareto criterion may also be consistent with subjectivism. Where utility is unmeasurable and interpersonally incomparable, there is no way for a subjectivist Paretian to judge economic welfare apart from the actual choices of individuals in a market setting. In this guise, Pareto optimality should be completely acceptable to an Austrian, even if the formulation says little more than that welfare is enhanced when gains from trade are realized. In fact, a subjectivist Paretian welfare economics bears a striking resemblance to Rothbard's reconstruction of welfare theory which purports to show that free trade maximizes welfare. Rothbard (1956, 250) argues that since whenever two people trade voluntarily, they both gain, all voluntary trades are welfare enhancing, a proposition with which most Austrians would agree. However, when the Pareto criterion is used in policy analysis, its differences from Austrian analysis become more obvious.

The first fundamental theorem of Paretian welfare economics is that a necessary condition for the achievement of welfare maximization is the attainment of general equilibrium in the absence of externalities and in perfectly competitive markets, while the second fundamental theorem states that any competitive equilibrium can be achieved via competition with the appropriate initial distribution (Feldman 1987, 889). The kinds of policy relevant questions that this approach invites all have to do either with identifying and devising remedies for market failures that prevent the attainment of a competitive equilibrium or devising alternative distributions of wealth endowments that will improve the welfare properties of the equilibrium achieved. Since the elimination of market failures or changes in wealth endowments will mean involuntary gains for some and losses for others, another principle is invoked to judge whether or not the policy change is a welfare improvement. The ways in which conflictual situations are evaluated all rest in one way or another on invoking the compensation principle. That is, if the winners gain enough to compensate the losers for their losses, a policy move is a Pareto improvement (Chipman 1987, 524).

Just as the Pareto criterion is not necessarily incompatible with Austrian economics, neither is the compensation principle. The acceptability of the compensation principle to an Austrian depends crucially on how one envisions this compensation being made. If compensation is actually required to be paid, as long as the amount of compensation is the result of mutual agreement between the gainers and the losers, the criterion should seem unobjectionable to a subjectivist. However, it also then becomes close to impossible to implement except in the simplest of conditions. And if the conditions are simple enough to permit mutually agreeable compensation to be paid, an Austrian economist has a right to ask why the profitable bargain has not already been struck by the market participants themselves. On the other hand, if it is only necessary that compensation could in principle be paid to the losers to identify a Pareto superior policy, one is then left to inquire how the gains and losses are to be measured. The familiar standard is to compare costs and benefits calculated at market prices. Besides the obvious violation of the individualist criterion that failure to pay compensation implies, the usual assumption that subjective values are actually measurable by market values where no voluntary trades have taken place is a clear violation of subjective cost theory (Buchanan 1969).

In sum, although the Pareto criterion for identifying an unambiguous increase in welfare is consistent with methodological individualism and it may also be consistent with subjectivism, it doesn't get us very far in policy analysis without violating at least one of the first two Kirznerian requirements for an Austrian welfare economics.

The differences in policy analysis between Paretians and Austrians is not epiphenomenal; instead, they reflect a fundamental difference in the way each understands market activity. And here we turn to Kirzner's third criterion for an Austrian welfare economics. In a Paretian world, the failure of markets to attain a perfectly competitive general equilibrium is considered prima facie evidence of a market failure that requires a corrective policy. Austrians who believe general equilibrium is a misleading construct at best, also believe that any assessments of economic welfare must be assessments about the ongoing nature of the market process rather than assessments about some artificially constructed conclusion of the market process. And once the continuous nature of markets is investigated, both judgments about economic welfare and economic policy take on a new character.

II. THE NATURE OF THE MARKET PROCESS

As Kirzner has pointed out throughout his work (for example, 1973, 1979, 1985, 1992), the most important feature of the market process is not that it achieves some externally definable equilibrium position. Indeed, given the dynamic nature of markets and the continual change in what conventional economics regards as parameters of the system, it is the market process itself that must be described and evaluated. What is remarkable about markets to Austrians is that within the context of continual "parametric" change, entrepreneurial activity brings about improved coordination among individuals' separately formulated plans. Through entrepreneurial market processes, the discordant plans and limited knowledge of market individuals become more synchronized with each other than was the case before. This is not a trivial theoretical insight nor a trivial empirical phenomenon. As Hayek has emphasized, what conventional economics glosses over in its focus on equilibrium conditions is the actual raison d'être of markets (Hayek 1948, 77).

Every entrepreneurial action of grasping a profit opportunity both reveals a previous lack of coordination among the plans of market participants: people who did not know that mutually profitable trading opportunities existed; and is itself a coordinating activity that brings plans into greater harmony.[1] The process of coordinating knowledge and plans is also the path through which new knowledge enters into the economic system. When Hayek called competition a discovery procedure (1978), he was referring to the fact that it was only through entrepreneurial market processes that the knowledge assumed by general equilibrium theory could ever be obtained.

Furthermore, as long as people continue to plan and learn (or as Lachmann might say, as long as time passes) the market process will never come to an end. What plans appeared to be coordinated before will be shown by alert entrepreneurs to have neglected some hitherto unrecognized aspect of other people's wants or actions. In such a world, the only way for perfect coordination to be achieved would be if all discovery, all innovation, all growth, and all potential for welfare improvements would cease. Since such an end is unthinkable where human beings have scope for action, surely a relevant welfare economics should focus not on the achievement of perfect coordination or general equilibrium, so much as on the implications of coordinating activity. No wonder, then, that Kirzner wants to substitute the act of coordination for general equilibrium as the measure of the achievement of welfare.

III. UNPACKING COORDINATION

Austrians, at least since the publication of *Competition and Entrepreneurship* (Kirzner 1973), have used coordination as their standard of market improvement. They regard every act of coordination, that is, every act that reveals an opportunity for pure profit, as an improvement in the welfare of individuals in the economy. By widening knowledge about costs and profits, coordinating behavior is the means to increasing economic well-being. Most Austrians take this for granted (as would most neoclassical economists who ignore second-best problems), but is this really so obvious? Is it really the case that every act of coordination is an unequivocal improvement in welfare in a general sense that fits the three necessary criteria for an Austrian welfare economics?

Consider the following example of simple arbitrage between two separate markets for, say, apples. Assume market A and market B are identical on the supply side, but different in the strength of demand for apples in each market. In market A, consumers tend to be poorer overall than in market B, hence demand in A is less than demand in B, and the price in A is lower than the price in B. A canny entrepreneur from market A visits market B, notices the higher price for apples and sees an opportunity for profit. He goes back to A, buys apples cheap and sells them dear in B. The familiar consequence is that the entrepreneur will tend to increase prices in A and reduce prices in B. Further, once the entrepreneur's actions become known, others are likely to imitate him, and prices will have a tendency to equalize between markets. Both neoclassical and Austrian economists will regard the result of the successful arbitrage as welfare enhancing, although they may explain their judgments in different ways. Neoclassical economists are likely to argue that as prices equalize, marginal rates of substitution in both markets will now equal the uniform prices and marginal social benefit will equal marginal social cost. Before, apples were undervalued in A relative to total demand and overvalued in B. Arbitrage has increased welfare.

Austrians will argue somewhat differently. Eschewing the notions of marginal social benefit and marginal social cost as violating the subjectivist principle, Austrians will nevertheless also argue that apples were undervalued in A relative to B given the true market demand, but their focus will be on the fact that knowledge of full market conditions has now increased and plans of all participants have now become more coordinated with one another. That is, potentially mutually beneficial trades are now taking place that went unconsummated before. Sellers and buyers were previously ignorant of profitable opportunities, but now they have discovered new sources of profitable action.

But does it also follow to say economic welfare has increased? If so, from whose perspective can this judgment be made? Surely consumers in market A will not report the increased coordination to be an increase in their welfare. As far as they are concerned, they have lost out in this entrepreneurial venture while consumers in B have gained. Consumers in market A now pay a higher price for apples and consume fewer of them. (What happens to suppliers is ambiguous without knowing about their previous level of profits and the nature of the competitiveness in each market.) Consumers in A might well regard themselves as better off if the two markets had not been brought into contact with each other. It would seem that a consistent subjectivist, methodological individualist could not claim that welfare has been enhanced from the perspective of *all* individuals in the economy. Some have been made better off and others worse off according to their own subjective assessments of their welfare. Yet, Austrians know in their bones that the successful arbitrage makes people better off. But in what sense can this be claimed?

Remember, one may not argue, as the utility theorists do, that total utility increases because market A was consuming too many apples given the utility functions of the consumers relative to B because not only are interpersonal comparisons of utility not permitted, Austrians deny that utility is something that can be totaled. Austrians may not argue that real income has increased as a result of the entrepreneurial action because the pecuniary gains to the winner more than offset the losses of the losers because they don't believe consumer surplus is measurable. Further, such an argument must "do violence to (the individual's) individuality." What kind of argument does Austrian economics offer to justify the pecuniary externalities that make some people better off than others as a result of catallactic competition?[2]

While it may seem that a quibble has been raised here, I think the problem is serious. One reason economists have a hard time convincing people of the benefits of the free market is precisely because of issues like this one. Substitute the market for rental housing in New York immediately before the imposition of rent control, or the price of meat in Russia as black markets become legal markets, for apples, and we see empirical examples of public outcry against "entrepreneurial coordinating behavior." This is even more true of the more complex forms of Kirznerian arbitrage in which entrepreneurs find better uses for inputs which then tends to drive competitors out of business.[3]

At this juncture, some might argue that the problem is merely a question of rights. The entrepreneur has a right to notice and act upon profit opportunities and those who lose out in market competition have no right to be protected. But where do these confident assertions of rights come from? Is this not the same as arguing that certain kinds of legal rights (to exchange one's property freely with others) are good while other kinds of legal rights (to protected markets) are bad? To those who believe they have a fully worked out theory of natural rights to back up their claims, such emphatic judgments may not be troubling. But to many people, the problem of who should have the right to do what with what resources is the main problem in establishing a regime of property and contract. To assert entrepreneurial rights to make bargains and dismiss rights in customers, for example, is to skip the analysis that makes such rights sensible. While Austrians do argue that markets rely on a regime of property and contract, exactly what kind of property and contract law is most conducive to economic welfare is one of the problems one presumably wishes to solve.

If we wish to adhere to the requirements that an Austrian welfare economics be both individualist and subjectivist, it is important to come up with an argument that shows how all market participants including the immediate losers from catallactic competition can be said to benefit from entrepreneurial coordination. While it may well be impossible to construct such arguments that are both individualistic and subjectivist from a static neoclassical framework, an Austrian approach that recognizes the dynamic nature of markets may be more successful.

What kinds of arguments might Austrians offer to show why the successful entrepreneurial venture in the apple market is of benefit even to those who now pay higher prices for apples? First, it might be argued that despite the immediate increase in the price of apples, the now larger market with more widespread knowledge might lead in the long run to a supply response that will eventually result in lower prices for apples overall. Where entrepreneurship is allowed to flourish, the lure of profit will provide an incentive for experimentation with new techniques of production or kinds of products that give all consumers greater choice of alternatives that will substitute for the forgone consumption of apples. The entrepreneurial regime could also well lead to greater worker productivity that will permit the poor apple consumers to increase their incomes sufficiently in the long run so they are no longer poor. Further, we might also point out that in markets, entrepreneurial activity is ubiquitous. To use economic policy to prevent entrepreneurial discovery from creating losses for some means also forgoing the gains that flow from entrepreneurial activities (Kirzner 1985, 136). Moreover, limiting market activity through government policy is itself costly and subject to the kind of government failure described in the public choice literature. Finally, following Mises, we might also invoke a slippery slope argument that a regime that allows government to intervene in the apple market will also permit it to widen the scope of its interventionist activities, eventually reaching markets that will injure the interests of the impecunious former apple consumers along with everyone else (Mises 1963, 856–861).

In sum, what an Austrian can offer is not a judgment on the welfare implications of any one market action for all individual consumers. Rather, an Austrian claim about the welfare properties of markets is a broad judgment about how individuals are likely to fair on average and in the long run in an ideal market economy. That is, despite their subjectivist theory, Austrians do not take the individual's actual reports about the state of his welfare as definitive. Instead, they describe the many ways unrestricted scope for entrepreneurial coordination is likely to benefit any random individual as compared to some alternative legal environment. Further, Austrians offer evidence of increasing welfare not by appealing to one particular feature of the market, but rather by describing the many salutary consequences of market activity and the many dimensions of markets that they believe people either do or should value if only they were well enough informed about the nature of markets.[4]

We might think of Austrian claims another way. By advocating a regime of unrestricted scope for entrepreneurship in markets, an individual is offered a lottery ticket with a very favorable payoff. If one buys a ticket to the market economy, one is agreeing to submit to market discipline and to take one's losses along with one's gains, but the expected overall welfare or level of satisfaction for any one individual will be higher than if one buys a ticket to another form of economic system.[5]

Clearly, such an approach to assessing welfare is individualistic in the sense of appealing to the welfare of individuals rather than of some supra-individualist collective as its bench mark. And clearly it takes processes seriously since it is the process of coordinating that leads to all the changes that require individual consideration and evaluation in welfare assessment. But it is subjectivist in only a very peculiar sense since it seems to appeal to a set of interests that individuals should have to be rational rather than the ones they may in fact believe they have.

This may be why in *Human Action*, Mises did not describe markets as leading to a harmony of (raw, untutored) interests, but rather to a harmony of *rightly understood* interests (1963, 673). In Mises's account of the market economy, laws of property and contract allow people to produce wealth by permitting a peaceful resolution of potential conflicts of resource use. What could otherwise be a Hobbesian war of all against all instead becomes a cooperative and orderly process of social interaction (273ff). In this order, people as producers are led to finding their most appropriate niches for serving consumer interests. Mises had no illusion that markets will necessarily give people whatever they want. Individuals may have unrealistic wants: a person might want very much to manage a big corporation, but if his abilities are not up to the job, the market lets him know by shifting resources out of his control to the control of someone better equipped to make decisions that satisfy consumer wants. While the would-be CEO may regard himself as misused by the market, in fact, he is no such thing. The market simply helps to direct him to a job that better suits his talents in serving consumers.

In Mises's view, in addition to resource constraints, individuals face the constraints imposed by other people's wants. The process of harmonizing people's competing interests with those of every other market participant means that some people will get what they want, while others will have to be content to want what they get. It is in everyone's rightly understood interests, however, to want a market economy given the many substantive claims that can be made about the properties of markets, and given the miserable conditions associated with all its alternatives. Whether or not a failed businessman will be convinced by Mises' argument, at the very least, Mises is giving him an interpretation of his predicament based on a theory about the nature of dynamic market processes that gives him reasons for supporting a market economy, despite his individual experience of loss.

IV. IS THIS WELFARE ECONOMICS?

Austrians emphasize that the fundamental property of markets is the activity of entrepreneurial coordination, the general activity by which all of the many dimensions of economic welfare are allowed to emerge. In that sense, coordination, or rather, scope for coordinating activity, is a necessary condition for markets to yield results that individuals are likely to regard as favorable. However, there is no way to measure degrees of coordination or to add up the consequences of various kinds of coordinating activities. Neither is there any way to predict with certainty which of the many possible consequences that may follow from any act of coordination will actually occur. The most Austrians seem to be able to offer the public policy debate is to describe general characteristics of market economies, and to recommend against instituting coercively imposed barriers to coordinating activity. This leads us to ask, then, does what Austrians say about markets even count as welfare economics? This may well be a case of a neoclassical formulation that does not fit a market process view of the problem to be addressed.

As already noted, welfare economics as commonly understood is primarily concerned with identifying market failure and potential gains from redistribution where political remedies are sought for identified market problems. Yet within the Austrian framework, it is very difficult to find a market failure that is both theoretically sound and empirically identifiable. Kirzner (1973, 103) and Rothbard (1962, 591), for example, have each offered definitions of monopoly that are both more in keeping with an understanding of market processes that either make monopoly a consequence of resource ownership or a privilege granted by government. In the first case, the potential harm caused by resource monopoly tends to be minimal, especially when understood in a dynamic context where substitutes are constantly thrown up by entrepreneurial discovery. In the second case, monopoly is an example of government failure, not market failure where the only policy remedy is to eliminate the barriers to entry.

The concern with the wastes of competition that occupied economists earlier in this century are similarly dispelled by the Austrian insight that competition is a discovery procedure in which what appears to be waste is the necessary cost of experimentation when the desired result is not known in advance (Kirzner 1973, 236).

Failure of markets to clear, we have already noted, is never a sign of a market failure to an Austrian, but simply the evidence of a dynamic and healthy market process.

And finally, while the notion of nonpecuniary externalities is in principle consistent with an Austrian account of market activity, in practice it is very hard to find one that Austrians would agree could be internalized by discretionary government policy. Externalities are generally recognized to result from some inability of individuals to contract with each other. Where the externality is due to incomplete property rights, Austrians would leave the resolution to the courts, unguided by Posnerian-like cost calculations, which they regard as impossible to make in any case.[6] When it is due to public goods problems, Austrians are likely to deny that there are really any such animals and where they do seem to exist, recommendations are to at least not preclude possible market solutions by banning competition with government providers.

The Austrian attitude toward market failure is not, as some may think, a byproduct of a dogmatic attachment to free markets no matter the costs so much as a recognition of the central role of the profit motive in bringing about the resolution of recognized problems in a dynamic market setting. Austrians emphasize the difficulty of distinguishing actual cases of market failure from transitory market adjustments. Further, Austrians have reason to believe that the same problems of dispersed knowledge and genuine error that exist in markets also exist and perhaps to a greater degree in government policy formation and implementation: any attempt to design government policy to fix up some perceived market failure not only is likely to be misconceived and poorly run; more importantly, it is likely to stifle the very entrepreneurial process that brings about the many benefits of market economies (Kirzner 1985b).

When it comes to distributional questions, again, Austrian analysis leads to the conclusion that Paretian welfare economics is misleading. Because of the dynamic nature of a market economy, production and distribution are not two separate variables. They are two consequences of the same process. Given the dynamic nature of that process, one cannot choose specific distributions, one can only choose rules under which distributions emerge. The same dynamic nature of markets also guarantees that whatever rules govern economic processes will lead to unintended or unexpected consequences (Hayek 1976, chap. 10).

It is evident that a so-called Austrian welfare economics has little in common with the neoclassical discipline with which it shares a name. Since there is no external benchmark such as general equilibrium by which to criticize actual market achievement, there is no corresponding notion of market failure that implies government correctives. What seems to be left is a description of the characteristics of market systems and the consequences of market activity (or attempts to thwart that activity through government) for individual actors. When Austrians conclude from their theories that individual welfare thrives where markets are allowed to flourish and where government's only role is to enforce laws of property and contract, they are offering a hypothesis about what economic conditions individuals value and showing how these conditions rest on a single phenomenon, the freedom of individuals to engage in noncoercive exchange of legitimate property.[7]

In this sense, Mises was essentially correct when he argued that he was not doing normative economics at all. He was simply describing the contours of a market order and leaving it up to the people to decide if they wanted to live in a market order or its alternative. He did not try to measure welfare or compare it between states. That could only be done by individuals participating within civil society. While it is true that Mises didn't believe that when individuals understood all the properties of a market economy, there would be much of choice—it was either the market economy or chaos (1963, 680)—it was nevertheless true that economics cannot make ultimate judgments of value, only individuals can.

V. THE ROLE OF THE ECONOMIST

Despite the pretensions of standard welfare economics, economics is not a discipline that is equipped to evaluate welfare in some abstract way. Where there is no quantum of utility to be summed, where prices do not "measure" marginal social cost, and where consumer surplus is merely a convenient analytic device with no real measurable correlate, there is no abstract scientific standard for judging some states of the world as necessarily preferable to others. Assessments of welfare at base are individual concerns. However, this is not to say that welfare is a purely random notion with no interpersonal meaning. In fact, there is evidence that many beliefs about the nature of economic welfare are shared across cultures (especially when people are able to act on their beliefs). If economists do not have abstract, a priori definitions of welfare to guide them, they certainly do have a variety of commonly held beliefs about welfare that can be held up to empirical assessment.[8]

It is completely appropriate for economists not only to provide theoretical interpretations of economic systems, but also to compare states according to a variety of more or less measurable criteria.[9] For instance, an economist who is charged with comparing the US economy with the former Soviet economy might simply say that the US economy was more coordinated than the Soviet economy in that mutual plans were more consistent with each other. But while that is undoubtedly true, it is also undoubtedly true that the consequences of this superior coordination were felt in the many aspects of individuals' economic well-being that they prize. Despite the imperfect nature of statistical measures, it is nevertheless possible to show on the basis of such measures as per capita income, availability of a variety of consumer goods, mobility of labor force, size of capital stock (crudely measured), rates of savings, and so forth, the material consequences of superior coordination. While there is no one metric by which to judge welfare a priori nor is there any privileged position that the economist has to unequivocally judge one society or economy better than another in total, we can investigate the economic variables that are important to people. We can also give analyses of the link between government policies and the economic consequences that flow from them.

Austrians see a vital connection between the scope for free trade and entrepreneurial activity that societies permit and the attainment of many states that people regard as desirable in those economies. Mises had faith that most people, if they could also understand that connection, would choose markets. In a way, his view is being vindicated by the repudiation of communism worldwide (at least in principle). But the repudiation was not accomplished by theory alone and especially not by welfare economics. The repudiation was largely a consequence of the crushingly obvious superiority of market-oriented economies over the so-called centrally planned nightmares that clinched the argument. It is a reasonable conjecture that economists can do far more good by striving to provide a combination of theoretical interpretations of market activity and empirical comparisons of actual economic practices than by trying to devise conversation-stopping proofs of some abstract welfare economics or other, especially since the latter ambition is unattainable. We can describe the economy, analyze it, and interpret it. Like good cobblers, we should stick to our lasts.

NOTES

1. Kirzner has been criticized by several writers (including the present writer [Vaughn 1994]) for ignoring the discoordinating features of entrepreneurial action. By grasping a profit opportunity, entrepreneurs strike new bargains that disrupt the plans of former trading partners. However, this criticism now appears to me to misunderstand Kirzner's use of the term "coordination." Coordination to Kirzner is not identical to plan fulfillment. While it is true that a new entrepreneurial venture may disrupt the plans of some people, the fact that it reveals the presence of previously unknown potential gains from trade is coordinating for the catallaxy as a whole. The plans that were held before the entrepreneur revealed knowledge that was previously hidden were plans now revealed to have been made in error. Had actors known then what they know now, they never would have made those erroneous plans. Hence, while people must revise their plans in light of new knowledge, the system as a whole is more coordinated because the new knowledge is taken into account.

2. Austrian economics is no worse off than neoclassical economics in regard to examining the welfare implications of pecuniary externalities. In fact, the consensus in neoclassical economics is that they are safely ignored (Laffont 1987, 264).

3. The belief that one is disadvantaged by the superior market performance of one's competitors surely is the motivation for "rent-seeking" behavior, trying to get government to offer protection from competition. While rent seeking is regarded to be welfare reducing because of "dead weight loss," what is sought is a form of property right that prevents others from trespassing on either markets or customers. To say, then, that markets require enforced property rights is unhelpful unless the kinds of desirable property rights for a market economy are specified.

4. Cowen (1990) has recently proposed several criteria for evaluating an economy according to innovation, complexity, and provision of consumer goods. While I have no quarrel with examining economies according to these standards, I wonder why individuals would regard the first two criteria as good in themselves. Innovation, complexity, and the provision of consumer goods are characteristics of modern economies that are potential means to the ends of increased well-being of individuals.

5. This is Hayek's basic point in *Law, Legislation and Liberty* (Hayek 1976, 126–128) where he argues that all that can be accomplished by good rules is to improve any individual's chances of success in a market order. "Even in a game with equal chances for all players there will be some winners and some losers . . . The aim of legislation, in laying down rules for an unknown number of future instances, can therefore be only to increase the chances of unknown persons whose opportunities will chiefly depend on their individual knowledge and skill as well as on the particular conditions in which accident will place them" (126).

6. For a thorough review of Austrian views of externalities, see Cordato (1992, 15ff). For a critique of the Rothbard-Cordato view of externalities, see Prychitko (1994).

7. In his recent book, Cordato (1992) argues that the appropriate welfare economics is one that does not attempt to evaluate particular market practices but rather confines itself to establishing the ideal institutional setting for markets. While this has some precedent in Hayek's (1976) discussions of the rules of just order in *Law, Legislation and Liberty*, I am skeptical that a complete set of ideal rules can be devised a priori by theoretical economists. See also Hamlin (1994).

8. Prychitko (1994) argues in a similar vein when he objects to abstract, formal welfare criterion and suggests the need for a more empirical defense of market economies.

9. One model for the kind of work that can be done to great effect is Peter Berger's (1988) book, *The Capitalist Revolution: Fifty Propositions About Prosperity, Equality and Liberty*. This book is an effective contribution to welfare economics from my perspective because it compares political-economic systems across many dimensions that most people would regard as important.

REFERENCES

Berger, P. 1988. *The Capitalist Revolution: Fifty Propositions about Prosperity, Equality and Liberty*. New York: Basic Books.

Buchanan, J. M. 1969. *Cost and Choice*. Chicago: Markham Publishing.

Chipman, J. S. 1987. "Compensation Principle." In *The New Palgrave Dictionary of Economics*, edited by J. Eatwell, M. Milgate, and P. Newman, 524–531. London: MacMillan Press.

Cordato, R. E. 1992. *Welfare Economics and Externalities in an Open-Ended Universe: A Modern Austrian Perspective*. Dordrecht, Netherlands: Kluwer Academic Publishers.

Cowen, T. 1990. "What a non-Paretian Welfare Economics Would Have to Look Like." In *Economics and Hermeneutics*, edited by D. Lavoie, 285–298. London: Routledge.

Feldman, A. 1987. "Welfare Economics." In *The New Palgrave Dictionary of Economics*, edited by J. Eatwell, M. Milgate, and P. Newman, 889–895. London: MacMillan Press.

Hamlin, A. P. 1994. "On the Possibility of Austrian Welfare Economics." In *Austrian Economics: Tensions and New Directions*, edited by S. Boehm and B. Coldwell.

Hayek, F. A. 1948. "The Use of Knowledge in Society." In *Individualism and Economic Order*, 77–91. Chicago: University of Chicago Press.

———. 1976. *Law, Legislation and Liberty*. Vol 2: *The Mirage of Social Justice*. Chicago: University of Chicago Press.

———. 1978. "Competition as a Discovery Procedure." In *New Studies in Philosophy, Politics, Economics and the History of Ideas*, 179–190. Chicago: University of Chicago Press.

Kirzner, I. M. 1973. *Competition and Entrepreneurship*. Chicago: University of Chicago Press.

———. 1979. *Perception, Opportunity and Profit: Studies in the Theory of Entrepreneurship*. Chicago: University of Chicago Press.

———. 1985a. *Discovery and the Capitalist Process*. Chicago: University of Chicago Press.

———. 1985b. "The Perils of Regulation." In *Discovery and the Capitalist Process*, edited by I. M. Kirzner, 119–149. Chicago: University of Chicago Press.

———. 1992. *The Meaning of the Market Process*. London: Routledge.

Laffont, J. J. 1987. "Externalities." In *The New Palgrave Dictionary of Economics*, edited by J. Eatwell, M. Milgate, and P. Newman. London: MacMillan Press.

Mises, Ludwig. 1963. *Human Action*. New Haven, CT: Yale University Press.

Prychitko, D. L. 1994. "Welfare Economics and Austrian Economics." *Critical Review* 7 (4): 567–592.

Rothbard, M. N. 1956. "Toward a Reconstruction of Utility and Welfare Economics." In *On Freedom and Free Enterprise*, edited by M. Sennholz, 224–262. Princeton, NJ: D. Van Nostrand.

———. 1962. *Man, Economy and State*. Princeton, NJ: D. Van Nostrand.

Vaughn, K. I. 1994. *Austrian Economics in America: The Migration of a Tradition*. Cambridge: Cambridge University Press.

Chapter 8
Hayek's Implicit Economics
Rules and the Problem of Order

From Menger to the present day, economists working in the Austrian tradition have displayed an ambivalent attitude toward the use of equilibrium constructs in economic analysis. On the one hand, they have repeatedly argued that economics should be primarily concerned with explaining economic processes that generate spontaneous economics orders. On the other, they have been reluctant to attempt to explain market processes without reference to some more or less standard notion of equilibrium to ground the analysis.

In Menger, the ambivalence shows itself in his references to prices that reflect the "full economic situation," despite the disproportionate weight that he gives to the growth of knowledge in explaining economic development. Similarly in Mises's *Human Action*, one finds a verbal analysis of evolutionary market processes as well as a justification for employing Mises's own notion of equilibrium, the evenly rotating economy, to illuminate aspects of a market order. Hayek's early work on capital theory makes full use of equilibrium reasoning while his positions in the economic calculation debate show his deep reservations about the appropriateness of the way equilibrium notions are employed by economists.

While the ambivalent attitude toward equilibrium has been a part of Austrian economics from its beginnings, it was largely Hayek's ruminations on the subject that called attention to the problematic nature of using equilibrium theorizing to capture the essence of a market process. In essays written

Originally published in *Review of Austrian Economics* 11, no. 1–2 (1989): 129–144. Republished with permission.

in the 1930s and 1940s, and especially his 1937 article, "Economics and Knowledge," Hayek raised questions about the meaning and use of equilibrium that led later Austrians to debate the usefulness of equilibrium analysis for explaining market processes. Israel Kirzner and Ludwig Lachmann were the main players in the debate of the late 1970s and early 1980s (Vaughn 1992), but the issue permeated the emerging American Austrian community and made for a temporary intellectual connection between Austrians and post-Keynesians.

Kirzner and his allies argued that it was crucial to describe the entrepreneurial function as "coordinating" where coordinating is a close cousin of, and sometimes a synonym for, equilibrating (Kirzner 1992, 3–37). Unless one could claim that entrepreneurs tended to coordinate otherwise discoordinated economic actions, Austrians would lose all claim to showing the fundamental order of a market economy, the order that they, along with Hayek, regarded as an empirical fact. To these Austrians, some notion that bore at least a family resemblance to conventional equilibrium was essential for preserving the theoretical explanation of economic order. Lachmann and his allies, however, argued from a Shacklean perspective that equilibrium (except of the individual actor) was utterly incompatible with theorizing about an ongoing market process that takes place in real time. If the future is created out of the undetermined choices of present actors, the notion of moving toward a particular equilibrium is incoherent (Buchanan and Vanberg 1991). When O'Driscoll and Rizzo (1985) attempted a reconciliation of the two views with their theory of "pattern coordination" (1985, 85–88), a theory that described a situation in which some features of a market action were perfectly coordinated (or in equilibrium) while others were open-ended and capable of generating Shacklean surprise, it satisfied neither side.[1]

Among neo-Austrians, the debates over the use of equilibrium that took place in the seventies and eighties appear to have died down. Many Austrians apparently accept the Kirzner-Garrison thesis that Austrian economics claims the "middle ground" between the perfect knowledge assumptions of general equilibrium theory and the total ignorance that they attribute to the Lachmann-Shackle position. In the middle ground, Kirzner argues, "Equilibrium is indeed never attained, yet the market does exhibit powerful tendencies towards it" (1992, 5). While others may find the "middle ground" unconvincing (Vaughn 1997), this is not the place to launch into a point-by-point critique. Rather, my purpose here is more constructive. I propose to demonstrate that an explanation of economic order that does not rely on commonly available equilibrium constructs and still demonstrates the systematic regularities that Kirzner rightfully insists upon is not only possible but is actually implicit in the writings of Friedrich Hayek.

It is well known that in "Economics and Knowledge," Hayek explored the assumptions about time and knowledge that must underlie a coherent use of equilibrium, and thereby (perhaps inadvertently) called the whole equilibrium notion into question. After that promising beginning, Hayek did not directly address the question of equilibrium again, yet the issues that concerned him in that essay shaped most of his later writings about markets and social processes in general. It is not surprising, then, that Hayek's later writings would contain the major ingredients for an account of market order that does not rely on conventional notions of equilibrium. It is also not surprising that such an important contribution to economic theory has not been more widely recognized since Hayek never specifically labeled his alternative formulation as "economics" per se. Yet, his many subsequent writings on social and political theory depend upon an implicit economics that for the most part is only alluded to in the context of other topics.

What is the central feature of Hayek's "implicit economics" that gives rise to increasing economic order? The key to economic order in Hayek's later writings is found in the role he sees for institutions as repositories of social learning. While he only explicitly described this role in the development of political and cultural institutions, his analysis applies perhaps even more usefully to the evolution of market institutions than it does to social and political ones.

Hayek's alternative embeds the Austrian appreciation of entrepreneurship within a larger institutional context of the market order. It is the institutional context that compensates for individual ignorance and makes it possible for people to formulate sensible expectations about the future. Only because human actors can take for granted as stable large areas of market activity, are they able to engage in the entrepreneurial experiments that can lead to the growth of market knowledge. Hayek's implicit economics describes a world of bounded, but unpredictable change where price equilibrium is a minor feature and may even be beside the point.

CONTRA SOCIALISM

It is relatively uncontroversial to claim that Hayek's critique of equilibrium was formulated within the context of the economic calculation debate of the late thirties and early forties[2] (Caldwell 1988; Kirzner 1988; Vaughn 1994). The market socialists, and especially Oskar Lange, he believed, were being led into a gross underestimation of the problem of central planning because of their "excessive preoccupation" with equilibrium to the exclusion of market processes (1940, 188). Hayek criticized the socialists for attempting to redesign the economy by using a theoretical construct that at best described a potential outcome of a market process and was made tractable only by assuming all market adjustments were instantaneous and all knowledge given.

We see this line of argument as early as 1935 in "Socialist Calculation II: The State of the Debate" (Hayek 1948, 148–180), where he begins to explore the relationship between the assumptions of general equilibrium and the actual market experience. Here are the beginnings of many of Hayek's later arguments concerning the nature of knowledge and the way in which market processes generate learning. Specifically, he makes three points that will figure importantly in his later writings on the market order: that information is not "given" to any one person but is dispersed among many individuals (155), that relevant market knowledge consists partly in "techniques of thought" for solving problems, and that market processes are in fact the product of the many small adjustments that people make to constant change (156). Even more surprising, he hints at his later argument, usually attributed to his 1969 article, "Competition as a Discovery Procedure," that market activity is a kind of trial-and-error process in which the most competent and knowledgeable succeed. He argues that to say that technical knowledge is given must mean that "people with all kinds of knowledge will be available and that among those competing in a particular job, speaking broadly, those that make the most appropriate use of the technical knowledge will succeed" (155).

In sum, Hayek maintains (a) that knowledge is diverse and (b) that competitive processes somehow will allow the most successful knowledge to emerge, a harbinger of his future accounts of social evolution. Further, the market process itself is a set of activities responding to constant change and not a static state of affairs. Markets reflect the numerous small adjustments that people make in response to perceived changes. While it may not "come near" the state of equilibrium described by a system of equations, that is not the point. "The essential thing about the present economic system is that it does react to some extent to all those small changes and differences which would have to be deliberately disregarded under the system (of central planning)" (156). This "essential thing," then, appears to be some sort of process of orderly change.

While Hayek chipped away at the particulars of the socialist planning schemes in a series of articles critical of central planning, it was specifically in his justly famous article, "Economics and Knowledge" that he raised the central issues of the use of equilibrium constructs that were to trouble Austrian economists more than forty years later.

ECONOMICS AND KNOWLEDGE

In "Economics and Knowledge," Hayek does not reject equilibrium theorizing out of hand. Instead, he seems to want to save the concept by reinterpreting it. Equilibrium to Hayek, means a relationship between proposed actions. To say that an individual is in equilibrium means that his actions are all part of one plan based on his subjective view of the world. The problem for economics is to explain how an individual's subjective beliefs ever come to conform with the "objective data" of the world around him. Similarly, equilibrium among several people is a state of affairs in which the beliefs of all individuals are such that they can all carry out their plans without disappointment. However, such a state requires that the mutual beliefs and expectations of these individuals are congruent with the objective facts of the world. The problem is made more difficult by the realization that one person's plans and actions become the "facts" that other people must take into account in their plans. The problem is to explain how markets enable people to learn enough about each other's plans so that they can coordinate their own actions to the actions of others. This requires, according to Hayek, empirical propositions about how people learn. As Hayek puts it,

> my main contention will be that the tautologies, of which
> formal equilibrium analysis in economics essentially con-
> sists, can be turned into propositions which tell us anything
> about causation in the real world only in so far as we are able
> to fill those formal propositions with definite statements
> about how knowledge is acquired and communicated (33).

Any such propositions will recognize the nature of knowledge in a market economy: that knowledge (or "data") consists of beliefs and expectations (49), that people learn from experience (46), and that knowledge is fragmented and reflects a "division of knowledge" (50). The division of knowledge, further, raises a central question of economics:

> How can the combination of fragments of knowledge
> existing in different minds bring about results which, if
> they were to be brought about deliberately, would require

a knowledge on the part of the directing mind which no
single person can possess? (54).

How, indeed? Stated in this fashion, the question is at the heart of our
understanding of economic order. It was Hayek's contention that equilibrium
theory as it was understood at the time, begged this central question. Since
the only justification for equilibrium theory is if there is a tendency toward
equilibrium in the real world, it simply is not useful to describe a set of equilibrium conditions unless one also has a theory of how those conditions can
be achieved.[3]

In "Economics and Knowledge," then, Hayek presents himself with a
complicated problem. If equilibrium is to be useful, it must explain how
people come to know enough to carry out mutually consistent plans, but
that means developing two auxiliary theories: a theory of how knowledge
is acquired and a theory of how divided knowledge can be interconnected.
That is, we must discover how people are able to acquire the knowledge
useful to them in a market economy and a theory of how people can use
other people's knowledge to their own advantage without themselves
acquiring it.

THE FIRST HALF OF THE SOLUTION—THE PRICE SYSTEM

Hayek makes his first pass at solving the problem he sets out in "Economics
and Knowledge" in his 1945 article, "The Use of Knowledge in Society" (Hayek
1948, 77–91). There he opens with a restatement of the economic problem
as he sees it: "how to secure the best use of resources known to any of the
members of society, for ends whose relative importance only these individuals
know. Or, to put it briefly, it is a problem of the utilization of knowledge which
is not given to anyone in its totality" (78).[4]

He makes it clear that the problem is an ongoing one for market participants, which requires them to continually adjust their actions to new
information:

> The continuous flow of goods and services is maintained
> by constant deliberate adjustments, by new dispositions
> made every day in the light of circumstances not known
> the day before, by B stepping in at once when A fails
> to deliver. (83)

Now, exactly how is it possible for people to adjust to constant changing circumstances in a manner that allows "A to step in when B fails to deliver"?

Hayek's answer in this essay is his justly famous paean to the price system.[5] The price system is a "marvel" that economically communicates relevant knowledge and allows people to take advantage of the knowledge of others at minimum cost to themselves.

To most economists, Hayek's account of the communication function of prices is unproblematic. Recently, however, it has generated criticism that Hayek's praise of the economy of prices is too neoclassical and conflicts with his earlier statements about knowledge. Desai (1996) has argued that for prices to function as Hayek says, they must be equilibrium prices, contradicting his earlier statements that markets never reach equilibrium. Kirzner (1992, 149) has gently chided Hayek for overemphasizing the information content of prices per se, while failing to emphasize that it is changing prices that really convey relevant information. While both criticisms have merit (in fact, Hayek does refer indirectly to equilibrium prices in summing up his argument [86]), the force of his argument is on how changing prices lead to subsequent adjustments, not on the equilibrium character of prices. Changing prices are a way of linking dispersed knowledge (knowledge of time and place) together in an economical way. Flexible prices make possible "constant deliberate adjustments" to changing circumstances (83). Granted, this does not entirely solve the problem of what information is conveyed by non-equilibrium prices, but neither does it preclude a later solution.

Hayek's praise of the price system has also suggested to some that he regarded the price system alone as *sufficient* for communicating relevant information (Fleetwood 1997; see Thomson 1992 for a contrary view). However, to interpret Hayek as arguing that prices are the only source of information for bringing about the coordination of plans must deemphasize (as Fleetwood does) both the context of the argument and several crucial qualifying statements included toward the end of the article.

There is no doubt that "The Use of Knowledge in Society" is an article extolling the price system. However, given Hayek's purpose, which was to bolster his arguments against administered prices in central planning schemes, perhaps the strong emphasis he places on the communicating properties of prices may be treated as exaggeration to make a point. Where Lange et al. were attempting to devise a system of arriving at equilibrium prices outside of genuine markets, Hayek was pointing out that if prices even approach equilibrium it is because individual actors can react to change. Hence the importance of emphasizing the role of flexible prices in a decentralized market for permitting the numerous "small adjustments" that generate efficient resource use.[6]

More important for our purposes, at the end of the article, Hayek places the price system in the context of a larger class of phenomena that we can loosely term the institutions of society. Even at this early date, Hayek notes both that institutions are a necessary feature of any set of social arrangements and that man did not consciously design the institutions that are so helpful to him in the carrying out of his plans:

> We make constant use of formulas, symbols, and rules
> whose meaning we do not understand and through the use
> of which we avail ourselves of the assistance of knowledge
> which individually we do not possess. We have developed
> these practices and institutions by building upon habits
> and institutions which have proved successful in their own
> sphere and which have in turn become the foundation of
> the civilization we have built up.
> The price system is just one of those formations which
> man has learned to use . . . after he had stumbled upon it
> without understanding it. (88)

It seems clear from this passage that at least by 1945, Hayek had hit upon the key to an account of the economic order that did not rely on conventional notions of equilibrium: that key was to view the economy as a set of institutions of which the price system was an important component, but not the only important component. Unfortunately, instead of going on to work directly on a more technical theory of how the price system was related to the other institutions of society to produce economic order, Hayek more and more turned his attention to "the philosophical and methodological issues" that underlay the economic planning debate (Hayek on Hayek, 79). Not that these were antithetical interests. In fact, by turning his attention to the larger issue of central planning and eventually the liberal order, he sketched the outlines of a more complete theory of the market process as well.

RULES AND SPONTANEOUS ORDER

Hayek's political and social writings are exercises in explicating the notion of a spontaneous order, a set of social arrangements that appear to be designed by some single intelligence, but in fact arise as the byproduct of human actions aimed at individual purposes. According to Hayek, spontaneous orders emerge as the consequence of rule-governed human action: social order is only possible because human beings follow rules, both formal and informal. Formal rules are the abstract rules of law that are enforced by the coercive powers of the government; informal rules are customs and habits of a social group enforced primarily through social approbation or disapproval. In both cases, rules function in two important ways in society. They increase predictability in social interaction, and they serve as a repository of knowledge that may not be fully understood by the actors who follow the rules.

While Hayek's most important writings on the nature of the social and political order date from 1960 (*The Constitution of Liberty*), the seeds of his arguments can be found as early as 1944 in *The Road to Serfdom*, his political as opposed to his economic response to the economic calculation debate. In *The Road to Serfdom* (as well as in some of his shorter papers written during the early 1940s) one can see his early objections to economic planning extended to the consequences planning would have for political society.

The central argument in *The Road to Serfdom* is that economic planning potentially leads to dictatorship and despotism. Planning requires establishing a hierarchy of ends, but humans have a multiplicity of disparate and often conflicting wants that cannot be aggregated into a unique hierarchy. Hence only the coercive powers of a dictator can bring about the necessary "agreement" about ranked goals that permit the plan to be fulfilled. Even worse, this spurious agreement will still not achieve the planners' ends because knowledge is limited and fragmented and the plan itself will bring about unintended consequences that can only be addressed by even more coercive methods. Hence, economic planning, far from being a benign supplement to democracy, could in fact destroy it. Only a system of decentralized decision-making guided by the rule of law is likely to preserve political liberty.[7]

Hayek's discussion of the rule of law here is a mere shadow of what it would become in his later works. However, by distinguishing between formal and substantive rules, he makes an important point that he will explore in greater depth later on. Formal rules are abstract and apply equally to all people. As a consequence, they allow people to predict some consequences of their actions, an indisputable advantage when formulating their own plans. If we remember that formulating plans that are capable of fulfillment is Hayek's definition of equilibrium, formal rules (or as he will later call them, abstract rules of order) are vital for bringing about a Hayekian equilibrium. In fact, the formal rules of law "could almost be described as a kind of instrument of production, helping people to predict the behavior of those with whom they must collaborate . . ." (1944, 73).

While his discussion of rules in *The Road to Serfdom* is suggestive, in *The Constitution of Liberty*, suggestions become a full-blown discussion of the importance of rules to social order. Here, however, he adds another dimension to the function of rules in social order: Both "the transmission in time of our accumulated stock of knowledge and the communication among contemporaries of information on which they base their action" are important in human social order (1960, 27). In earlier writings, he emphasized the communication problem at a moment in time; here, he explores the role of institutions as transmitters of knowledge through time to subsequent generations. In this issue we see the seeds of his later theory of social evolution.

The later Hayek became famous (or infamous) for his theory of social and cultural evolution. It was the one aspect of his work that generated criticism from friend and foe alike.[8] While most criticism focused on his formulation in *Law, Legislation and Liberty*, he actually puts forth a reasonably complete argument about the nature of social evolution in *The Constitution of Liberty* and does so in a way that undercuts later criticisms. For our purposes, it is important to note that both here and in *The Road to Serfdom* he understands cultural evolution first by analogy to an economic phenomenon: the evolution of "tools" or technology.

Hayek explains that techniques of production evolve gradually as people learn to modify existing tools to better suit their purposes (cf. Smith 1976, 20). The result is often that the original model of a modern tool might well be unrecognizable to current workmen. Traditions and institutions are like tools "which the human race has evolved and which enable us to deal with our environment. These are the results of the experience of successive generations which are handed down. And once a more efficient tool is available, it will be used without our knowing why it is better, or even what the alternatives are" (1960, 27). Traditions and institutions of society are like tools in that they, too, embody cumulative learning about solutions to problems that has taken place through perhaps millennia of experimentation.

Hayek continues with a terse description of a process of social evolution that will form the basis for his later trilogy, *Law, Legislation and Liberty*:

> Every change in conditions will make necessary some
> change in the use of resources, in the direction and kind of
> human activities, *in habits and practices* (italics mine) . . .
> Thus every change in a sense creates a "problem" for society,

even though no single individual perceives it as such; and it
is gradually "solved" by the establishment of a new over-all
adjustment. (Hayek 1960, 28)

The consequence of this problem solving is "successful adaptations of society
that are constantly improved and on which depend the range of what we can
achieve" (34).

ADAPTATION AND THE ROLE OF INDIVIDUAL ACTORS

But how is successful adaptation brought about? How are problems solved if
no individual "perceives it as such?" That is, what is the mechanism for social
evolution that allows previous learning to be embedded in the traditions and
institutions of society? Hayek has sometimes been criticized for allegedly failing to ground his evolutionary theory in individual action, but a close reading
of his account of social evolution here should lay that criticism to rest. He
clearly argues that innovations occur because in an essentially rule-following
society, some individuals are willing to bear the disapproval of their fellows
to solve problems in novel ways. The growth of human knowledge proceeds,
then, "by the selection and imitation of successful habits" (Hayek 1960, 59).
"The existence of *individuals* (italics mine) and groups simultaneously observing partially different rules provides the opportunity for the selection of the
more effective ones" (63). Evolutionary progress does not depend exclusively
on simple observation and imitation, however; it also proceeds through per-
suasion: "Advance consists in the few convincing the many" where "individuals act according to their own designs" (110).

To reconstruct the argument: Societies are characterized by a system of
overlapping rules (traditions, customs, practices). Individuals attempt to solve
their own economic "problem," often with novel actions. Insofar as others can
observe the novel action, they choose either to imitate it or to condemn it.
Novel actions which appear to enhance their own ability to further their aims
are likely to be adopted and spread. In this way, novel practices can be introduced into a society and may even cause it to splinter into new social arrangements. Insofar as the new practice also serves to solve some larger, unperceived
social problem as a byproduct of individual action, it represents a successful
social adaptation.

The question of the relationship between individual actions and imitation
of those actions and the degree to which the new practice is really "more effective," is an important one. While the implicit criterion for judgment is the

degree to which the practice furthers individual aims, what benefits an individual in the short run might not prove to be beneficial to others who follow this lead in the long run. The problem arises because of the imperfections in judging from the "outside" what has led to individual success and partly because in a complex reality, individual experimentation is never controlled. It might be that the short-run success of an individual will give way to long-run failure after all factors have had time to operate. In short, even an apparently successful practice may or may not foster the flourishing of the group that adopts it. Hayek only alludes to the problem here, but he addresses it head on in his next major work: *Law, Legislation and Liberty*. His answer there was to develop his much criticized theory of group selection.

GROUP SELECTION

Hayek's theory of group selection was a logical continuation of the evolutionary theory he had begun to develop earlier. Individuals may adopt rules that appear to them to enhance their ability to achieve their ends, but there would be no way to know whether or not the new rule would have negative consequences to themselves and/or to others over time. In so far as the rules were to be adopted by a whole society (or some large subset thereof), its efficacy could only be tested in the long run, and in competition with groups that followed alternative rules. Groups would rise or fall depending upon how well their commonly shared rules allowed them to compete for resources with other groups.

While Hayek's presentation of his group selection theory admittedly was often murky, it is important to point out that whatever its problems, Hayek was not at all expunging individual agency from his theory of social evolution as some critics have argued. Consider the problem he was addressing: How do people come to acquire new knowledge and new technologies when there is no "given" knowledge or no recipe book to read from. The adoption of rules, no matter how initiated, is always subject to testing through the experience of using them. Some sort of selection process is operable in human social orders whether we like it or not. But humans live in groups. Social evolution by definition is the evolution of rules followed by groups of human beings. Hayek, however, pointed out that it is individual minds that conceive of problems and new ways to solve those problems, and it is individuals who choose whether or not to follow a new rule. Evaluating, choosing individuals are the first step in introducing and selecting any novel course of human action.

The unintended consequences of novel actions are unforeseeable and affect the ultimate selection of social rules.

FROM SOCIAL RULES TO CATALLACTICS

While it is widely recognized that Hayek began his investigations into the nature of social order as a consequence of his work on economic systems, it is generally not recognized that Hayek's theory of the evolution of social order is most convincing when used to explain the evolution of market institutions. Indeed, if we tie together the arguments Hayek makes in his political writings with his economic essays, we see a coherent account of economic order that does not rely on conventional equilibrium analysis emerge as pieces of jigsaw puzzle.

Unfortunately, Hayek did not himself try to rewrite economic analysis in light of his work on social institutions. However, he did bring some of the pieces together in two important pieces: "Competition as a Discovery Procedure" (Hayek 1978, 179–190) and volume 2 of *Law, Legislation and Liberty* (Hayek 1976, 107–132).

"Competition as a Discovery Procedure" is important for several reasons. It contains one of Hayek's first clear references to tacit knowledge in economic affairs (Vaughn 1994; Fleetwood 1997). Fleetwood has argued that it is evidence of a Hayek III who recognizes the reality of social knowledge. For our purposes, however, even more important is the distinction Hayek makes here between an economy and a spontaneous order. An economy "is an organization or arrangement in which someone deliberately allocates resources to a unitary order of ends" (Hayek 1978, 183). A market order, or catallaxy, as he now calls it, is composed of individuals with a multiplicity of often competing ends. The market order facilitates the achievement of individual ends through competition, and the process of competition generates the knowledge that economists often regard as given.

But how to describe the characteristics of this order? Hayek once again is critical of conventional notions of equilibrium. The term equilibrium is "unfortunate" because it "presupposes that the facts have already all been discovered and competition, therefore, has ceased" (184). Conventional equilibrium is most appropriately applied to an economy. The term is not useful to describe the properties of a market in which knowledge is continually being discovered. A market society is an "order" (or spontaneous order) that can reflect varying degrees of "orderliness" and can be maintained through a process of change. While here, Hayek compares the catallaxy to a "self-organizing system"; he does not go into detail about how the system works.[9] In fact, it isn't until 1978 in volume II of *Law, Legislation and Liberty* that he attempts a fuller explanation of the nature of a catallactic order.

THE GAME OF CATALLAXY

A spontaneous order, according to Hayek, is a recognizable pattern of actions that emerges because the elements follow specific rules. A catallaxy is "a special kind of spontaneous order produced by the market through people acting within the rules of the law of property, tort and contract" (Hayek 1978, 109). Laws of property, tort, and contract support a set of exchange relationships that contributes to the cooperative meshing of plans among a wide interdependent network of human beings. The consequence of these exchange relationships is continually growing wealth for those so connected. Wealth grows because people can innovate with their own property, and the returns to their efforts accrue to them. Hayek calls this the "game of catallaxy." Gains can be measured because the price system and its derivative, cost accounting, is available as a sign of the benefit of the effort to others. In the game, the discoveries of some are communicated to all: "It is by conveying information in coded form that the competitive efforts of the market game secure the utilization of widely dispersed knowledge" (117).

Notice that once again, Hayek emphasizes the role of prices in maintaining catallactic order. However, here he notes that the price system has its limits. The market proceeds by trial and error, which means that there will be a constant stream of disappointments as people find their expectations falsified. If change is too rapid, Hayek implies, people will find it difficult to use the price system to formulate reasonable plans. Change is continual in human life, but people can only cope effectively with constant change if it is not too rapid or disruptive.

In a well-functioning market order, current prices must always "provide some indication" of what future prices will be for people to plan. For the "negative feedback" of the market to function to bring about more and more plan coordination, two conditions are necessary: that there be a "fairly constant framework of known facts, (and) only a few of them change . . . (and) . . . so long as the price mechanism operates as a medium of communicating knowledge which brings it about that the facts which become known to some, through the effects of their actions on prices, are made to influence the decision of others" (125). The implication seems to be that for markets to do their jobs, there must be large areas of stability to give a basis for handling changes at the margin.

This is a very provocative idea that Hayek himself did not plumb for further insights. In fact, as others have noted (Burczak 1994), he seems in the rest of this chapter to fall back on more equilibrium-saturated notions such as production possibilities curves and the law of one price. Yet, if we try to flesh out Hayek's sketchy argument here, there may be a way to reconcile his equilibrium-like arguments with his more compelling discussion of coping with change. To proceed, we must ask first what in Hayek's thought creates the "constant framework of known facts" that changes only gradually.

It seems reasonable to interpret the constant framework as the relatively stable set of institutions, practices, and traditions that constitute a market order. This set of regular practices is likely under normal conditions to change slowly so that coping with change is largely an exercise in making marginal adjustments to a more or less intact set of plans.

The institutions and traditions of a social order are recurring patterns of actions that in fact define the substance of the market order. By their very existence, they provide a degree of predictability in human behavior that allows actors to take vast areas of human experience for granted. In markets, humans come to rely on more or less stable market institutions to give them a basis for formulating their economic plans. While Hayek does not specifically call attention to them, markets are really defined by the institutional arrangements for trade. All trades have rituals or expected behaviors associated with them. Not to know them means not to be able to trade. Such rituals or behaviors are characteristics of all firms, personal relationships (to which Hayek explicitly called attention), and locations for trade. By inverting Hayek's original insight, we can even think of technologies as traditions or rules for action that embody past knowledge and create a certain basis upon which to plan.

Hayek's emphasis in all of his writings is on markets as means of adapting to change and on the concomitant growth of knowledge. Consider, however, what he means by knowledge. Certainly, it is universal scientific knowledge, but he is more concerned with local knowledge and with tacit knowledge. In all cases, knowledge is knowledge of some rule. What markets generate is growing knowledge about how to do things to improve one's wealth. It is not much of a stretch to call this knowledge, rules of market behavior.

A market order or catallaxy, then, is a network of overlapping institutional arrangements that facilitate the actions of entrepreneurs to create wealth in two ways: (a) the institution of monetary exchange gives rise to prices that enable entrepreneurs to make judgments about the expected profitability of a proposed venture and (b) their expectations and judgments are informed and constrained by their knowledge of the relatively stable structure of market, political and social institutions. Entrepreneurial actions are undetermined and even creative, yet there are reasonable bounds to what is likely to emerge in any given market order. The future is unknowable, as Lachmann was always ready to remind us, but the range of imagined possible futures is constrained enough by the institutional environment to make some futures far more likely than others. It is this bounding of the future by the institutions of any particular market order that makes the achievement of human plans generally possible. We can achieve our goals as often as we do because not everything changes at once, and because we know (or at least some people guess correctly) which institutions are more likely to change than others. In normal circumstances, then, Hayek suggests that most markets will likely be relatively stable with prices changing infrequently and/or by small amounts. These markets will be closest to the neoclassical notion of equilibrium and make account for Hayek's reversion to equilibrium notions in his account of the catallaxy.

However, a well-functioning catallaxy should also enhance individuals' abilities to cope relatively successfully with significant, major changes brought about by, say, important new innovations or even natural disasters. Major changes will upset individual plans more drastically and require major institutional adjustments. In a healthy catallaxy, however, existing webs of interconnections should provide enough resiliency to incorporate the emergence of new institutions as people learn the implications of changing market situations. The important question, then, is what characteristics of a catallaxy contribute to its ability to deal with major changes? One can only infer that Hayek believed that in some circumstances, markets would have a more difficult time dealing with catastrophic changes than "small adjustments". Large changes would be likely to break too many connections in the market and distort or render obsolete too much knowledge of time and place. However, except perhaps in his early writings on business cycle theory or his writings on inflation in the 1970s, he did not take up this important question. Instead, Hayek focused his analysis on the way in which political and legal institutions could affect individuals' ability to act within the market order.[10]

If this reading of Hayek is correct, we are led to an entirely different picture of a market order than is portrayed by general equilibrium theory. The value of general equilibrium is partly to show the interconnectedness of the market order, but professional focus has been limited to examining equilibrium prices and the welfare consequences that follow therefrom. In Hayek's implicit economics, these issues are sidelights. What is in full focus is the interconnectedness of the institutional structure with its regular trading relationships and established channels of communication. Within these channels, actors are constantly making all those "small adjustments" incited often, but not always, by price changes that keep goods flowing at costs as low as anyone knows how to make them. Prices, then, are vitally important in communicating information within the web of trading relationships and for facilitating economic calculation, but prices do the job within the context of a relatively stable institutional structure.

CONCLUSION

Clearly, the outline of the market order offered above is a reconstruction, not an exposition, of Hayek's understanding of a spontaneous market order. Further, it is just the beginning of such a reconstruction. It seems clear, however, that as the details are worked out, conventional notions of equilibrium as some destination of a market process or as a criterion for evaluation will be irrelevant. And it also seems clear that this will in no way increase the difficulty of explaining a coherent and wealth-creating market order. The worries that many Austrians have expressed—that rejecting equilibrium theory (even as an endpoint of a market process) means giving up any explanation of the coherence of markets will hopefully be revealed to have been for naught.

The market process is motivated by the efforts of actors to improve their own well-being. The consequence of market action is a continual increase in useful knowledge brought about as successive solutions to economic problems. This useful knowledge gets embodied in new market institutions and practices. What must be emphasized is that markets work not solely because people are entrepreneurial but also because they are entrepreneurial within a particular institutional structure. Human beings cannot learn or find solutions to problems in a vacuum. They always start from some basic knowledge of "time and place," which in large part consists of knowledge of the local institutional structure. This knowledge is necessary to a reasonable assessment of the consequences of their actions.

Entrepreneurship can only be exercised if the entrepreneur already knows a great deal about the circumstances surrounding the opportunity he believes he has identified. That is, an entrepreneur can exploit profit opportunities only insofar as he knows how to buy in one market and sell in another with all the rich detail that those activities encompass. This knowledge of "how to" is knowledge of at least the relevant parts of the institutional structure that makes up a market economy. While such knowledge does not guarantee entrepreneurial success, it does load the dice, so to speak, in the entrepreneur's favor. Or rather, it means that entrepreneurial hunches or judgments will be based on large substrata of relatively predictable behavior that will make their own ventures more likely to be successful than if no such substrata existed. So, in so far as entrepreneurial knowledge is in the middle ground between perfection and perfect ignorance, it is because there is a well-developed and relatively stable institutional structure to have knowledge of.

Austrians for years have acknowledged the importance of institutions in market society without fully examining their theoretical role. It is now time to follow in Hayek's footsteps to complete the integration of institutions and prices that he began. Only then will a full account of the functioning and benefits of a market society be developed.

NOTES

1. See the reviews of *The Economics of Time and Ignorance* written by Israel Kirzner and Ludwig Lachmann, which were published simultaneously in *Market Process* in 1986 and now reprinted in Boettke and Prychitko (1994, 38–51).

2. This does not mean that Hayek's work on capital theory was unimportant to his thinking about equilibrium. In fact, the problems of intertemporal equilibrium that he was addressing in his business cycle theory may well have stimulated his objections to the socialists' too-facile attempt to pattern new economic institutions on the Walrasian model. Hayek knew too well from his capital theory the difficulties in even defining an equilibrium position in a complex capital using economy over time to think "solving" for equilibrium prices in the socialist commonwealth would be a simple matter. On this issue, see Foss (1995).

3. For a full discussion of Hayek's various uses of equilibrium, see Rizzo (1990, 1992).

4. Stated this way, it seems as if he is limiting himself to explaining the dissemination of existing knowledge through an economic community. However, in light of his subsequent statement that "the economic problems arise always and only in consequence of change . . ." (82) it seems likely that Hayek took for granted that new knowledge would arise as part of the market process as well. On the other hand, he did not specifically address the question of the discovery of new knowledge in this article. That discussion did not appear until 1968.

5. "In a system in which the knowledge of the relevant facts is dispersed among many people, prices can act to co-ordinate the separate actions of different people in the same way as subjective values help the individual to co-ordinate the parts of his plan" (85).

6. Hayek's continual emphasis on small adjustments in the market reflect his later attitude toward the possibility of catallactic order. In fact, it is likely that he believed that most prices tended to be stable or varying only slightly in a well-functioning market.

7. *The Road to Serfdom* is a much-undervalued work, in part because Hayek himself referred to it as polemic. He claimed that he lost so much academic credibility by writing it, that he had to produce a very scholarly work to regain his reputation. While the world can be grateful that his sense of scholarly embarrassment led to the publication of another monumental work, *The Sensory Order*, given the careful reasoning and measured argument characteristic of the book, Hayek seems entirely too diffident about the contribution he made in *The Road to Serfdom* (Vaughn 1984). For similar assessments of the work, see Boettke (1995) and Barry et al. (1984).

8. See, for example, Gray (1986), Buchanan (1986), Vanberg (1986). For a more favorable view, see Vaughn (1994) and Whitman (1998).

9. For a discussion of the relationship between Hayek's theory of spontaneous order and modern complexity theory, see Vaughn and Poulsen (1998).

10. It could well be that he believed that government was the primary source of destabilizing change and that markets would not in themselves generate major disruptions. In any case, this is an area in Hayek's approach that requires much more attention.

REFERENCES

Barry, N., et al. 1984. *Hayek's "Serfdom" Revisited: Essays by Economists, Philosophers and Political Scientists on "The Road to Serfdom" After 40 Years*. London: Institute of Economic Affairs.

Berczak, T. A. 1994. "The Post-Modern Moments of F. A. Hayek's Economics." *Economics and Philosophy* 10:31–58.

Boettke, P. 1990. "The Theory of Spontaneous Order and Cultural Evolution in the Social Theory of F. A. Hayek." *Cultural Dynamics* 3 (1): 61–83.

———. 1995. "Hayek's *The Road to Serfdom* Revisited: Government Failure in the Argument Against Socialism." *Eastern Economic Journal* 21 (1): 7–26.

———. 1997. "Where Did Economics Go Wrong? Modern Economics as a Flight from Reality." *Critical Review* 11 (1): 11–63.

———, and L. P. David. 1994. *The Market Process: Essays in Contemporary Austrian Economics*. Cheltenham, UK: Edward Elgar.

———, and D. Prychitko, eds. 1994. *The Market Process: Essays in Contemporary Austrian Economics*. Cheltenham, UK: Edward Elgar.

Buchanan, J. M. 1986. "Cultural Evolution and Institutional Reform." In *Liberty, Market and State*, edited by J. M. Buchanan, 75–85. New York: New York University Press.

———, and V. Viktor. 1991. "The Market as a Creative Process." *Economics and Philosophy* 7:167–187.

Caldwell, B. 1988. "Hayek's Transformation." *History of Political Economy* 20 (4): 513–542.

Desai, M. 1994. "Equilibrium, Expectations and Knowledge." In *Hayek, Coordination and Evolutions: His Legacy in Philosophy, Politics, Economics and the History of Ideas*, edited by Jack Birner and Rudy van Zijp. London: Routledge.

Fleetwood, S. 1996. "Order Without Equilibrium: A Critical Realist Interpretation of Hayek's Notion of Spontaneous Order." *Cambridge Journal of Economics* 20:729–747.

———. 1997. "Hayek III: The Necessity of Social Rules of Conduct." In *Hayek: Economist and Social Philosopher, A Critical Retrospect*, edited by Stephen R. Frowen, 155–178. New York: St. Martin's Press.

Foss, N. 1995. "More on Hayek's Transformation." *History of Political Economy* 27 (2): 345–364.

Gray, J. 1986. *Hayek on Liberty*. 2nd ed. Oxford: Basil Blackwell.

Harper, D. A. 1996. *Entrepreneurship and the Market Process: An Enquiry into the Growth of Knowledge*. London: Routledge.

Hayek, F. A. 1948. "Socialist Calculation II: The State of the Debate." In *Individualism and Economic Order*, 148–180. Chicago: University of Chicago Press.

———. 1948. "Economics and Knowledge." In *Individualism and Economic Order*, 33–56. Chicago: University of Chicago Press.

———. 1948. "Socialist Calculation III: The Competitive Solution." In *Individualism and Economic Order*. Chicago: University of Chicago Press.

———. 1948. "The Use of Knowledge in Society." In *Individualism and Economic Order*, 77–91. Chicago: University of Chicago Press

———. 1956. *The Road to Serfdom.* Chicago: University of Chicago Press.

———. 1960. *The Constitution of Liberty.* Chicago: University of Chicago Press.

———. 1967. *Studies in Philosophy, Politics and Economics.* Chicago: University of Chicago Press.

———. 1973. *Law, Legislation and Liberty.* Vol. 1: *Rules and Order.* Chicago: University of Chicago Press.

———. 1976. *Law, Legislation and Liberty.* Vol. 2: *The Mirage of Social Justice.* Chicago: University of Chicago Press.

———. 1978. *Law, Legislation and Liberty.* Vol. 3: *The Political Order of a Free People.* Chicago: University of Chicago Press.

———. 1978. *New Studies in Philosophy, Politics, Economics and the History of Ideas.* Chicago: University of Chicago Press.

Kirzner, I. 1988. "The Economic Calculation Debate: Lessons for Austrians." *Review of Austrian Economics* 2:1–18.

———. 1992. *The Meaning of the Market Process.* London: Routledge.

O'Driscoll, G. P., and Rizzo, M. 1985. *The Economics of Time and Ignorance.* Oxford: Basil Blackwell.

Rizzo, M. 1990. "Hayek's Four Tendencies Toward Equilibrium." *Cultural Dynamics* 3 (1): 12–31.

———. 1992. "Equilibrium Visions." *The South African Journal of Economics* 60 (1): 117–130.

Smith, A. (1776) 1976. *An Inquiry into the Nature and Causes of the Wealth of Nations.* Vol. 1. Edited by R. H. Campbell, A. S. Skinner, and William B. Todd. Carmel, IN: Liberty Fund.

Thomsen, Estaban F. 1992. *Prices and Knowledge: A Market Process Perspective.* London: Routledge.

Vanberg, V. 1986. "Spontaneous Market Order and Social Rules." *Economic Philosophy* 2 (1): 75–100.

Vaughn, K. 1992. "The Problem of Order in Austrian Economics: Kirzner vs. Lachmann." *Review of Political Economy* 4 (3): 251–274.

———. 1994. "Can Democratic Society Reform Itself? The Limits of Constructive Change." In *The Market Process: Essays in Contemporary Austrian Economics*, edited by P. Boettke and D. Prychitko. Cheltenham, UK: Edward Elgar.

———. 1997. "Economic Order Once Again: The Meaning of the Middle Ground." Working Paper.

———, and L. Poulsen. 1998. "Is Hayek's Social Theory an Example of Complexity Theory?" George Mason University Economics Department Working Paper.

Whitman, D. 1998. "Hayek Contra Pangloss on Evolutionary Systems." *Constitutional Political Economy* 9: 45–66.

Chapter 9
Hayek's Theory of the Market Order as an Instance of the Theory of Complex, Adaptive Systems

1. INTRODUCTION

In recent years, a new approach to economics has begun to emerge that models economies as evolving complex systems rather than as optimization problems. Although becoming increasingly widespread, this approach, an application of the more general and also recently developed science labeled "complexity theory" by its practitioners, is still largely associated with the Santa Fe Institute and the work of Brian Arthur. In a recent interview about the new science of complexity, Arthur was quoted as saying, "Right after we published our first findings [about the implications of complexity theory for economics], we started getting letters from all over the country saying, 'You know, all you guys have done is rediscover Austrian economics' . . . . I admit I wasn't familiar with Hayek and von Mises at the time. But now that I've read them, I can see that this is essentially true" (Tucker 1996, 38). The purpose of this paper is to explore the degree to which Arthur's claim is itself "essentially true," at least with respect to the economics of Friedrich Hayek. Does complexity theory really capture a Hayekian understanding of a market economy?

Austrians might well be skeptical of claiming a linkage between Hayek and complexity theory. Complexity theory is both mathematically sophisticated and to a great degree the product of the development of bigger and faster

Originally published in *Journal des Économistes et des Études Humaines* 9, no. 2–3 (1999): 241–256.
Republished with permission.

computers that can generate solutions to large systems of nonlinear equations. As such, complexity theory employs techniques of analysis that are totally foreign to traditional Austrian modes of explanation. Further, complexity theory purports to find similarities across a broad spectrum of scientific areas, from astronomy to physics to biology, and now to economics. As a consequence, some, and not just Austrians, have been inclined to dismiss a theoretical construct that appears to claim to explain everything of interest in the world as more hype than science.[1] Austrian skepticism, additionally, could be exacerbated by the tendency of some complexity theorists like Arthur or, more recently, Paul Krugman, to use complexity theory to reveal more and more instances of potential market failure. However, despite these very real worries, it seems inescapable that Arthur's statement about "rediscovering" Austrian— or at least Hayekian—economics is in large part correct.

I will argue in this paper not only does the theory of complex, adaptive systems capture the main features of Hayek's theory of spontaneous market order, in fact it would be surprising if it did not do so. Indeed, Hayek was himself in some sense a pioneer in developing the theory of complex systems in the 1950s, when the scientific problems that were precursors to modern complexity theory were being discussed. I will further argue that the theory of complex, adaptive systems may provide a useful analogy to help in explicating the theory of spontaneous market order to the scientifically minded, and in particular, can buttress Hayek's critique of central planning. Finally, I will argue that Hayek's insights about spontaneous market orders can themselves help to interpret the results of complexity theory as they are applied to real world conditions.

2. WHAT IS COMPLEXITY THEORY?

Complexity theory is the name given to a set of ideas that have emerged in the last three or four decades from several disciplines such as computer science, information theory, evolutionary biology, and cognitive psychology.[2] In general, complexity theory deals with nonlinear systems with many interdependent variables. Because of the nonlinearity of complex systems, the history of the development of complexity theory is closely linked with the development of computer technology. Without computers, most complex systems are impossible to investigate.[3] Computer scientists discovered earlier in this century that they were incapable of programming a computer directly to find the optimum solution to a large system of nonlinear equations. Consequently, they began to investigate such systems indirectly by using genetic algorithms, rules of operation that mimic competition among artificial agents who possess alternative strategies for achieving some end. These artificial agents compete for computer time, and those strategies that yield the highest payoffs come to dominate in the solution set. Even these more indirect methods of solving nonlinear systems are highly computationally intensive, and they do not yield clearly defined maxima, but they do give better solutions than any possible alternative.[4] The claim is that such artificial agents operating according to defined rules based on local information mimic many complex systems found in nature such as weather patterns, the movements of astronomical bodies, chemical interactions, biological systems and even some human institutions.

All complex systems, whether cosmological, biological, or artificial, display several common properties. As John Holland describes it, all complex systems are networks of many independent "agents" that interact with one another according to some internal set of rules or strategies.[5] At the simplest level in biology, for example, molecules are either attracted or repelled by other molecules in a particular environment, while more complex collections of molecules have a repertoire of strategies to call upon to navigate through their environment and to reproduce themselves. The interaction of these agents gives rise to the development of "emergent properties" that are different from the properties of the individual agents and cannot be explained simply with reference to the properties of the component agents. For example, we may know a great deal about the details of individual water molecules, and we may know that clouds are composed of water vapor. We cannot, however, explain the behavior of clouds by referring solely to the properties of water molecules because the behavior of clouds depends upon the interactions among the molecules.

Emergent properties are said to be the consequence of self-organization because they arise solely from the inherent behavioral strategies of the agents acting on their local knowledge: there is no central controller to "tell" agents to form larger units, nor does any agent have complete knowledge of the circumstances surrounding its actions.

Complex systems often tend to be hierarchical in the sense that each level of emergent properties serves as building blocks for more complex arrangements. Genes organize into chromosomes which form the building blocks of cells, which form the building blocks of tissues, which organize into organs, which organize into bodies, which organize into social groups. Each level is composed of elements from the simpler level. Further, the more complex level is only possible because of the prior organization of the simpler level. Obviously, the hierarchical nature of complex adaptive systems implies that the course of development is path dependent: the characteristics of one level depends upon the emergent characteristics of the simpler level.[6]

Most important for our purposes, complex systems also tend to be *adaptive* systems. That is, the agents in these systems in some sense learn better to deal with their environment. They are continually organizing and reorganizing their building blocks according to the payoffs they receive from their activities—that is, according to the reproductive success of their new organization. Since the payoffs agents realize depend heavily upon the actions of other agents, they tend both to cooperate with some agents and to compete with others to improve their environmental adaptability. What primarily drives such behavior is the agents' ability to learn from their environment.

Learning is at the core of the theory of complex, adaptive systems. *What* the agents learn in a complex system are new strategies of action. If we think of strategies as "predictions" of the consequences of their actions (if I do x, y will follow), revising strategies depends upon some form of feedback from their actions (I did x, but z followed, try doing w instead). Where feedback exists, the system continues to become more and more mutually adapted.

As in genetic evolution, adaptability is really another word for what works in a particular environment—what leads to reproductive success. But since in complex adaptive systems, the environment is composed of other agents all pursuing their own strategies, a highly adapted system is one in which agents adapt to the strategies of each other through competition and cooperation.[7] This continual process of prediction (i.e., choosing an available strategy to fit the circumstances) and feedback (receiving the payoffs of the strategy) leads to greater and greater levels of organization. It also leads to more variation in the system as the adaptive strategies of some agents open up niches for other agents to exploit. Consequently, complex adaptive systems never settle down to a determinate equilibrium. They constantly generate novelty via opportunities to be exploited by other agents in a process that Austrians will find reminiscent of the Kirznerian entrepreneur.[8]

Certainly, there are apparent similarities between Hayek's account of a market economy and the major propositions of complexity theory. Complexity theory is about self-organization of individual units into unexpected groupings that contain properties beyond those descriptive of the units alone. Hayek's theory of "spontaneous order" is concerned with explaining social order as an unintended, undesigned outcome of purposeful human actions. Complexity theory is essentially about information; its organization, communication, and evolution while Hayek's philosophy of science, his theory of the brain, his understanding of a market economy and his theory of social evolution all revolve around his essential insights about the nature and limitations of human knowledge. Complexity theory is based on nonlinear relationships among many variables for which there is no unique solution; Hayek has long argued that economics because of its complexity cannot be a predictive science. And finally, complexity theory is about systems that have the capacity to change but are also bounded by rules that facilitate the evolution of even more complex arrangements, a very suggestive parallel to Hayek's theory of the evolution of rules of social order.

The overlap between complexity theory and Hayek's theory of spontaneous social order is more than a surface similarity, however. Indeed, given the way in which Hayek's ideas on the subject emerged, it is reasonable to argue that Hayek's theory of spontaneous market order was a verbal description of a complex, adaptive social system that at least partially drew its inspiration from the early scientific literature that eventually led to complexity theory.

3. HAYEK ON THE ECONOMICS OF CENTRAL PLANNING

It is now well known that Hayek was inspired to develop his theory of spontaneous social order as a consequence of his involvement in the debate over the economic calculation under socialism. The main issue under consideration was whether or not a socialist system could arrive at economic prices without private property and market exchange. A variety of solutions to the problem were offered that essentially relied on conventional economic theory to show how prices could be determined either mathematically, statistically, or through a process by which the central planners could iterate toward a "solution" by trial and error. To conventional economists, the economic problem of socialism was solved as long as it could be shown that the equilibrium prices were not logically inconsistent with socialist institutions (Vaughn 1980, 1994; Lavoie [1985] 2015).

To Hayek, the so-called solutions to the problem of making rational decisions in a socialist economy did not even identify the problem correctly, let alone solve it. The nub of his criticisms of socialist plans all concerned the problem of knowledge: how could planners ever know enough to direct and coordinate the actions of all of the many participants in an economy? Saying that solutions were mathematically consistent, Hayek argued, was not the same as saying that they were applicable to the real world of individual actors with heterogeneous, dispersed, and imperfect knowledge. Market economies function because individuals are able to plan their own actions based on their local knowledge of "time and place" and to revise their own plans in light of new knowledge. The price system is the means by which individuals are able to coordinate their actions with one another despite their limited knowledge. As a consequence, market exchange indirectly enables an economic system to benefit from far more knowledge than could ever be employed by a central planner.

Implicit in Hayek's criticisms of socialist planning was a criticism of the naive manner in which economists at the time were attempting to apply Walrasian general equilibrium theory to redesign the institutions of society. General equilibrium theory presumes that all knowledge is given and known equally to everyone. If that were the case, central planners would have relatively little difficulty in calculating shadow prices to help them direct resources to their highest valued uses. Hayek, however, argued that the real problem was not what to do when the planner has perfect knowledge; it was rather how to make economic decisions when knowledge was not given to any one person. The problem facing society, he argued was, "How can the combination of fragments of knowledge existing in different minds bring about results which, if they were to be brought about deliberately, would require a knowledge on the part of the directing mind which no single person can possess?" (Hayek 1948, 54). Markets are the result of a vast number of individuals pursuing their own ends who must make decisions with only partial knowledge of the relevant facts. The problem facing the economist is to explain how individual plans can be coordinated so that each person can best achieve his purposes in conjunction with the actions of others. Conventional economics simply did not address this question.

While Hayek's arguments were not dismissed out of hand by his colleagues, neither were they considered decisive critiques of the economics of socialism. Even economists who agreed with Hayek's political conclusions did not believe the knowledge problem would present serious problems for socialist planning (Knight 1940; Schumpeter 1942). In retrospect, it seems apparent that Hayek's critique was considered of minor importance because he was implicitly struggling to articulate a view of a market economy that did not fit well within conventional general equilibrium theory. It is no wonder, then, that Hayek turned his attention to investigating the methodological and philosophical foundations of his understanding of market economies. What emerged in these methodological writings was a set of ideas that points the way to a theory of the economy as a complex system.

4. THE THEORY OF COMPLEX PHENOMENA

Hayek's methodological essays date from the mid-1940s up until the early 1960s. In these methodological works, one theme that Hayek develops over and over is the peculiar nature of a social system that has a coherence that seems to be the outcome of a single plan but in fact is the unintended consequences of the actions of many independent agents operating separately. In *The Counter-Revolution of Science* for instance, Hayek calls attention to the undesigned nature of the outcome of human action (1952b, 38–39) and argues that a social theory must explain how individual actions can lead to unintended collective outcomes. He invokes both Adam Smith and Carl Menger as social scientists who understood how "spontaneously grown institutions" could develop as a byproduct of human action yet appear to be created for a purpose (83).

One characteristic of these unintended orders is that they emerge from the actions of a large number of separate variables, which means that "The number of separate variables which in any particular social phenomenon will determine the result of a given change will as a rule be far too large for any human mind to master and manipulate them effectively" (Hayek 1952b, 42). As a consequence, the scientist will rarely be able to do more than explain "the principle on which certain phenomena are produced" (42). Hayek points out that "explanation of the principle" is not confined to social science, but is also applicable to evolutionary biology.[9] One can explain the relationships between the variables, describe a process after the fact, but cannot predict precise outcomes. In economics, he argues, the best example of explanation of the principle is Walrasian general equilibrium. Hence, we see Hayek's objection to a socialist economics that relies on general equilibrium to control and predict supported by a general principle of what is theoretically possible in a certain class of sciences: general equilibrium is only suitable for explaining the principle by which prices and commodities are related to each other in a market economy. By implication, it is not a suitable tool to use to direct economic activity itself (1967, 43).

Hayek's notion that in some sciences, "explanation of the principle" is the best that can be achieved appears again in an article written in 1952, "Degrees of Explanation." Here, he specifically links explanation of the principle to the complexity of the phenomenon to be explained and argues that as science progresses in the explanation of complex phenomena, explanation of the principle may become the rule rather than the exception. Of particular importance for our argument is his statement that "Certain developments of recent years, such as cybernetics, the theory of automata or machines, general systems theory, and perhaps also communication theory, seem to belong to this kind" (1952b, 20). Each of these theoretical subjects contributed in some way to modern complexity theory. Obviously, as Hayek was struggling to articulate the nature of a social order, he was looking to these related fields to illustrate his understanding of a complex system.[10]

The influence of the precursors to complexity theory is even more pronounced in Hayek's 1964 paper, "The Theory of Complex Phenomena."[11] There, Hayek describes a set of attributes for complex phenomena that is identical to some of the attributes of complex systems articulated by theorists such as John Holland and Stuart Kauffman. Hayek's main argument, again, was that some phenomena are so complex that models at best can serve to explain past action and to predict patterns of outcomes but cannot predict individual events. In particular, he specified evolutionary biology and economic systems as examples of complex phenomena.

Systems are perceived by human beings as patterns of events that require explanation. The complexity of a system, Hayek argued, depends upon "the minimum number of elements of which an instance of the pattern must consist in order to exhibit all the characteristic attributes of the class of patterns in question" (1967, 25). The more related elements necessary to describe a system, the more complex it is. Complex systems, moreover, demonstrate "emergent properties" (26); that is, the system has characteristics that cannot be simply reduced to an account of its individual parts. There appears to be a chain of "increasing complexity" found in nature, ranging from the simplest inanimate systems to more complex biological systems to the most complex of all, human social systems.[12]

Once again, Hayek took evolutionary biology as his prime example of a complex phenomenon to illustrate his point that the exact outcome of evolution depended upon relationships between an overwhelming number of variables, the exact relationships among which could never be fully specified. Similarly, theories of social structures are also so complex that they cannot be predictive in the conventional sense. They can, however, explain particular patterns of action and rule out impossible futures.[13]

Again, as in his previous essay, Hayek uses Walrasian general equilibrium as an example of a complex system in social science. General equilibrium describes a particular pattern of price relationships more or less observed in the real world but the theory itself can never be predictive of actual prices because the initial conditions can never be fully specified. The primary value of general equilibrium theory, he argued, was not to predict the future course of events, but only to provide a general description of a particular kind of order.

While Hayek's description of complex phenomena is much like later accounts of complex adaptive systems, his use of general equilibrium as an example from economics is poorly chosen. It is true that Walrasian general equilibrium systems are composed of a large number of independent agents, but the relationship among those agents is really quite simple. Contrary to modern complex, adaptive systems, in general equilibrium, the agents themselves never interact with each other, instead simply maximizing their own objective functions subject to parameters known to all agents. Because the parameters are available to all alike, each agent essentially has global knowledge of the "true" value of the solutions set. Further, the equations that represent the agents must be linear if a unique solution is to be found. This means that general equilibrium systems can in principle be solved for an optimum using linear programming techniques as long as the equations are fully specified.

By focusing solely on the number of variables in a system and the difficulty of specifying the equations as the marks of a complex system, Hayek did not identify the *defining* features of modern complex adaptive systems: nonlinearity of the elements and the path-dependent interactions among them. This is surprising considering that Hayek's verbal descriptions of the economic order were very much in the spirit of modern complexity theory. Further, many of Hayek's later criticisms of general equilibrium amounted to attacks on the "linearity" of the assumed relationships even more than on the difficulty of specifying the initial conditions. Indeed, Hayek's whole later emphasis on the process of learning in a market suggests nonlinearity and path dependency. Why, then, did he use general equilibrium as an example of a complex phenomenon? The obvious reason is that at this point in his intellectual journey, Hayek had no other fully developed model than general equilibrium for describing the contours of an economic system.[14] It was only in his subsequent writings as he worked out his theory of the market order that he abandoned all references to general equilibrium.

Despite the inaptness of his illustration of general equilibrium as a complex system in the modern sense, there is no doubt that Hayek was at the time struggling to articulate an understanding of the market order as a complex system in the modern sense. As we have seen, he was deeply immersed in the early literature that gave rise to complexity theory. In "The Theory of Complex Phenomena," he cites von Neumann's important article on "The General and Logical Theory of Automata," a classic contribution to the theory of artificial intelligence; L. von Bertalanffy on the complexity of biological systems; Lloyd Morgan on the nature of "emergent" properties; Steven Toulmin on the ability of biology to rule out possible futures; and Noam Chomsky on the method of linguistics as related to economics. Hayek's familiarity with this literature, revealed in much of his methodological work after 1952, is important since at this time he was beginning to work out his evolutionary theory of social rules.[15] While the major influence on Hayek's social theory was probably biological evolution,[16] biological evolution is itself one of the most convincing examples of a complex adaptive system in the modern sense.

5. HAYEK AND SPONTANEOUS MARKET ORDER

Most of Hayek's work during the 1960s was preparatory to writing his three-volume masterpiece, *Law, Legislation and Liberty*. The lynchpin of his "statement of the liberal principles of justice and political economy" was his notion of spontaneous order.[17] Spontaneous orders are social patterns that emerge as "the result of human action but not of human design"; that is, "from the bottom up" through the actions of individuals directed to their own purposes. The spontaneous social order is unplanned in the sense that it was not designed by some higher intelligence or central planner. The reason that an order can emerge from the self-directed actions of individuals is that individual actors are not only purposeful, but they are also rule followers (1973, 38–46). It is the rule-following behavior of human beings that generates the order that makes society possible. Even more, the spontaneous social order is an evolutionary process in that rules that make society possible result from a selection mechanism that rewards groups who follow more successful rules (1973, 44; 1967, 68–81).[18] These rules consist of law, customs, and habits (the institutions of a social order) that emerge as an unintended consequence of individual action—"emergent properties" in the parlance of complexity theory.

Hayek regarded the economy (or catallaxy, as he preferred to call it [1976, 108]) as a special case of spontaneous social order, one that was guided by the laws of property, tort, and contract. That is, these laws are the rules that agents must follow to permit the spontaneous order to emerge. As in his earlier economic essays, Hayek emphasized the dispersion and heterogeneity of knowledge that made markets necessary and argued that coordination of the system comes about through competition of agents for profits aided by the price system. Unfortunately, apart from his insistence on the nature of the catallaxy as the interactions of individual agents who have no common goal, his account of "the game of catallaxy" (1976, 115) is too limited in purpose to give a complete account of the market order as a complex, adaptive system.

However, by piecing together Hayek's descriptions of a market economy from his various writings, it seems clear that his understanding of markets is much closer to a complex, adaptive system than it is an example of Walrasian general equilibrium.[19]

A. As in all complex adaptive systems, a catallaxy is composed of many separate agents pursuing their own advantage. There is no objectively determined hierarchy of aims (1978, 109).

B. There is no globally available knowledge: individuals are always groping their way around their local environments with limited knowledge of "time and place" (1948, 80). Hence, the economic problem is one of interaction among independent agents each seeking their own optimum; it is not a simple global maximization problem.

C. Because "one person's actions are the other person's data" (1948, 38), agents learn to revise their plans (or strategies) to better achieve their purposes. The result is that agents learn through their experiences and hence become more adapted (46); that is, individuals learn to improve their ability to create wealth by learning what works and what does not. They learn through trial and error how to exploit niches in their environments.

D. This leads to the creation of new structures or "emergent properties" in the form of new products, new technologies, new firms, new market customs (1948, 92–106). Each of these emergent properties cannot be explained solely by the individual actions that led to them. Further, these emergent structures permit the development of more and more complex and specialized forms and institutions. A modern industrialized economy is a veritable web of interlocking and supporting markets and institutions.

E. Finally, the constant change that agent learning brings about means that catallaxies are path dependent. What people learn depends upon what they know and what kind of problems they face. The existing capital stock greatly influences the shape of new investment, just as the kinds of tools and production techniques available in any one time influence the specific nature of technological innovation that occurs (1960, 27).

It seems evident that all of these elements add up to a reasonably complete description of the catallaxy as a complex, adaptive system.

6. POTENTIAL USES OF COMPLEXITY THEORY FOR AUSTRIAN ECONOMICS

Even if it is true that Hayek's account of the catallaxy was a verbal statement of a complex, adaptive system as the term is understood today, does it matter? Specifically, is there anything important to be gleaned from studying this relatively new science, or are the verbal analyses Austrian have been content to employ sufficient to do Austrian economics?

While many may remain skeptical,[20] I am cautiously optimistic that the science of complexity, by clarifying the characteristics of nonlinear, adaptive systems may prove to be an aid to articulating a more Hayekian understanding of the market order. For instance, the mature theory of complex adaptive systems can help support Hayek's central argument against central planning.

Consider the "mathematical solution," which held that all one needed was to set up a system of simultaneous equations to generate equilibrium prices that could guide planners (Dickinson 1933). At the time of the economic calculation debate, computers were not available to attempt to set up and solve those equations, so even the socialist sympathizers agreed that such a scheme was "practically" impossible, at least for the immediate future. Oskar Lange's "trial and error" solution to the problem of factor pricing was a fallback to achieve the same goal without computers (Lange and Taylor 1938). However, Lange never gave up on the possibility that one day, computers could be used to direct a centrally planned economy, making his clumsy trial and error solution obsolete (Kohler 1997). The science of complexity can finally put that fantasy to rest, and at the same time, vindicate Hayek's insight.

We recall that computer scientists learned from experience that nonlinear, many-equationed systems cannot be solved by programming them "from the top, down." Indeed, the closest computers can come to a solution is to essentially try out solutions and compare them to each other. Even then, the method of "comparing" the solutions that works best is an indirect one. That is, computer scientists approach solutions to these complex problems by devising artificial agents who are given simple but varying decision rules, providing specific payoffs to their various actions and then allowing the agents to compete with each other for computer time. In a process remarkably like economic agents attempting to make a profit, the most "successful" artificial agents get more time as they come up with better and better solutions to the specified problem. The point is that to solve much simpler problems than presented by a vast economy, computer programmers have had to simulate market-like activities to come up with workable solutions. Hence, rather than computers substituting for markets to run an economy, markets have had to be incorporated into computer programs to solve problems far less complicated than are presented by real economic systems. To duplicate the relative efficiency of a market economy would require a program as complex as the market itself and contain agents as intelligent as real human beings. Even then, it could not be used to predict and direct so much as to explain. It seems that when Hayek tried to claim that the "mathematical solution" of optimizing a social objective function simply did not come to grips with the real problem faced by markets, he was even more correct than he realized.

The challenge to today's Austrians, however, is no longer the threat of central planning. Today, the supposed pervasiveness of market failure is the justification for government interventionism. Unfortunately, models of complex systems can incorporate positive feedbacks and path dependencies that appear to demonstrate inefficient market results that seem to cry out for government remedy. Brian Arthur's work on network externalities and technological lock-ins (1989) is one important case in point.[21] Yet, if we agree with the complexity theorists that economies are more like nonlinear systems than linear ones, what is an Austrian to make of these proofs of new ways in which markets can fall short of the neoclassical ideal?

This is one area in which complexity theorists can learn from Hayek. Perhaps the simplest answer is, "Why should the neoclassical ideal be taken seriously when one understands the real nature of a complex market system?" Perfect, fully complete markets is an analytic fiction that does not apply to the real world just as it did not apply to the problem of socialist planning. Market "failures" are only failures to achieve the result of an inapplicable model. The salient point is that individual actors, operating in a regime of property and contract, are capable by trading with one another of creating an ever growing amount of wealth despite their limitations. The Hayekian question to ask is not how many ways might markets fail, but why, as a matter of empirical observation, do they so often succeed? Or, to rephrase that in the parlance of complexity theory, why do markets so often appear to act like simple linear systems when nonlinearity seems to be a more realistic assumption for human interaction?

Recently, Stephen Margolis commented that the useful aspect of Brian Arthur's work on path dependency and lock-ins was not to point out a potential market failure, but to force us to ask how entrepreneurs deal with the problem.[22] If lock-ins and network externalities can potentially exist, but we find few or no real world examples, that must mean that entrepreneurs have found ways for the latecomers to even up the playing field with the first entrant in a new market. By identifying a potential market problem such as network externalities, we perhaps explain behavior directed toward solving the problem that might not have been comprehensible before. For instance, trial discounts may be a way of overcoming a lock-in while bundling of services might be a way of overcoming a network externality. People are not perfect, but they do search for ways to overcome their limitations. Models that incorporate nonlinearities give us more tools to identify the problems that real world institutions have arisen to solve.

This approach has been deliberately followed by Axel Leijunhufvud. Recently, Leijunhufvud has been examining what he calls "out-of-bounds" situations such as hyperinflation, situations he argues are nonlinear and characterized by positive feed-backs (1995). He argues that by analyzing such situations, we can get a better grip on those aspects of the economy we take for granted. His work on high inflation, for example, shows that intertemporal markets of all kinds disappear as inflation increases, belying the neoclassical prediction that markets would find ways to contract around increased uncertainty about future prices. This points to the importance of predictable institutions for intertemporal planning, and predictable monetary value in particular. Furthermore, his analysis suggests an important new theory of how price stability in particular markets is necessary to extend planning ever further into the future.

Both Margolis's comment and Leijonhufvud's recent work suggest an appropriate use of complexity theory. At the very least, at this stage of its development, it can serve as a foil to investigate the characteristics of real economic systems. That is, it may well provide a alternative for Mises's Evenly Rotating Economy that allows us to address more sophisticated market phenomena than his simple model. By providing a set of possible undesirable outcomes from assumed nonlinear relationships, economists are directed to searching for the particular institution or practice that individuals have discovered to solve the problem.

Additionally, by articulating a set of common characteristics of all complex, adaptive systems, complexity theory can help sharpen the Austrian analysis of the market process. By describing the processes by which other systems adapt and change, it can offer an analogy to be adapted to the particular case of social change. Certainly, a theory that incorporates learning and change, the evolution of new forms and increasing variety has far more to offer economics than any previously employed scientific analogy. Like all analogies, comparisons of economies to the artificially created complex adaptive system of computer simulations will be incomplete and must be handled with care. But even incomplete analogies are often instructive. As long as Austrians don't repeat the neoclassical vice of thinking the analogy is equivalent to the real world and trying to change the world to fit the model, we can cautiously explore gains from trade with the new science of complexity.

NOTES

1. See, for example, Horgan (1995).

2. There is no one universally accepted definition of a complex system, but a very general definition given by Rosser, "that a dynamical system is complex if it endogenously does not tend asymptotically to a fixed point, a limit cycle, or an explosion," captures most of what people are including when they speak of complex systems (Rosser 1999, 4). My account of complexity theory is both more circumscribed and more historical and follows directly from Coveney and Highfield (1995) and Waldrop (1992).

3. Non-linear equations generate multiple solutions exponentially as the number of variables increases. A mere 10-variable equation system can generate approximately 181,440 possible solutions, any of which could be a maximum.

4. A simple example of such an approach that is familiar to economists is Axelrod's work on the origin of cooperation that yielded the "tit for tat" strategy (Axelrod 1984). Another is the recent work by Robert Axtell in which he generates firms through the wealth-maximizing behavior of independent artificial agents with preference for wealth and leisure (Axtell 1998).

5. While the language used to describe the behavior of complex adaptive systems tends to be anthropomorphic, it should be emphasized that the so-called agents in these models are not generally conscious, self-reflective choosers of strategies and interpreters of feedback. They are elements that follow certain rules of action, from molecules to living organisms. In computer simulations, the rules are programmed into the agent; the actual patterns of behavior that emerge are unpredictable since they depend solely on the agent's application of the rules to its local environment.

6. It should be noted that complex systems do not always lead to increasing hierarchy. In some cases, the complex hierarchy can break into smaller units as the hierarchy ceases to provide the best-known solutions to the agents' problem. See Axtell (1998) for a simulation that shows firms growing and decreasing in size as the agents' payoffs change.

7. The obvious example of a complex adaptive system is, of course, evolutionary biology. And while the exploration of complex adaptive systems is common in physics and cosmology and is closely connected to attempts to create artificial intelligence, much of the language comes directly from biology.

8. John Holland, as summarized in Waldrop (1982, 145–147).

9. Like economic systems, biological systems is an area where it is intuitively appealing to infer purpose where none exists: "in biological organisms we often observe in spontaneous social formations that the parts move as if their purpose were the preservation of the wholes" (Hayek 1952b, 82).

10. What led Hayek to the precursors of complexity theory was undoubtedly his work on *The Sensory Order*, published the same years as *The Counter-Revolution in Science*. *The Sensory Order* was a contribution to what would later be called cognitive psychology that described the brain itself as something of a spontaneous order. At issue was how humans processed and categorized sense perceptions and made use of these perceptions to solve novel problems. In support of his arguments, he cites the same contributors to information theory, systems theory, and evolutionary biology that he refers to in this article. See Weimer (1982).

11. Reprinted in Hayek (1967).

12. Note the similarity to John Holland's description of emergent properties forming building blocks of even more complex systems described above.

13. Like evolutionary theory, economic theory can rule out classes of outcomes as impossible because its "empirical content consists in what it forbids" (Hayek 1967, 32). For example, the rules of genetic variation and selection rule out the possibility that a horse could give birth to a foal with wings.

14. It is clear that Hayek was dissatisfied with the manner in which general equilibrium posed the economic problem. However, while it is true that Hayek criticized the simplistic application of general equilibrium theory to socialist economies in the socialism debate, he did not give up the model as an explanatory apparatus until his 1969 article, "Competition as a Discovery Procedure" (Hayek 1978, 184). For a fuller discussion of Hayek's gradual abandonment of equilibrium theory, see Vaughn (1999a).

15. In "Notes on the Evolution of Systems of Rules of Conduct" in Hayek (1967), he also cites L. S. Penrose on "Self-Reproducing Machines" written in 1959, an important player in the development of the theory of complex adaptive systems (Hayek 1967, 66).

16. See in particular, "Notes on the Evolution of Systems of Rules of Conduct" (Hayek 1967, 66–81), where the analogies between biological systems and human cultures is pervasive, with numerous references to experts in the field of animal societies.

17. Although Hayek began systematic study of the nature of unintended orders in *The Counter-Revolution in Science,* he did not introduce the term "spontaneous order" until *The Constitution of Liberty,* where he attributes the term to Polanyi (Hayek 1960, 160).

18. While many have criticized Hayek's resort to group selection to explain the evolution of rules, I argue in Vaughn (1999b) that group selection is a necessary implication of the social nature of rules in Hayek's system.

19. For a fuller account of Hayek's mature understanding of a market economy, see Vaughn (1999a).

20. See Boettke (1997).

21. See also Krugman (1994).

22. Oral presentation at the Austrian Economics Seminar, George Mason University, October 1997.

REFERENCES

Anderson, Ph. W., K. J. Arrow, and D. Pines. 1988. *The Economy as an Evolving Complex System.* Vol. 5 of *Santa Fe Studies in the Sciences of Complexity.* Reading, MA: Addison-Wesley.

Arthur, B. 1989. "Competing Technologies, Increasing Returns, and Lock-In by Historical Events." *Economic Journal* 99:116–131.

Axelrod, R. 1984. *The Evolution of Cooperation.* New York: Basic Books.

Axtell, R. 1998. "The Emergence of Firms in a Population of Agents: Local Increasing Returns, Unstable Nash Equilibrium and Power Law Size Distributions." Unpublished paper.

Bergson, A. 1948. "Socialism." In *A Survey of Contemporary Economics,* edited by Howard Ellis, 1:412–488. Homewood, IL: Richard D. Irwin.

Boettke, P. 1997. "Big Think, Hype Think: Complexity and its Relationship to Austrian Economics." Unpublished paper.

Coveney, P., and R. Highfield. 1995. *Frontiers of Complexity: The Search for Order in a Chaotic World.* New York: Ballantine Books.

Dickinson, H. D. 1933. "Price Formation in a Socialism Community." *Economic Journal* 43 (June): 237–250.

Hayek, F. A. 1948. *Individualism and Economic Order.* Chicago: University of Chicago Press.

———. 1952a. *The Sensory Order*. Chicago: University of Chicago Press.

———. 1952b. *The Counter-Revolution in Science*. Glencoe, IL: Free Press.

———. 1967. *Studies in Philosophy, Politics and Economics*. Chicago: University of Chicago Press.

———. 1973, 1976. *Law, Legislation and Liberty*. Vols. 1 and 2. Chicago: University of Chicago Press.

———. 1978. "Competition as a Discovery Procedure." In *New Studies in Philosophy, Politics, Economics and the History of Ideas*, 179–190. Chicago: University of Chicago Press.

Heyman, D., and A. Leijunhufvud. 1995. *High Inflation*. Oxford, Clarendon Press.

Horgan, J. 1999. "From Complexity to Perplexity." *Scientific American*. http://www.scientificamerican.com/explorations/0695.trends.html.

Kauffman, S. A. 1999. "Antichaos and Adaptation." *Scientific American*. http://www.scientificamerican.com.explorations.0624 96kaufman.html.

Knight, F. 1940. "Socialism: The Nature of the Problem." *Ethics* 50.

Kohler, H. 1997. *Economic Systems and Human Welfare: A Global Survey*. Mason, OH: South-Western College Publishing.

Krugman, P. 1994. "The Economics of QWERTY." *Peddling Prosperity*, 221–244. New York: Norton.

Lange, O., and F. Taylor. 1938. *On the Economic Theory of Socialism*. New York: McGraw-Hill.

Lavoie, D. (1985) 2015. *Rivalry and Central Planning*. Cambridge: Cambridge University Press Reprint, Virginia: Mercatus Center at George Mason University.

Leijonhufvud, A. 1997. "Macroeconomics and Complexity: Inflation Theory." In *The Economy as an Evolving Complex System II*, edited by W. B. Arthur, S. N. Durlauf, and D. A. Lane, 321–335. Reading, PA: Addison-Wesley.

Polanyi, M. 1951. *The Logic of Liberty*. Chicago: University of Chicago Press.

Rosser, J. B. 1998. "On the Complexities of Complex Economic Dynamics." Unpublished paper.

Schumpeter, J. 1942. *Socialism, Capitalism and Democracy*. New York: Harper and Row.

Tucker, W. 1996. "Complex Questions: The New Science of Spontaneous Order." *Reason*, January 1996.

Vanberg, V. 1994. *Rules and Choice in Economics*. London: Routledge.

Vaughn, K. I. 1980. "Economic Calculation Under Socialism: The Austrian Contribution." *Economic Inquiry* 18 (October): 535–554.

———. 1994. *Austrian Economics in America: The Migration of a Tradition*. Cambridge: Cambridge University Press.

———. 1999a. "Hayek's Implicit Economics: Rules and the Problem of Order," *Review of Austrian Economics* 11:129–144.

———. 1999b. "Institutions and the Coordination of Plans in Hayekian Economics: A Preliminary Look." Unpublished paper.

Waldrop, M. M. 1992. *Complexity*. New York: Simon and Schuster.

Weimer, W. B. 1982. "Problems of Complex Phenomena: An Introduction to the Theoretical Psychology of the Sensory Order." In *Cognition and the Symbolic Processes*, edited by W. B. Weimer and D. S. Palermo, 2:241–285. Hillsdale, NJ: Lawrence Erlbaum Associates.

Chapter 10
Can Democratic Society Reform Itself? The Limits of Constructive Change

This paper argues that constitutional reform, reform of the basic rules of the game in a democratic society, is fully compatible with an evolutionary view of social change. It further argues that constitutional reform can only take place piecemeal and at the margins of governmental procedures if the reform has any hope of being beneficial. There is no trick to getting bad reforms. Indeed, that seems to be the specialty of twentieth-century democracies. But if the aim is to institute political reforms that enable men to more effectively pursue their purposes in peace with their neighbors, then there are definite limits to the amount of reform that can successfully be accomplished in a modern, stable Western democracy. In order to support this, however, it is first necessary to show that the idea of reform itself is an acceptable one to those of us imbued with the Hayekian spirit.

Buchanan and others have recently pointed out a possible inconsistency between Hayek's emphasis on the gradual evolution of spontaneous orders in society on the one hand, and his call for reforms of the legislature and the money supply on the other.[1] Buchanan, who in his work over the last ten years or so has consistently called for constitutional reform of the role of government in the economic order, has criticized those who might display a too faithful adherence to some possible implications of Hayek's evolutionary theory

Originally published in *The Market Process: Essays in Contemporary Austrian Economics*, edited by Peter J. Boettke and David L. Prychitko, rev. ed. (1994; repr., Virginia: Mercatus Center at George Mason University, 2018), 229–243. Republished with permission.

of social institutions. If one takes too seriously the argument that social institutions contain a spontaneously developed wisdom in their traditions, one
might be led to a "council of despair,"[2] a feeling that any rationally conceived
social change is necessarily "constructivist rationalism" leading inexorably to
a worsening of whatever problem it was constructed to solve. Clearly, Hayek
himself does not believe that, nor could anyone who expends breath or energy
in trying to change people's minds about the nature of an ideal society. Yet neither Hayek, nor others that I know of in the broadly liberal tradition, has spent
much time discussing how reform is possible, or even more generally, how
change takes place in social institutions. This is the question I will address here.
More specifically, I will question (a) how does social and political change come
about? (b) what are its limits? and (c) what are the chances that future social
change can be in the direction of the "good society" as conceived by one
who values freedom? We focus on reform in a democratic society, as Hayek
points out, because democracy is the only political tradition so far in which
there is a mechanism for peaceful change in government.[3] Obviously, political
reform can be brought about by armed revolution, but our interest is in political reform that occurs through peaceful and willing acquiescence to change.

THE EVOLUTIONARY MODEL OF SOCIAL CHANGE

One of the persistent themes of Hayek's *Law, Legislation and Liberty* is that the
rules of social behavior encompass more knowledge than can be possessed
by any one participant in that society. These rules evolve gradually. They are
never fully articulated by anyone, nor are they in principle articulatable, yet
they are understood and obeyed implicitly. Further, they serve purposes that
are often unknown but important to the survival of the community. Hayek's
explanation for this phenomenon is that these "rules of behavior" have evolved
along with man and in a sense define what man is. Man and culture develop
together, man did not evolve first and then create culture to suit his purposes.
He is not a purely rational being who can exist or even think completely apart
from his culture. He chooses his purposes within the context of his culture.[4]

Hayek's vision seems to be of a primitive time, an early pre-history of
humanity in which language, social customs, religion, trade, money, and
sexual mores all evolved as adaptive responses to the exigencies of a difficult
natural environment. In this early time, man fought an evolutionary battle
with both other species and other cultures. Those institutions and mores which
represented more successful behavioral strategies won out relative to others
and became dominant. The more successful strategies became embedded in

tradition, and the original survival value of the behavior was lost to conscious knowledge, if it ever had been consciously recognized in the first place. In this way, tradition developed as the repository of unarticulated knowledge that contributed to successful culture.

Hayek uses this conjectural history to elucidate his concept of spontaneous order. Spontaneous order arises as the unintended consequences of human action. The individual actions themselves are directed at particular purposes, but the order that results serves no purpose designed by any one human mind. The ultimate "purpose," success of the culture, emerges solely through the agency of some sort of process of natural selection.[5]

While the evolutionary model of human development does seem to suggest a gradual building up and tearing down of traditions over long stretches of time, even gradual change has an ultimate source. Evolutionary models of spontaneous orders need to incorporate a means of change in order to be complete. The theory of biological evolution relies on mutation or genetic accident to explain species creation; theories of social evolution must have some comparable instrument of introducing novelty into the society. The possible agencies of change one can suggest for human society are divine intervention, genetic accident, or human creation—either intentional or inadvertent. Of the three, the only acceptable source of change in society to a social scientist would seem to be human action. I emphasize this because the term "spontaneous" in spontaneous order can be misleading if not carefully defined. It conjures up visions of spontaneous combustion or spontaneous generation—things that seem to spring up without explanation. Yet even in Hayek's version of spontaneous order, the order is an unintended result of an intended action. Hayek focuses on the unintended result. I wish to focus on the intentionality. Humans, after all, have as part of their genetic make-up the ability to learn and to transmit ideas and ways of doing things. They also have the ability to imagine futures different from the past. It is this ability that accounts for innovation and discovery, and it is innovation and discovery that is the well-spring of social change.

HUMAN ACTION AS THE SOURCE OF CHANGE IN SOCIETY

Social change is a tension between human creativity and daring and human reluctance to disturb the known patterns of their lives. Man is part dreamer and part follower of rules. Hayek has emphasized the important implications of man the rule-follower, but he has surprisingly downplayed the role of man the dreamer in bringing about the desirable social change. Consider, for example, Hayek's explanation of how common law (rules of just behavior) develops. Common law develops on a path conducive to spontaneous order because common law judges do not believe they are making law but discovering it. The underlying presumption of the judges is that what constitutes law exists independently of their ideas, and their task is to discover the implications of the law for any particular case they are called upon to decide.[6] Hayek points out that in the process of trying to render judgments in hard cases, the abstract concept of what the law is may well change, but this is an unintended consequence of a judicial process, that is, a process of applying abstract, incompletely articulated rules to particular concrete cases.[7] This kind of process can also explain the development of human conceptions of morality and ethical behavior. Where the "correct thing" is in dispute among men who share a basic commonality, the very notion of "correct" will undergo gradual change.

This gradualist version of the evolution of rules of behavior is an appealing one. It is consistent with how humans think and use language. Language is imprecise and words have shades of meaning, sometimes encompassing ambiguities and ambivalences that make language only an imperfect proxy for the thought underlying it. The very notion of searching for an abstract rule within the confines of language seems to guarantee a social process of dispute, compromise, resolution, and gradual change of shared ideology. Yet even in this extreme gradualist explanation of social change, someone has to originate a new idea, a new interpretation or new vision. Man is a rule-follower once he understands the rules. It is man the dreamer who fashions the rules for himself and others to follow. The real question Hayek is asking in *Law, Legislation and Liberty,* and the real question in all "conservative" theories of social change, then, is how can man the dreamer channel his dreams into socially desirable ends?

To explicate the problem, I turn back to the biological theory of evolution once again. The biologists tell us that in any species, genetic mutations occur with surprising frequency, but most mutations are evolutionary dead ends. They are either irrelevant to the organism, or harmful in some way. Organisms that suffer from serious mutations are usually physically defective and/or sterile and hence present no danger to their species from interbreeding with normal individuals. Where the mutation does get passed on, if it is of some benefit, it confers a competitive advantage on those individuals who inherit it, and they tend to dominate the species.

In human culture, innovations, the "mutations" of social change, are also more likely to be harmful to the society than beneficial. The introduction of social novelty is probably not as random in effect for society as a whole as genetic accident is for a biological organism since social novelty is introduced by a thinking, planning being. But even though individuals have rational minds, their ability to perceive the effects of deliberate innovation is limited by the competence of their models of social reality and by the irremediable uncertainty of a non-preordained future. In such a world, a conservative attitude toward social change can be a valuable survival technique for any group. This is especially true of primitive societies, which have very little margin for error in their struggle so close to the edge of survival. Rule-following makes sense when the consequences of deviations can be disastrous for one's group. Yet without the ability to adapt to changing circumstances, and without the ability to introduce novelty where the novelty can improve the chances for survival, a particular culture can easily stagnate and eventually die out. Somehow, the prudential features of social conservatism must be combined with a certain amount of willingness to take risks on innovation for a society to remain viable. One technique available to social orders to test out innovation in a relatively low-cost manner is to somehow isolate the intellectual "mutant" until the worth of his suggested innovation is evaluated. If this can be done, a social order can increase the probability of embracing beneficial change while rejecting innovation that would prove disadvantageous to society.

One possible way a social order might isolate the innovation from contaminating the group until its worth is proven is to socially ostracize the innovator who refuses to follow some of the established rules. For relatively innocuous deviations, isolation can take the form of social disapproval, not being treated as a social equal, and being shunned by one's neighbors. For more serious deviations, it can take the form of expulsion from the group. Expulsion is the ultimate group protection from a failed innovation, but it also insulates the group from any possible benefits from new ideas. If ostracism were the only means society had to protect itself against dangerous novelty, one would expect innovations to be incorporated into cultures at an excruciatingly slow pace.

We contrast the technique of social ostracism to another technique that has evolved to isolate the innovators, to internalize the costs and benefits of his activities: the technique of residual claimancy in a market economy based on private property. The entrepreneur is the residual claimant in a market economy and he is also the source of innovation in a market order. Schumpeter, interestingly, saw him as a "creative destroyer" who disrupts established patterns to introduce progress as he searches for personal gain.[8] Kirzner sees him as essentially an arbitrager, alert to profitable opportunities others fail to perceive.[9] The crucial feature of the entrepreneur for our purposes here is as the earner of profit and loss. His personal financial stake in the outcome of his venture is what isolates the effects of his innovation until the worth is proven to society. If the entrepreneur makes an error, the consequences are limited to his own personal wealth loss (and perhaps some external effects within his immediate neighborhood). If his visions and judgments are correct, he profits personally from his actions and his success encourages others to imitate him thus disbursing his innovation throughout society. Because of the ability of the market order to isolate the entrepreneurial experiment until the test results are in, this kind of order can afford to assimilate change of a much larger magnitude and at a much faster rate than would be possible in a more communal environment. Perhaps this helps to explain the great economic progress of Western civilization that takes place alongside a depressingly stagnant set of ideas about political and social relationships.

SPONTANEOUS ORDER AND CONSTRUCTIVE REFORM

I have tried to establish so far that in an evolutionary theory of society, change normally takes place only gradually and at the margins of accepted rules of behavior.[10] Errors are costly to the group, and unless a mechanism such as a market order arises to internalize the errors of innovators, gradual change is a valuable survival strategy (except obviously in the case of catastrophic environmental changes that must be adapted to rapidly). Further, I have argued that even in evolutionary theories of social orders such as Hayek's, the agent of social change is still some intentional human action.[11] The order may evolve as an unintended consequence of that action, but to the extent that a change is intended, all change is constructivist in some sense.

The problem this paper addresses, however, is not the possibility of any kind of change in society, but a particular kind of change—reform. Reform does not fit easily into an evolutionary theory of society. Reform seems to imply a discrete jump of some kind, a conscious break with an established tradition. Even if the reform is intended to return to an earlier way of doing things, a return is still a conscious break with the present. The problem here is, can a general theory that stresses the unintended outcomes of individual human actions also encompass conscious reform? More specifically, does the fact that orders arise from the unintended results of human action limit or nullify the possibility of reform?

There are two problems buried in this question. The first is positive: Where human actions have unlooked-for consequences, can there ever genuinely be a constructed reform that achieves a desired end? The second is normative:

Even if reform is possible, is it desirable or is it merely a destructive influence in a benign social process?

Hayek has justly denounced a particular kind of reform he calls "constructivist rationalism." Constructivist rationalism refers to the attempt to sweep away all or most existing institutions and to replace them with a new set that is the product of someone's model of how society *should* be. Society is mentally rebuilt from the ground up, so to speak, in an attempt to clear away the inefficiencies and immoralities inherent in the existing set of institutions. Looked at in this way, constructivist rationalism is simply a product of human intelligence (or hubris) and human longing for improvement. Rational constructivism would seem to be a temptation particularly of intellectuals who specialize in allowing their imaginations free reign to contemplate the "good life," but any human being could well become afflicted. Merely reflecting on the evils of present-day society—any present-day society—leads one inexorably to explain the evils and to design ways of correcting them.

This longing for a better way has manifested itself in a long history of utopian thought and utopian action. A large number of philosophical writings consist of this kind of rational constructivism, from Plato's *Republic* and More's *Utopia* to Nozick's *Anarchy, State and Utopia*. And there have been throughout history many attempts by individuals to put their alternative visions into practice through voluntary means. Religious orders, religious sects that have formed quasi-governmental structures, attempts at communal living, are all examples of experiments in rational constructivism. As we implied earlier, these social experiments probably serve an important service in introducing and testing particular kinds of social deviations at minimum cost to the larger group. Because of the inherent conservative bias of human beings, only a few participate at any one time, and hence errors in construction are borne by members of the group. To follow our analogy above, the "mutation" is isolated until its worth is proven, and society gains in knowledge. As a practical matter, such experiments are usually dismal failures to the extent that they attempt to change too many customary institutions too radically, but where the changes are at the margins, the experiment may lead to discovery of a social improvement (or at the least, an equally acceptable way of doing things). Obviously, this kind of constructivism is simply an instance of the evolutionary model of society. When a utopian group attempts to force its vision on an unwilling population, however, a harmless social experiment can become a deadly virus infecting the social order.

Hayek's objection to constructivist rationalism is really an objection to the *forced* imposition of a comprehensive new set of social institutions that are designed of a piece by some social reformer. As an historical note, Hayek first became aware of the problem of rational constructivism during the economic calculation controversy of the 1920s. That controversy involved a group of "market socialists" who wanted to eliminate private ownership of the means of production and the market exchange private ownership implies, and to replace it with a form of central direction they believed would duplicate the successes of the market while correcting its failures. Hayek centered his criticisms of the socialist schemes around the problem of information in the market economy. On one level, he argued that the advantage of private property and markets rests with the fact that it allows people to take advantage of a specialization of knowledge that could not exist in a centrally planned economy. On a more abstract level, however, he also argued that no one mind could understand all the complex functions existing institutions served and hence no one mind could possibly design a system to take care of all the potential problems existing institutions evolved to solve.[12] While Hayek's arguments were not taken seriously at the time he wrote, events in soviet-type economies have certainly borne out Hayek's view of the importance of the division of knowledge to economic efficiency. Even more to the point, Communist China under Mao and more recently, Cambodia under Pol Pot have borne out Hayek's more general view of the knowledge limitations that doom rational constructions on a grand scale. Indeed, Cambodia is a tragic example of what any sane person should call "irrational destructivism," the forcible tearing away of all civilized customs and institutions to replace them with the nightmare visions of a demented mind.

The difference between a New Harmony[13] and a Pol Pot is, of course, one of voluntarism. An experiment like New Harmony, as we have shown, is part of a process of acquiring knowledge from voluntary attempts in alternative lifestyles that do not threaten the overall fabric of society. Decentralization of experiments serves to limit the consequences of a failed vision. Pol Pot forces everyone into his mold of a "good life" and thereby threatens the entire society if his mold is defective. The unrestrained power of government is the power to turn constructivist dreams into the reality of oppression. But where government is seen as the guardian of independently existing rules of just conduct, the dangers from the Pol Pot kind of rational constructivism are minimal. This is the crux of Hayek's distinction between the rule of law and the rule of men. The rule of law serves to constrain the power of political leaders to enforce their will on an unwilling population. Constitutional democracy is a form of government that peacefully limits the degree to which any guardian of the rule of law can violate his trust.

GOVERNMENT VERSUS SPONTANEOUS ORDERS

In a sense, Hayek's objections to constructivist rationalism are not directly relevant to the problem of reform as conceived here. The question addressed is "Can Democratic Society Reform Itself?" The title should read, "Can Democratic Government Undergo Genuine Reform by Its Citizens?" Is reform something that one group somehow imposes on the political process, or is reform something that emanates from within the process itself? Is government itself part of the grand spontaneous order that describes the evolution of human societies or is it an impediment to that order? In what sense, in simpler language, do people get the government they deserve?

One can agree that orders exist that obey no known purpose, that these orders evolved through no conscious design of any one mind or group of minds and also believe that government itself is not primarily a spontaneous order. Government is then conceived of as being imposed upon spontaneous orders affecting the way in which orders evolve and function. This is largely the view Buchanan espouses. He sees government as the result of a social contract, an agreement men enter into to submit to a shared set of rules that set the framework within which voluntary orders can arise.[14] Hayek similarly sees government as the forum for articulating rules of just conduct and imposing the rules on a more or less willing society. One needs government because the application of abstract rules to particular instances is not above dispute, and because not everyone is equally scrupulous in following the abstract rules that are accepted by the group.[15]

Both Buchanan and Hayek, then, view government essentially as an organization with a definable purpose that is in some sense agreed to by the population it serves.[16] The problem the society subject to a particular government faces is that a "spontaneous order" develops within the structure of government, which in many instances runs contrary to the stated purposes of the organization. Indeed, that is the theme of most public choice literature from Mises's *Bureaucracy* through *The Calculus of Consent* to the present esoteric works on agenda control. But the governmental "order" develops after the imposition of the organization on the social structure, and it affects how the organization performs its designed functions. The order within government—the way things are *really* done as opposed to how they are supposed to work—is actually an unintended product of the organizational design itself. This seems to dictate the conclusion that perverse consequences resulting from organizational design can only be corrected by some kind of constructivist redesign of that organization. Once a particular design is in place, however, redesign may be extremely difficult. Our modern dilemma is how to redesign our present governmental organization to overcome obvious faults, despite the fact that many individuals profit from those faults and most people do not recognize the faults for what they are.

When it comes to the question of how to redesign our current political institutions, an interesting paradox presents itself in the work of Hayek and Buchanan. Buchanan the social contractarian rests his hopes for reform on a quasi-spontaneous process leading to agreement on the rules of the game, while Hayek the evolutionist draws a blueprint for the design of good government. The paradox is only apparent, but it is an interesting one to dissolve.

Buchanan believes that reform must emerge from a genuine social contract. Good political institutions can only emerge when men choose them without regard to their place within a particular society.[17] Buchanan does not actually imagine any population actually sitting around behind a veil of ignorance deciding on a just set of political institutions to govern them.[18] Rather, he uses this construct as a model for evaluating particular sets of institutions. In an analogy with Pareto optimality in the theory of exchange, Buchanan offers only those institutions that could emerge from agreement within the genuine social contract as candidates for an acceptable set of rules of the game.[19] This criterion does not dictate any one set of institutions—the ignorance of any one man or group of men about the consequences of their decisions precludes the prediction of which institutions might emerge—but it does delineate a range within which political reform can rationally and honorably take place. Within this range, the fact that a set of rules could emerge from agreement will ensure that the polity will serve the social order rather than the social order exist only for the sake of the polity.

Buchanan's model is a good starting place for intellectually choosing among political institutions. However, it suffers from being essentially a static model of political organizations. Once the social contract is entered into, Buchanan pays no attention to provisions for maintaining the abstract rules agreed upon. This is particularly disturbing because historically the United States had an acceptable social contract—the Constitution—which was gradually transformed into the sorry competition of special interests we see today. Hence, while Buchanan describes a method of choosing among reforms, he has not turned his attention to the problem of how to bring about needed reform or how to protect the social contract from another process of decay.[20]

Hayek shares Buchanan's view that political institutions are necessary to set the rules within which the spontaneous orders within society can flourish, but his emphasis has been on articulating an ideal organization of government that will interfere least with the order of society. Hayek recognizes that the "rules of just behavior" are subject to continual reevaluation and reinterpretation in human life. Hence, he has designed a political organization that will institutionalize the reevaluation process to ensure that it is done in a manner that comes close to duplicating Buchanan's genuine social contract. His scheme is to set up a bicameral legislature where one house is concerned solely with articulating the rules of just conduct, while the other is concerned solely with matters of political organization. Hayek offers no suggestion about how we might approach such an ideal constitution, however, and indeed he discourages anyone from using his blueprint to undertake major reform in a country with an established constitution.[21] While Hayek's reluctance to endorse major reform is understandable, if we are not to give up hope of better government even in the relatively free countries of the West, we need some theory of how we can at least approach the ideal.

POLITICAL REFORM IN A DEMOCRATIC SOCIETY

In attempting to answer the question "How do we get from here to there?" I really have only two insights to call upon. The first is drawn from Buchanan's call for constitutional reform. This suggests that human intelligence must be involved in the designing of man's political institutions. To rely on the long sweep of cultural evolution is to consign intelligent men to evolutionary traps and dead ends within losing cultures. The second insight is drawn from Hayek's theory of the gradual evolution of social orders. This suggests that any designed change in political organizations must be gradual and at the margins of existing organizations if it is to be both acceptable to an inherently conservative population and beneficial in its unintended consequences. Hayek convinces us that no matter how careful our designs, no human intelligence can foresee all the consequences of an imagined course of action. Even the most carefully thought-out changes in the "rules of the game" will have unexpected results if for no other reason than that people are creative in finding ways to use rules to their own advantage, a fact that partly explains our drift away from the old "implicit constitution." Gradual reform allows us to catch our errors before they lead us too far away from our original intention, while minimizing the wealth loss to those who have learned to function honestly within the old rule.[22]

The paradox that remains is this: Although in practice, gradual reform is required to minimize our chances of still greater error, reform in a direction libertarians and conservatives would favor, toward greater personal liberty under a rule of law, will not come about unless committed individuals have a clear idea of the nature of a fully constructed, radically free society. One *must* be a constructivist rationalist in the sense of carrying a vision around in one's mind in order to have any hope of achieving the rules we desire in a society that chooses through democratic means.

Reform in a modern democratic society where outcomes depend in large measure on convincing others to agree with the reformers requires the activities of ideological entrepreneurs. People don't vote exclusively according to their self-interests. They vote for political packages that have mixed implications for their own wealth positions. Hence, they have to make judgments among candidates on some ideological basis that encompasses both a view of how the world works and a set of moral judgments about the rightness of a policy. This composite view is what ideological entrepreneurs sell. They sell consensus, and in this way ideological entrepreneurs are the political counterpart to the economic entrepreneurs who coordinate activities and bring about change in the economic order. However, although they both bring about "reform" in some sense, they achieve social change in ways that are diametrically opposed to each other.

The economic entrepreneur acts to achieve his own purposes, which generally involve increasing his pecuniary wealth. He acts on the basis of particular knowledge of specific circumstance—he possesses knowledge of "time and place," to use Hayek's phrase[23]—which enables him to take advantage of opportunities others miss. He operates to coordinate small pieces of the economic order, but his individual efforts cojoin with those of other entrepreneurs to bring about an overall coordination of the economic order intended by no one conscious being. Actions in the small bring about coordination in the large. The entrepreneur himself has no need for an awareness of his role in the grand design and indeed, most entrepreneurs have no idea of their value or place in bringing about catallactic order. They are unconscious agents of Adam Smith's "invisible hand," who serve the common good through no intention of their own.

The ideological entrepreneur, on the other hand, does have an awareness of a grand design. That is why he is valuable. He has visions of how society should be, of how all the pieces fit together and of how it can be guided or molded to the ideal shape. In having such a vision, he shares some of the characteristics of the constructivist rationalist Hayek decries, but his vision might easily be one of competing spontaneous orders that does not partake of the constructivist fallacy. He is entrepreneurial in that he takes advantage of numerous small opportunities to bring about the larger end he desires. The economic entrepreneur lacks a grand vision, but because he sees the small opportunities for gain, he helps to bring about a larger end. The ideological entrepreneur can only act to bring about his larger end because he has the vision that enables him to take advantage of small opportunities. He cannot identify the small opportunities without the larger vision. The irony is that the economic entrepreneur who recognizes only small opportunities for gain, by his actions inadvertently brings about an overall order. The ideological entrepreneur begins with the grand design, but because of the nature of the democratic process, he can only hope to bring about marginal changes in the political organization.[24]

Ideological entrepreneurs have existed throughout history (I am reminded most forcefully of Beatrice and Sidney Webb), but even if they did not exist, we would have to invent them to bring about the political reform we desire. In a democracy political change rests on agreement, and agreement on the constitutional level, as Buchanan calls it, will not come about spontaneously as humans independently recognize the same sources of evil and the same methods for institutionalizing the good. Even in relatively homogeneous societies, individuals differ both in their values and in their understanding of the social order.

It has been said that people want to do right, and they want to do well. They have values and they have interests. To be able to know what actions will help them fulfill either one or both of these aims, they must rely on their own observations, the knowledge transmitted by their teachers, and the moral instruction meted out in their lives—religious and otherwise. They have to be convinced that any particular kind of reform is possible, practical, and "fair." This means communicating a particular model of the social order and invoking a shared sense of values that the order supports. The ideological entrepreneur, then, must be part teacher and part preacher.

It must be further recognized that there are all kinds of ideologies for sale and as many entrepreneurial efforts aimed at selling them. Unfortunately, in any competitive struggle, the "best" does not automatically win and "right" does not always triumph without efforts directed toward ensuring its triumph. Ideological entrepreneurs expend those efforts. The successful ones will have to combine plausible arguments with correct models, good ideas with good packaging. And being in the right place at the right time is as much an asset to the ideological entrepreneur as it is to his economic counterpart.

In this competitive struggle of ideologies, those who believe in the value—the rightness—of political freedom and the rule of law will have to grab entrepreneurial opportunities to proselytize for their program. Successful proselytizing, however, requires that there be a consistent, coherent program to present to the public on all levels. To develop it, we need to study the principles of a free society, the history of its emergence and recession, and to explore possible practical means for its restoration. But overall, we need to understand the moral basis of the free society since it is on the moral arguments that the principles of freedom generally lose to the easy fallacies of the left.

The moral justification of a free society is far less articulated than the economic justification, although ultimately it will prove to be far more profound when fully understood. It will be a moral justification that takes account of man's individuality in an uncertain world, that judges processes rather than outcomes. In charting this moral argument, we will have to take care to address the hard questions that too often have been sloughed over in the past. For example, it does no favor to the ideal of freedom to pretend that freedom yields only winners and no losers.[25] And it does no good to the cause of free markets to pretend that self-interested businessmen are altruists after all.[26] There are always individual costs to any change in social structure, there are mean ends and noble ones, there are always injustices and accidents of fate. We live in an uncertain world which by its nature can never live up to any human conception of perfection. Hence, we need to develop a morality that accepts the fact of uncertainty, revels in it and places its faith in the ability of humans to plot a course through the unknown.

NOTES

This paper was awarded first place in the N. Goto prize contest sponsored by the Mont Pelerin Society at their meeting in West Berlin in September 1982. The Mont Pelerin Society holds copyrights.

1. James M. Buchanan, *Cultural Evolution and Institutional Reform*, working paper (Center for the Study of Public Choice, George Mason University, 1982). See also Buchanan, "Law and the Invisible Hand," in *Freedom in Constitutional Contract* (College Station: Texas A&M Press, 1977).

2. Buchanan, *Cultural Evolution and Institutional Reform*, 3.

3. F. A. Hayek, *Law, Legislation and Liberty*, vol. 1–3 (Chicago: University of Chicago Press, 1979), 4. (Hereafter, *L, L & L*.)

4. *L, L & L*, "Reason and Evolution," 1.

5. "The Error of 'Social Darwinism' was that it concentrated on the selection of individuals rather than on that of institutions and practices, and on the selection of innate rather than on culturally transmitted capacities of the individuals" (*L, L & L*, "Reason and Evolution," 1:23).

    Buchanan is much less sanguine about the outcomes of a natural selection process among institutions. The natural selection model is consistent with the survival of many different cultures enjoying very different levels of material success. As Buchanan has pointed out, above a very minimum level of subsistence, there is a great latitude of material wealth that can support a human culture. As long as differing cultures are isolated from each other, relatively more successful and relatively less successful ones can exist simultaneously. Obviously, there is no basis for arguing, then, that survival in itself is a criterion for judging a "good" culture relative to a bad culture. The same can be said of institutions existing within a culture (*L, L & L*, "Reason and Evolution," 1:6–8). See also Buchanan, *Freedom*, 31.

6. *L, L & L, Rules and Order,* 1:76–78.

7. *L, L & L, Rules and Order,* 1:81–82.

8. Joseph Schumpeter, *Capitalism, Socialism and Democracy* (New York: Harper & Row, 1950).

9. Israel Kirzner, *Competition and Entrepreneurship* (Chicago: University of Chicago Press, 1973).

10. Obviously, change also follows great cataclysmic upheavals, but it might be argued that after the first shock of cataclysm subsides, society once again reverts to a form of "business as usual."

11. *L, L & L,* vol. 1, *Rules and Order.*

12. Karen Vaughn, "Economic Calculation Under Socialism: The Austrian Contribution," *Economic Inquiry* 18 (October 1980): 535–554.

13. New Harmony was a well-known social experiment based on the ideas of Robert Owen in the nineteenth-century American Midwest.

14. Buchanan, *Freedom.*

15. *L, L & L, Rules and Order,* 1:43–46. Hayek's argument for why a society resorts to government is very Lockean. Although Locke believed a natural law exists and is discoverable by reason, he also believed that there would be hard cases where the abstract rules would not be easily applied to particular property disputes and an official arbiter would have to be imposed. He also suggested that men were not given to strict observance of the rule of law when their own interests were in dispute. See Karen Vaughn, *John Locke: Economist and Social Scientist* (Chicago: University of Chicago Press, 1980), 94–95.

16. Hayek distinguishes between orders which have no purpose of their own other than the individual purposes of the participants in the order, and organizations that are designed to serve a particular end. My argument here is that government is an organization that is imposed on order. See *L, L & L, Rules and Order,* ch. 2.

17. Buchanan, *Freedom,* 128–130.

18. "Individuals do not participate in a 'social contract' that involves organizing everything from scratch. They do participate in social decision processes that involve changes in organizational structure, changes from what exists to what might be" (Buchanan, *Freedom,* 278).

19. Buchanan, *Freedom,* 223–225.

20. Buchanan does recognize the problem of gradual decay of the social contract and regards this as an unintended result of the political process that requires reform to correct (Buchanan, *Freedom,* 174–275).

21. *L, L & L,* "The Political Order of a Free People," 3:105–127. "I certainly do not wish to suggest that any country with a firmly established constitutional tradition should replace its constitution by a new one drawn up on the lines suggested" (107).

22. People have capital value accumulated in understanding a given system. To change that system too rapidly depreciates their capital and imposes wealth losses on essentially innocent victims caught in a change. The possible way to deal with this problem is to buy off the losers in some way, but the information problems inherent in this course of action may frequently be insurmountable. Gradual change still imposes losses but gives people more time to learn new strategies to offset the obsolete strategies they once followed.

23. F. A. Hayek, *Individualism and Economic Order* (Chicago: University of Chicago Press, 1948), 80.

24. The idea of the ideological entrepreneur was inspired by Buchanan's discussion of the difficulties of the usual kind of entrepreneurial behavior in bringing about structural social change. See *Cultural Evolution,* 15–18.

25. This is the naive interpretation of consumer sovereignty that overlooks such obvious facts as that some renters gain from rent control and some workers gain from minimum wages.

A moral basis for free markets must show how those particular kinds of gains are not only inefficient in some sense but also unfair.

26. This is the startling claim made by George Gilder in *Wealth and Poverty* (New York: Basic Books, 1981). To argue that entrepreneurs are really altruistic muddies the notions of altruism and self-interest. It would be far more satisfying intellectually to argue that there are spillover benefits from self-interested behavior.

Chapter 11
The Constitution of Liberty from an Evolutionary Perspective

orty years ago, in the pages of *The Road to Serfdom*,[1] Friedrich Hayek described with alarming vividness the symptoms of a decaying liberal order. The message of this troubling book was not only that there was really very little difference between the national socialism of Nazi Germany and the communism of Soviet Russia but, even more disturbing, that the same kinds of attitudes and philosophical beliefs which gave rise to the two most despicable régimes in modern history were also dominant among the intelligentsia and political pundits in the liberal West.

1. HAYEK'S TWOFOLD MESSAGE ON ECONOMIC PLANNING

The immediate targets of Hayek's book were the social planners who wanted to "rationalize" economic activity. His message to that audience was twofold. He argued, first, that no individual or group could, in principle, plan an economic system in all its infinite detail since there were simply too many unspecifiable variables to take into account in the plan. Hence, attempts to satisfy consumer demands through the agencies of government were destined to be dismal failures if judged by the stated goals of the planners.

His second and more important contention in this context was about the long-run consequences of attempts to engage in comprehensive economic

First published in 1984 by the Institute of Economic Affairs, London, in *Hayek's "Serfdom" Revisited: Essays by Economists, Philosophers and Political Scientists on "The Road to Serfdom" after 40 Years*, edited by N. P. Barry (London: Institute of Economic Affairs, 1984), 119–143. Republished with permission.

planning. Hayek argued forcefully that economic and civil liberties are two sides of the same coin. Those who are blind to this congruence have failed to understand that to be even remotely successful, economic planning requires the restriction of individual choices in a manner inconsistent with the kind of personal freedom that has characterized modern Western liberalism.[2]

According to Hayek, the institution that most protects the political freedoms of individuals is the rule of law, which binds both private and public individuals alike.[3] In order to carry out a comprehensive economic plan, however, the state would necessarily have to become involved in the most detailed aspects of everyday life, including deciding what occupations people could pursue and where and under what conditions they could practice them. Clearly, where the state required such power, the rule of law could only be a hindrance to state planning, and personal autonomy would inevitably give way to the needs of the state. Hence, the *Road to Serfdom* was really about the gradual erosion of liberty that accompanies the erosion of the rule of law in the realm of economic activity. The only difference Hayek then saw between the England of 1944 and Nazi Germany or Communist Russia was the 30 or 40 years' head start the totalitarian states had in the decline of belief in the principles of liberalism. The disturbing implication of Hayek's analysis was not only that "it could happen here" but that "it"—a totalitarian government—was likely to come about unless conscious steps were taken to preserve the tradition of individual liberty which accounted for the material and spiritual superiority of the West. What were the steps to take?

The Importance of *The Constitution of Liberty*

After the publication of *The Road to Serfdom*, Hayek believed it was imperative to articulate the principles of economic freedom and the rule of law in order to halt our progress on the road to serfdom, the ultimate destination of all comprehensive state plans. It was to this task that he turned his attention during the 1960s. That he titled one of his major works of that period *The Constitution of Liberty*[4] emphasized the importance he placed on devising the right set of political rules to enable a liberal order to thrive.

In describing the characteristics of a free society, Hayek built on Adam Smith's notion of a social order as one that results from the unintended consequences of human action—halfway between a "natural" (that is, biological) order which arises from purely physical relations and a consciously created organization which is the product of deliberate design.[5] An economy is a spontaneous order which emerges from the purposeful actions of individuals but is, as a whole, intended by no one. It cannot be said to have a purpose of its own, but only serves the purposes of the individuals whose actions create the order. Such an order is only possible, however, because individuals follow rules that make certain features of their behavior predictable. Rules are important to set the framework within which individuals can make their plans and pursue their interests.[6] To a large extent, therefore, the kind of spontaneous order which emerges depends on the rules individuals follow, both in their private dealings with one another and in their dealings through the state. Hence the importance of designing the "right" rules.

The immediate implication of Hayek's work on defining the rules of a liberal society was that governments interfere in the particular operations of the spontaneous order at their (and their citizens') peril. Attempts to replace a spontaneous order with a conscious, comprehensive plan for society simply cannot work according to the planners' expectations. However, the very description of a spontaneous order led Hayek to another, more difficult problem. If we accept that human societies are in large part the unintended outcomes of individual acts and that human actions have unlooked-for consequences, does that not also apply to the rules of social order? Perhaps the rules themselves are also the unintended consequences of other actions, and perhaps they emerged as part of a larger spontaneous order. But if that is so, the very idea of designing the constitution of liberty becomes problematic. How can we design a system of rules to protect individual liberty when we cannot foresee the consequences of our schemes? On the other hand, if we cannot in some sense design the rules by which we live, can we ever hope to change them for the better?

In order to answer this question, Hayek sketched out a sweeping theory of social change that was broadly evolutionary in its structure.[7] His theory was an ingenious attempt to provide an explanation for social change that takes account of the limitations of human knowledge. When it comes to an explanation for the emergence of and changes in the rules of social order, however, Hayek went both too far and not far enough in his recognition of these limits.

2. THE EVOLUTION OF RULES

In his three-volume work, *Law, Legislation and Liberty*, Hayek builds on the notion of a spontaneous order arising from human action but not from human design to explain the emergence of the rules of social behavior as the product of an evolutionary process. He argues that, to a large extent, some of the most fundamental aspects of human culture—language, values, and laws—were adaptations to primitive man's struggle for existence. In some prehistoric time, man was engaged in an evolutionary competition both with other species and with competing human cultures. Those institutions and cultural norms which gave some groups more successful behavioral strategies won out relative to others and became dominant. The more successful strategies became embedded in tradition and continued to be practiced long after the reason for doing so became lost to conscious knowledge. Indeed, the value of a particular strategy might never have been consciously recognized by anyone since success did not depend at all on any individual knowing why the rules worked—just so long as members of the group followed them.[8]

The Survival of Rules and Cultures

Not all the rules that survived and became embedded in tradition, however, were necessarily crucial to the success of the community. What survived were bundles of rules in which important practices would be mixed with irrelevant or perhaps even harmful ones. Yet, so long as the entire set of rules was better adapted than any other existing set, the culture would thrive. Since no one knew for certain the purposes of a particular rule, it would be difficult for individuals consciously to break apart the bundles and reject less-preferred rules in favor of better ones. Since the danger of eliminating a crucial rule would normally outweigh the benefits of introducing a potentially better one into the group, the most viable strategy for a group to follow would be to permit very few changes in the rules. It was therefore not human consciousness but the differential survival of cultures that discriminated among various social rules.

The limitations of man's knowledge is a powerful argument against attempts to introduce drastic change into the accepted rules of social order. While change undeniably does, and often must, take place (otherwise there would have been no human cultural evolution), Hayek infers from his analysis that only when it proceeds slowly and at the margins of a culture will the dangers be minimized of making fatal errors which could seriously undermine the viability of a society. Tradition is valuable, human rationality has limits, and the benefit of the doubt should be given to the *status quo*. And, at least in Hayek's "rude and elementary state," good rules will, apparently, win out in an evolutionary competition.

This is admittedly a conservative message—so conservative indeed that some commentators have argued that it could inspire either an attitude of individual impotence in the great sweep of history (a feeling that there is no purpose in individual efforts directed to the improvement of society), or an unwarranted optimism that everything will work out in the end.[9] Yet neither attitude is justified by a closer examination of this evolutionary theory of the rules of social order.

The Implausibility of the Hayekian Account in Complex Societies

Hayek's account of the origin of rules seems plausible for the early dawn of human culture. It is, however, far less plausible an explanation of the survival of rules in modern, complex societies. There is no question that there are limits to the kinds of rules which will allow cultures to persist; for instance, a culture which requires its members to practice celibacy obviously will not flourish, as the Shaker community in the United States discovered earlier this century. Yet casual empiricism reveals a wide degree of cultural variety consistent with the survival of a group in the modern world.[10]

It may be true that the amount of cultural variability consistent with survival was much smaller in prehistoric times because of a very primitive technology or a very parsimonious environment. It may also be true that the kinds of cultural norms which evolved in the prehistory of the human race were of a very general, basic nature that we would take for granted as defining the characteristics of a human being. For example, such traits as parental involvement in child rearing, and an ability to form co-operative groups or to subordinate one's immediate goals to a more long-range purpose may have been the basic cultural traits which evolved first before the wide variety of practices we call "culture" could begin to emerge. Yet these most basic traits may have been the ones which distinguished successful from unsuccessful human groups. The variety of cultural practices and the artefacts which accompany them may have developed only with advancing technology long after the cutting edge of survival ceased to be a ruthless discriminator among societies. But if, at least in the modern world, physical survival is not the screen by which various rules of social order are selected, what is? Or is there no screen at all?

No Rule-Selecting Evolutionary Process in Politics

I shall argue that, at least in the case of ideas about appropriate political rules, there is no valid evolutionary explanation in the sense of describing unidirectional change and a selection mechanism which operates in favor of some rules above others.[11] While there are many aspects of human culture that can be explained by the use of evolutionary models incorporating selection mechanisms, the rules of the political order simply change. More importantly, there is no sense in which "good" rules—that is, rules consistent with individual freedom—necessarily win out in an evolutionary struggle. Good rules of political organization must be constructed and vigilantly maintained by active partisans whose ideas may or may not prevail in competition with others.

Hayek to some extent shares this view. If we examine his work over the last 40 years, it is obvious that he believes the case for a free society must be articulated and advocated. He certainly does not *in practice* rely on the long sweep of evolution to bring about the optimal rules of a just order. Indeed, the major thrust of his arguments has been that the hallmarks of civilization—the ideas of the rule of law and of limited government—have deteriorated in Western culture. Essentially, for 40 years Hayek has been trying to restore a tradition that has gone into decline. The wisdom inherent in the deliberations of the Founding Fathers of America and in the Gladstonian era in Britain has, Hayek believes, been lost. And the unhappy consequence is that our political institutions have been gradually eroding individual liberty. His intellectual activities have therefore been aimed at changing the way in which people understand political and social reality, and at changing their values in order to make it possible to reform the structure and rules of government. For all his emphasis on tradition, Hayek's program has been revolutionary. To seek to bring about a transformation of popular political ideology is revolutionary, even if the transformation is back toward an earlier set of views.[12]

For someone who explains the emergence of rules as a product of evolution, this ideological activism would seem to be a contradiction. Yet when we consider the mechanism by which cultures—and the ideas of which they consist—evolve, there is no real contradiction. In any evolutionary explanation of social phenomena, the ultimate source of novelty and hence of change must be human choice. Spontaneous orders may emerge as the product of the unintended consequences of human action, but the actions themselves originate from human intention.[13] And, while the intentions of human beings are rarely fulfilled according to their expectations, the only way we have a chance of influencing the outcome is to participate in the game. The outcome is in no sense preordained: it depends on who the players are and on how well they play.

In order to assess the possibility of success for such a revolutionary venture, I want first to explore the reason for the ideological decline which Hayek so decries. The interesting question here is how an evolutionary explanation of the rules of social order can be compatible with a degeneration into a less "adapted" state. We can imagine that it might take a long time for the particularly felicitous notion of limited government to emerge, and we can accept that it might emerge not in some triumphant march of progress but from a lucky accident—as Tollison and Ekelund have recently argued.[14] But given that ideas such as limited government and the rule of law *did* emerge within a society to the great benefit of the population, how then do we account for a deterioration or retrogression of political ideology within that society?[15] While notions of improvement and deterioration are admittedly difficult to pin down in theories of social change, it is a puzzle why, in a democracy allowing individuals some political choice, a political organization which yields obvious material benefits and expands personal autonomy should be so vulnerable to attack from opposing ideologies.

Special-Interest Groups Undermine Democracies

Hayek's answer, and the dominant explanation among economists today, is that unconstrained democracies provide an open invitation to special-interest groups to compete for ways to use government to further their own ends at the expense of the general welfare of the community.[16] Although this is a powerful explanation of the mechanism by which limited government breaks down, it only partly answers the question. First, the United States did not begin as an unconstrained democracy. It began as a constitutional republic in which "superior" notions of republicanism gave way to "inferior" ideas of democracy. Even more to the point, changes in the rules of a democratic society have in some sense to be agreed upon by the population—or at least not arouse vigorous opposition. Why, therefore, even in an unconstrained democracy, are interest groups so able to operate to the detriment of society as a whole? How do they so easily convince others to go along with their activities when the result is not only a decline in the rule of law but also in the material and spiritual benefits which have accompanied it?

The economist's ready answer to this question, which I fully accept so far as it goes, points to the relative costs and benefits of interest-group action. Interest groups have much to gain by lobbying for special favors from government, while the average individual citizen stands to lose very little by their actions. Hence, interest groups have a much stronger incentive to organize to seek gain through preferential treatment than individuals have to organize to stop them.[17] While that explanation is important, there is surely more to the story. Specifically, no interest group ever lobbies publicly for its own direct benefit; it always claims that its activities are in the public interest in some sense. Thus, it must be believed that people generally are not in favor of using government for personal gain—otherwise there would be no purpose in trying to construct elaborate public-interest cover stories for essentially selfish requests. My question, then, is this: Why is it so easy for interest groups to win on the ideological plane? Why, for example, has Lee Iacocca[18] emerged in the United States as a pop hero rather than an unpopular figure? The answer is that democracy (and, to a lesser extent, republicanism) requires individuals to make political decisions as if they possessed more knowledge than it would ever be worth their while to possess. Moreover, for some issues, it may even require citizens to act as if they had more knowledge than it is even in principle *possible* for them to possess.

3. KNOWLEDGE AND POLITICAL REALITY

One of the defining characteristics of a democracy is that its citizens choose their leaders and have influence over government policy. Let us consider, then, the contrast between an individual attempting to participate intelligently in the political process with the same individual attempting to make intelligent decisions in the market process. In order to use the market to achieve his purposes, it is not necessary for him to know why it works; he needs only to know how to use it. In this sense, participating in market institutions is much like learning to drive a car or use a word-processor. There is a complicated theory, known to someone, which explains how the device functions; but an individual user does not have to understand the theory to benefit from its services. Furthermore, because he has the ready measure of prices available to him in markets, an individual can easily assess the value to him of a particular market transaction. And when particular market institutions emerge to help organize transactions, an individual can decide without difficulty whether the institution is to his benefit. He can learn to use the institution either directly or by imitating others, and he can determine its efficiency by referring to his profit-and-loss statement.[19] When a market institution helps individuals to improve their profits, the institution will spread as people avail themselves of its advantages—and it will tend to become an established practice. (A good example is the rapid advance of money market funds once the idea occurred to someone to organize banking in that way.)

For aspects of culture such as the growth of economic institutions (or changes in technologies) where individuals can fairly easily acquire information about the consequences of an innovation, there is an obvious selection process at work. If an innovation is "efficient" in the narrow economic sense of that word, it has a competitive advantage over other techniques and will succeed. Individuals seek to improve their own well-being, but the unintended consequence of their actions is a more complex, integrated social order. Because this model of an evolutionary system where the "fittest" survive permeates the literature of economics, it is not surprising that Hayek, an economist, should have wanted to generalize the model to other forms of cultural change, including the emergence and selection of rules of social order.

Individuals and Rule-Changing Decisions

This can be contrasted with the problem facing a citizen in a democratic society who is required to take a position on a proposed change in political rules. In the first place, while we might think of him attempting to use the political system for his own purposes, the latter are complicated because they include some desire to live in a "good" society—whatever that may mean to an individual. Thus, his purposes involve some idea about how people's activities, including his own, should be constrained. One problem is that such preferences are generally not articulated clearly by an individual. Even if we assume they are, he still faces a considerable difficulty in making a reasoned political decision. To make an intelligent decision on some change in political rules—some change in constitutional design, perhaps—an individual must try to understand the rule, determine its possible consequences, assess the impact of those consequences on him, and then make a moral judgment about the desirability of the new rule. All this implicitly requires an individual citizen to develop a theory of social causation and to apply it to particular instances. He may not develop a particularly profound or carefully reasoned theory; but political judgments are nevertheless based on some kind of social theory which relates rules to certain outcomes and includes moral judgments about those outcomes. The problem for the individual is that there is no political equivalent of a profit-and-loss statement to help him determine whether he has made the right judgment about the political process. The political party is a poor substitute.

Ideology as an "Economizing" Device

In part, citizens resolve this problem by subscribing to an ideology—a set of beliefs an individual holds about the world and his role in it. An ideology is composed of a set of theories about social causal relationships combined with a set of values pertaining to those relationships. It can be thought of as an economizing device for dealing with a complex reality, most of which individuals cannot investigate completely in order to choose their actions. Since individuals are faced with the unavoidable problem of having to make decisions and act on the basis of very little information, they use their ideologies as proxies for the missing information. Ideology is not only important for the individual because it gives him a basis for making judgments about the appropriateness of certain actions—his own and those of others; it also has a social value in that insofar as a society is characterized by a shared ideology, it enables people to predict large areas of social reality. That people generally take their ideology for granted at any one time is probably of the highest significance. And, like the unconscious adherence to the rules of social order which Hayek describes,[20] most people hold as part of their ideologies an unarticulated set of beliefs which may very well have contradictory parts. Hence, an ideology does not have to be an accurate picture of reality in order to serve a useful social function. As long as it is "good enough" to allow the individuals to function in the social realm, it serves its purpose. However, when for some reason an individual finds his ideology no longer to be "good enough"—when, for instance, he is faced with some crisis or with the necessity of making a decision among alternatives that call on contradictory or missing elements in his beliefs—then he is forced to make a conscious alteration in his beliefs—in his causal model of the world and/or in his values.[21] The problem is that, for the most part, he has very few markers to help him choose which alteration to make. More to the point, in many instances there is no one correct choice available to him—no "right" course of action open to him if only he would take the time to search for it.

In all aspects of his deliberations about political policies (except, ideally, in his formation of a moral judgment), an individual is in much the same position as a social scientist trying to develop theories of social change. In arriving at political judgments, a citizen of a democracy—insofar as he participates in the political process—must act as a social scientist. But that also means he faces the same limitations as does a social scientist. The problem the social scientist faces in attempting to test his theories is that he confronts a complex reality where it is impossible to make crucial empirical experiments. The tests of his theory, either in terms of logical coherence and/or indirectly through statistical inference, are never conclusive. No test of a hypothesis, even if it is both statistically significant and logically coherent, is immune from attack from those who offer an alternative explanation based on another logically coherent theory.[22] Professional scientists have developed methods for dealing with these problems which define what is considered to be an adequate explanation for a particular event. While the methods are not without problems, there is a community of specialists who at least agree to the rules of the game. Nevertheless, because of the problems of experimentation with a complex reality, social scientists never manage to reach the degree of agreement that characterizes many of the "hard" sciences. Clearly, if it is difficult for social scientists who specialize in the production of theories of social reality to reach theoretical agreement, how much more difficult will it be for an ordinary citizen to arrive at a reasoned choice of rules? It is no wonder, therefore, that the average citizen solves this problem, not by joining some scientific community, but by subscribing to and making use of an ideology.

Unpredictability of Change Where No Objective Social "Truth" Exists

We can assume that, when faced with the necessity of making a decision that does not fit conveniently into his existing ideology, an individual will attempt to alter his ideology to make it more consistent with reality. And given the difficulties involved in this exercise, he will search for a consensus among his peers—perhaps guided by the advice of experts he trusts. But this only substitutes one information problem for another. How does he judge among competing experts? Where there is no objective social "truth," no theory which is widely accepted—even among experts—about the consequences of alternative rules for a social order, then changes in ideology are unpredictable at best. Indeed, I would go so far as to argue that shifts in political ideology frequently have a large random element when evaluated from the perspective of the cogency of the idea. What gets adopted probably depends more on who is advocating an idea and how it is packaged than on the quality of the idea itself.

Summary of the Thesis

To return to the original problem, how can we explain the degeneration of a political system which has obviously benefited its citizens? The answer seems to be that the causes of the benefits are not obvious to most people, including those the population at large regards as experts. The argument which attributes material wealth to a free society and the argument that political and economic freedom are inseparable are very difficult abstractions; and even when they are understood, they cannot adequately be "proven" at the level of the individual. Since, in a democracy, people are required to make important decisions on the basis of such abstractions, it is not surprising both that most of them fail to get it right and that the political system is vulnerable to decay. Unlike changes in technologies and economic institutions where private ownership—including equity ownership in joint stock companies—disciplines results, there is no mechanism for weeding out failure in political ideas which does not put the entire society at risk. Innovation in the political realm necessarily binds the entire society to the dominant opinion, and mistakes cannot be contained.

Neither is it possible to choose better political institutions simply by observing the successes and failures of others. In a complex reality, simple observation will not enable us to distinguish the particular causes of success or failure, as Hayek has often argued. For instance, one observer of the Soviet Union could argue that its standard of living is so low because of its central planning, while another could equally argue that it is as rich as it is *only because* it has centrally planned its economy. There is no physical (unintended?) constraint on the production and dissemination of political ideology that will automatically select those ideologies which serve individual long-run purposes. It is more likely that no bad idea ever really dies; it simply hovers in the recesses of someone's mind to be trotted out in a slightly different verbal garb when people are searching for a solution to a new crisis.

In some ways this is a very pessimistic message. We cannot rely on the unintended consequences of human action to generate a "spontaneous order" of rules—at least, not of rules that will permit other spontaneous orders to flourish. So, what is left? Only a vigorous ideological activism on the part of all who value the Great Society.[23] The idea of the Great Society is not "natural" in any biological or sociological sense of the word. It is not something which must, in any determinate sense, emerge from a natural process of cultural evolution. Human beings are capable of creating it and functioning in it, but they are also capable of many lesser social orders. Hence the values which make the great society possible must be taught and re-inforced if they are to be preserved.

Reason and Rules

Hayek laments the passing of the time when people were willing to obey a set of rules they did not understand—the rules which made the Great Society possible.[24] If there ever was such a time, however, it cannot be reinstated. In modern, complex democratic societies, people must be convinced of the *reason* for rules. And they must be shown which rules will make society possible. The growth of technology and economic institutions attest to the creativity and imaginativeness of human beings when they are free to experiment with ideas. We cannot assume creativity and imagination applied to innovation in technology, science, and economic institutions and, at the same time, also assume that people will not attempt to be creative and imaginative about their political institutions or that they will be willing to submit to rules the purposes of which they do not understand. The more open the society, the more likely that creative and intelligent individuals will insist on thinking through the rules of behavior they follow and the more experimentation—for better or for worse—we will observe. Hence the overwhelming importance of ideological activism to convince people of the value of a free society.

Toward a Reversal of the *The Road to Serfdom*

One optimistic implication of my analysis is that the evolution of ideas is *not* uni-directional. There is no presumption that, because a good idea has been lost, the loss is irrevocable. *The Road to Serfdom* can indeed be a two-way street if the inducements to change direction are strong enough and the arguments in favor of freedom persuasive enough. Much progress has already been made in the arguments for liberty. At least for the present, the case for comprehensive economic planning has been demolished. We now have a much better under-standing of how markets work (due in no small part to the seminal work of Hayek), and we have a much more realistic understanding of how government functions.[25] What still needs to be accomplished is to complete the argument Hayek began in *The Road to Serfdom*—the argument that liberty is all of a piece and that economic and political freedom cannot be separated for very long. There is mounting evidence that, in the communist East, the failure of economic planning is proving to be a very good argument in favor of economic and political freedom. In the West, the case for economic freedom has yet to be made (indeed, there seems to be a serious retrogression in the United States despite the popular perception of the ideological bent of the Reagan administration). But to the extent that people value certain civil liberties, there is still a basic shared ideology upon which to build that case. We still do not know enough about the transmission of ideas and the role of intellectuals and specialists in disseminating them. This is the gap that must be tackled because the task in the years ahead is to disseminate the principles and the practices of liberty in a way that builds on what current consensus there may be.

We must also expect that the case for liberty will never be completely won. It is in the nature of these ideas, as has been shown, that they can never be tested conclusively and thus are always vulnerable to counterargument. We might, however, take some comfort from the hope that, if people can be con-vinced of the importance of the rules which permit a free society to flourish, the widely disbursed material benefits which flow from genuine liberty will give few people cause to re-evaluate their political ideologies—at least for a very long time.

NOTES

1. F. A. Hayek, *The Road to Serfdom* (University of Chicago Press, 1944); Phoenix Books edition including the Foreword written in 1954—referred to hereinafter as *Road*.

2. *Road*, especially chap. VII, "Economic Control and Totalitarianism," 88–100.

3. "Nothing distinguishes more clearly conditions in a free country from those in a country under arbitrary government than the observance in the former of the great principle known as the Rule of Law" (*Road*, 72).

4. F. A. Hayek, *The Constitution of Liberty* (University of Chicago Press, 1960), hereinafter *Constitution*. In addition, he published *Studies in Philosophy, Politics and Economics* (Chicago: University of Chicago Press, 1967), hereinafter *Studies*.

5. *Studies*, 96–105.

6. Especially *Constitution*, chap. 15, 220–233, in which Hayek discusses the implications of following a rule of law for economic policy.

7. Hayek's evolutionary social theory is expounded principally in the three volumes of F. A. Hayek, *Law, Legislation and Liberty*—Vol. 1: *Rules and Order* (Chicago: University of Chicago Press, 1973); Vol. 2: *The Mirage of Social Justice*, 1976; Vol. 3: *The Political Order of a Free People*, 1979. (Hereinafter referred to as *L, L & L*.)

8. *L, L & L*, 1:17–18, and 3:153–165.

9. For example, James M. Buchanan, *Cultural Evolution and Institutional Reform*, Working Paper, 1982. Also, James M. Buchanan "Law and the Invisible Hand," in *Freedom in Constitutional Contract* (College Station: Texas A&M Press, 1977), hereafter *Cultural Evolution*.

10. Buchanan advances this argument in *Cultural Evolution*, 6–8.

11. Jack Hirshleifer lists the following criteria for an evolutionary explanation: change cannot be random for the phenomenon we wish to explain; there must be an element of irreversibility in the process—once something evolves it cannot go back; changes at the macro level result from accumulated changes at the micro-level; and changes are somehow "unintended." *Research in Law and Economics: Evolutionary Models in Economics and Law*, vol. 4 (Newton, MA: JAI Press, 1982). I argue that, while changes in rules and ideas about what rules should be may result from unintended micro-changes, what emerges is largely random and reversible. It is often *possible* to go back to older, discarded notions of political order.

12. "The fundamental principle that in the ordering of our affairs we should make as much use as possible of the spontaneous forces of society, and resort as little as possible to coercion, is capable of an infinite variety of applications. There is, in particular, all the difference between deliberately creating a system within which competition will work as beneficially as possible and passively accepting institutions as they are" (Hayek, *Road*, 17).

13. Karen I. Vaughn, "Can a Democratic Society Reform Itself? The Limits of Constitutional Change," in *For a Free Society in the Coming Decade* (The Mont Pelerin Society, 1983). (Also published as "Kann sich eine demokratische Gesellschaft ohne Revolution reformieren? Die Grenzen konstruktiven Wandels," in *Zeitschrift fur Wirtschaftspolitik* 32, no. 2 (1983): 7–8.)

14. Robert D. Tollison and Robert B. Ekelund, Jr., *Mercantilism as a Rent-Seeking Society* (College Station: Texas A&M Press, 1981). Tollison and Ekelund argue that a free society emerged as the unintended consequence of the political competition between Parliament and the Crown in the 17th century to monopolize the disbursement of rents to supplicants. Interestingly,

Hayek also traces the idea of the rule of law to the 17th and 18th centuries. He argues that it was "consciously evolved" during the liberal age. Presumably, this means that it emerged through the conscious intellectual efforts of successive thinkers directed toward an abstract problem (*Road*, 81.)

15. Hayek's reference to the idea of a "just" distribution of wealth as an atavism should be recalled: "the long-submerged innate instincts have again surged to the top. Their demand for a just distribution in which organised power is to be used to allocate to each what he deserves is thus strictly an *atavism*, based on primordial emotions." (*L, L & L*, 3:165.)

16. *L, L & L*, 3:13–17.

17. The most recent exposition of the interest-group theory of government and its disastrous consequences for a liberal order is in Mancur Olson's *The Rise and Decline of Nations* (New Haven, CT: Yale University Press, 1982). Olson argues that once interest groups get a lock on a democratic system, the only way economic freedom can be attained is through some kind of cataclysmic event which destroys them.

18. Lee Iacocca is the president of Chrysler Corporation who managed to arrange a multi-million dollar "loan" from the Federal Government to save Chrysler from bankruptcy—a bankruptcy which many analysts have attributed to earlier bad management.

19. That particular economic transactions are difficult for some people to master provides opportunities in the market for others who are more skillful at market dealings to make money by offering to serve as agents for the less adept. Mutual funds are an example. Markets provide an incentive for the production and dissemination of information about how to benefit from the market process. There is nothing equivalent in the political process. Political parties provide information, but it is not necessarily accurate information.

20. *L, L & L*, 1:19.

21. Hayek argues that the internal contradictions in people's beliefs will be an engine of constant ideological change in society: "modern man is torn by conflicts which torment him and force him into ever-accelerating further changes" (*L, L & L*, 3:159.)

22. Hayek has advanced this argument repeatedly: for example, *Studies*, 22–34. Also, Ludwig von Mises, *Human Action* (New Haven, CT: Yale University Press, 1963): "The champions of logically incompatible theories claim the same events as the proof that their point of view has been tested by experience. The truth is that the experience of complex phenomena—and there is no other experience in the realm of human action—can always be interpreted on the ground of various antithetic theories" (42).

23. This is Hayek's term for the advanced, complex industrial society which results from economic and political freedom (*L, L & L*, 1:14).

24. "The refusal to yield to forces which we neither understand nor can recognise as the conscious decisions of an intelligent being is the product of an incomplete and therefore erroneous rationalism" (*Road*, 205).

25. Our better understanding of how government functions is due to the work of the public-choice theorists, and primarily to those of the Virginia School.

Chapter 12
The Limits of Homo Economicus
in Public Choice and in
Political Philosophy

1. INTRODUCTION

In recent years, the subdiscipline of public choice has made dramatic inroads into the traditional fields of political science and political philosophy. By applying a consistent model of human action originally developed in order to study behavior in market settings to the study of behavior in political settings, public choice economists have to a large extent "taken the blinders off" the way we look at our political institutions. By making the simple assumption that the same kind of people act in political settings as act in markets, the field of public choice has deromanticized our view of government. We have come to see not only economic reasons behind much public behavior, but also the way in which public trusts can be and have been used for private purposes. Public choice teaches us to be skeptical of public professions of ideological motivations and apparently selfless actions. We have come to expect that in public life, people say one thing and mean another. The implication drawn is that good science requires us to assess what people actually do and what the consequences of their actions are, rather than what they say they want and what they expect will happen. In public life as in market settings, saying is not to be trusted. Doing is what matters.

And what do people do? The assumption behind positive public choice models is that individuals are narrow, self-interested maximizers who do

"The Limits of Homo Economicus in Public Choice and in Political Philosophy," originally published in *Journal Analyse & Kritik* 10, no. 2 (1988): 161–180. Republished with permission of Oldenbourg Wissenschaftsverlag GmbH.

not restrain their self-seeking according to any ideological or moral principles. This model of man as homo economicus is of course derived from economic theory[1] which, when properly interpreted, has generated so many fruitful theories of market phenomena. The point of this paper is to argue that homo economicus is not equally sufficient to generate fruitful theories about some important areas of the political process. While there is no question that economic science owes its success to a stylized view of human nature, it is not also true that the same stylized view is equally applicable to all empirical settings nor that it allows us to say everything there is to say about human action. The position I will argue below is that there are areas of political action that can only be understood if one takes the moral and ideological views of the actors into account. I further argue that one cannot make any policy prescription at all without presupposing some moral or political philosophy as the guide to the good.

2. THE GENERALITY OF THE ECONOMIC PARADIGM

Economic analysis and its subset, public choice, begins with a simple and perfectly general model of human action. Indeed, it is the simplicity and the generality of the model that gives economic analysis its explanatory and predictive edge over other social sciences. Economists conventionally begin with the empirical given that human beings, by the nature of the material world within which they live and their finite life spans, are confronted with scarcity and hence cannot have everything (or even much of) what they want. Hence, humans must make choices. From that simple beginning, economists add empirical observations to their basic framework in order to try to provide satisfying accounts of why some choices are made with predictable frequency while others are not. In order to carry out this program, they start from the premise that individuals are rational or "self-interested," but at this level of generality, all self-interest means is that individuals have purposes and projects which they wish to accomplish. These purposes and projects are not necessarily confined exclusively to those that will bring personal benefit in a narrow sense. It is perfectly within the scope of the self-interest assumption for individuals to want to improve the welfare of others rather than their own.[2] To say that individuals choose rationally among alternatives to achieve their purposes simply means that individuals will never knowingly sacrifice a greater end for the sake of a lesser one or will never knowingly choose a more expensive means to their end than is necessary. Both are ways of saying that rational action means economizing action.

The formal neoclassical statement of these assumptions is the constrained maximization formulation where individuals are modeled as maximizing their "utilities" subject to the constraints they face. As is well known, at this level of generality, the formulation is empty of any content and any real explanatory power. It simply says that individuals choose what they choose because that's what they want. "Rationality" in this context can be made consistent with any kind of action imaginable so long as the actor is conscious and not mentally deranged.[3] We *impose* the rationality construct on human choices because it is the only way we can make sense out of individual actions. Indeed, at this level of generality, the rationality formulation is simply a translation of what human beings recognize and define as an explanation of a human action. To say someone acts rationally is simply to say that his choice had a recognizable purpose (Mises 1963, 18–21).

In order to develop predictive theories about human action, it is necessary to fill the framework of rationality and self-interest with content, to specify the purposes and to identify the constraints that individuals face. The particular assumption that positive economics generally makes is that human beings have a strong preference for material wealth, or rather, the kind of wealth that can be evaluated in money terms. While most people, including most economists, would recognize that the preference for money wealth is not the sole preference individuals exhibit, most people, including noneconomists do recognize that the preference is an important one. Much of the debate between economists and those who accuse them of methodological imperialism, then, seems to revolve around the relative weights one observes people giving to pecuniary and nonpecuniary preferences and to what extent non-pecuniary preferences can be said to dominate individual choices.

Clearly, the hypothesis that the desire for pecuniary wealth explains *all* human action is demonstrably false. Where they have real choices, individuals are often observed to choose alternatives other than those that maximize monetary wealth. For example, we observe people choosing leisure over work when they have the option of working more, choosing to specialize in occupations that are financially less rewarding than real alternatives, choosing to give money away to charities, engaging in acts of kindness that either do not add to or may even detract from pecuniary wealth and a host of other nonmoney-wealth enhancing activities. While real hardline advocates of the wealth-maximizing hypothesis might try to argue that some of these activities are directed toward long run wealth improvement, that approach is impossible to sustain for all such activities.

Economists generally recognize this and argue that people observed to be engaged in activities that do not maximize their money wealth are actually maximizing their *subjective* wealth. This, of course, brings us back to the general formularization of self-interest and hence, as analytically precise as this may seem to say that an economic actor is maximizing subjective wealth, the fact is that saying that people maximize subjective wealth is simply another way of saying that people want many different things, some of which are of a nonpecuniary nature. These nonpecuniary things might include not only leisure, but also good fellowship, love, social status, association with others of a like nature, or a sense of rectitude or personal integrity; any one of which could dominate specific choices and falsify economic predictions.[4]

Unless we have some notion of what it is that people want, we cannot devise predictive theories of choice; we can at best share a language with which to discuss people's actions ex post. The positive economist who assumes pecuniary wealth maximization to explain action knows this and is making an empirical generalization that need not be totally descriptively accurate to make his point. It need only be "good enough." The point of this paper is simply that this particular empirical generalization is less likely to be fruitful for genuine explanations of events when applied to political action than when it is applied to market activity. There are two reasons I have to offer for this assertion. The first is that in political action more than in market action, people's values and ideas of what constitute the good society enter into their choices. The second reason is that in analyzing and describing political choice, the application of the model of deliberative rational choice itself becomes problematic. Citizens have limited and faulty information about the consequences of political choices and hence often have no idea what would constitute a rational decision even if they were disposed to make one.

In order to discuss the first claim, that moral and ideological beliefs influence political choice, we must first consider how to account for notions of morality in our standard model of human behavior. Homo economicus, broadly conceived, has preferences and is limited by constraints. To which category do we relegate moral values: to preferences or constraints? The answer to this question has implications for the kinds of public choice models one can fruitfully construct.

Consider the following situation: Two men are engaged in a heated argument. They hurl insults at each other until it seems inevitable that they will come to blows. One of the men, however, with great effort, controls his temper and walks away from the confrontation. In the language of revealed preference, the economist might say that obviously, the man who walked away preferred to give up rather than to fight. While on one level that is correct, on another level, it violates conventional discourse to describe the situation in that way. The man himself might claim that he really preferred to fight, but he knew that was wrong and so could not permit himself the luxury of punching his opponent. In the first instance, we describe the moral behavior in terms of preferences; while in the second, the moral conviction is a constraint on behavior. It seems more in concert with conventional language to accept the second characterization where the moral code is a constraint on behavior, but to do this means the observer must believe the participant's verbal account of his behavior rather than relying only on observation alone, something positive economists are reluctant to do. Treating morals as rules that constrain behavior, then, must of necessity place us outside of the positive economists' world right from the beginning.

If people conduct themselves according to rules of personal behavior to which they ascribe moral weight so that following these rules may result in short-term suboptimal choices, clearly it is not descriptively accurate to model them as narrow pecuniary maximizers in any setting. However, the descriptive inaccuracy is more pronounced, it seems to me, in modeling political action than in modeling market action. Markets are useful to actors precisely because they aid people in enhancing their material wealth. The polity, on the other hand, is valued by individuals for other reasons as well. Public choice emphasizes the Hobbesian aspects of the state, the delegation of authority to create the order that makes wealth possible. The state also seems to many people to be symbolic of shared values and shared notions of the good life. Since political action is as much concerned with establishing the rules by which citizens will live as with the exploiting of the rules for one's own benefit, it seems obvious that people will choose rules at least partly for their moral content. If this is so, then politics cannot be successfully modeled purely as economics.

3. ECONOMIC MAN AND POLITICAL CHOICES

One obvious area in which narrow economic analysis has failed to provide an interesting explanation of political behavior is the analysis of voting behavior.[5] It is a well-known irony that public choice theory, the theory of how public goods are demanded, produced, and allocated in a democratic society, cannot provide a satisfactory explanation of why people vote. Economic theory predicts that since the likelihood of any one person's vote influencing the outcome of an election is almost infinitesimal, as long as there are any costs at all associated with voting, it is irrational for an individual to vote. Yet we commonly observe individuals turning out to vote in huge numbers in national elections. Why?

The fact is, the paradox is only a paradox if one insists on looking at voting as an act of choice among real alternatives open to the individual, the purpose of which is wealth maximization. Few citizens seriously believe that his/her vote will decide an election, yet people vote nevertheless. Common explanations in the literature all must move outside of the model of pecuniary advantage to provide an explanation. Buchanan and Brennan, for example, compare voting to a kind of consumption activity like rooting for a sports team (Brennan and Buchanan 1984). It is also possible that people vote because they have a sense of civic responsibility that only allows them to approve of their own behavior if they take the time to vote. They vote at some immediate cost to themselves not because it is an act of consumption but because their internalized set of moral constraints makes voting something that is not a matter of immediate choice. They provide evidence to themselves and to their peers that they are "good" citizens.[6] Whatever the explanation, the act of voting can only be explained by some appeal to nonpecuniary values. One can think of other examples of civic behavior that do not fit the normal calculus; for example, volunteering for the army in war time, and carrying litter to a litter basket rather than dropping it on the ground are two that range from the dramatic to the mundane.

This is not to argue that the economists' cost-benefit calculations are irrelevant to the individual's political acts. At the margin, one would expect to observe less of the behavior in question when the costs are higher than when they are lower. For example, election turnouts are higher in good weather than on rainy days, enlistments are higher when the threat of the draft is more imminent, and more litter ends up in baskets on beaches when the baskets are placed at convenient intervals.[7] However, the average amount of such behavior is largely a function of the moral values and ideologies of the actors. It is always in one sense "irrational" to hold litter for the litter basket when rationality means maximizing pecuniary advantage (see the article by Vanberg and Buchanan in this issue). Clearly however, that is not the sum total of what motivates human action.

The positive public choice economist might counter that in economic theory, it is margins, not averages that count. Even though individuals claim to hold values that do not maximize their pecuniary wealth, the fact is that at the moment of choice, the model of pecuniary maximization will predict behavior better than any other. Hence, it makes scientific sense to ignore nonpecuniary interest. This is, of course, an empirical question, but there is at least some evidence that exists in the literature to support the a priori appealing notion that ideology or nonpecuniary values do count in the way people vote (Rubin and Kau 1979). Indeed, there are good reasons why individuals could not even formulate an opinion about the relative merits of various candidates in an election without some set of moral presuppositions to guide them.

I am not disputing that pecuniary wealth maximization is *a* goal of individuals acting in a political setting. That is, I am not arguing that public choice has missed the boat entirely. It seems perfectly appropriate to model individuals as wealth maximizers within a system of established rules. Hence, positive public choice models are useful for explaining such things as lobbying behavior and productivity and labor relations in a bureaucracy, for example. However, when it comes to modeling the way in which individuals choose their rules (and their representatives) or how the basic structure of a political society is developed, positive public choice is simply inadequate. There are other goals besides pecuniary wealth maximization which people expect the political system to provide for them and these goals affect behavior and outcomes.

4. IDEOLOGY AND PUBLIC CHOICE

My second claim was that for some political choices that individuals make, the application of a deliberative choice model is probably inadequate because choosers have very little information upon which to base a deliberate choice. Political ideologies and, on a more immediate level, political parties seem to be the natural implication of the limited information and the radical uncertainty faced by voters in a democracy.

There are obviously many political decisions individuals must make for which they have very poor information, or where they would be unable to calculate their self-interest even if they had good information. For instance, are the interests of world peace served by the Star Wars defense system currently advocated by the Reagan administration? If in principle, interests are served, is the system technologically feasible and is it worth the cost? Does the public debt have important consequences and if so, is it better to reduce the debt by increasing taxes or reducing spending? Both these questions are examples of problems where the "experts" do not agree on even the theoretical level of the problem. Clearly, the nonexpert citizen is totally incapable of making a correct decision on the merits of any proposal that requires his consent. It is even more unlikely that the citizen could take a position on these questions that reflected his pecuniary self-interest in the matter. What, then, is the citizen to do?

In markets, where information is poor and difficult to obtain, entrepreneurs have a financial incentive to provide that information. Competition among entrepreneurs ensures that where accurate information is possible, accurate information is generated and made available to an otherwise ignorant public. Or perhaps it would be better to say that the market process of competition allows consumers to discover the information relevant to their own needs. In political settings, however, the kind of information that people need in order to make intelligent decisions is often the kind that no one knows even in principle. Individuals must not only assess what public goods it is in their interest to demand (a far more difficult problem than assessing what kind of car one should buy), they must also determine which elected representative will best serve their purposes and what the consequences of present legislation are likely to be for their own future welfare.

While there are plenty of political entrepreneurs willing to offer voters their opinions on the answers to these complex questions, there is no effective testing process in politics to weed out errors and incorrect information comparable to the competition in markets. Political entrepreneurs supply individuals with what they think they want, but what they think they want may have very little resemblance to what they would want if they were correctly informed. Since on many of these issues, information is only in the form of untested theories, voters are led to economize on this very difficult decision process by adopting a political ideology to aid them in their choices. Even if the public choice theorist were to assume that men are solely pecuniary wealth maximizers, he could not hope to understand the political decision process without understanding the information individuals ascribe to their ideologies.

Achieving this understanding is no easy task. Political ideologies usually consist of statements of broad values (like "political equality is a good thing," or "people shouldn't be poor") and of theories about how those values can be accomplished (like "allowing eighteen-year-olds to vote will promote equality and redistribution of income will reduce poverty"). Actual political party platforms, on the other hand, are imperfect translations of those values and theories into specific sets of policies that may or may not be either internally consistent or empirically workable. What people think the ideological and practical implications of a party platform are may be different from what they really are. The public choice theorist has generally conducted his analysis of public policy by first applying his theory to calculate the policy's consequences and then assuming that those who support the policy understand the consequences and have a pecuniary interest in them, even if the predicted consequences are different from those supporters claim they will be.[8] They tacitly assume that anyone who supports the policy for non-wealth-maximizing reasons is lying in order to conceal his potential gain from others. While this may often be the case, it may also be the case either that policy advocates simply do not understand the wealth implications as well as the public choice theorist understands them, or it may simply be the case that advocates of a particular policy support it for nonmoney wealth-maximizing reasons. Their reasons for supporting a particular policy may simply be what they claim them to be.

For example, assume that it is calculated that a bill to subsidize higher education will increase the expected incomes of college teachers and redistribute wealth to the middle class. From this, the public choice theorist might try to predict the disposition of the bill according to the size and political clout of the coalition. Note that there are two parts to this formulation, an explanatory and a predictive. If the public choice economist ignores ideology where ideology happens to be important to making a decision, he will construct a model that provides an inaccurate explanation of events even if the predictions of the model hold—which may or may not be the case.

First of all, it may be the case that many higher educators genuinely believe that it is appropriate national policy to provide higher education to anyone regardless of ability to pay and do not understand the redistributive consequences of their actions. Or they may understand them but think, nevertheless, the consequences are fair. While the educators may be beneficiaries of the bill also, it is simply not accurate to explain their actions solely in terms of the pecuniary income they can expect as a consequence. Secondly, voters may also believe that higher education should be subsidized regardless of the fact that university faculty and middle-class families with children benefit disproportionately. They may fully believe that the importance of widespread access to higher education supersedes any redistributive consequences.[9]

The public choice theorist might argue that whether or not he is correct in the motives he ascribes to individual actors, the predictive power of his model is nevertheless protected. The fact is that regardless of what people say, at the margin, pecuniary self-interest is a good predictor of resource allocation. Yet if for some goods, either because information is so incomplete or non-pecuniary values are so important, people choose according to ideological considerations rather than self-interest, the strict application of homo economicus can only be correct by accident. The fact is, there are always people who support public measures even when they don't gain; even, in fact, when they personally may stand to lose.[10]

Consider, again, the widespread support for public education. It is of course true that most voters believe they and their children will be better off financially if the cost of education can be spread to all taxpayers rather than borne by themselves alone. But the demand for public education seems also to have another component to it that is far more prevalent in political decisions than in market choices; that is, a desire to affect the way others behave. A typical argument for public education is that society is "better" if more people are literate and educated. Here, "better" means not only wealthier, but also more stable and better governed. While I suppose "more stable" and "better governed" could be translated into "wealthier" as well, I believe the sense of the argument has more to do with the kinds of people with which one wants to live. The nonpecuniary value of having others behave in certain ways is very important to political choices. Clearly such values are self-interested, but only in the tautological sense in which all values are held by a self. Politics is largely about creating a society of shared values and establishing a set of shared behaviors. In political society, "utility" is a function of the behavior of others as well as of one's measurable wealth. Economists sometimes call the demand for shared values and shared behaviors "meddle-some preferences" (Sen 1970), but this seems to miss the central point of human culture. We are interested in each other's behavior because that is how we define and judge ourselves. The simple narrow model of homo economicus cannot do justice to this important characteristic of human beings.

5. EFFICIENCY AND SOCIAL INSTITUTIONS

One may grant that individual human beings act according to many values, some of which are not self-interested in the narrow sense, and still argue that positive economic analysis provides the best tools for explaining social phenomena including political institutions. One argument that has been made is that the outcomes of social action do not depend so much on the ends that human beings pursue as on the constraints they face. In this view, largely associated with the Chicago School although not limited to it, no matter what individuals hold as moral beliefs and no matter what kinds of nonpecuniary goods they may choose in the short run, in the long run the only thing that explains social change are changes in relative prices brought about by shifts in constraints. The implication is that the only economic, political, and social institutions that will survive are those that maximize the pecuniary wealth of the population (or some important segment thereof?). In saying this, I am creating something of a straw man since it is difficult to find any one economist who will hold to this line without wavering. As we have noted above, most economists argue that men maximize utility, not pecuniary wealth. However, utility is not a useful concept for positive economics unless we are able to specify the arguments in the utility function. Those economists who postulate material wealth as the maximand at least are saying more than people try to get the most of what they want. What this argument seems to say is that no matter what they think they want, what they get is maximum pecuniary wealth since action that leads to that particular end will be differentially rewarded in a competitive struggle (for example, see North and Thomas 1973).

Such "survivalist" arguments borrow the language of evolutionary biology and interpret social institutions as the result of some form of competition in which only the fittest or most efficient can survive. Any attempt to explain a phenomenon in evolutionary terms must, however, describe a process by which competing elements are selected and inefficiencies weeded out. For social institutions, it would be important to explain how innovative social arrangements are introduced and how humans act to select among these institutions either consciously or unconsciously. In the argument under consideration, there is some vague notion that social institutions compete much in the same way that firms compete, and hence efficient institutions will drive out inefficient ones in the competitive struggle. But what is an efficient institution?

It is tautologically true that in evolutionary explanations, the efficient survive, but only because survival is the definition of efficiency. One might apply the same reasoning to social institutions but only with some difficulty. For instance, the social scientist could observe what institutions and societies have in fact survived competition and then search for explanations for why the survivors are adaptive to their environment. Those who hold that only efficient social institutions can survive may hypothesize that wealth maximization is the major explanatory variable in institutional survival. In that case, it would be imperative for the theorist to specify how he defines wealth and then to describe a process by which maximizing this definition of wealth leads institutions to survive before the proposition is tested. So far, no one has attempted to follow such a procedure.[11]

Discussion of the efficiency of *economic* institutions, whose major purpose is to allow individuals to improve their economic well-being, at least makes some intuitive sense because we have a theory that allows us to define what constitutes an efficient economic institution (it allows individual actors to effect more transactions at lower cost than without it) and to describe a process by which efficient institutions survive and others fail (those institutions like business firms that are profitable survive while those that make losses fail). More inclusive institutions like a banking system or a stock exchange, that is, institutions that consist of regularized trading arrangements—survive that improve the profits of the individuals who use them for their own purposes. In either case, the fact that individuals who choose to participate in the institution have purposes they wish to satisfy and have a clear measure, profit, by which to judge whether or not the institution is serving their needs, allows us to describe a process by which efficient institutions can evolve. An evolutionary approach to the study of *economic* institutions, then, may prove fruitful because we can hypothesize a recognizable goal and describe a process by which efficient institutions are selected by the competition among self-interested human actors. However, when one attempts to describe an economic process by which other forms of social institutions are selected, the problem is not nearly so clear cut.

What is an efficient political organization? If we wish to be consistent with our notion of economic efficiency, then it must in some way reduce the costs of individuals pursuing their own interests (as, for example, Hobbes and Locke explained the reason for government). Clearly, we can see how some political organization may be better than no political organization, but this is not the same thing as arguing that the most efficient political organization from the perspective of the wealth-maximizing activities of individual citizens necessarily is the one that will survive international competition. An evolutional theory of political organization might start from the hypothesis that those political organizations that can command the greatest number of resources in times of stress are the most efficient and hence most likely to survive political competition. This seems a reasonable empirical hypothesis, but it does not have any readily apparent connection to the wealth-maximizing actions of individuals. And it certainly does not imply that individuals cannot successfully pursue other goals besides pecuniary wealth maximization. The course of human events has been altered more than once by the ideas and values of individuals who were not pursuing either individual or national material wealth.[12]

Political organizations are systems of power as well as economic resources. A successful polity probably depends as much on variables such as intelligent military strategy, willingness to wage defensive wars, canniness of leaders in world and domestic affairs, a sense of national purpose based on shared values, and a host of other intangibles that cannot be adequately proxied by measures of wealth. Given the wide variety of relatively long-lived political institutions of all different shapes and sizes, it seems clear that wealth maximization alone cannot account for the survival of all of them.

6. PUBLIC CHOICE, PUBLIC POLICY, AND THE CHOICE OF INSTITUTIONS

So far, this paper has been concerned with the limitations of the narrow homo economicus assumption for positive public choice, the economic theory of individual political behavior. Now we turn to the difficulties associated with assuming narrow homo economicus in normative public choice, the exercise of devising political institutional rules to improve the way that government functions to serve the purposes of its citizenry.[13]

Normative public choice begins with the assumption that insofar as individuals want government to provide public goods, the public choice economist is in a position to design institutional rules to help them achieve their purposes more efficiently. I rather call this activity "prescriptive" public choice since it prescribes methods for achieving given goals; it is not strictly positive science since it does not attempt simply to analyze and explain what is, nor is it normative policy since it does not explore goals or values, nor does it choose among them. It does, however, presuppose the norm that using fewer resources to achieve one's goal is better than using more.

One method by which to engage in prescriptive public choice is to apply a simple calculus of benefits and costs to all public policies, and to attempt to design rules and procedures that maximize the ratio of benefits to costs.[14] The calculations are made in money terms and nonmarket values are given money proxies. The presumption in this exercise is that all preferences count equally and that all consequences can be effectively measured in money terms. So, for example, if it would have been cheaper to buy up all the slaves in the antebellum South and manumit them than to fight the Civil War, prescriptive policy would have argued for the former course of action.

There is much merit in this approach to public policy. It provides some framework for comparing the consequences of alternative policies and some rough and ready measure of the magnitudes of those consequences. Calculating the potential costs of a war and then figuring out how much you could pay the opposing soldiers not to fight at least gives the citizenry some basis upon which to judge the degree to which they believe the war is in their national interests. It might even open up a debate on possible peaceful alternatives. If one views the public policy economist's (or the prescriptive public choice theorist's) role as offering some measure of the relative costs of various policies, cost-benefit analysis is useful and important. However, given the multiplicity of values people hold as citizens, it should not be surprising if the so-called efficient policy is not followed. What is efficient in terms of money calculations may not be efficient in terms of the nonpecuniary goals individuals as citizens hold.

When it comes to designing political institutions, however, the cost/benefit approach to prescriptive policy cannot even in principle be applied. To say something is efficient implies that one is judging it according to some end one has in view. We have already argued that the goal of political institutions is not limited to promoting wealth maximization of the citizens of a polity *even in the eyes of the citizens themselves*. Hence applying a rational calculus to devising, say, voting rules or distributions of rights is meaningful only in a very general sense. Certainly, a rational calculus based on pecuniary wealth maximization could easily lead to the development of rules that conflict with individuals' notions of fairness or rights.

Consider, for example, the controversy surrounding the Coase theorem. Coase showed that in any conflict of externalities that is to be settled by specifying property rights, who gets the right to the property in question is irrelevant from the perspective of efficiency. Regardless of who gets the right to use the hitherto common resource, the person who can make most efficient use of it (that is, generate the most market income from its use) will end up with it so long as the property is tradable in the market. Clearly, however, even if the terms of the settlement of the property right are irrelevant to the eventual emergence of efficient use of the resource, it is not irrelevant in terms of rights. It is not legitimate to infer from the Coase theorem that maximizing market value is the only—or even the most important—consideration in solving disputes over property (Coase 1960).

Efficiency is an end-state notion. It implies that the desired outcome should be arrived at in the cheapest possible way. It also implies that the ends and the means to achieving them are known to the decision maker. The rules of political society, on the other hand, are process notions. Part of the "end" that is desired is a way of living and a way of doing things. The rules of social order are important precisely because there is no one agreed upon set of ends for the society as a whole that are to be maximized nor are the full consequences of rules known at the time of adoption. Hence the term "efficient rules" would seem to be an oxymoron—that is, self-contradictory.[15]

It is the difficulties with the conventional notions of efficiency that motivate James Buchanan's contractarian approach to government or "constitutional economics."[16] Buchanan's contractarian model is partly prescriptive in nature, although it is different from the uncomplicated utilitarianism of cost/benefit analysis. Generalizing from subjectivist insights into the choice process, Buchanan realizes that individual evaluations of alternatives are always subjective and that money equivalents can't always reflect individual subjective evaluations. Consequently, Buchanan argues that the only test of the efficiency of either immediate policies or of more long run institutional—in his case, constitutional—rules is the agreement of participants in the institution. This is a generalization from the subjectivists' insight that the only evidence we have of the gains from trade is that the trade was entered into voluntarily (Buchanan 1985a).

Buchanan recognizes that for the exercise of prescriptive public choice especially at the constitutional level, the simple calculation of money gains and losses may not be a good guide to the kinds of policies and rules to which a collection of individuals will agree. So, for instance, in the case of the Civil War, Buchanan's approach can accommodate the fact that Southerners and Northerners both saw values like moral rectitude, regional autonomy, and ingrained life-styles at stake, and a policy of "buying out the opposition" would have been unacceptable to either side. This is not to say that at the level of immediate policy, calculating benefits and costs in money terms is not a useful exercise to aid decision-making. Indeed, it may be the only way for decision makers to understand the trade-offs involved in some policies. However, at the level of constitutional design, the level of deciding what actions are permissible and impermissible to the state and to individuals, the simple calculation of money benefits and costs is impossible. It begs all the questions of mine and thine that must be answered before money values have meaning.

Buchanan's alternative to the utilitarian brand of prescriptive public choice is to attempt to devise constitutional rules that might command agreement if actually put to the test. The rules he proposes are long-range constitutional rules where calculation of immediate gains and losses to individuals is difficult, but where procedures for making decisions and limitations on government power can be agreed to because of the uncertainty each person faces about his own position in the future. Since Buchanan does not believe there is a spontaneous order by which political processes lead to unintended beneficial outcomes for citizens, his contractarianism is a way of designing constitutions that provide the benefits that spontaneous processes generate in market settings. The constitutional contractarian serves a useful role in this political process specifically because there is no benevolent spontaneous order; there are no processes by which information about the characteristics and consequences of constitutions can be generated in order for individuals to make informed choices, nor is there a process by which an analysis of the unintended consequences of individual actions leads to the discovery of this information in an unambiguous manner. The constitutional-contractarian, then, himself serves as a political entrepreneur who "discovers" information about constitutions and, having discovered the information, is in a position to serve as a political broker offering potential bargains until the right one is struck among political traders. Given the fact that the constitutional broker does not know the preference functions of individual parties to the bargain, he only knows if he has hit on an efficient trade if the bargain is in fact made.

At this level, Buchanan provides the prescriptive public choice theorist with a role to play in public policy formation that has its justification in an information failure in the political process. It is practical in this exercise (and not misleading) to use the homo economicus construct as a first approximation to arrive at potential political bargains since actual human beings will be deciding just how close to the mark the proffered bargain is to their own value structure. At another level of abstraction, however, Buchanan's contractarianism moves out of the range of prescriptive public choice and into the realm of normative political philosophy. At this level, homo economicus is not nearly so benign an assumption to make. We arrive at this level through the discussions of the conceptual contract.

Buchanan argues that because it is impossible to actually put constitutional rules to the test of actual agreement, the constitutional political economist must devise constitutions that could in principle command unanimous agreement among those who will be governed by the constitution. He starts from the normative premise familiar to economists that only individuals count and that all individuals count equally regardless of their preferences (or moral values or personal characters?), and that the only moral basis for a political society is agreement. However, since we don't have actual empirical tests of agreement to legitimize governments, we must model those humans who might participate in the social contract in order to theorize about the kind of government upon which they might be able to agree.

The only legitimate governments are governments upon which real human beings would be able to agree. Notice that the moral presuppositions of this approach are minimal, but strong. Individual values are not to be questioned. All individuals must count equally in the contract, negotiation is the only legitimate process and agreement the only way to legitimize an outcome.

Since the conceptual contract is never put to the market test yet is intended to serve as a means of judging existing or potential constitutions, the characteristics of the people one presumes are party to the contract are important. If we begin with the subjectivist assumption that no one but the individual himself can know his utility function, then finding the appropriate model of the human beings who are a party to the contract can be problematic. Buchanan solves this problem by peopling his social contract with beings that look remarkably like homo economicus. Buchanan's contractors all have different tastes and different endowments to begin with, but the long-run nature of constitutional rules tends to mute these differences as the consequences of adopted rules are only realized in the future. More significant are the characteristics they all have in common. They are all rational, adult, mentally competent, and concerned exclusively with their material well-being. More significantly, they know everything the economist knows about the functioning of society. Even more importantly, they have no interest in the behavior of others except insofar as it directly affects their own pecuniary interests. They are not real people but ideal types who capture the essence of the rational, economic man.

We have already argued that narrow economic man is descriptively incorrect and analytically too restrictive a concept to judge economic policy. Certainly, it is even more off the mark to model men in this narrow way for the purpose of devising conceptual contracts. By definition, the conceptual contract is conceptual because the contract cannot in fact be put to the test. Hence, it is all the more important to take seriously the subjectivist presumption that people not only have different tastes and preferences, but also different moral beliefs and different ideologies. People think differently about the world.

To model men in the conceptual contract as strictly homo economicus either presumes that that is in fact the best description of human beings, or it implies that that is the way men should behave. We have already argued that the first alternative is incorrect. It is doubtful that any contractarian would want to subscribe to the second alternative. Hence, unless we want to assume that some rational ethic can be built into the social contract,[17] which puts us further away from a real contract and blunts the individuality of persons even more than the fictional social contract normally does, we must assume something about the moral philosophies that these rational beings will bring to their bargaining. Otherwise, it is impossible to come up with criteria by which to judge existing or potential contracts in the absence of actual agreements. The contractarian who takes individuals as the source of all values, I think, must logically take individuals as the source of information about values as well. This implies that moral presuppositions must be assumed to be part of the package that individuals bring to the social contract. This, of course, makes the role of the contractarian philosopher far more difficult than that of the contractarian economist. If the requirements of the differing moral systems must be added to the calculations of the different alternative rules in order to have some rational basis for judging their efficiency in the absence of actual agreement, how do we deal with conflicting moral systems?

The contractarian position is that all individuals who are a party to the contract must be counted equally in arriving at the rules of the game. Yet, there may be some cases involving the definition of common standards of behavior (as for example, whether or not abortion is legitimate) where coming to agreement may be almost impossible.[18] One also must question whether all moral beliefs, no matter how repugnant to other members of the community, must be counted equally. Should the beliefs of the primitive tribesman who takes it as religious dogma that infant girls should be sexually mutilated command the same respect in the social contract as the beliefs of those who oppose the practice simply because both want to live in the same political order? While a large degree of moral relativism is necessary in a pluralistic society, it is not clear that a philosophical contractarian can be totally agnostic on the question of which moral values count.

7. CONCLUSION

This paper has been concerned with the limits of the narrow model of homo economicus that ignores the role of moral rules and ideological commitments in the actions of human beings. The recent fashion in economics is to extend the model of homo economicus into other fields besides economics, to engage in a proud kind of economic imperialism. In general, there is something to be gained from this adventure, especially in those fields like political science and sociology where the effects of narrow economic calculation had hitherto been completely ignored. However, this essay is offered as a cautionary tale to those crusaders of the economics faith who long to spread the Word into all corners of the intellectual world. The economists' model does not translate perfectly into other languages or other cultures, and to fail to recognize the truth of this observation can lead to a total misperception of the phenomenon under consideration. In the specific case of the analysis of political activity, the economists have made great gains in understanding the way in which special interests can use the political process to gain an advantage. But to say that this is the only useful way of understanding the political process is in itself an ideological position that would command little agreement among participants in the intellectual debate.

NOTES

1. This is an extreme version of what economists seem to believe. Very few would actually adhere to such a hard line if they were forced to do so explicitly, but the argument is implicit in the way in which some economists dismiss the investigations of all other disciplines, such as philosophy or sociology, with a contemptuous wave of the hand. In the typical lunch time conversation among "hardnosed" economists, the typical attitude suggests that *only* economic self-interest is important in explanation—or appropriate personal behavior.

2. Kirzner (1963, 5). Kirzner's formulation follows Mises's view of a man as a purposeful animal, and it is far superior to the more standard self-interest formulation since it implies nothing about the content of interests. People may or may not be selfish, but they do have ends or purposes for which they will choose among alternative means. Jack Wiseman prefers to model men as making plans that are subject to revision, thereby including the notion of time and learning in human action. See Wiseman (1983, 18–20).

3. Gary Becker, for instance, has modeled altruistic behavior within families by assuming that individual utility functions depend in part on the utility of other family members. See Becker (1981).

4. Merely including such arguments in individual utility functions does not eliminate the possibility of economic explanation in the broad sense since one can still want more or less of these values at different "prices," but it does suggest that a conventional empirical economics of, say, love or duty will be problematic since an act performed for the sake of love or duty may not be amenable to analysis with money proxies.

5. For a brief summary of arguments on the paradox of voting, see Mueller (1979, 120–123).

6. It might be argued that both rooting for a team and exercising one's "civic responsibility" are just two forms of consumption. However, it is at least as likely that they are fundamentally different forms of behavior in that the individuals behave differently in response to changes in incentives. While a marginal increase in the price of voting from, say, rain or distance from the polls will normally reduce voter turnout in an election, an increase in the price of voting from political repression or violent confrontation has induced some people to increase rather than decrease their voting behavior. Insofar as voting is considered a right of citizenship, attempts to thwart its exercise can lead to more rather than less assertion of that right.

7. James Buchanan uses the example of the litter on a beach to illustrate the need for rules of social order. "Law and the Invisible Hand," in Buchanan (1977).

8. This is the tacit assumption of the interest group theory of public policy. While I do not disagree with much of the empirical results that follow from this assumption, I think it is overly ambitious to assume that it explains all policies. There are cases where there are simply unintended redistributive consequences to public policy that are secondary to the main purpose of the policy. Gordon Tullock makes this point in Tullock (1983, 9–10). Of course, Tullock points out that once a mistake is made, the benefited group is likely to fight to keep its benefits.

9. Or they may not think of it as redistributive. The public might regard higher incomes for university faculty as payment for services rendered, and subsidies to middle-class taxpayers as an unavoidable consequence of making higher education available to all citizens.

10. I suppose one could argue that the reason something is of overriding importance is precisely because the costs are difficult to calculate and that if the calculation could be made in a way that would capture the attention of the voter, the "importance" of the goal would diminish greatly.

11. I understand from verbal reports that Friedrich Hayek is working on an evolutionary explanation of political societies where population maximization is the survival principle. While at the moment this sounds an unpromising line of argument, one can only wait until the full elaboration is published to judge fairly.

12. This argument is not to be confused with the interest group theories of the state mentioned above that attempt to explain particular policies according to which interest groups gain *within* a state. The argument I am criticizing here tries to explain the survival of a particular state itself in terms of wealth maximization.

13. The theory of normative public choice is outlined in Buchanan and Tullock (1962).

14. This is the position that Gordon Tullock takes. See Tullock (1971).

15. On the inability to define an efficient political institution, see Coleman (1984).

16. The best statement of Buchanan's position is in Buchanan (1975).

17. This is exactly what David Gauthier tries to do in his 1986 book, *Morals by Agreement.*

18. James Buchanan took a step in that direction in his recent paper (1985b), in which he included behind the veil a recognition that men would become attached to the goods they produced. In other words, he worked out some implications of an emotional attachment to a primitive notion of property for the social contract.

REFERENCES

Becker, G. S. 1981. *A Treatise on the Family.* Cambridge, MA: Harvard University Press.

Brennan, G., and J. M. Buchanan. 1984. "Voter Choice." *American Behavioral Scientist* 28 (2): 185–201.

Buchanan, J. M. 1975. *The Limits of Liberty: Between Anarchy and Leviathan.* Chicago: University of Chicago Press.

———. 1977. *Freedom in Constitutional Contract.* College Station: Texas A&M Press.

———. 1985a. "Rights, Efficiency and Exchange: The Irrelevance of Transaction Costs." In *Liberty, Market and State: Political Economy in the 1900s*, 92–107. New York: New York University Press.

———. 1985b. "Community and Coercion: The Relationship Between Taxation and Liberty." Unpublished paper.

———, and G. Tullock. 1962. *The Calculus of Consent: Logical Foundations of Constitutional Democracy.* Ann Arbor, MI: University of Michigan Press.

Coase, R. 1960. "The Problem of Social Cost." *Journal of Law and Economics* 3:1–44.

Coleman, J. 1984. "The Foundations of Constitutional Economics." In *Constitutional Economics*, edited by R. B. McKenzie, 141–156. Lexington, MA.

Gauthier, D. 1986. *Morals by Agreement.* Oxford: Oxford University Press.

Kirzner, I. 1963. *Market Theory and the Price System.* New York: New York University Press.

Mises, L. 1963. *Human Action.* New Haven, CT: Yale University Press.

Mueller, D. 1979. *Public Choice.* Cambridge: Cambridge University Press.

North, D., and R. Thomas. 1973. *The Rise of the Western World.* Cambridge: Cambridge University Press.

Rubin, P., and J. B. Kau. 1979. "Self-Interest, Ideology and Log-Rolling in Congressional Voting." *Journal of Law and Economics* 22:365–384.

Sen, A. K. 1970. "The Impossibility of a Paretian Liberal." *Journal of Political Economy* 78:152–157.

Tullock, G. 1971. *The Logic of the Law.* New York: Basic Books.

———. 1983. *Economics of Income Redistribution.* Dordrecht, Netherlands: Kluwer Nijhoff.

Wiseman, J. 1983. *Beyond Positive Economics.* London: Macmillan.

Chapter 13
Friedrich Hayek's Defense
of the Market Order

Friedrich Hayek was a prodigious scholar whose work spanned almost seven decades and ranged over contributions to economics, scientific methodology, political philosophy, law, psychology, and social theory. Despite the impressive span of fields that he covered, the driving force for all his work emerged from his original study of economics and his belief in the overwhelming benefits of a market economy for human flourishing. He honed his distinctive contributions to economics during the 1930s and 1940s in debate with socialist economists over the technical feasibility of central economic planning—contributions that led to his being awarded the Nobel Prize in 1974. Yet, he regarded as his major life's work his writings on the broad topic of the nature of the liberal order, in particular his best-known works, *The Constitution of Liberty* and *Law, Legislation, and Liberty*, and his final work, *The Fatal Conceit*.[1] That Hayek should shift so dramatically from writing about technical economics to broader philosophical issues was no fluke: the issues that increasingly characterized his economic work led him to consider the wider context within which economic activity takes place. Unlike most economists who see exchange as a purely economic phenomenon, Hayek understood markets as embedded in a cultural and political context: what people value and the means they choose to achieve their ends are contingent upon rules and expectations of the society within which they reside. And while exchange is ubiquitous and

Originally published in *Wealth, Commerce, and Philosophy: Foundational Thinkers and Business Ethics*, edited by E. Heath and B. Kaldis (Chicago: University of Chicago Press, 2017), 341–358. Republished with permission.

serves as an engine of human progress, the engine can be slowed or stalled by an inhospitable culture or political regime. He saw as his task to articulate rules of political and social order that are most conducive to the growth of wealth and thus to the flourishing of civilization.

Despite the ideological motivation for Hayek's work, he was foremost an economist and as such saw himself as a scientist, not an ethicist. His brief was to focus on explaining the nature of the market order and its consequences for human beings without passing final judgment on its ultimate goodness or badness. Insofar as he had an ideological purpose, it was to discover the political and legal system that allowed human beings to achieve their own ends as they saw fit. Hayek believed that for a social scientist to pass judgment on the ultimate moral worth of human arrangements is an exercise in intellectual hubris. He believed that there was no extrahuman authority to reveal the nature of the good nor any objective means for defining the ultimate good apart from the perceptions and beliefs of individual actors. The scientist must take the values of actual human beings as his starting point for analyzing how various social structures affect the achievement of human ends. Individuals could then use the scientific appraisal of market action to assign value to the market economy for themselves. And while Hayek did not presume to argue that maximum material wealth was an ultimate value, he noted that most people desire material wealth for the simple reason that material wealth is a means to the achievement of other human values, whether selfish or altruistic. Despite his adherence to a scientific agnosticism with regard to ends, he firmly believed that if people were truly to understand that extending the market order means, among other benefits, the reduction of "starvation, filth and disease,"[2] there would be few who would not choose a political environment that supported markets.

The argument of this essay proceeds as follows. The opening section delineates how Hayek's dissatisfaction with the economics profession's enthusiasm for central planning in the interwar years led to his critique of mainstream economic theory and, in particular, its conventional assumption of perfect knowledge. How to cope with the limitations of human knowledge became a central theme of his later work on social and political theory. The subsequent section, on the market order, examines Hayek's exploration of the ways in which exchange in markets permits people to benefit from each other's specialized knowledge. The mutual benefits from trade lead to reduced violence and discord in human life. The third and fourth sections of this essay take up Hayek's evolutionary account of the growth of the market economy and its reliance on social and political rules to constrain individual behavior so as to lead to growing prosperity. The last section, on social justice and prescriptive morality, sets forth how Hayek did not judge the morality of either the market itself or the actions of individuals within the market. He limited his argument to noting that societies permitting the greatest scope for market exchange constrained by rules of property, tort, and contract tended to be the wealthiest, and that wealth was widely shared among the population.

THE POSSIBILITY OF ECONOMIC PLANNING

Hayek began his career as an economist, but one who early on grew increasingly out of step with his profession. In the 1930s, as a rising figure at the London School of Economics, he was viewed as John Maynard Keynes's most important rival for professional prominence.[3] While he was primarily known for his original approach to the theory of capital and money, in the middle part of the decade he became involved in an academic controversy over the feasibility of central planning that radically changed the direction of his research. During the interwar period, both the seeming achievements of the Soviet Union and the disruptions caused by the Great Depression served to fuel strong intellectual sentiment in the West for replacing the "chaotic" market with "rational economic planning," a sentiment that was shared by many mainstream economists. Hayek, on the other hand, believed that central planning was a system that would lead to declining wealth, increasing economic disruptions, and greatly reduced personal liberty, a view that led him to write a series of articles that would change the course of his life's work.

Pro-planning arguments, though socialist in sentiment, owed little to Marxist ideology. Instead, they were an exercise in determining whether or not the tools of conventional economic theory could be used to devise an efficient system of central planning that could overcome some of the perceived shortcomings of real market economies. Pro-planning economists in the 1920s and 1930s formulated schemes to achieve the goals of socialism, state ownership of the "means of production," greater rationality in capital investments (which they believed would bring about an end to business cycles), and greater income equality and security, all based on general equilibrium theory and its underlying theory of perfect competition. These economists were referred to as "market socialists" because they recognized the important role prices play in allocating resources efficiently but wanted to find a means of bypassing genuine market exchange to arrive at "economic" prices—prices that accurately represented relative resource scarcity. With the correct set of prices, they believed, a central planning board could manage the production of goods in state-owned firms more efficiently and more equitably than was possible in the "chaos" of the market. While early attempts to devise an alternative to actual markets depended upon determining statistically generated supply and demand functions that could then be solved for equilibrium prices, an approach abandoned in recognition of the "practical" difficulties surrounding such a project, the most widely respected theory of market socialism, and the one that the economics profession agreed was a genuine alternative to actual markets, was a system of "trial and error" pricing proposed by Oscar Lange.[4]

Lange proposed that "the means of production" be organized in state firms, where managers would be told to use planned prices in their output decisions. He reasoned that since equilibrium prices are set in markets through a process of trial and error much like an auction, all the central planners had to do was to list any set of prices and then instruct managers of state-owned firms to equate price to marginal cost in order to maximize return. The central planners would then observe resulting surpluses and shortages to adjust prices accordingly to reach equilibrium, and they would use "profit" and "loss" to guide capital investment in the state firms. This way, the allocative function of price could be preserved, allowing central planners to make rational decisions about resource use. Hayek's direct response to the economics of socialism was to write several articles that criticized the details of the socialist schemes,[5] which he regarded as naively misinformed about the nature of market activity. More important, the debate over the economics of socialism led Hayek to publish a series of articles that presented a different view of how markets function from the one implied by general equilibrium theory.[6]

This is not the place to go into a detailed discussion of Hayek's technical reasons for criticizing Lange's scheme. As might be expected, he catalogued a myriad of difficulties that would be encountered by a central planning board, such as defining what constituted a product, what was proper firm size, how managers would be chosen and evaluated in the absence of genuine profit or loss, how often to adjust administered prices, and how to deal with changing circumstances. But at the heart of all his objections to central planning were two methodological issues that were generally not the subject of economic inquiry—the importance of time in economic action, and the nature of the knowledge that informs decisions.[7]

In order to explain market prices, the model of perfect competition, which underlies general equilibrium theory, was essentially timeless: change was understood as comparative statics, the movement from one equilibrium position to another. Change itself was modeled as exogenous shocks that were by definition outside the parameters of the model. With such a model, it is understandable that one might think that central planners could determine a set of equilibrium prices that could guide production decisions from one period to another. But in the real world of constant change, Hayek argued, an exclusive focus on achieving equilibrium conditions diverts attention from understanding the essential nature of the market process. Central planning boards can gather statistics about past prices and quantities traded, and they might be able to gather specifications about existing production processes, but economic activity is not an exercise in endlessly repeating past patterns of behavior; it is about dealing with changing circumstances that require novel adjustments that in turn introduce more change into the system.[8] The market order that economists attempted to capture in the metaphor of general equilibrium theory could not describe this unending process of change and adjustment to change that was the central characteristic of market economies.

The timeless nature of perfect competition was further supported by the assumption that knowledge of technologies was essentially an engineering problem that could be easily shared, and that market conditions were known equally to all actors. Hayek believed that these simplifying assumptions left out the very feature of the human condition that makes markets necessary to economic order: that humans live in a world where they plan for an unknown future, and they do so in light of the unique knowledge each possesses about their own circumstances. The problem facing economic theory, according to Hayek, was to explain "how the spontaneous interaction of a number of people, each possessing only bits of knowledge, brings about a state of affairs . . . which could be brought about by deliberate direction only by somebody who possessed the combined knowledge of all those individuals."[9] What Adam Smith called the "invisible hand" of the market, Hayek was to call a "spontaneous order": an orderly process of human interaction that is planned by no single intelligence yet results in patterns of action that enable individuals mutually to achieve their ends in concert with one another.[10]

Hayek was especially disturbed by the simplifying assumption of perfect knowledge that economists took for granted. He argued that human knowledge, far from being "homogeneous" and perfectly available to all, is differentiated and personal. Knowledge is not an abstract thing to be looked up in some authoritative text. It resides in millions of human minds in fragmented form. The knowledge people possess may be technical, practical, circumstantial, or simply "techniques of thought"[11] that allow an individual to see the world differently from others. This kind of market-relevant knowledge allows individuals to form conjectures about the consequences of potential courses of action based on their own unique experiences. Most importantly, economically relevant knowledge grows in the process of people trading with each other. No one knows in advance what will be the best technology, or who will be the most skillful producer, offer the best service, or what products will most satisfy wants. That knowledge comes about only as people act upon their beliefs and bear the consequences of their actions. Further, and perhaps most important, in the process of participating in market exchanges, individuals not only revise and enhance their knowledge; they benefit from the knowledge of other market participants, knowledge embedded in the products consumed and the technologies that produced those products. When individuals trade with each other, they are trading not only goods and services, but the unique knowledge each possesses.[12] As Hayek was to later call it, a market order is a "discovery procedure,"[13] an arrangement of trading practices that permit knowledge and the fruits of knowledge to grow. Intellectuals might focus on abstract theoretical learning as the significant achievement of human progress, but Hayek was equally impressed by practical knowledge acquired through market activity, knowledge whose application could improve lives dramatically.

Central to the advance of market knowledge is that people pursue their own interests, projects, and plans, and use their own resources to trade with others. One can consider the pursuit of one's interests as a set of problems to be solved: how to best use what I have and what I know to best achieve my goals. This, of course, is the economic problem that neoclassical economists render as "maximizing utility." What neoclassical economics and, by implication, market socialists fail to account for, however, is that "maximizing" is not an automatic process, and the solution to the maximizing problem, never obvious, must be discovered. What may be discovered can range all the way from which brand of jeans offers the best fit to a new use for an existing resource to the discovery of new resources and new ways of using them that revolutionize how we live.[14] The technological and organizational change that we have come to take for granted is a product of people pursuing their interests in the marketplace.

Human society flourishes when as much knowledge as possible that is discoverable by individual human minds is used in ways that benefit others. Like Adam Smith before him, Hayek argues that this happy result flows from allowing people to make their own economic decisions based on their own notions of their best interests: insofar as people are free to trade with each other, each has an incentive to use his own knowledge and skills as best he can to enrich himself. The consequence, as Adam Smith taught us,[15] is that by pursuing his own interests in the marketplace, each enhances the welfare of others. Or, as Hayek might put it, without addressing any notion of ultimate worth, by using his unique knowledge and skills for his own purposes, an economic actor creates value that allows others to benefit from his actions. Smith called this the "simple system of natural liberty,"[16] and invoked the metaphor of the "invisible hand"[17] to explain how the freely chosen actions of separate individuals lead to orderly patterns of trade and economic growth that seem to be the product of a planning intelligence. In Hayek's case, he offered his notion of a spontaneous order: an order that appears to be the result of a plan but is actually the unintended result of individuals going about the business of making a living through trade constrained only by commonly followed rules of behavior.

THE MARKET ORDER OR CATALLAXY

Hayek regarded the term *economy* to be a poor description of what actually goes on in a market order. From the Greek word for the art of household management, *economy* implies a manager who chooses to maximize the welfare of a household according to his evaluation of what is best for those under his care. Yet given human differences in valuation, the metaphor of a single mind is clearly misplaced. While humans might share broad notions of what contributes to economic flourishing, they differ greatly in how that applies to their own well-being. Humans might agree that they all need food, clothing, shelter, companionship, and community, but how much of one is worth how much of another will differ from one person to the next. There is no unitary, undisputed ranking of social values by which to judge the welfare maximum of a society.[18]

A market order is better analyzed as a network of trading relationships that allow people to reshuffle things they value in such a way as to make them all come closer to satisfying their most pressing diverse interests.[19] These diverse interests cannot be aggregated into a common hierarchy of values that would satisfy all members of the group.[20] Thus, Hayek preferred to describe the phenomenon under consideration as a "catallaxy," rather than an "economy." He coined the term based on another Greek word, *katallattein*, which had a double meaning, "to trade" and also "to admit into the community" or "to change an enemy into a friend,"[21] a double meaning that Hayek found particularly significant. While the first meaning emphasizes the specific character of a market order as facilitating wealth creation through trade among diverse people, the second refers to the civilizing effects of trade. When humans see others as rivals, there is potential for conflict and violence, but where they see others as useful to their purposes, as they do in mutually beneficial acts of trade, they have an incentive to act peacefully and cooperatively. One need not think that seeing others as means to one's ends is a salutary motivation for human interaction and yet be able to appreciate the value of reducing the scope for intergroup violence in human society.[22] Hayek believed "changing a stranger into friend" was both the source of economic development and one of the foundations of civilization. There is supporting evidence for his claim.[23]

Humans evolved over the course of several million years, at first living in small bands of about fifty individuals who made a living by hunting and gathering. There is accumulating evidence that while early hominid life was surely not solitary (human ancestors, like modern-day chimps and apes, were social creatures), a case can be made that it was, indeed, poor, brutish, and short.[24] Significantly, death by violence was a common occurrence, through either unfortunate encounters with wild animals or outright warfare with rival tribes. While a person had to cooperate with others in his tribe to survive, people outside the tribe were de facto enemies, rivals for territory and resources (again like modern-day chimps and apes—and surviving hunter-gatherer tribes). In such an environment, there was precious little scope for the division of labor and the gains from trade, as evidenced by millennia of almost nonexistent technological change. The welfare of the group would be dependent on natural elements beyond anyone's control, and populations would wax and wane largely with the availability of food. Yet somewhere between 10,000 and 40,000 years ago, a major change took place. Some tribe or tribes discovered a way to trade with strangers from other tribes without killing them first, and the consequences were revolutionary. Tribes that discovered how to trade peacefully with others outside their band would necessarily expand their market, giving scope for the division of labor and all the benefits that arise therefrom.

While it is impossible to know exactly how some human groups first managed to find a way to trade with each other, Hayek points out that a group that eventually learned to suspend hostilities long enough to trade with strangers from outside of their tribe would have a great evolutionary advantage over nontrading tribes.[25] Trade would have enhanced the tribe's wealth, which would have resulted in more children surviving to adulthood and more adults dying from disease and old age rather than malnutrition and conflict. Greater wealth would have meant greater population, and as the population of traders grew, they would come to crowd out nontrading groups in the competition for resources. It is also likely that some nontrading tribes would wish to copy their wealthier rivals and themselves become traders. In either case, the resultant growth in trading populations would cause their trade-favorable practices to dominate less-advanced groups. The consequences were that within the span of a few millennia, social rules that permitted widespread trade were common throughout Europe, the Middle East, and Asia. Within a geological blink of an eye, humans moved from a nomadic lifestyle to a settled one, then to agricultural communities, and then to large cities, which characterized ancient civilizations. And while the human condition cannot be said to have reached perfection by any means, and while it is the case that the upper echelons of political hierarchies dominated the less powerful and captured a disproportionate share of wealth created through the extension of trade, it is undeniable that populations grew, life spans increased, and an individual had a much greater chance of dying of old age or disease than from an ax to the skull. How this came about was to a large degree explained by the adoption of new rules of social order that favored trading with strangers.

THE IMPORTANCE OF RULES

If anything captures Hayek's approach to understanding social order, it is his emphasis on the importance of rules in social interaction.[26] All human action is bound by rules for the simple reason that the world is uncertain. Yet if purposeful humans are to achieve their goals, they must be able to form predictions about the possible outcomes of their projects and plans. In particular, they need to have some idea about the way in which others will react to their endeavors. Thus, Hayek argues, society is possible only because humans have developed rules of behavior that govern their interactions, and not the least of these are the rules that govern the interactions of people in markets.[27] Market rules may be informal, such as the etiquette surrounding bargaining or the degree of small talk that must precede serious negotiation, or they may be formally codified into law. Fundamental to the expansion of trade were settled laws of property, tort, and contract. Without laws upholding private property, an individual's right to use resources to produce goods for sale would be at best uncertain and subject to challenge from other potential claimants. Nor would complex trades be possible without some form of assurance that contracts would be upheld in the eyes of society and wrongdoing punished. In the early stages of economic development, it is likely that rules of property and contract would have been subject to informal enforcement; as civilization grew and political authority asserted itself, significantly, informal rules would have been codified into law enforced by the power of the state.

From a Hayekian perspective, what distinguishes laws from informal rules is the method of enforcing compliance. If one fails to follow social conventions that signal a desire to enter into a negotiation, or if one does not understand the difference between goods that are acceptable objects of trade and ones that are off-limits in a culture, one very likely will lose the opportunity to profit from a trade. Egregious violations of informal rules of trade might also in the extreme lead to social ostracism. In any case, people who violate informal rules of trade can suffer short-term financial losses but ultimately can learn from their failures. Formal rules, on the other hand, are laws backed up by the power of the legal authority: they constrain behavior through the threat of force if they are not followed. While failing to follow an informal rule can hamper one's ability to profit from a potential deal, failing to follow a formal rule can mean socially sanctioned loss of wealth or freedom. This difference is crucial for understanding the forces of economic development.

Recall that Hayek saw the market as a "discovery procedure," in essence an experimental process by which people act upon their own conjectures about possible outcomes and learn from bearing the consequences of their actions. The greater the scope for experimentation, the greater will be the potential growth of knowledge that flows from entrepreneurial action, and greater knowledge leads to more wealth for the entire society. Hence, Hayek believed that societies that allow individuals the greatest degree of discretion to determine their own actions in the marketplace would be the richest societies.[28]

Just as technologies evolve as humans learn better ways of enhancing their productivity, the rules of trade also evolve with human experimentation and learning. New habits and customs surrounding trade will evolve to support new technologies and expanding markets. As long as the consequences of acting against an established social norm involve no cost greater than potentially losing money or incurring public displeasure, entrepreneurs will try out new ways of interacting in the market, and where their innovation is wealth enhancing, it will be copied by others and become established as a new norm.[29] Where norms are codified into law, however, experiments that potentially violate formal social rules will be severely limited and slow to change. This is as it should be: laws need to be predictable to allow people to plan their actions in an uncertain world. But it is also true that changing technologies that result from economic development will require changes in laws of property and contract to reflect the new economic environment.[30] If laws are too rigid or the process of adapting laws to new circumstances too inflexible, economic development will be slowed or, in extreme cases, halted entirely.[31]

THE CHARACTER OF GOOD RULES

As we have seen, for Hayek, what distinguishes a progressing nation from a stagnating one is the scope for market experimentation. In particular, this means freedom to use one's resources on the basis of one's own conjectures about the consequences of one's action. Since progress requires employing an ever-increasing stock of knowledge, much of which exists only in dispersed form, successful societies will be ones that have rules of social order that encourage individuals to deploy that knowledge to economically beneficial uses.[32] There is no certainty in life, and in a complex, evolving market order, every action contains the possibility that the consequences will differ from the actor's hopes. Each deployment of one's resources and each trade are a sort of market experiment from which one learns more than one knew before.

Learning through one's actions in the marketplace has two components. First, one must be able to risk one's own wealth in a market endeavor; traders must have clear property rights in the goods and services they wish to trade. The potential for gain or loss encourages an actor to tap into all of her market knowledge to make the best guess possible about how to profit from the action. Second, the actor must bear the consequences of the action. To be deprived of the gains from one's actions will reduce market experimentation and the deployment of knowledge that benefits society. To be insulated from losses is equally harmful. Without the discipline of losses from one's miscalculations, there is little incentive to make the best decision possible, and there is little learning from one's mistakes. In either case, society loses, a circumstance recently observed by government bailouts of businesses deemed "too big to fail."

Hayek tells us little about what specific rules fulfill these general requirements, and for good reason. The specific rules of property and contract, he argues, will be culture dependent, and they will change with changing economic circumstances. Law, he believed, was the product of an evolutionary process that allowed societies to adapt to changing conditions.[33] But, while he did not think he or anyone else was competent to design the perfect set of laws to govern economic interaction, he did describe several characteristics of such laws that would make them consistent with a progressing extended market order: they must consist of general rules that constrain certain actions, but do not command specific behaviors, and they must be impartially applied to all people.[34] Both are important for permitting individuals to use their knowledge effectively to achieve their purposes in the marketplace. To prescribe certain behavior (such as in what manner a product must be produced, or what goods one must purchase) takes away individual discretion, substituting the will of the authority for that of the actor. To enact laws that single out some for benefits or handicaps that do not apply to others violates the principle of equality before the law. Hayek believed both to be a violation of liberty, but even if one does not share his perspective, there are practical disadvantages to violating the tenets of good economic rules.

Where political authorities prescribe specific actions, or where they try to play favorites and pick winners, they are substituting their own judgment for that of market actors. This necessarily reduces the amount of knowledge employed in a decision and stifles adaptation to change, slowing and often preventing the process of entrepreneurial discovery and the growth of wealth.[35] On the other hand, a political regime that permits free employment of one's resources constrained only by impartially enforced laws of property, tort, and contract, and tempered by the need to bear the consequences of actions is a political regime that encourages the sharing of knowledge that leads to economic growth and development.

THE MIRAGE OF SOCIAL JUSTICE

Even if we grant Hayek's argument that the extended market order leads to the production of the greatest amount of material wealth possible for the greatest number of people, does this constitute a moral defense of the extended market order? After all, Hayek, himself agrees that material wealth is not an ultimate value in any sense: it is merely what people desire in order to achieve their other varying purposes. These purposes can be praiseworthy, such as supporting their families or donating to charity, or they can be morally unattractive, such as wanting to wallow in sybaritic pleasures. It is not markets per se that can be judged moral or immoral; rather, it is people's actions in markets that can be so judged. In general, there are two kinds of criticisms of the extended market order that are commonly asserted. The first is that market activity may preclude the pursuit of some values that people think of as good. Perhaps the clear benefits derived from self-interested behavior in markets crowd out altruistic behavior, and perhaps the incentives to compete with others undermine actions that lead to a sense of community and solidarity.

Hayek had little patience with this argument, nor did he address it in any depth. While he might agree that people often behave in unethical ways in markets, he would likely argue that people have been known to behave badly in all social settings. If anything, the desire to prosper in market activity encourages sociability and conformity with ethical norms: success in market endeavors requires that others be willing to trade with you.[36] The great contribution of a market economy is that large areas of behavior are constrained by the need to benefit others to achieve our own purposes. Hayek finds it no accident that societies that permit greater economic freedom historically have not simply been wealthier, but more charitable as well.[37] Of course, there is no guarantee they will be so: how people use economic freedom depends upon their moral convictions. There is reason to believe, however, that markets encourage, in fact, teach, such virtues as honesty, self-reliance, and accountability because people who practice them tend to prosper. Further, Hayek pointed out, the only kinds of actions that can be given moral import are noncoerced choices, the kinds one is able to exercise within market settings. Hence, freedom in economic as well as political society permits people both to exercise virtuous behavior and to learn virtue from the responses to their actions.[38]

Hayek regarded as far more serious the second common indictment of a market order, that wealth is not distributed equally among actors. He found complaints about disparities in wealth dangerous because while fundamentally misguided, they provide ideological justification for both socialist planning and the advanced welfare state. His worry was that intolerance for wealth inequalities that follow from economic freedom, and the concomitant demands for redistribution that intolerance engenders, could seriously undermine the market order and reverse all of the benefits that modern civilization has come to take for granted. Hayek's concern is reflected in the subtitle of volume 3 of *Law, Legislation, and Liberty: The Mirage of Social Justice.*[39]

Calls for social justice, he argues, stem from the belief that differences in wealth that follow from market action are unjust, a claim that Hayek regarded as a misuse of the notion of justice. Justice can apply only to the acts of individuals. Unlike a society, a person is an independent mind that can choose her actions, and because the person has a choice, she can be held accountable for the consequences of her actions. If a person has no choice, no moral evaluation can be assigned to her actions. "Society" is not a single choosing entity. Rules guide individual actions within the society, but there is no single intelligence that can be held accountable for the consequences of following the rules. When actors who adhere to a common set of rules make choices among alternatives, the outcomes that emerge from their choices form recognizable patterns, but they are nevertheless unpredictable and uncontrollable.[40] Further, since no one can control the outcomes of the rule-following behavior of individuals in markets, there is really no meaning to the term "social injustice." Insofar as individuals' market transactions are consistent with the rules of property, tort, and contract that are applicable to all people, the actions are just, and the outcomes of the actions must be just.[41] The fact that people will prosper differentially in a market order is irrelevant.[42]

While one might agree with Hayek that unequal outcomes from market action cannot be avoided where there is even a modicum of economic liberty, it is also true that people often find offensive the differences in wealth that emerge from market activity. When people claim that the market is "unfair," they usually mean that market rewards do not reflect nonmarket notions of merit. Successful traders are not necessarily the strongest, the smartest, the most personally lovable, or even the most skillful in a recognized activity. And while certainly knowledge, hard work, and skill play some role in economic success, so does luck. Everyone knows someone who is honorable and hardworking but nevertheless suffers market reverses due to circumstances beyond his control. It seems unfair that a worthy person can do badly, while others, perhaps not so worthy, become wealthy because they were in the right place at the right time or guessed correctly what consumers would regard as the next "hot item." Yet, according to Hayek, the very feature that people find objectionable—that markets do not necessarily reward merit—is really one of its major strengths.[43]

If Hayek's claim[44] seems counterintuitive, consider the following: in an extended market order, personal profit accrues only to those who provide services valued by others. This central truth about market success applies to rock stars and sports heroes as well as people going about the more mundane tasks of life in a market economy. We don't choose doctors because they are kind to their families or donate to multiple charities, and we don't prefer a highly educated but incompetent plumber to one who can stop the sink from leaking. As consumers we try to deal with sellers who provide us with the greatest service for the least price regardless of their many other attributes. The income derived from market exchange, then, is an assessment of the worth of one's actions to other people. Market rewards are in essence a social judgment about the relative importance of various productive activities. Redistribution, on the other hand, substitutes some other non-agreed-upon standard for assigning rewards for productive actions, standards that can be maintained only by imposition from a political authority. Some might be quite willing to supply an alternative standard to be imposed through political means as the popularity of welfare state transfers attest, but redistribution is not a costless exercise in altruism by proxy. Further, and not incidentally, laws aimed at redistributing the wealth that actors create in market transactions will have the perverse effect of reducing the amount of wealth available in society.[45] In markets, people are motivated largely by the chance of material gain.[46] At some point, attenuating the chance of gain also chips away at the motivation to provide services for others, slowing economic growth and reducing wealth not only for the wealthy, but for all who benefit from cheaper and more plentiful goods, which are the hallmark of a vibrant market economy.[47]

CONCLUDING REMARKS

Perhaps because he was not primarily interested in formulating precepts for how people should live, Hayek was a firm believer in the importance of economic liberty. To be free to use one's own resources to shape one's own life, he believed, was both a value in itself and instrumental to the achievement of other values, not the least of which was the growth of material wealth. Material wealth, after all, is the means by which so many human purposes can be achieved. And economic growth is not simply about having more stuff: it is also about the eradication of disease, the extension of life spans, the reduction in infant mortality, and the luxury of leisure to allow the pursuit of arts and letters.

Hayek believed that twentieth-century socialist ideology, with its railing against the purported shortcomings of the market order, failed to appreciate the interconnectedness between economic liberty and economic growth that improved the material well-being of an entire people. For the economically advanced countries of the world, such as the United States and the countries of Western Europe, a slowing and eventual cessation of economic growth would mean a slow decline in living standards that, while unpleasant, could persist for decades. The Third World would face a very different future. A slowing down or stagnation of economic growth would at best remove from the poorest of the world's population their chance to escape their poverty. At worst, Hayek dramatically argued, it would lead to even greater poverty, increasing misery, and even death through starvation and social upheaval.[48] While Hayek's argument may seem exaggerated to twenty-first-century readers, when one remembers that the examples he had in mind were the USSR and Communist China, the specter of mass starvation following the elimination of a market order is not at all far-fetched.

Hayek's answer to critics of the market order was straightforward. It may be true that in the "game of catallaxy,"[49] there will always be losers as well as winners, and some players could well find themselves worse off than they would have been under some other rules of order.[50] However, the net result of an extended market will be that the greatest number of people will have the best chance to improve their own well-being and that of their children. There is no other system of human arrangements yet discovered that has allowed as many people to better their circumstances as they see fit or raised the standard of living of even the poorest "by assuring to all an individual liberty desirable for itself on ethical grounds."[51]

So, is there a moral defense of the market order? If with Hayek, we believe that the only judge of the value of a market order is the evaluations of individual actors, then perhaps there is. As Hayek concludes his last book,

> If one considers the realities of "bourgeois" life—but not utopian demands for a life free of all conflict, pain, lack of fulfillment, and indeed, morality—one might think the pleasures and stimulations of civilisation not a bad bargain for those who do not yet enjoy them. . . . The only objective assessment of the issue is to see what people do when they are given the choice. . . . The readiness with which ordinary people of the third world—as opposed to Western-educated intellectuals—appear to embrace the opportunities offered them by the extended order, even if it means inhabiting for a time shanty towns at the periphery, complements evidence regarding the reactions of European peasants to the introduction of urban capitalism, indicating that people will usually choose civilisation if they have the choice.[52]

NOTES

1. Friedrich Hayek, *The Constitution of Liberty* (Chicago: University of Chicago Press, 1960). Friedrich Hayek, *Law, Legislation, and Liberty* is a three-volume work published by the University of Chicago Press: vol. 1, *Rules and Order* (1973); vol. 2, *The Mirage of Social Justice* (1976); and vol. 3, *The Political Order of a Free People* (1979). Friedrich Hayek, *The Fatal Conceit: The Errors of Socialism* was also published by the University of Chicago Press, in 1988.

2. Hayek, *Constitution of Liberty*, 53.

3. For an insightful account of Hayek's career, see Bruce Caldwell, *Hayek's Challenge: An Intellectual Biography of F. A. Hayek* (Chicago: University of Chicago Press, 2004).

4. Oscar Lange and Fred M. Taylor, *On the Economic Theory of Socialism* (New York: McGraw-Hill, 1938).

5. All three articles—"Socialist Calculation I: The Nature and History of the Problem" (1935); "Socialist Calculation II: The State of the Debate" (1935); and "Socialist Calculation III: The Competitive 'Solution'" (1940)—were published in Friedrich Hayek, *Individualism and Economic Order* (Chicago: University of Chicago Press, 1948), 148–208.

6. "Economics and Knowledge," 33–56; "The Use of Knowledge in Society," 77–91; and "The Meaning of Competition," 92–106, in Hayek, *Individualism and Economic Order*.

7. For a comprehensive treatment of Hayek's role in what came to be known as "the economic calculation debate," see Karen I. Vaughn, *Austrian Economics in America: The Migration of a Tradition* (Cambridge: Cambridge University Press, 1994), chap. 3.

8. "The practical problem is not whether a particular method would eventually lead to a hypothetical equilibrium, but which method will secure the more rapid and complete adjustment to the daily changing conditions in different places and different industries." "Socialist Calculation III," 188.

9. Hayek, "Economics and Knowledge," 51.

10. Although Hayek introduces the term "spontaneous order," in *Constitution of Liberty*, 160, a detailed development of the notion is found in *Law, Legislation, and Liberty*, vol. 1.

11. Hayek, "Socialist Calculation II," 156.

12. Hayek, "Economics and Knowledge," 33–56. Although learning in markets is probably most often thought of in terms of technological innovations, in fact, the simple act of shopping in a mall exposes shoppers to new products and supplies information about prices and available quantities. In turn, consumer purchasing *decisions* give useful information to sellers that influences what they supply in the future.

13. Friedrich Hayek, "Competition as a Discovery Procedure," in *New Studies in Philosophy, Politics, Economics, and the History of Ideas* (Chicago: University of Chicago Press, 1978), 179–190.

14. One has only to think of the microprocessor to grasp the point.

15. Adam Smith, *An Inquiry into the Nature and Causes of the Wealth of Nations*, ed. R. H. Campbell, A. S. Skinner, and W. B. Todd (Indianapolis, IN: Liberty Fund, 1981), IV.ii.10 (p. 456).

16. Smith, *Wealth of Nations*, IV.ix.51 (p. 687).

17. Smith, *Wealth of Nations*, IV.ii.9 (p. 456).

18. Obviously, Hayek is denying that there is any such thing as a social welfare function that truly reflects some aggregate, agreed-upon relative valuation of alternatives. *Law, Legislation, and Liberty*, 2:109–111.

19. As a network of relationships, a market does not have a single purpose, despite what some business ethicists might claim. The entire thrust of Hayek's work renders nonsensical the claim that "the purpose of business is to provide for the prosperity of the entire society" (Robert Solomon, *Ethics and Excellence: Cooperation and Integrity in Business* [New York: Oxford University Press, 1992], 20). Without doubt, of course, business enterprises lead to greater prosperity, so in some sense one might say that is their function, but no one *assigns* that purpose to them. Purposes are individual, and there are unintended and largely beneficial consequences to organizing production in business enterprises. Crucially, no businessman can know exactly what the "prosperity of the entire society" means. He can know only whether or not the organization is making, a profit.

20. Friedrich Hayek, *The Road to Serfdom* (Chicago: University of Chicago Press, 1944).

21. Hayek, *Law, Legislation, and Liberty*, 2:107–111.

22. Or as Adam Smith so aptly put it, "Man has almost constant occasion for the help of his brethren, and it is vain for him to expect it from their benevolence only. He will be more likely to prevail if he can interest their self-love in his favour. . . . Give me that which I want, and you shall have this which you want [is] . . . the manner that we obtain from one another the far greater part of those good offices which we stand in need of." *Wealth of Nations*, I.ii.2 (p. 26).

23. For an account of current anthropological research that supports Hayek's evolutionary view of markets, see Matt Ridley, *The Rational Optimist: How Prosperity Evolves* (New York: Harper Collins, 2010). See also Nicholas Wade, *Before the Dawn: Recovering the Lost History of Our Ancestors* (New York: Penguin Books, 2006), for corroborating evidence from genetics.

24. We make no judgment about its ultimate nastiness.

25. Hayek, *Law, Legislation, and Liberty*, 3:155.

26. Recall the subtitle of volume 1 of *Law, Legislation, and Liberty: Rules and Order*. Hayek's thesis is that without rules there is no social order, and the character of the emergent order is dependent upon the nature of the rules by which it is governed. See esp. *Law, Legislation, and Liberty*, 1:17–19.

27. Hayek, *Constitution of Liberty*, 148–161.

28. Hayek, *Constitution of Liberty*, 156.

29. Violations might include trading with a socially unacceptable partner or offering to trade a good that was previously considered outside the scope of the market.

30. Hayek's model for a legal process that supports market innovation was English common law. Because judges apply precedent to new situations, the law would be changed gradually to accommodate economic discovery. *Law, Legislation, and Liberty*, 1:82–88.

31. Slowing or reversing the process of economic development, Hayek will argue, is not simply an inconvenience, however, or even a choice among lifestyles. It is a calamity for the society that suffers stagnation or decline. One could think of Europe after the fall of the Roman Empire or of China, which suffered close to a thousand years of economic stagnation, during which the overwhelming majority of the population lived in poverty while the politically powerful lived in relative opulence (Ridley, *Rational Optimist*, 179–184).

32. An action that is "economically beneficial" is one that benefits all those with whom one trades. In a market economy, one only benefits by providing benefits to others.

33. Hayek, *Law, Legislation, and Liberty*, 1:72–91.

34. Hayek, *Constitution of Liberty*, 149.

35. Hayek was not arguing against all economic regulation per se. He was merely warning that regulation that specifies certain actions comes at a high cost and should be employed sparingly if at all. See *Constitution of Liberty*, 253–396, for a detailed examination of regulatory issues.

36. Answers to the numerous critics of market values abound. See, for example, Deirdre McCloskey, *The Bourgeois Virtues: Ethics for an Age of Commerce* (Chicago: University of Chicago Press, 2006).

37. "Free societies . . . in modern times have been the source of all the great humanitarian movements aiming at active help to the weak, the ill, and the oppressed. Unfree societies . . . have as regularly developed a disrespect for the law, [and] a callous attitude toward suffering." Hayek, "The Moral Element in Free Enterprise," in *New Studies*, 230.

38. Hayek, "Moral Element," 231.

39. See especially chap. 9, which is entitled "'Social' or Distributive Justice."

40. A wide body of research supports Hayek's claim by showing that economies are complex, adaptive systems (or emergent orders, as in evolutionary biology) where individual rule-following agents create orderly patterns of action that lead to emergent structures more complex than their constituent parts (e.g., bilateral trades become organized markets). In complex, adaptive systems, specific outcomes cannot be predicted, although patterns can be perceived. See, for example, Scott E. Page, *Diversity and Complexity* (Princeton, NJ: Princeton University Press, 2011). Complexity science had its origins in the 1950s and 1960s in what was then called "systems theory," features of which Hayek incorporated into his writings on methodology and into his theory of spontaneous order. See Karen I. Vaughn, "Hayek's Theory of the Market Order as an Instance of the Theory of Complex, Adaptive Systems," *Journal des Économistes et des Études Humaines* 9, no. 2/3 (June/September 1999): 241–256.

41. Robert Nozick, *Anarchy, State, and Utopia* (New York: Basic Books, 1974), 150–153, makes a similar argument.

42. Hayek was not tone deaf to people's differences in life chances. He favored, for example, an income safety net to cushion people from devastating loss, as well as several provisions of the modern welfare state. He simply opposed attempts to level incomes through direct intervention in market contracts or to impose massive redistribution through tax policy in the name of justice (*Constitution of Liberty*, 259).

43. *Constitution of Liberty*, 85–99.

44. "One of the great merits of a free society is that material reward is not dependent on whether the majority of our fellows like or esteem us personally. . . . So long as we keep within the

accepted rules, moral pressure can be brought on us only through the esteem of those whom we ourselves respect and not through the allocation of material reward by a social authority." Hayek, "Moral Element," 233–234.

45. Hayek, *Law, Legislation, and Liberty*, 2:98.

46. Of course, motivations for specific actions are complex. People choose professions not simply to maximize material income: the desire for status, to do good, or just to enjoy life all play a role in how and what one does with one's working life. The argument here is simply that reducing the financial reward of any occupation will have consequences for how much of a service is provided and how well it is accomplished. Even saints need to eat.

47. Hayek, *Law, Legislation, and Liberty*, 1:98.

48. Hayek, *Fatal Conceit*, 134.

49. Hayek, *Law, Legislation, and Liberty*, 2:115–120.

50. Sadists, for example, did very well as torturers under despotic governments, but found themselves less in demand as democracy followed expanded markets.

51. Hayek, *Law, Legislation, and Liberty*, 2:71.

52. Hayek, *Fatal Conceit*, 134.

Chapter 14
Why Teach the History
of Economics?

I. INTRODUCTION

Nineteen ninety-three is an auspicious year for the History of Economics Society. Almost exactly twenty years and one month ago, the first gathering of historians of economic thought took place in Chicago. It was not exactly the first meeting of the Society since it was officially formed only in 1974 and the first official meeting took place that year in Chapel Hill, North Carolina. However, the 1973 meeting demonstrated that there was sufficient interest in the subject to form a society. Hence, this is both the twentieth annual meeting of the History of Economics Society and the twentieth anniversary of its inception.

Anniversaries that are multiples of ten or of twenty-five are cause for reflection and for celebration. For my presidential address, then, I propose to offer both a reflection on the nature of the history of economic thought and a celebration of its contribution to academic life. In particular, I want to show why the history of economic thought deserves a place of honor in any graduate economics curriculum. Not surprisingly, I will claim far more importance for our chosen field of study and for our Society than most of our economics colleagues would think reasonable.

Historians of economic thought are frequently on the defensive about their chosen field of study. Our prestige among our peers is modest—to err on the side of overstatement—and our courses are often considered a frill.

Originally presented as a presidential address at the Twentieth Annual Meeting of the History of Economics Society in Philadelphia on June 28, 1993, and published in *Journal of the History of Economic Thought* 15, no. 2 (1993): 174–183. Republished with permission.

Indeed, the attitude reported at some of our most highly esteemed graduate programs is that it is a waste of time to read anything written in economics that was published more than five years ago (Klamer and Colander 1990). In addition to considering our field of only minimal importance, many of our colleagues tend to disparage the skills of historians of economic thought. Since our papers are generally not highly mathematical nor do they make use of the latest (or for that matter almost any) statistical techniques, the field is sometimes considered "easy," mere verbal history rather than hard theory.

So here we are, practitioners of a so-called easy subdiscipline that is itself considered more or less a waste of time. No wonder we band together so tightly once a year at our annual meeting. We relish our annual three days together because it may be the only time during the year that we experience the collegiality that we anticipated finding in academic life. Yet, if the experience of the Society is indicative of the vitality of our subdiscipline, we should conclude that our star is rising.

Twenty years ago, 81 people answered a call to gather in Chicago to discuss the history of economic ideas. There were five sessions with 12 papers given and a round table discussion (Samuels 1974, 243–245). Nineteen years ago, the Society was formed, with 210 original members. The first official meeting in Chapel Hill had 75 participants and no concurrent sessions (Vincent Tarascio 1993, personal communication). This year, the membership is up to 500 and our meeting has 31 sessions and 150 participants. Twenty-five years ago, in 1969, the first journal dedicated to the history of economic thought, *History of Political Economy*, was begun with fear and trembling. By 1974, the year of the founding of our society, *HOPE* had increased its publication rate from twice yearly to four times a year. In 1979, we published the first issue of the *HES Bulletin*, a skinny little thing devoted to notes and announcements.[1] The very idea of someday turning it into a journal at the time seemed fantastic: could there really be enough good papers written in the field to warrant another publication? However, by 1988, the *Bulletin* began to look like a real journal and by 1990, it evolved into the *Journal of the History of Economic Thought*. Furthermore, the Society now publishes an annual collection of essays, *Perspectives on the History of Economic Thought*, and cosponsors a book series. Clearly the field is alive and well, and its specialists are intellectually and professionally active.

Yet, despite all the signs of intelligent life in our disciplinary universe, we as a group remain apologetic about our idiosyncratic interest in the economics of dead economists. In an early issue of *HOPE*, George Stigler wrote an article that still reflects our own anxiety, "Does Economics Have a Useful Past?" (Stigler 1969). In that paper, Stigler gave a few reasons why the history of our discipline is "useful," but he ended on a cautionary note: "Many useful commodities and services are not produced in a society because they are worth less than they cost: it remains the unfulfilled task of the historians of economics to show that their subject is worth its cost" (230).

Not surprisingly, tonight I will argue not only that economics has a useful past but also that it is worth its cost. I will also argue that the question: "Is it worth its cost?" makes no sense unless we additionally ask the more economically relevant question: "As compared to what?"

II. JUSTIFICATIONS

The claim that there is no room for the history of economic thought in a graduate program presumes a certain view of the nature of economics: that economics is a progressive science, and that the sole purpose of graduate education is to train professional economic scientists. The implication seems to be that there is little point in reading the mistakes of dead economists except for fun, and who ever said graduate school should be fun?

Even if one were to take this rather strong view, however, one can still defend studying the history of economic thought in graduate school on several grounds. Indeed, Stigler himself in his 1969 article took the view that the history of economic thought was useful in teaching the young how to read a book carefully and objectively, claiming that it is easier to learn from the old masters than from the modern writers (218). (Did he mean to imply that modern economics is usually badly written, I wonder?) There are other reasons as well. One can agree that all that is important for contemporary theory is contained in the journals of the last few years, but since economics is not as rigorous as physics, mistakes can sometimes reoccur. Economists are better off knowing the mistakes of the past so they will not repeat them. Besides, identifying and correcting the mistakes of the past sharpens students' techniques and makes them more proficient economists. One can also argue, as Stigler did, that although economics is mostly progressive, there are areas of current theory that are "underdeveloped," and in these areas we might still learn from our relatively recent ancestors (217).

These arguments are good as far as they go. Even if economics is a progressive science, it may still make sense for students to have some passing acquaintance with the history of their discipline as long as the study is not taken too seriously. And certainly there is little reason to learn anything but the history of economic analysis, narrowly construed. These arguments imply that an historian of economic thought is a good thing to have around the economics department as long as he or she does not take up too much space and as long as he/she knows his/her place, which is the academic equivalent of the back of the bus.

This view of the place of the history of economics also implies something about what kind of study of the history of the discipline is appropriate: the kind Mark Blaug once called "absolutist" history of thought (Blaug 1978, 2) and what he now, following Richard Rorty, calls "rational reconstruction" (Blaug 1990, 28). This is also what Paul Samuelson recently referred to as Whig history of thought (Samuelson 1987); that is, presenting the ideas of past economists in modern theoretical terms, locating their errors and omissions and thereby finding evidence of progress in science, or less moderately, combing the ancient texts for evidence of "anticipations" of modern ideas.

This kind of work, obviously, requires close reading of older texts and expertise in modern economic theory, but it requires no necessary acquaintance with the history, intellectual background, philosophical preconceptions, or biography of the past thinker. Instead of recreating the full flowering of a human mind, these exercises remind me of nothing so much as dissecting a corpse for the purpose of discovering the cause of death.

I agree with Blaug (1990, 30) that there is nothing wrong with this kind of exercise as far as it goes. Autopsies do serve an important function, after all. However, unlike medical students, economics students have living bodies to dissect, so if the major purpose of studying the history of our discipline is as a pedagogical device for sharpening theoretical techniques by identifying analytical errors of other economists, it might well be more cost effective to train students on contemporary texts. For one thing, finding a contemporary mistake is a much surer road to publication.

A stronger argument for including the history of economic thought in graduate education, however, sees the field as more than simply instrumental in teaching young scientists about the tools and techniques of their science. If we only train students in theory and techniques, we might argue, we make them narrow and unimaginative. Moreover, we isolate them from the rest of the intellectual community. They will have no understanding about the relative place of economics in either the social sciences or in the liberal arts. As members of an academic community, they will not be able to talk to anyone else on a liberal arts faculty and they will be hopeless on any kind of university committee because they will have no conception of how other people think or phrase arguments.

Clearly, this justification for teaching the history of economics implies that the history of economic thought is more than just absolutist, rational reconstruction or Whig history. To develop an appreciation for the place of economics in the larger intellectual community presupposes that when one approaches an older thinker one asks not simply how close did he come to what we know, but why did he think as he did. Our job here is to place a past thinker within his intellectual and historical context, and to discern the questions that were important to him; to aim for historical reconstruction (Blaug 1990, 28) as well as rational reconstruction. Obviously, such an exercise cannot help but be more interdisciplinary and will of necessity acquaint the student with adjacent fields such as history, philosophy, political theory, and the history of science in placing a thinker in his context.

While most of us gathered here would find this argument convincing, our colleagues at home might still retort that however worthy disciplinary perspective may be, it is still not worth the cost. Besides, who wants to talk to the rest of the liberal arts faculty, anyway? Further, this argument seems to suggest that at most, the history of economic thought might be useful to teach, but not actually to specialize in. The history of economic thought then gets relegated to the residual course to assign to whoever does not have something more important to teach this semester. After all, can't anyone read a textbook and teach simple verbal material?

A proper justification for teaching the history of economics is also a justification for reading, studying, and writing the history of economics. Unless we can show why it is respectable to be a specialist in a field, the teaching of that field can only be regarded as a second-class activity. Blaug recently addressed that question and argued that economists inevitably do history of thought when they present novel ideas. The subject is "unquenchable," and as long as it is going to be done, there may as well be professionals to do it (Blaug 1990, 36). This is the economics equivalent of "Its a dirty job, but someone has to do it."

This seems to me a singularly half-hearted defense! To make it seem a reasonable occupation for a grown-up to spend his or her time reading and making sense out of ancient texts requires a much bolder counterattack to our nonhistorically minded colleagues then this. We need to say straight out that the history of economic thought is "useful" not because it helps students to sharpen theoretical skills or because it gives them a little interdisciplinary breadth, but because it can affect how they understand economic theory itself, its potential accomplishments, and its important limitations.

To be sure, one important reason to be an historian of economic thought is to provide the kind of disciplinary perspective I have already mentioned. But the disciplinary perspective is itself important for a deeper reason: Because economics is not the kind of progressive science that many of our colleagues back home think it is. Not all that is important in the past has been incorporated into the last journal article in the *American Economic Review*. The progress of economics is not always away from darkness and toward light. While some questions about economic activity have been tentatively answered, many have been left dangling. Mistaken views do not always die, correct views do not always survive. It is not even always clear what words like "mistaken" and "correct" mean in economics. Propositions are generally correct or incorrect within a context of a larger theoretical system. In order to evaluate older economics, then, we need to understand the context of the propositions and not just our system for interpreting the world.

Such a view of economics is an expected consequence of the study of its development. Historians of economics by definition study the unfolding of economic ideas and cannot help but be reflective about how economics is done.[2] And by such study and reflection, we tend to lose our naivete about current certainties. We see how often the advanced doctrine of one era was the mistake of another (John Stuart Mill's pronouncements on the labor theory of value come to mind), how endless debate in one period was wiped away by a refocusing of the problem at a later date (consider the late eighteenth- and early nineteenth-century debate over productive versus unproductive labor). And more to the point, how the metaphors and moral views of previous eras inform our current notions of science. (I, myself, am partial to describing current welfare economics as a combination of the ethos of the medieval just price theory with Aristotelian notions of an exchange of equivalents.)

But if economics is not the unimpeded triumph of light over darkness, then the history of economics takes on a whole new importance in graduate study. Students in all good conscience can be asked to read Aristotle or John Locke or Adam Smith or Carl Menger not simply for antiquarian interest or to give them perspective—although both are available in abundance in these works. Students can read these thinkers to help develop into good economists. Reading creative thinkers from the past can have several salutary results: It may reduce the arrogance quotient among young economists who cannot imagine that anything important was written before their time. It also makes students aware of grand systems of thought that might serve to lift their sights above the mind-numbing specialized papers that are the routine fare of economists today. By giving students both great ideas and broad systems to chew on, we might stimulate them to think a few great thoughts themselves.

We can, however, claim more than providing inspiration and intellectual humility as benefits of study of our discipline. We can also argue that study of our ancestors can lead to contemporary enlightenment as well. If not all that is true in the past is contained in the journals of the present, that must mean there are more true things out there for us to recapture. If some discarded ideas were prematurely rejected, we might be able to identify and reconsider them. If questions that were once ignored are now of crucial importance, we might, if we know the literature well, be able to re-ask them.

My colleague David Levy likes to compare the history of ideas to a bulletin board upon which unanswered questions in economics are posted to challenge future generations. I like this metaphor, but I would add that even the supposedly answered questions need rethinking from time to time and that can only be done if one understands the contingent nature of our current theory.

I am particularly sensitive to this last issue because of my recent work on Carl Menger and the Austrian school (Vaughn 1987, 1990, 1994). Austrian economists for several decades have claimed that Menger was misunderstood by his neoclassical interpreters who judged him to have been a budding but at times confused neoclassical founder of modern economics. This view, by the way, is supported by rational reconstructions. The Austrians argue, on the other hand, that Menger was the founder of a distinctive approach to economics. To investigate that claim required a historical reconstruction to find out what Menger himself thought he was about and how he might have been right or wrong within the context of his own system. My own attempt to do just that led me to the conclusion that despite his theory of diminishing marginal use and several references to equilibrium prices and situations, Menger was most usefully thought of as a neoclassical economist. He was more interested in explaining economic processes and institutions than equilibrium conditions.

I found this important not only because I felt it settled an interesting issue of interpretation, to my own satisfaction any rate. I thought the result was important because I became convinced that Menger was on to something missing in modern economics. He began with different questions, questions of growth through time rather than allocation and maximizing, and he was interested in different problems—what people know and don't know and how their knowledge is shared and improved upon through trade with each other, more than what equilibrium prices will be established in a perfect world. In Menger's case, a rational reconstruction alone is misleading for understanding Menger since what it identifies as his mistakes are really his strengths from another perspective. But the value of historical reconstruction was more than just "getting Menger right." The historical reconstruction led me to understand how the kind of theory we use dictates the kinds of questions that can be asked. This led me to look at contemporary economics differently. Most of you, and especially those who study J. M. Keynes or Karl Marx or J. R. Commons or Thorstein Veblen, probably have all had similar experiences.

III. HES AND THE HISTORY OF ECONOMIC THOUGHT

This leads me to an observation about the importance of the History of Economics Society itself rather than the field in general. Those who are drawn to study the history of economics are often people whose hearts belong in other eras or other, non-neoclassical worlds. It has frequently struck me that in addition to our Smith and Ricardo specialists, our students of ancient and medieval writers, our seventeenth- and eighteenth-century buffs, this society has a disproportionate number of people interested in institutionalism, Austrians, Marx, and Keynes at each meeting. There is a good reason for that. People who are drawn to other, non-neoclassical interpretive structures have no place else to go to talk to people who do not either automatically agree or automatically disagree with them. Out-of-favor paradigms do not get much of a hearing at more general professional meetings. Sessions organized around institutionalist, Austrian or post-Keynesian themes are generally attended by the faithful. When others wander in to listen, the criticism tends to be hostile or dismissive. Yet when only the faithful listen, comments take the form of "insider" criticism that does not help to communicate with the mainstream.

At meetings of the History of Economics Society, papers on out-of-favor paradigms tend to be couched in terms of what an illustrious ancestor said and how that relates to either his contemporaries or our own. Hence, criticism can be on more neutral grounds than when our own pet beliefs are directly challenged. Interestingly, such more or less "objective" discussions often lead to genuine engagement about the relative merits or demerits of the ideas themselves.[3]

Thankfully, this Society is a place where basic assumptions can be challenged, grand schemes can be examined and where wisdom is preferred to technical knowledge. We are a society of good conversationalists, which Donald McCloskey (1985) would remind us means that we are also a society of good scientists. We are also that rare thing in modern academics, a community of scholars who listen to each other before they speak.

IV. CONCLUSION

I still have to answer George Stigler's question of a quarter century ago. Even if our past is useful, is it enough to justify asking hard-pressed students to devote the time necessary to its mastery? As our economics expertise tells us, the appropriate response here is: "Is it useful compared to what?" What is the opportunity cost and how do we evaluate it? Since value is determined at the margin, we need to be clear about the nature of the margins under consideration.

Here we can be confident of our contribution. If the choice is between one more course in mathematical economics that teaches students advanced techniques that have no application to any real-world problem that anyone cares to solve or a course in the history of economic thought in which they get to read how Aristotle, Aquinas, or Smith grapple with the central questions of economic life, I put my money on the history of economic thought. If the choice is between one more course that teaches the latest sophisticated econometrics, when most questions that anyone wants to answer can be approximated with a hand calculator, or a course in which they get to read Mill or Marx or Marshall, the history of economic thought gets my vote. Historians of economic thought at least use original data!

The same arguments can be made for the relative merits of our research. If the choice is one more article squeezing a reluctant world into the narrow confines of the maximization paradigm or another article trying to understand the expansive mind of Adam Smith, it seems to me there is no contest. Indeed, if we had to sell our product directly to the consuming public, the ultimate marginal evaluation, we would do well relative to our colleagues. Our articles are written in words and contain interesting ideas, colorful personalities, and a plot.

So let me conclude by suggesting that the original question was incorrectly formulated. Everyone agrees that the past has some use; the question is how much of it is worth how much of the present? Or how much learning from the present at the margin should we trade off for what increment of learning from the past? Economics may not be a fully progressive science, but we do know that choices are not all or nothing—and at the current margins of decision, the history of thought is greatly undervalued!

NOTES

1. As first editor of the *Bulletin*, I am permitted a mildly disparaging evaluation.
2. This is probably why there are so many methodologists among us as well. Otherwise, there would be no necessary logic to the professional linking of the history of economic thought and methodology that is customary.

3. This genuine engagement of ideas also, unlike in many other forums, invariably takes place in an atmosphere of good will. More than once I have seen serious discussion that began during a session which included some combination of Austrians, institutionalists, post-Keynesians and conventional economists continue long after the session in an aura of congeniality over coffee or cocktails.

REFERENCES

Blaug, Mark. 1978. *Economic Theory in Retrospect*, 3rd ed. Cambridge: Cambridge University Press.

———. 1990. "On the Historiography of Economics." *Journal of the History of Economic Thought* 12 (Spring): 27–37.

Klamer, Arjo, and David Colander. 1990. *The Making of an Economist*. Boulder, CO: Westview Press.

McCloskey, Donald. 1985. *The Rhetoric of Economics*. Madison: University of Wisconsin Press.

Samuels, Warren J. 1974. "A Report on the Chicago Conference of the History of Economics Society." *History of Political Economy* 6 (3): 243–246.

Samuelson, Paul A. 1987. "Out of the Closet: A Program for the Whig History of Economic Science." *History of Economic Society Bulletin* 9 (1, Fall): 51–60.

Stigler, George J. 1969. "Does Economics Have a Useful Past?" *History of Political Economy* 1 (2): 217–230.

Vaughn, Karen I. 1987. "Carl Menger." In *The New Palgrave: A Dictionary of Economic Theory and Doctrine*, edited by John Eatwell, Murray Millgate and Peter Newman, 438–444. London: Macmillan Press.

———. 1990. "The Mengerian Roots of the Austrian Revival." *History of Political Economy* 22 (Suppl.): 379–407.

———. 1994. *Austrian Economics in America: The Migration of a Tradition*. Cambridge: Cambridge University Press.

Chapter 15
Economic Policy for an Imperfect World

I. INTRODUCTION

It has been four years since the total collapse of even the pretense of central planning in the former Soviet Union. Since that time, there has been almost universal agreement among the nations of the world that market economies are necessary for the production of wealth. The mounting problems of the highly bureaucratic and rigid Soviet economy in the last decade of its existence are now common knowledge. Pundits who once feared the economic "superiority" of a centrally planned Soviet system now seem to be counting the days until even a diehard like Fidel Castro bows to the inevitable and agrees to reform the Cuban economy. Yet those who would take this turn of event to mean that the case for "the free market" is now "won" are declaring victory prematurely. While to be sure, almost no one of any stature still holds out hope for total central planning, the alternative that is considered is not "free markets" so much as a regulated market economy. That is, most of the countries undergoing transition to market economies are searching for the appropriate rules and policies to avoid the excesses of capitalist development, and they are looking toward Western-style welfare and regulatory states for guidance. Meanwhile, many of the European welfare states, which are facing problems of increasing public expenditures, stagnating economies, and high unemployment are themselves beginning to reexamine the question of the right mix of government and market. And in the United States, the forces supporting more market and less government are increasingly making their voices heard on the political scene.

Originally published in *Southern Economic Journal* 62, no. 4 (1996): 833–844. Republished with permission.

The question I want to explore here is the following: what role can conventional neoclassical economic theory play in helping to inform this historic moment? As political regimes worldwide are struggling to find the appropriate role for the market in the political order, or conversely, the appropriate role for government in a market order, what can contemporary economic theory contribute to the debate?

This may seem a ridiculous question to most of you. Obviously, economists using standard economic theory are continually participating in policy formation at home and abroad. There is a veritable flood of economic advisors to formerly communist countries helping them to install market economies. Here at home, regiments of policy analysts, think tank dwellers, advisors to political parties, congressional committees, and presidential panels continually pronounce on things economic. Regulatory agencies are especially blessed in this department. But my question isn't whether they do it, it is on what basis do they do it. What standards are they applying to inform policy? What is the scientific status of the policy recommendations made? What can economic theory tell us about the role of government in the economy?

This is not an idle question. More than a decade ago, Frank Hahn (1982) argued that general equilibrium theory tells us that the invisible hand needs a visible assist from government to keep it from paralysis. More recently, Joseph Stiglitz (1994) has argued that there is no scientific argument to support a belief that free markets work. Those who advocate them do so out of an ideological commitment. If we consider also recent "revisionist" work on two policy areas in which economists once were in overwhelming agreement: Card and Kreuger (1994) who argue that minimum wages do not necessarily reduce employment, and Richard Arnott (1995) who argues that well-designed rent control may bring about good economic effects, it is clear that the question of what theory informs economic policy is important.

My argument will be as follows: The rationale for most economic policy is the enhancement of economic efficiency. Yet our definition of efficiency is based on equilibrium models of perfect markets, and there is the rub. Perfect market models serve less to explain how markets work than to identify imperfections in economic order that interfere with the achievement of perfectly efficient outcomes. These imperfections, in turn, appear to be ripe for some policy intervention. But to go from an equilibrium model of a perfect market to real world imperfections to policy correctives requires several leaps of logic that call the whole exercise into question. We must presume first that the model is sufficient to identify the ideal state, second that the imperfections are correctable, and third that a policy even in principle can be designed to eliminate the imperfection. None of these steps is unproblematic. In fact, I argue that our models are not sufficient to identify an ideal state of the world. Even if they were, it is not clear that any policy we are able to devise could bring it about. Finally, those features of the real world we call imperfections are often integral parts of a market process that we are only beginning to understand.

II. THE THEORETICAL BASIS FOR ECONOMIC POLICY FORMATION

For most of the twentieth century, economic theory has been dominated by one or the other of two related models: Perfect competition, both the mainstay of partial equilibrium analysis and a necessary condition for the achievement of the second, more encompassing market model: general equilibrium.[1] Perfect competition is perfect because in equilibrium, production is perfectly efficient: prices equal marginal costs, goods are produced at minimum average cost and economic profits are zero. These equilibrium conditions guarantee that there is no way to reorganize production to get more of the good at a price consumers will pay. General equilibrium is perfect in a related but more stringent sense, in that all markets are in perfectly competitive equilibrium such that no improvement in the entire economic system is capable of being made.

It is often maintained that the economic case for unrestricted markets is based on these models of perfect competition and general equilibrium. But if these models are the sole defense of free markets, the defense is a poor one at best. Quick examination reveals that these models do not support the contention that unrestricted market competition within a set of minimal rules results in efficient outcomes. Instead, they offer more support for a regulated market economy. The same theory that describes the efficient nature of perfect competition also suggests that in many, perhaps even most instances, perfect competition doesn't apply. And if one takes a general equilibrium view of market economies, it is clear that full equilibrium could never be obtained by a free market. The reason is the widespread existence of market imperfections such as monopoly power, imperfect information, incomplete markets, and externalities that all lead to market failure.

Let us dwell for a moment on the rhetorical impact of the term "market failure." "Market failure" sounds very ominous indeed. It seems to conjure up a devastating flaw with dire consequences—perhaps like brake failure or heart failure. More accurately, however, market failure simply means some condition of market exchange that prevents achievement of full equilibrium as described by an abstract model. Any identified "market failure" says nothing about the overall strength of competitive forces, nor the overall health of the economy. While it seems to be the case that real economies manage to chug along quite productively despite the presence of as myriad of imperfections, we don't seem to have a theoretical language to explain such real-world robustness in the face of putative market failure, although economists often argue about the practical seriousness of one market failure or another. Indeed, an economist's political views are largely a consequence of how important a factor s/he believes market failure to be in real economic affairs.[2]

But whether one believes that market failures are important and widespread as do the New Keynesians, or that they are of small consequence in a typical market economy as do Chicago economists, the fact remains that market failure to most economists suggests a defect in the market place that at least in principle could benefit from some well designed government intervention. But can we legitimately go from identifying market failures to making a case for government policy in one logical leap? Given the nature of our economic models and the limitations of our knowledge about market entities, the leap is at the very least, suspect. It may or may not be the case that markets will work better when government takes on a regulatory role: But simple identification of market failure is not sufficient to establish the case.

III. THE PUBLIC CHOICE VIEW

You will all remind me that I am not the first one to make this point. Since the 1960s and the publication of the *Calculus of Consent*[s] (Buchanan and Tullock 1962), it is inexcusable, and increasingly unlikely, for an economist to blithely advocate regulatory policy without taking into account the problem of "government failure," the inability of government to develop policies that satisfy voters' preferences. Public choice economics, by applying the same model of human action used in economics to political decision-making, shows that policy formation is far more complicated than the "there oughta be a law" sentiment suggests. This body of literature has analyzed the ways in which democratic governmental processes involve a variety of motives that belie an easy path to correcting market failures (Mueller 1989). There are unintended consequences both in the formation and execution of economic policy. Factors such as interest group politics in the design of policy, and the need to implement policy via a bureaucracy that follows its own rules and encompasses a variety of conflicting agendas lead us to be wary of calling for more market correctives than the political system can effectively handle.[3] Buchanan (1979) has called public choice politics without romance, and not the least of its achievements is to deromanticize the politics of economic policy formation.[4]

One might be tempted to stop there and argue that little more needs to be said about the theoretical requirements of economic policy formation. Market imperfections lead to market failure, but then political imperfections lead to government failure. The sensible course to adopt when a market imperfection is identified, then, is to weigh the costs of the economic imperfection against the costs of trying to implement a policy to correct it.[5] Economic policy is in this sense the recreation of political economy after a century of neglect, but this time political economy consists of a pragmatic weighing of political options in order to get the most efficient outcome possible.

As sensible as this approach seems on the surface, it only addresses part of the problem I wish to articulate. Yes, weighing the likely costs and consequences of administrative processes against the costs of market failure surely leads to better policy than not doing so. But that is not enough. The public choice approach is a necessary counterweight to what Demsetz (1969) has called "nirvana" style policy formation, but as long and insofar as it is wedded to conventional notions of perfect markets and conventional definitions of efficiency, it too will be insufficient to guide economic policy. To weigh policy alternatives properly, one needs to know what the alternatives actually are, and I am not at all convinced that our current models of perfect markets which yield neat equilibrium conditions are appropriate tools to aid us in this investigation.[6]

IV. PERFECT MODELS VS. IMPERFECT REALITY

As useful as our models are for many worthy purposes, perhaps out of excess admiration for our own work, when it comes to proposing regulatory regimes, economists may be guilty of confusing models with the real world.[7] As we tell our students, models are helpful abstractions of a complex reality that hopefully lay bare important characteristics of the real world we want to understand. But this does not mean that they are viable alternatives to that reality.

In particular, there is no reason to believe that the result of perfect competition is an achievable state of affairs in the real world, no matter what rules and regulations are imposed on competitive behavior. As a model, perfect competition is useful for the purpose of highlighting relationships between market variables such as prices, costs, profits, and quantities supplied and demanded. To make these relationships clear the model takes certain pervasive features of market competition and defines them in such a way as to establish limit-ing conditions: widespread competition among many producers becomes a market with enough firms so that all firms are price takers; similar products become homogeneous products; widespread information about relevant mar-ket phenomena becomes perfect information perfectly known to everyone; ease of entry and exit of firms becomes costless entry and exit. While it is true that limiting conditions make the model more tractable, it is at the cost of eliminating complicating features of reality that may very well be important for other purposes, especially for the purpose of trying to alter and control the economy.[8]

As a model, perfect competition is simple—even naively so—for the pur-pose of answering specific and limited questions. Why do prices tend to equal costs in a competitive environment? Why do prices increase as supply decreases and vice versa? Certainly, there is no presumption that such a simple model should enable us to answer every important question about market activity, let alone duplicate its simplicity in a complex world.

We may easily lose sight of the fact that perfection and imperfection are characteristics of the model we use, not descriptions of real-world processes. To call competition "perfect" or "imperfect" in this sense implies nothing about its desirability or undesirability and carries no normative weight. An imperfection is a characteristic of the world that has been deliberately assumed away in constructing an abstract model; no more and no less. Yet, economists routinely equate the strictures of the simple model of perfect competition with desirable features of the real world, thereby imparting normative significance to a supposedly scientific construct.

A minute's reflection on this procedure should inspire a certain wariness in us. To illustrate my objection, consider the following analogy. The economist who proposes policies to fix up the deficient world because of its failure to achieve perfect efficiency in perfect equilibrium is in many respects similar to the physicist who builds a model of a perfect vacuum and then judges the world inadequate because feathers don't really fall as fast as lead balls when dropped from the Leaning Tower of Pisa. Of course, the analogy would only be complete if the physicist would also join a commission to devise policy tools to eradicate the earth's imperfect atmosphere. Obviously, physicists don't do that because they realize that the simplified model of a perfect vacuum is not a normative description of what the world should look like, but a first approximation that helps them to understand the more complex phenomena of the real world. Friction is not a defect of the world. Friction is an integral part of a complex physical reality that enables us to walk around on the surface of the earth, among other useful things. Is it perhaps conceivable that market "imperfections" are also integral features of the social world that serve important systemic functions? We will return to this idea later.

V. BUT WHAT ABOUT WELFARE?

Like the model of a perfect vacuum, the assumptions of perfect competition should not be regarded as descriptions of a perfectly desirable reality. Nor are they recipes for bringing about some normative result. Why then do economists insist on judging the world deficient when it doesn't achieve outcomes that match their models of efficiency?

The simple answer to that question is that the achievement of perfectly competitive equilibrium across all markets represents the maximization of something we call "welfare," and welfare has policy significance. And since equilibrium is required for the maximization of welfare, anything that interferes with its attainment seems to provide strong grounds for proposing economic policy to correct the deviation.

While we may regard the improvement of economic welfare as part of the project of modern scientific economics, in truth, the style of argument is nothing if not reminiscent of the just price theories of the Middle Ages. Following Aristotle's understanding of price as an exchange of equivalent values (1953, 151–153), the scholastic doctors of the medieval church agreed that the exchange of equivalents was the criterion for justice and proceeded to ask what circumstances would bring about a just price. While, as Schumpeter (1954) says, the medieval churchmen did develop surprisingly sophisticated theories of value, markets, and money following this procedure, their primary aim was to form the medieval version of economic policy. They used their theories to decide what economic actions promoted economic justice and therefore should be permitted and which actions were unjust and should be regarded as sinful. ("May a man lawfully sell a thing for more than its worth? No, because this violates the just price. Is usury lawful? No, because it represents a perversion of the proper use of money" [Spiegel 1983, 63–65].)

Modern general equilibrium theory and its corollary, welfare economics, bears more than a passing resemblance to a modern, more complicated version of just price theory. (Should monopoly be permitted? Only if the deadweight loss is small. Should natural monopolies be regulated? Yes, because on their own, they will produce too little consumer surplus.) Only now the just price is the long run competitive equilibrium price where price equals long run marginal cost, and sin is disequilibrium brought about by market imperfections.

I say this not to be facetious (well, not *only* to be facetious) but to point out a real misuse of our models. It seems more a religious than a scientific exercise to identify what we want the outcome of people's actions to be in advance and then try to devise means to bring about our desired result. A scientific model should serve to help explain the world as it is, not serve as a reproach to a defective reality.

But haven't I missed an essential point here? Isn't it true that welfare economics is really on a firmer scientific footing than medieval just price doctrine? After all, welfare economics only formalizes the agents' notions of their own well-being. Since we model agents as acting to maximize their own utility, is it not also acceptable to model the conditions that would maximize their collective utility given the initial constraints? General equilibrium describes conditions under which people get the most of what *they* want, given initial endowments, technology, their preferences, and the preferences of others. Economists do not substitute some external valuative criteria for the preferences of the agents we are studying; we assume their purpose is to get the most of what they want and then see if "free trade" or some regulatory regime gives it to them. From there, the only normative step required to justify corrective economic policy is the assumption that people should get what they want. The rest is science.

Well, yes and no. Yes, it is sensible to begin analysis of human behavior with the agents' own view of their welfare. It is not sensible to presume that either perfect competition or its big brother, general equilibrium theory gives us a rich enough understanding of what people do in pursuit of their own welfare in markets to allow us to posit some state of welfare maximization, let alone devise policies to bring it about. Both models simply leave out too much that is important about market activity. In particular, what are identified as imperfections in these models are not defects of the market, but reasons why the market is important in the first place. The reason that markets are valuable instruments for achieving agents' purposes is because the world is "imperfect." Markets solve problems that imperfect life creates.

VI. WHAT'S SO BAD ABOUT IMPERFECTION?

What I am advocating here is a reversal of the perspective on the marketplace usually implied by welfare economics. It is a perspective that many economists instinctively take in their empirical work, but it was explicitly articulated by Friedrich Hayek in 1946. In his article, "The Meaning of Competition," Hayek proposed an alternative way of looking at market phenomena: Instead of investigating why markets fail, he argued, economists should be more concerned with why they might ever be successful in the first place (Hayek 1948, 105). Given the daunting nature of the economic problems that humans face, that markets should ever succeed is more of a puzzle than that they might from time to time fall short of our expectations. That simple restatement of the economist's explanatory problem opens up doors to developing a richer, more fruitful economic research program and a more modest but more sensible approach to economic policy.

Hayek's main concern in this and in several other articles he wrote during the 1930s and 1940s was with the role of knowledge in market transactions.[9] Where standard models assume "given" knowledge or "perfect" knowledge, Hayek rightly asked, given to whom? and perfect with respect to what? He pointed out that knowledge is not given in the sense that it is perfectly public. Knowledge does not (nor cannot) exist concentrated in one mind (or computer program) nor is it equally possessed by all people. While perfect competition regards incomplete and dispersed information as an imperfection in the world, Hayek regarded this as the reason why markets are necessary in the first place.

The fact is that in the social world there is a division of knowledge that needs to be overcome: People know different things just as people have different skills. And just as people can benefit from employing their skills in the service of others in markets, they can benefit from employing their knowledge as well.[10] By acting upon their own knowledge to gain personal advantage within markets, individuals inadvertently share the benefits of their knowledge with others.[11] Without the lure of gain from market exchange, however, less information would be employed for the creation of wealth.

But the market process implies more than just sharing dispersed knowledge. Another defining feature of human life is that we are temporal beings. The fact that time passes means, among other things, that we live with the specter of Knightian uncertainty. We make plans for the future, but we simply cannot know in any definitive sense whether our plans will be fulfilled or not, nor can we know in advance if our schemes are workable or not. The only test of the feasibility of a proposed action in the market is to try it out and see if it works. Hence, as Hayek says, competition in markets is a "discovery procedure" (1978). The trial and error of actual market competition is required to discover whether or not a particular innovation works, whether or not a particular product will sell, whether or not a production technique is an improvement over our current practices. Again, the information that we generally assume exists like production functions, cost functions, even utility functions are all generated through experimentation in markets.[12] And this process of knowledge creation does not stop at any preordained position. It is a continuous process. Hence, imperfect information is not an argument for government but an argument for markets. Without markets, information would be even more "imperfect" than it is with them. And there is no reason to believe that government can mobilize more relevant knowledge than can market processes.[13]

VII. WHAT IS THE ECONOMIC PROBLEM?

If we take as our task to explain the sources of order in economic life before we tackle cases of disorder, our first job is to correctly identify the environment in which individuals operate. Economists universally recognize that human beings have to navigate in a world of scarcity. More of one thing means less of another. But it is just as true that they have to make a living in a world in which they have limited and specialized knowledge about the conditions that will allow them to fulfill their plans, and in which they have a knowable past and an unknowable future. These are existential conditions that cannot be eradicated from human consideration. That is, human beings make choices under conditions of scarcity as we commonly recognize, but they also must make plans and choices in a world of time and ignorance.[14] We would never countenance an economics that abstracted away from scarcity, but it makes as much sense to abstract away from time and ignorance as it does to abstract away from scarcity.

If we do start from an extended notion of the economic problem as want satisfaction in the face of scarcity, time, and ignorance, we can't help but once again embark upon Adam Smith's original inquiry: we will want to know why and how markets enable people to cope with their limitations well enough that they have created unintended order out of potential disorder. How have ignorant, imperfect individuals working with scarce resources managed to create ever increasing wealth in market economies?

Two years ago, in this same forum, Robert Clower (1994) called for turning economics into an inductive science. Part of that project is to explain an increasingly evident empirical reality: market economies create wealth and order far better than nonmarket economies. It is perverse to develop a theory of market failure as deviations from the ideal when the real question is how do we get as much order as we do knowing as little as we do? The economists' problem is to explain the source of economic order and the causes of economic growth. This requires understanding the connection between individual actions and the development of complex economies. It also means among other things, examining the persistent empirical characteristics of market orders. When we do that, we notice that market economies look nothing like the pictures our ideal models paint. Rather than settling down to some equilibrium, they grow and become increasingly complex. Prices fluctuate, products proliferate and fill more and more niches, firms develop different organizational strategies and technologies, services become more important and more arcane. We also notice that technological innovation swamps capital accumulation as source of growth. All of this needs to be understood and explained, but the job is hopeless if we start from some a priori notion of perfect markets that look nothing like this roiling, seething world of business out there.

Once we start thinking of our project as one of explaining markets rather than engineering them, a whole host of interesting questions present themselves. For instance, instead of asking when monopoly should be regulated, we can ask what role monopoly plays in economic development and what are the competitive forces that may or may not undercut long run monopoly. We can ask if the whole concept of monopoly as currently defined makes sense in a dynamic, ever changing context.[15] Instead of stigmatizing differential and specialized information, we can ask not only how markets allow people to profit from and generate differential information, we can also ask what role concealing information might play in market development (Moss 1991). And we can examine the importance of talk to the market process. It is astonishing to have theories of competitive markets in which no one is supposed to talk to anyone else. Yet talk is not only a means of sharing information, it is also a short cut to imitation of successful market experiments. We can ask how individuals learn about their preferences and how they carve out areas of certainty in an uncertain world. We can ask why the proliferation of economic institutions is important to economic growth and development.

With this kind of economic project, equilibrium conditions are beside the point, and descriptions of perfection are useless because we could never identify it or measure it apart from the existing market process. In the real world, all we can know is better or worse, more or less efficient with respect to known alternatives. And in a changing world, there is no reason to think there is some predictable, describable endpoint that can be modeled.

VIII. ALREADY PART WAY THERE

I am not suggesting that all these ideas are brand new. Actually, I believe much work has already been done to develop a deep understanding of the market process. While the posing of the problem has been largely the province of modern Austrian economists, economists from many other perspectives have already begun the job of fleshing out this more interesting project. Indeed, when most practicing economists talk about markets rather than model them, they demonstrate a deep understanding of market processes. Of course, this talk is often disparaged as "mere story telling" or a bit less condescendingly as "appreciative theory" or "informal theory" that requires "formalization" (Williamson 1993). However, these stories are the real arguments that make us think the models are useful. Without them, we have no claim to connecting our theoretical propositions or our empirical research to real world events.

The most interesting economics of the last twenty years have been variations on the theme of finding out what actors really do in markets to overcome their limitations and bring about economic order, rather than investigations of the mathematical properties of irrelevant models. I think most immediately of several recent strands in economic literature: most prominently, the new institutional economics that looks at institutions as ways of dealing with uncertainty and limited information (Furubotn 1994); evolutionary theorists who see organizations as evolving institutional routines to deal with recurring problems (Nelson and Winter 1982); and the transactions cost literature that in some hands is an exercise in identifying market failure, in others is an exploration of how people organize themselves in markets to deal with the problem. Property rights economics also asks similar questions when it focuses on who has the right to make what decision about what pieces of the world. Old style Chicago economics and its offspring at UCLA exemplified a method of reasoning about economic problems that kept formal equilibrium conditions in the background and concentrated on providing sensible explanations of real-world phenomena.[16] What all these theoretical literatures have in common is an emphasis on explaining real-world problems with stories about processes attached to them. And the emphasis is always on how people cope with their limitations, not on why they are imperfect.

IX. WHITHER PUBLIC POLICY

I titled this talk, "Economic Policy for an Imperfect World." So, where's the policy? If we start from our revised project about how to understand the market economy, the old policy assumptions no longer apply. What point is there about talking about rate regulation when you admit that you don't know what an equilibrium rate should be? What point is there to antitrust legislation when the ultimate impact of an apparent monopoly is unpredictable, and eliminating it may be even more detrimental to wealth creation than leaving it alone? What point is there to outlawing certain collusive practice when it could well be the case that talk among rivals is necessary for good information sharing? We simply don't know enough from the old models to guide us into sensible policy. From that perspective, we would do well to develop our own version of the Hippocratic oath and vow, economists, first do no harm.

I do think that recognizing the existential character of incomplete knowledge and of learning reinforces the view that markets should be the default assumption in public policy debate. In a world where knowledge must be discovered both at a cost as the information cost literature points out, and serendipitously in the course of taking advantage of economic opportunities, as the Austrian literature highlights, there is little reason to believe that government can outguess the market in picking winners or losers or in judging specific economic practices. Government intervention will instead bias information flows and truncate the discovery process in markets. There may be good reasons to do this from time to time, but they will be political reasons rather than economic reasons.

However, my arguments do not automatically imply that as far as public policy goes, all we need to say is "laissez faire-laissez passer" and be done with it. All economic action takes place within the context of some regime of property rights and contract law, and within some legislative tradition. But the specific contours of property and contract law is not a given, and the particular legislative tradition will affect the long run stability of the economy. So at the very least, a full appreciation of the processual nature of markets implies an investigation of the impact of alternative structures of property and contract on market activity, and the relationship between the constitutional constraints on government and economic performance, two projects which are already underway in the law and economics and the constitutional economics literatures. But where law and economics and constitutional political economy primarily focus on incentives inherent in various legal and constitutional regimes, recognizing the importance of time and ignorance in economic life suggests that another focus be added to the investigation. That is, we need to ask how various rules structures affect human learning and error correction. Markets foster learning and error correction on the part of economic actors as they compete for profits. We might also ask how learning and error correction take place in hierarchical, bureaucratic structures (the kind that must always implement any policy directive) compared to decentralized markets in an effort to see what kinds of decisions are best rendered in each environment.[17]

In sum, the central problem of an economic policy for an imperfect world is to ask what political regime is most likely to allow economic agents to pursue their own goals and least likely to interfere with their own incentives to find cooperative solutions to the problems raised by their limitations. What rules and procedures aid individuals in making good economic plans with some hope of being fulfilled in light of scarcity, time, and ignorance? This project is truly a reinvigoration of the older notion of political economy; this time more self consciously based on a fuller understanding of human limitations and human capabilities to transcend those limitations.

NOTES

Presidential Address delivered at the sixty-fifth annual meeting of the Southern Economic Association, New Orleans, Louisiana, November 19, 1995. I wish to thank Garrett Vaughn, Peter Boettke, and Richard Wagner for helpful comments on an earlier draft of this paper, and the Earhart Foundation for financial support during its preparation. All errors are, of course, my own fault.

1. For a fascinating account of how this came about, see Frank Machovic's (1995) *Perfect Competition and the Transformation of Economics*.

2. A case in point is the literature of a few decades ago on the costs of monopoly. There the urgency of economic policy depended to a large extent on how extensive welfare losses due to monopoly really were. The empirical measures varied all the way from Harberger's (1954) low of .07 percent of GNP to Cowling and Mueller's (1978) high of 13 percent of GNP. Harberger provided reasons to argue that monopoly was such a small problem that it wasn't worth worrying about, while Cowling and Mueller certainly suggested that control of monopoly would bring about big gains.

3. In light of the public choice literature, one could easily claim that conventional argumentation about economic policy is backwards. In recognition of pervasive government failure, it is more reasonable to argue that imperfections in governmental processes should imply market correctives, than the other way round. Why shouldn't markets rather than government be our default assumption when considering public policy? Certainly, if it is true that there is, as Stiglitz says, no theoretical argument for the proposition that markets work, there is even less evidence that governments work.

4. One of the encouraging indications that public choice considerations have entered the mainstream is the increasing attention that the economics of regulation is paying to the regulatory process in devising market failure correctives. This has led to the formulation of far more sophisticated regulatory policies than simple "fix up the market" approaches once implied. Some of these proposed policies attempt to use "market-like" processes to inform the regulatory regime and minimize potential intrusions. See, for example, the regulation text by Spulber (1989).

5. This is the position that Gordon Tullock has espoused in a number of articles and books. See in particular, Tullock (1988).

6. The inadequacy of equilibrium models to fully guide public policy formation was first espoused by James Buchanan himself in *Cost and Choice* (1969) where he showed that the subjectivist nature of costs would make cost/benefit calculations unreliable. I argued, further (Vaughn 1980a), that the higher the degree of perceived market failure, the further away market prices will be from equilibrium, therefore the less reliable will cost/benefit analysis be.

7. Machlup (1958) has called this the "fallacy of misplaced concreteness." Clower (1995) more recently identified it as the "Pygmalion Syndrome."

8. This was exactly the problem highlighted by the economic calculation debate of the 1930s and 1940s where the market socialists tried to construct a socialist economy by duplicating features of a Walrasian general equilibrium model in the real world. Market socialism was doomed to failure not because the model was wrong in some sense, but because it left out too many features of the social world that are important in making markets actually work. The market socialists tried to use equilibrium models as blueprints for society rather than as tools of explanation. See Vaughn (1980b).

9. The articles were collected in *Individualism and Economic Order* (Hayek 1948).

10. More to the point, a skill is a kind of personal knowledge that allows its possessor to profit from market interaction.

11. Hayek (1948, 85–86) illustrated this principle by showing how when people respond rationally in response to a price increase without knowing the cause of the increase, they are benefiting from other people's knowledge without having to acquire detailed knowledge themselves. Market prices disperse information that might otherwise remain hidden. Some have taken this to mean that Hayek believed prices were perfectly efficient, but this is a misreading of Hayek's project. Rather he was illustrating one way in which markets allow people to use more knowledge than they themselves possess. He said nothing to suggest that prices contain every relevant bit of information one might like to have in order to make an economic calculation. It is perfectly consistent with Hayek's story that a manufacturer, for example, might want to know not just that prices have in fact changed, but the reason for a change in price of a resource in order to make better long-run plans. However, he is still better off with price information than without it.

12. Kelvin Lancaster (1969, 62–70) developed an interesting technique for constructing a production function that implicitly incorporated the importance of experimentation in discovering the information assumed in economic models. He showed how a production function was the optimal segments of a series of process rays that could be interpreted as the "survivors" of a series of experiments and discoveries about production techniques. The only "Hayekian" element missing from Lancaster's device is the recognition that the whole of the production function is never gathered in one place.

13. As Hayek wrote: "If we can agree that the economic problem of society is mainly one of rapid adaptation to changes in the particular circumstances of time and place, it would seem to follow that the ultimate decisions must be left to the people who are familiar with these circumstances, who know directly of the relevant changes and of the resource immediately available to meet them" (Hayek 1948, 83).

14. See O'Driscoll and Rizzo's (1985) book, *The Economics of Time and Ignorance* for a discussion of the implications of time and ignorance for understanding economic phenomena. In particular they show, following Oscar Morgenstern, that perfect knowledge and perfect certainty is inconsistent with the achievement of an equilibrium (83–85).

15. This was one of the main points of Kirzner's (1973) *Competition and Entrepreneurship* where he argued that in an ongoing market process, defining monopoly as a firm that faces a downward sloping demand curve makes little sense. In a dynamic setting, firms may find temporary monopolies constantly undercut by competitors.

16. While new style "equilibrium ever" Chicago economics goes too far in believing people have enough information to live in a Pareto efficient world, there are nevertheless some close affinities with the perspective I am advocating here. Their analysis at least always presumes people are doing things for a purpose and if on the surface something seems to be inefficient it may be the problem of the economist and not the economy.

17. On this, see Thomas Sowell's (1980) important and under-appreciated book, *Knowledge and Decisions* where he examines the economic, political, and social institutions from the perspective of their ability to aid participants in learning from their mistakes.

REFERENCES

Aristotle. 1953. *The Ethics*. Translated by J. A. K. Thomson. Baltimore, MD: Penguin Classics.

Arnott, R. 1995. "Time for Revisionism on Rent Control?" *The Journal of Economic Perspectives* (Winter): 99–120.

Buchanan, J. 1979. "Politics Without Romance." *IHS Journal* 3: B1–B11.

———. 1969. *Cost and Choice: An Inquiry into Economic Theory*. Chicago: Markham Publishing.

——, and G. Tullock. 1962. *The Calculus of Consent*. Ann Arbor: University of Michigan Press.

Card, David, and A. B. Krueger. 1994. "Minimum Wages and Employment: A Case Study of the Fast Food Industry in New Jersey and Pennsylvania." *American Economic Review* (September): 772–793.

Clower, Robert. 1994. "Economics as an Inductive Science." *Southern Economic Journal* (April): 805–814.

——. 1995. "Axiomatics in Economics." *Southern Economic Journal* (October): 307–319.

Cowling, K., and D. Mueller. 1978. "The Social Costs of Monopoly Power." *Economic Journal* (December): 727–48.

Demsetz, H. 1969. "Information and Efficiency: Another Viewpoint." *Journal of Law and Economics* (March): 1–22.

Furubotn, E. G. 1994. *Future Developments of the New Institutional Economics: Extension of the Neoclassical Model or New Construct?* Jena, Germany: Max Planck Instituts zür Erforschung von Wirtschaftssystemen.

Hahn, F. 1982. "Reflections on the Invisible Hand." *Lloyd's Bank Review* (April): 1–21.

Harberger, A. C. 1954. "Monopoly and Resource Allocation." *American Economic Review* (May): 77–92.

Hayek, F. A. 1948. *Individualism and Economic Order*. Chicago: University of Chicago Press.

——. 1978. "Competition as a Discovery Procedure." In *New Studies in Philosophy, Politics and Economics*. Chicago: University of Chicago Press.

Kirzner, I. 1973. *Competition and Entrepreneurship*. Chicago: University of Chicago Press.

Lancaster, K. 1969. *Introduction to Modern Microeconomics*. Chicago: Rand McNally.

Machlup, F. 1958. "Equilibrium and Disequilibrium: Misplaced Concreteness and Disguised Politics." *The Economic Journal* (March).

Machovic, F. M. 1995. *Perfect Competition and the Transformation of Economics*. London: Routledge.

Moss, L. S. 1991. "The Chicago Intellectual Property Rights Tradition and the Reconciliation of Coase and Hayek." *Eastern Economic Journal* (April–June): 145–156.

Mueller, D. C. 1989. *Public Choice II*. Cambridge: Cambridge University Press.

Nelson, R. R., and S. Winter. 1982. *An Evolutionary Theory of Economic Change*. Cambridge, MA: Harvard University Press.

O'Driscoll, G. P., and M. J. Rizzo. 1985. *The Economics of Time and Ignorance*. Oxford: Basil Blackwell.

Posner, R. A. 1975. "The Social Cost of Monopoly and Regulation." *Journal of Political Economy* (August): 807–827.

Schumpeter, J. 1954. *History of Economic Analysis*. New York: Oxford University Press.

Sowell, T. 1980. *Knowledge and Decisions*. New York: Basic Books.

Spiegel, H. 1983. *The Growth of Economic Thought*. Durham, NC: Duke University Press.

Spulber, D. F. 1989. *Regulation and Markets*. Cambridge, MA: MIT Press.

Stiglitz, J. 1994. *Whither Socialism?* Cambridge, MA: MIT Press.

Tullock, G. 1988. *Wealth, Poverty and Politics*. New York: Basil Blackwell.

Vaughn, K. I. 1980a. "Does It Matter That Costs Are Subjective?" *Southern Economic Journal* (January): 702–715.

——. 1980b. "Economic Calculation Under Socialism: The Austrian Contribution." *Economic Inquiry* (October), 535–554.

Williamson, O. 1993. "The Evolving Science of Organization." *Journal of Institutional and Theoretical Economics* 149 (1): 36–63.

Chapter 16
Does Austrian Economics Have a Useful Future?

The historians of economic thought in the audience (and I guess that is most of you) will recognize the rhetorical reference in the title of my talk. It is a deliberate takeoff on George Stigler's article written almost 30 years ago, "Does Economics Have a Useful Past?" The article appeared as the lead in the second issue of *History of Political Economy (HOPE)* at a time when even the journal's founding editors were not sure about the correct answer to Stigler's question. I am reminded of that article tonight for two reasons. The first and obvious one is that, like the historians of economic thought in 1969, Austrian economists in 1997 suffer from an insecurity about their place in the academic world. *HOPE* was launched in part to argue for the legitimacy of the subdiscipline that was increasingly being marginalized in academic departments: the SDAE (Society for the Development of Austrian Economics) has been organized in part to give members already marginalized in their academic employment a sense of academic community and a forum for development.

My second reason for recalling Stigler's article is less innocent. Stigler chose the first volume of *HOPE* to deliver a message that was mildly subversive of the subdiscipline of the history of economic thought. He suggested that the history of economics, while interesting for its own sake and perhaps useful in teaching young economists how to read a book carefully (1969, 218) might in the end be too expensive an indulgence to include in graduate training in economics.

Originally published in *Advances in Austrian Economics*, vol. 5 (London: JAI Press, 1998), 3–14.

Hence, while economics might have an interesting past, the implication was that it might not have a useful one, where useful meant contributing to current economic theory.

While I do not intend to be nearly so critical of Austrian economics as Stigler was of the history of economic thought, neither will I take the opposite tack of limiting my comments to celebration of our accomplishments and importance. Last year, at this event, in the first of the "presidential addresses" (in that case, given by someone who served as our guiding inspiration rather than as an actual president) Israel Kirzner quite rightly chose to inaugurate our society by reminding us of those characteristics that unite us, and urged us to put our differences aside in order to continue the Austrian tradition. Israel Kirzner's inspiring talk last year invites us to look forward in a spirit of self-searching to ask ourselves "how, exactly, do we continue the Austrian tradition?" Tonight, my remarks are intended to offer some suggestions about how to carry on the Austrian tradition in a way that ensures that it has both an interesting and a useful future.

I. OUR PLACE IN THE PROFESSION

Austrian economics at the moment is regarded as a heterodox school within the larger economics professions. This in itself is progress since little more than 25 years ago, those who heard of it at all probably thought of it more as crackpot ideology than as legitimate economics. Being viewed as heterodox represents a certain hard-won respectability. And being heterodox is not really such a bad thing in itself. When one is a member of a heterodox school, one arguably has freedom to range far and wide with one's imagination. Heterodox thinkers don't have to guard their respectability quite so much as those committed to the received doctrine, so they can take risks in their thinking and writing that more standard colleagues could not afford. Being part of a heterodox group also tends to confer a certain sense of purpose, a certain zeal, that is absent in the land of the orthodox. So it can be great fun. But this freedom comes at a steep price, one exacted by the very orthodox academic establishment we seek to challenge.

Existing on the periphery of the profession means relying on the open-mindedness of journal editors and tenure review committees (a quality that often appears to be in exceedingly short supply) for permission to exist in the academy. One is thus forced into a defensive posture that is not always conducive to developing a genuine Austrian research program. As Peter

Boettke recently argued (1994), the academic game forces Austrians to engage in "strategic writing": writing articles that may have little to do with one's real interests but are close enough to conventional economics to get into "respectable" journals. While this strategy contributes to the important goal of staying employed, it does little to develop a distinctive Austrian approach to economics. Strategic writing also has the unfortunate consequence of convincing one's neoclassical colleagues that Austrian economics is no different from and often inferior to their own brand of work.

These are the facts of life in any scientific community, and there is no point tearing our clothes and beating our breasts about it. Indeed, it is probably, on net, a good thing that heterodox views are scorned and ignored until they prove so compelling that they force themselves upon a reluctant scientific community. None of us would really like to see a thousand intellectual flowers bloom where Austrian economics is just one of the multitude. After all, we happen to think we are right about some issues, and we want a scientific community that stands for something to become convinced. But that leaves us with the puzzle of how to do Austrian work—and how to continue to develop an Austrian economics—in a neoclassical world.

On one level the answer is simple: do what we have been doing. Continue to write strategic articles that contain an Austrian point in language congenial to the mainstream; form an academic society to provide a forum to share more "sectarian" Austrian work; talk to each other; talk to others who have something to teach us; build bridges to people who share some of our interests in the hope of expanding our numbers along with our own understanding of economic phenomena. This is the practical side where we are already good and getting better. But having people to talk to and a place to share our work makes it imperative that we address the next question. Now what do we talk about? How do we go from here to developing a full Austrian research program?

II. TAKING CRITICS SERIOUSLY

In times of self-reflection and uncertainty about the way forward, it is often helpful to think about what one's critics are saying. Critics who take you seriously can be the most valuable resource for improving the quality of one's argument. That the Austrian approach is as coherent and articulated as it is can be attributed to the many conversations Austrian writers have had over the last 20 years with friendly but unconvinced critics.[1] At this juncture in the development of the Austrian research program, what is needed are more, not fewer, friendly and informed critics to help sharpen arguments and rethink old positions.

However, before I get carried away with this theme, let me quickly point out that there are some kinds of criticisms that I do not think we should take seriously, at least not seriously enough to spend much time debating. Some are so far away from grasping the potential Austrian contribution that spending too much time answering them would prove more of a diversion than a learning experience. In this category I am reminded of a talk that Sherwin Rosen gave at the 1996 meeting of the Mont Pelerin Society (now published in the *Journal of Economic Perspectives* [1997]). In what was supposed to have been a conciliatory talk to explore whether or not there are "gains from trade" between neoclassical and Austrian economics, Rosen highlighted the contributions Austrians made to the theory of entrepreneurship. Now, one would have thought this alone was proof of gains from trade between the two paradigms. On the contrary, however, Rosen argued that while the Austrian theory of entrepreneurship certainly fills a gap in neoclassical economics, in the end it "lacks operational definition and cannot be quantitatively measured. . . . If we cannot measure that total volume of entrepreneurial activity, there is no way of assessing its economic importance and rate of return, nor of the social and legal environments that nurture it or suppress it" (149).

What could one say to a critic like that without going into a lengthy methodological debate that would make him yawn and doze off long before one had a chance to change his mind? The idea that what can't be operationalized or measured in the conventional neoclassical way can't be important misses the point of Austrian economics by such a wide margin that to take it seriously enough to try to answer would just divert attention away from more interesting pursuits.[2] This is a genre of criticism that can only be answered by simply doing good economics.

However, there is another kind of critic who we definitely should pay heed to. One who knows the literature, appreciates many of the ideas and still finds the project wanting. This is the kind of critic who can really help to move Austrian economics forward because he can spot weak points that the rest of us might be too close to notice. In this category I call your attention to one critic who gives us something to chew on: Nicolai Foss, and his recent book *The Austrian School and Modern Economics* (1994). Foss calls himself an Austrian fellow traveler because of his obvious deep understanding and appreciation of the Austrian literature but refuses to include himself in the Austrian camp for reasons he offers in his book.

In his book he makes two important arguments. The first is the satisfying one that much of the most interesting ideas in modern economics such as property rights, asymmetric information, problems of intertemporal coordination, the new institutional economics, and evolutionary processes, all had their origin in the works of Mises and Hayek. Indeed, he argues that if "Austrian insights emerging in these two decades (1920s and 1930s) had not been swept so decisively away by the Keynesian tide and the emerging Walrasianism, economic theory would have progressed faster than it has done, and done so in a sounder way" (Foss 1994, 10). Obviously, this is a sentiment with which we can heartily agree as we congratulate him for his perceptiveness.

However, we will not be so pleased with his second proposition, that currently Austrian economics is a degenerating research program in that no new propositions or theories have been added to contemporary economics by the new Austrians (Foss 1994, 190). In particular, Foss argues that possibly because of the commitment to "thorough-going subjectivism," Austrians focus too much on the "negative heuristic" in doing their work. That is, they pay more attention to what not to do (aggregative economics, mathematical economics, identifying equilibrium conditions) (187) than what to do. The positive heuristic, as far as it goes, tends to be rather vague: "explain events in invisible hand terms, allow for indeterminacy in human action, explain economic phenomena in strict methodological individualist terms, focus on analyzing processes rather than equilibrium" (188). While all those instructions are consistent with subjectivism, they are so general as to make it difficult for an economist to figure out what to do next. As a consequence, Austrians face too much "task uncertainty" uncertainty about what problems to work on. Because of this, he argues, most Austrian research has been of two kinds: exegetical—what did Mises, Menger, or Hayek say about something? or critical—why orthodoxy is mistaken about an issue. What Austrians haven't done, he argues, is engage in problem solving: explaining puzzling features of the world in novel ways.

Now these criticisms are not made from ignorance (nor is he the first person to enunciate them), so perhaps we should pay some attention to them. What can we say in answer to him? You will all immediately respond, quite accurately, that even if there is some truth in Foss's charge, it is not entirely fair. Where a good chunk of one's career must be devoted to "strategic articles" as we have already noted, criticism and exegesis are routes to publication. That is one reason why so many Austrians (as well as post-Keynesians) for so long tended to be methodologists or historians of economic thought. Also, Foss's criticism ignores the constructive work that has been done in monetary theory and banking history, law and economics, comparative economic systems, constitutional political economy and, to some extent, economic development in the last decade.

We might also point out that scientific progress requires a core of people working together, in communication with each other. But the number of Austrians has been quite small and geographically dispersed (which is, of course, one of the deficiencies that the formation of this society is intended to correct).

Additionally, and this point may be controversial to some of you, it took some time for the new Austrians to articulate what is now distinctive about Austrian economics. Both Mises and Hayek, during their heydays, regarded themselves as economists—not hyphenated economists. The designation "Austrian," where that meant something distinctive from mainstream economics, was only reinvoked when it was perceived that mainstream economics had moved decidedly away from the Mises and Hayek variety of economics. Mathematical economics, increasingly formal models, concentration on equilibrium conditions, and Keynesian macroeconomics all put distance between the Mises–Hayek approach and the mainstream. Younger economists who were attracted to the Austrians couldn't help but think of Austrian economics in terms of what it was not—mathematical, Keynesian, equilibrium—rather than what it distinctively was. Even Mises and Hayek (in this case, more so of Hayek) wrote in opposition to then current debates. *Human Action* (1966), for instance, was a treatise aimed at earlier audiences that by definition could not take into account economics developed after 1950. Further, it was so complex a text that there was no common understanding of the implications of its central features for Austrian economics.

For this reason, the debates of the 1970s and the early 1980s about the nature of Austrian economics were very productive, indeed crucial to getting us to where we are today. It was necessary to continually ask, "What is Austrian economics?" to ever get the answer, the economics of "time and ignorance" (O'Driscoll and Rizzo 1996). We now know that what the Austrian tradition can contribute to economic understanding stems from widening the core assumptions of economic theory beyond scarce resources and unlimited ends: Humans strive to achieve their ends in the face of scarcity, the passage of time, and ignorance of at least some of the circumstances relevant to their choices. These ideas were implicit in the "founding documents" of Menger, Mises, and Hayek, but making the implicit explicit in contemporary discourse is part of any research program. Once the starting point is clearly articulated, the Austrian focus on market process becomes not only understandable, but imperative. The way is cleared for much progress.

III. WHAT NOW?

It is one thing to identify Austrian economics as the economics of time and ignorance and another to translate that into substantive propositions about how the world works. What *is* the positive heuristic to guide Austrian research? Or to put it another way, what problems and puzzles do we give graduate students to work on, and how do we advise them to go about solving them? Figuring out the answer to this question is the next step in developing Austrian economics as a viable research program. After all, Austrian economics will rise or fall depending upon how well it helps people explain the world around them, and explanation is the product of a robust positive heuristic.

Now, as a believer in evolved orders, I do not think a positive heuristic can be dictated from above. This is tantamount to making those methodological pronouncements that Leland Yeager (1995) is always criticizing as being coercive—what McCloskey (1985) calls conversation stoppers. Science itself is largely a spontaneous order, and I, certainly, am not about to try to dictate to you about how to do your work. Nevertheless, let me offer the following suggestions in the spirit of contributing toward the articulation of a positive heuristic. (Let me also hasten to add that I am by no means advocating giving up methodology or the history of economic thought. Both are worthy areas of study, but it might be worth remembering that those fields are only marginally more prestigious than Austrian economics!)

First, it seems inescapable that taking time seriously means incorporating human learning into all our accounts of human action. Human beings learn through experience, they are inductive learners and they don't all learn the same things from the same experience.[3] We need to explicitly acknowledge that human learning is fundamental to any account of market processes, from price adjustment to resource use to technological progress to product creation. Learning is central to all explanations of economic growth and development, and economic growth and development is one of the central concerns of Austrian economics.

While the Austrian literature is replete with allusions to learning and/or discovery (think of Menger on the growth of knowledge, Hayek on knowledge and discovery, Kirzner on entrepreneurial alertness), we need to go further to understand the relationship between the context of learning and what discoveries are likely to be made. Hence, refocusing our accounts of human action on processes of learning and discovery leads us naturally to ask what it is that people learn. Menger emphasized the crucial role to human progress of discovering the causal relationship between a thing and its capacity to satisfy a human need (1976, 52). A promising area of research is to investigate the way in which people learn about the causal relationship between *actions* and their capacity to facilitate satisfying human needs: that is, the strategies, ways of doing things, routines, paradigms, solutions to problems, that people learn to adopt through experimentation and imitation.

It will be fruitful to consider these patterns of action as solutions to problems that once learned are repeated in all like situations. What people learn, then, in some sense are institutionalized behaviors that form part of their repertoire of actions aimed at want satisfaction. Mises recognized the important role that habits and routines play in everyday living (1966, 47) but beyond arguing that they, too, were objects of choice, he said little about them. A further development of Mises's ideas would be to show how habits and routines become part of purposeful action, how they are developed and what circumstances lead to change.

I believe that this particular area of research has exciting possibilities for developing an Austrian research program. On the one hand, pursuing the role of habits, routines, and recurring strategies for acting human beings can show a link between Austrian and neoclassical concerns. Equilibrium can be interpreted as a situation in which patterns of action learned through experimentation get repeated until a better solution to a problem is discovered. As for the Austrian concern with growth and development, we can think of firms as codifiers of learned production strategies, and capital goods as artifacts of learned routines and practices. In this sense, the accumulation of production strategies and capital goods is the substance of economic development. Once again, such a view finds its roots in Menger (1976), who argued that progress is the growth and proliferation of market institutions that embody human learning. Now we need to know much more about the interactions between institutional environments and human learning in all its forms: rote learning, imitation, creative problem solving, alertness, and serendipitous discovery.

To my mind, it is the natural course of Austrian argument to examine human action within institutional structures. Learning never takes place in a vacuum, hence can never be considered in an institution-free context. However, the very nature of learning and its subset, discovery, implies that humans can learn things that change the institutional structure as well. Obviously, this was a main point of Hayek's later work (1973). We can learn much from examining the ways in which human beings act and interact to both maintain and change institutional structure. We can also begin to see how institutions provide the shared social context that permits a measure of common understanding to subjective actors, the shared culture that makes order possible.

Finally, paying attention to learning within institutional structures will inevitably lead to paying more attention to real world events. Institutions are contingent factors in the world; hence, they are the province of what Mises called economic understanding as opposed to praxeology (1966, 51–58). To understand the world means to know specific things about it. Foss makes the interesting claim that too much attention to praxeology has led Austrians to neglect focusing on contingent claims about the world, that too much focus on theory leads to neglect of empirical concepts (1994, 192–193). Yet what makes economics a valuable science is its claim to illuminating features of the real, contingent world.

I think it would be enormously productive to the development of an Austrian research program if each of us became an expert on some contemporary issue of applied economics. Perhaps one could choose a developing country and give an account of its progress from an Austrian perspective: Or a country in transition, a particular industry, a particular area of economic policy. By talking about something concrete, we show the payoff to the Austrian approach far more effectively than by arguing for it in the abstract. Of course, developing propositions about real-world events and institutions would require that we pay more attention to how to marshal evidence to support our claims. We would need to ask what makes for a convincing argument? What counterevidence might we face and how might we account for it? In other words, think seriously about the methods of "understanding" and develop a set of tools to conduct empirical analysis that avoids the standard Austrian objections to econometrics. Here is an area where being pluralistic in our empirical methods is absolutely necessary.

IV. CONCLUSION

With a more real-world-oriented market process theory, one that builds change via human learning and discovery into its "positive heuristic," I believe the Austrian tradition has an important contribution to make to economics. But even if we all became exemplary and hardworking Austrian "problem-solvers," I do not mean to suggest that Austrians will then automatically be respected in the Ivy League. Old ideas and methods are too entrenched in an academic power structure for even our best work to impress many of the most respected economists in the mainstream. But so what? If the cost of Ivy League respectability is to do work that we do not believe in, I say the cost is too high. One thing that characterizes Austrians is a passionate belief in the correctness of their path that makes it impossible for them to write what they don't believe. Hence, success in the Ivy League is not even an option at the moment.

However, if no Austrian is going to make it in the Ivy League in the near future, neither do I think the price for doing interesting work is going to be academic exile, either. My guess is that there are far more fellow travelers out there in academe than we suspect: people fed up with the tyranny of the "top journals" and mathematics for its own sake, people who love economics, who love thinking about markets and the human ingenuity they represent, who want to know how the world works and not how a model performs. (If we are a book culture, that means someone is buying the books!) They are our natural colleagues, and they are the ones who will respond to (and want to contribute to) an Austrian economics that is straightforward, lively, and helps to make sense of the world around us.

This society was founded on the belief that the best of the Austrian tradition has the potential to provide an organizing framework for a revitalized economic science. The belief may be no more than wishful thinking; or less charitably, grandiose delusion on the part of the organizing committee. But on the other hand, it just might be correct. In the game of bridge, when faced with a doubtful hand, the advice to the declarer is that if there is only one position the cards can be in for the contract to be made, play as if the cards are there. In our community we might profit from following much the same advice. Play the game as if the future is ours, and maybe, just maybe, in the end we will find we have won the contest. At the very least, we will have an interesting future. At the most, we could have a useful one as well.

ACKNOWLEDGMENT

The author would like to acknowledge the generous support of the Earhart Foundation during the preparation of this paper.

NOTES

1. I think here of people like James Buchanan, Warren Samuels, Kenneth Boulding, and Axel Leijunhufvud, to name just a few who come quickly to mind.

2. Leland Yeager's response to Rosen, also published in the Fall 1997 *Journal of Economic Perspectives*, was originally entitled "Neoclassical Self-Congratulations." Yeager's comment on the entrepreneurship issue was that Rosen's argument reminded him of "jokes about keys and lamp posts."

3. Recent work by Vanberg (1995), Harper (1994), and Choi (1992) are all trying to give accounts of how people learn and how they act on the basis of their learning.

REFERENCES

Choi, Y. B. 1992. *Paradigms and Conventions: Uncertainty, Decision Making, and Entrepreneurship.* Ann Arbor: University of Michigan Press.

Boettke, P. J. 1994. "Alternative Paths Forward for Austrian Economics." In *The Elgar Companion to Austrian Economics*, edited by P. J. Boettke. Aldershot, UK: Edward Elgar Publishing.

Foss, N. J. 1994. *The Austrian School and Modern Economics.* Copenhagen, Denmark: Munksguaard International Publishers.

Harper, D. 1994. *Entrepreneurship and the Market Process.* London: Routledge.

Hayek, F. A. 1973. *Law, Legislation and Liberty.* Vol 1. Chicago: University of Chicago Press.

McCloskey, D. 1985. *The Rhetoric of Economics.* Madison: University of Wisconsin Press.

Menger, C. 1976. *Principles of Economics.* New York: New York University Press.

Mises, L. 1966. *Human Action* (3rd rev. ed.). San Francisco: Fox & Wilkes.

O'Driscoll, G. P., and M. J. Rizzo. 1996. *The Economics of Time and Ignorance.* London: Routledge.

Rosen, S. 1997. "Austrian and Neoclassical Economics: Any Gains from Trade?" *Journal of Economic Perspectives* 4:139–152.

Stigler, G. 1969. "Does Economics Have a Useful Past?" *History of Political Economy* 1 (2): 217–230.

Vanberg, V. 1995. "Rational Choice vs. Adaptive Rule Following." In *Rules and Choice in Economics*, edited by V. Vanberg. London: Routledge.

Yeager, L. B. 1995. "Tacit Preachments Are the Worst Kind." *Journal of Economic Methodology* 2 (1): 1–33.

———. 1997. "Austrian Economics, Neoclassicism, and the Market Test." *Journal of Economic Perspectives* 11 (4): 153–166.

Acknowledgments

I wish first of all to thank Peter Boettke, who encouraged me to gather together a selection of my essays on Austrian economics to be reprinted as a book. I am a reluctant author, and without his support, this book never would have appeared. For the better part of 40 years, Pete has been one of my most trusted colleagues. His insights into and enthusiasm for Austrian economics are a source of constant inspiration.

I thank Karla Segovia who, with the help of Stefanie Haeffele, was charged with the arduous task of securing permissions to reprint my articles from a wide variety of sources while dealing with all of the intricacies of organizing a publication like mine. I am especially indebted to Karla for gently keeping me on task—no easy job when dealing with a habitual procrastinator such as myself. I also thank Logan Hansen for careful copyediting.

I must also acknowledge several people who only indirectly contributed to this book, but who were nevertheless important to my growth as an Austrian economist: Israel Kirzner, who was the first economist to convince me that Austrian economics was important and worth studying, Don Lavoie with whom I had many discussions that pushed me to new and fruitful directions with my research, and Mario Rizzo and Jerry O'Driscoll who, with the publication of their pathbreaking book, showed me for the first time that Austrian economics is "The Economics of Time and Ignorance."

And finally, for everything I have ever accomplished in my career—and in my life—I thank my husband, Garry. For 53 years he has supported me with love and constant encouragement. I can't imagine what my life would have been like had we never met.

Index

About the Author

Karen I. Vaughn is emerita professor of economics and distinguished senior fellow with the F. A. Hayek Program for Advanced Study in Philosophy, Politics, and Economics at the Mercatus Center at George Mason University. She was a professor of economics at George Mason University from 1978 to 2004 and served as department chair from 1983 to 1989. She is a former president of the History of Economics Society, Southern Economics Association, and Society for the Development of Austrian Economics. Professor Vaughn is recipient of a Lifetime Achievement Award from the Society for the Development of Austrian Economics in recognition of her central role in forming the society and her scholarly work advancing Austrian economics. She is the author of *Austrian Economics in America: The Migration of a Tradition* (Cambridge University Press, 1994) and numerous articles on Austrian economics and the history of economic thought.

Source Acknowledgments

Chapter 1: "Economic Calculation under Socialism: The Austrian Contribution." Originally published in *Economic Inquiry* 18, no. 4 (1980): 535–554. Republished with permission.

Chapter 2: "Does It Matter That Costs Are Subjective?" Originally published in *Southern Economic Journal* 46, no. 3 (1980): 702–715. Republished with permission.

Chapter 3: "Hayek's Ricardo Effect: A Second Look," by Laurence S. Moss and Karen Vaughn. Originally published in "History of Political Economy" 18, no. 4 (1986): 545–565. © 1986 Duke University Press. All rights reserved. Republished by permission of the rightsholder. www.dukeupress.edu.

Chapter 4: "Profit, Alertness, and Imagination." Originally published in *Journal des Économistes et des Études Humaines* 1, no. 2 (1990): 183–188, available at http://www.bepress.com/jeeh/. Republished with permission.

Chapter 5: "The Mengerian Roots of the Austrian Revival." Originally published in *History of Political Economy* 22 (Suppl. 1990): 379–407. © 1990 Duke University Press. All rights reserved. Republished by permission of the rightsholder. www.dukeupress.edu.

Chapter 6: "The Problem of Order in Austrian Economics: Kirzner vs. Lachmann." Originally published in *The Review of Political Economy* 4, no. 3 (January 1992). Reprinted by permission of the publisher (Taylor & Francis Ltd, http://www.tandfonline.com).

Chapter 7: "Should There Be an Austrian Welfare Economics?" Originally published in *Advances in Austrian Economics*, vol. 2, part A (London: JAI Press, 1995), 109–123. © Elsevier. Republished with permission.

Chapter 8: "Hayek's Implicit Economics: Rules and the Problem of Order." Originally published in *The Review of Austrian Economics* 11, no. 1–2 (1999): 129–144. Republished by permission from Springer Nature.

Chapter 9: "Hayek's Theory of the Market Order as an Instance of the Theory of Complex, Adaptive Systems." Originally published in *Journal des Économistes et des Études Humaines* 9, no. 2–3 (1999): 241–256, available at http://www.bepress.com/jeeh/. Republished with permission.

Chapter 10: "Can Democratic Societies Reform Themselves: The Limits of Constitutional Change." Originally published in *The Market Process: Essays in Contemporary Austrian Economics,* edited by Peter J. Boettke and David L. Prychitko (Cheltenham, UK: Edward Elgar Publishing, 1994), 229–243.

Chapter 11: "The Constitution of Liberty from an Evolutionary Perspective." First published in 1984 by the Institute of Economic Affairs, London, in *Hayek's "Serfdom" Revisited: Essays by Economists, Philosophers and Political Scientists on "The Road to Serfdom" After 40 Years,* edited by N. P. Barry (London: Institute of Economic Affairs, 1984), 119–143. Republished with permission.

Chapter 12: "The Limits of Homo Economicus in Public Choice and in Political Philosophy." Originally published in *Journal Analyse & Kritik* 10, no. 2 (1988): 161–180. Republished by permission of Oldenbourg Wissenschaftsverlag GmbH.

Chapter 13: "Friedrich Hayek's Defense of the Market Order." Originally published in *Wealth, Commerce, and Philosophy: Foundational Thinkers and Business Ethics,* edited by E. Heath and B. Kaldis (Chicago: University of Chicago Press, 2017), 341–358. Republished with permission.

Chapter 14: "Why Teach the History of Economics?" Originally published in *Journal of the History of Economic Thought* 15, no. 2 (1993): 174–183. Reproduced with permission.

Chapter 15: "Economic Policy for an Imperfect World." Originally published in *Southern Economic Journal* 62, no. 4 (1996): 833–844. Republished with permission.

Chapter 16: "Does Austrian Economics Have a Useful Future?" Originally published in *Advances in Austrian Economics,* vol. 5 (London: JAI Press, 1998), 3–14. © Elsevier. Republished with permission.